# END-TIME

## THE DOOMSDAY CATALOG

Compiled and Edited
by WILLIAM GRIFFIN

Merry Christmas
1982
and much love as
always, from your
Sister,
Gloria Jean

**COLLIER BOOKS**
*A Division of Macmillan Publishing Co., Inc.*
NEW YORK

LIBRARY OF CONGRESS CATALOGING IN PUBLICATION DATA
Main entry under title:

Endtime: the doomsday catalog.

    Bibliography:  p.
    1.  Eschatology—Collected works.  I.  Griffin,
William, 1935-
BT819.E5     236      79-22671
ISBN 0-02-085250-9


Macmillan Publishing Co., Inc.
866 Third Avenue, New York, N.Y. 10022
Collier Macmillan Canada, Ltd.


First Collier Books Edition 1979


*Designed by Philip Grushkin*


Printed in the United States of America

# CONTENTS

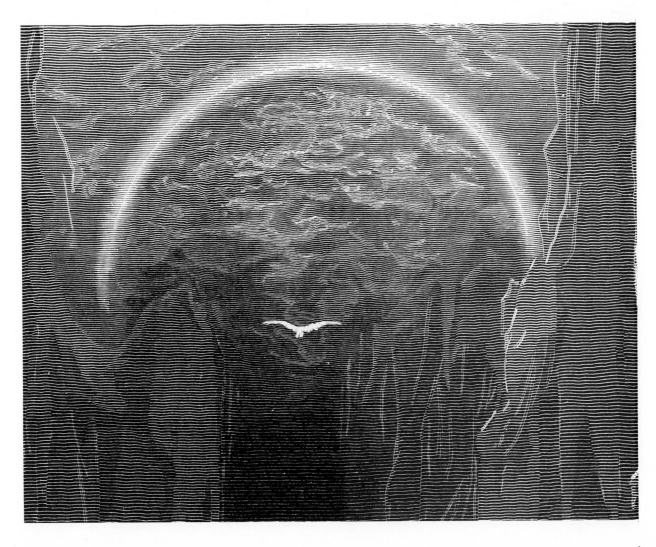

*in memory of*

ALICE

*the girl in wonderland*

*who found books*

*without pictures*

*and conversations*

*dull*

# INTRODUCTION

CHRISTIANS HAVE BEEN THINKING about the end since the beginning. Commenting upon the wonderfulness of the architecture of the temple, the apostles got their first rude hint. Jesus said that the temple of Herod—white limestone, gold appointments, gilded pinnacles—would be destroyed, gutted, leveled.

Later, lazing about the grassy slopes of Olivet, trying not to appear anxious, the apostles casually asked Jesus if the temple really had to be destroyed, did it mean the end of the world, would it happen in their lifetimes, was he really going to come again, and if so, when.

Jesus just as casually declined to give a precise time but, to allay their anxiety, he did give them a sort of timetable. Before the end would come, before he would come again, there would be wars and rumors of wars, plagues and famines, hurricanes and earthquakes, massacres and martyrdoms, and false prophets.

The temple of Herod was indeed destroyed in A.D. 70, as Flavius Josephus reported. Since that time hardly a day has gone by that the earth has not trembled. Hardly a night has passed that hundreds have not starved to death. Day and night the false prophets strut by as if in a parade. But no matter how much prayed for, no matter how often preached about, Jesus has not come back.

Those who do not believe in Jesus laugh at the prophecies he made but did not keep, but those who do believe wait. Some, in the first few centuries of the Christian era, fled to the deserts of Egypt, there to weave mats one day, unweave them the next, waiting prayerfully for Jesus to come again. Others, realizing that Jesus will come when he will come and not a moment before, set about to market the mats woven in the desert and to witness their faith in the marketplace.

Although there are as many styles of waiting as there have been Christians, these seem to be the basic two. The weavers focus their thinking and praying on the figure of Jesus coming with a rush on a cloud to judge. The marketers have as the model for their lives the son of God plunging himself into human existence and plashing about in the human enterprise.

Whatever one's style as a Christian, whatever age one lives in, the *eschata*—Greek word for "endthings"—must be accounted for. In apostolic times one could count endthings on the fingers of one hand: death, judgment, hell, and heaven. In medieval times one would have to use the fingers of both hands, distinguishing between two judgments and adding intermediate state, second coming, resurrection of the dead, and end of the world. In modern times one has to take off a shoe to include tribulation and millennium.

*Endtime* is one person's attempt to come to grips with the endthings, no matter how enumerated. The book is an anthology of the writings of others, an eschatological catalog, an *omnium-gatherum*, an informal encyclopedia of information on most, if not all, the phenomena surrounding the end for a Christian. Some of it is evidence, some of it exegesis, some inspirational, some perspirational, all of it motivational. To read, to reflect, perhaps to pray, perhaps even to take some appropriate action—that, no more, no less, is the purpose of *Endtime*.

In a way, *Endtime* is a symposium, a dinner to which a number of interesting and entertaining Christians have been invited. After bread has been broken, wine drunk, and thanks offered, the Christians speak of one or another aspect of endtime.

- Augustine of Hippo tells how the death of a friend devastated him at first but led him eventually to his dramatic conversion.

- Jerome had the fear of Jesus scared into him, he says, the night he dreamed of judgment.

- Martin Luther tells why Jesus will prefer him to Moses at the last judgment.

- John Henry Newman notes how well the hour of death is described as evening since evening has scripturally been the time for divine visitation.

- Hal Lindsey recounts his faltering answer to an amputee who had asked whether his resurrected body would have legs.

- Fulton J. Sheen goes back into the storehouse of his memory to fish out a few mounted and framed examples of heaven.

Although the guests hail from different centuries, they are all, to use the words of J. V. Langmead Casserley, "contemporaries in Christ." What they have in common is, to use the words of Richard Baxter which C. S. Lewis was to find so meaningful, "mere Christianity": that body of doctrine that constitutes the barest, merest minimum held in common by the majority of Christians since the Christian era began.

This is not to say that all the authors whose excerpted works appear in *Endtime* agree in each and every detail. The fifth trumpet, as John the Divine describes it in Revelation, is a plague of locusts. One exegete fully expects to see real locusts swarming across the fields; another interprets the chewing and chomping insects as symbols of what will corrode and consume; a third dons his helmet against locustlike helicopters ready to spray automatic weaponfire from their stingers.

Christians even of the merest sort have not always been known for their uniformity. Purgatory, long considered a doctrinal necessity by Roman Catholics, caused nothing but discord in the sixteenth century. But in the twentieth, C. S. Lewis, a non-Roman if ever there was one, felt that purgatory, even if it were not doctrinally necessary, might be medicinally desirable. Like antiseptic mouthwash after a tooth extraction.

Disunities aside, the Christians invited to participate in *Endtime* find they have much to talk about and much to share. First-century authors chatter with twentieth. Lettered discourse with unlettered. Europeans ramble with Americans; both are amazed by Africans and Egyptians. Chilly theologies transmit the warmth of their hearts to theologies that glow but whose hearts are ice. The authors of *Endtime* are, to use Thomas R. Kelly's words, "a holy fellowship, a blessed community."

Also entertaining but no less edifying at the after-dinner eschatology are the illustrators whose work accompanies the text:

- Albrecht Dürer, whose woodcuts of Revelation scenes, crowded with hyperactive figures, are full of sixteenth-century zow and pow;

- William Blake, whose inventions-for-etching of souls and bodies at death, judgment, and resurrection are truly waltzlike;

- Gustave Doré, whose steel engravings of human anatomy suffering the tortures of the damned are sadistically correct;

- Hans-Georg Rauch, whose antiwar, antiestablishment drawings are flooded with humanism;

- Brad Holland, whose dark creatures with symbolic limbs look as though they leaped from the Book of Revelation;

- Susannah Kelly, whose drawing for *The New York Times International Economic Survey* is a perfect illustration of how difficult it is for the rich person to get into heaven.

What we are to think of dying, especially of

dying before endtime, is the subject of the first chapter.

Doctors of both body and soul express a variety of opinions. Death is the result of life in its incredible profusion, observes a surgeon. Death is the result of sin originally committed, remarks more than one theologian. We are born dying, concludes a psychoanalyst; it is the central fact of life. We should practice dying, suggests a twentieth-century monk, the easier to let go when the time comes. We should do little else but practice, counsels a fifteenth-century monk; people are dropping like flies.

The day one dies in this world, suggests some first-century Christians, is the day one is born into the next; it is a time for joy and celebration. The day Jesus died was indeed one for horns and hats, streamers and noisemakers; as a medieval mystery play reminds us, Adam, David, Elijah, John the Baptist, and a host of others who had been waiting patiently were harrowed from hell, liberated from the limbo of the just.

The first five minutes after we die, promises a nineteenth-century pastor, will be full of the same sort of pyrotechnics. The soul will go to court, his or her case will be heard, particular judgment will be handed down. The verdict, describes a twentieth-century bishop, will be heaven, or hell, or perhaps a limbolike state wherein the soul undergoes a cleansing process which some theologians call purgatory.

What we are to make of waiting for endtime is the subject of the second chapter.

Christians have been waiting for so long that they have developed it into a fine art. Some spend their time weaving definitions one day (realized, inaugurated, apocalyptic)—and unweaving them the next (unrealized, future, prophetic). Others go into the warning business, establishing an eschatological DEW line to detect at the earliest possible moment the coming of the Lord.

The most perplexing question facing the professional eschatologist is *when*. Scripturally, there is a climax a-building, says one evangelist. Prophetically, this is the terminal generation, says another evangelist. Dramaturgically, it will come without warning, says an English scholar, like a knife in the back of the First Servant in *King Lear*.

Some professionals draw spiritual fruit from the eschatological countdown. Of that there can be no doubt. But others take deliberate pleasure in ticking off the hours, minutes, seconds before the end. These latter, by the way, have not escaped the scathing notice of the cartoonists who comment on our society. But the list of Christians who have waited for the end, patiently, holily, but for whom the end did not come, is too long for us to laugh too loudly.

The second most perplexing question about the end is *how*. With a bang, surmises a NASA astronomer; the universe that had an explosive birth will have an implosive death. With a whimper, says an English poet, that being the only sound a tepid society can muster. Other possibilities for the merely curious, suggests a *New York Times* science writer, are planet collision, supernova explosion, solar radiation, carbon dioxide, contagious disease, and resource depletion.

When Jesus comes for the second time, subject of the third chapter, there will be much to hear, to see, and not to see.

There will be a word of command, a shout from an archangel, a blast from the trumpet of the Lord; this is what Paul told the Thessalonians. Those who died in the Lord will rise from the dead. Those living in the Lord will be raptured; that is to say, swept or snatched or scooped up into the air to meet the Lord. (The word *rapture* is developed from the Greek verb Paul used to describe the sweeping or scooping movement.)

In this part of the book there is much glorious speculation about the resurrected body, reflecting perhaps our childlike concern that Jesus might not be able to put our bodies back together again. It is as though we imagine him pulling out a shoe box full of parts that were once posable dolls. What we want to know, once he dumps the parts on the floor, is whether he can snap the right limbs onto the right

torsos and will he know whose head goes on which body.

Rapture and wrath, or tribulation, seem to go hand in hand in the New Testament, but New Testament scholars seem hard-pressed to make them walk together. Some say the rapture will take place before the tribulation; some say during the tribulation; some say after the tribulation. Others say not all believers will be raptured. Still others say there will be no rapture, no tribulation, indeed no millennium, before the eternal state of heaven.

Also at the beginning of the end, or so the Book of Revelation tells us, is the tribulation, subject of the fourth chapter.

Tribulation is a period of seven years during which God will visit the earth with scourges or punishments. John the Divine says there will be twenty-one such visitations, or judgments, and they will come in three series: seals, trumpets, and vials, or bowls. There will be seven of each, and each will be delivered by an angel.

Playing major parts in the scenario of the tribulation are four foul but fascinating characters.

• Satan, his leash lengthened, is permitted to bag as

many souls as possible; his time is short; he has the power to kill.

• Antichrist, an attractive figure on the stage of world politics, goes about denying the existence of God the Father and the divinity of God the Son.

• False Prophet, sidekick to Antichrist, can call down fire from heaven and ventriloquize a dummy of Antichrist.

• Whore of Babylon, garishly bedraped and bejeweled, has a filthy mouth and with her vodka she mixes the blood of Christians freshly martyred.

These four would be most ingenious and interesting literary creations if they were not destined to play such prophetic and destructive roles in human history.

Horrific as the tribulation judgments are and horrid as the tribulation characters seem to be, they are also pleasurable. Christians enjoy doom, especially when it is impending on someone else. They seem to revel in doomsday books like *The Late Great Planet Earth* and *There's a New World Coming* by Hal Lindsey, proponent of the nuclear-bomb interpretation of seals, trumpets, vials.

Armageddon has become a growth industry, *Time* magazine has noted on more than one occasion, and eschatologists both sacred and profane seem to be merely cashing in on collective fear. What the critics and commentators fail to notice is that endtime pyrotechnics are based on the Book of Revelation and that John the Divine in chapters six through nineteen out-Hollywoods Hollywood.

The final battle of the forces of good and evil in the tribulation period is pure Panavision.

Picture Armageddon, the broad flat plain where Palestine pounded, and got pounded by, many an enemy.

Approaching on one side, as described by John the Divine, riding a white horse, easy in the saddle, is the warrior Christ.

Snapping in the wind is his cloak already stained red, a bloody reminder of casualties already inflicted.

Behind him, also riding white horses, clad in highly visible white linen, are his fellow warriors.

Unsheathed and held high, steel-tipped, sword-pointed, is his only weapon—a word, the word of God.

Trotting, cantering, galloping, the white cavalry charges across the plain.

Lumbering toward them, as interpreted by Hal Lindsey, are treaded, camouflaged creatures: the mechanized, perhaps nuclear-armed, jet-powered forces of Antichrist.

Fire. An exchange of most unfriendly fire.

When the smoke clears, Christ is victorious, Antichrist is dead, and Satan is committed to solitary confinement for a thousand years.

How the millennium will unfold is the subject of the fifth chapter.

Millennium is like the coming of summer, says one scholar, only more slowly and on a grander scale.

Cantering back across the battlefield will be Christ and his victorious cavalry.

On his garter the words "King of Kings, Lord of Lords" are plainly legible.

Scorched grasses green again. Coming quick as dandelions, joy is everywhere.

Plans for a summer wedding are made. Long affianced, the fullness of time having come, Christ and his Church will be joined in holy matrimony.

For the devoted, invited saints, no doubt there will be pavilions with chandeliers, crystal with champagne, china with chicken à la king.

Of course there will be an epithalamium, a poem for the occasion by a third-century Christian, almost anonymous, perhaps a bishop and martyr.

And the thousand-year reign of Christ the King will have begun.

Unlike other model societies in the history of the world, the kingdom of Christ will be perfect in both theory and practice. Its many and varied perfections, however, are not a piece of cake—at least, not a piece from the wedding cake. The kingdom has been interpreted nine different ways, shrugs one scholar. The kingdom has five sure signs, grins one evangelist. And the kingdom is chronologically uncertain: it may have already begun; it is about to begin; it will begin at some point in the definite future.

What we are to think of judgment at world's end is the subject of the sixth chapter.

The dead are summoned to the great white throne, according to John the Divine, and God will pore over the book of life. Sheep will be separated from goats, says the evangelist Matthew, the former heading for greener pastures, the latter for fiery furnaces.

It is called "the general reckoning" in a fifteenth-century morality play. It is termed "the great assize" by an eighteenth-century evangelist. It is a spectacle unrivaled, as the engravings of Blake and Doré panoramically detail.

The judge may be gracious, says a nineteenth-century pastor, or he may be wrathful, says a thirteenth-century theologian; but the defendant, when his or her day in court comes, will surely be apprehensive, says a fourth-century monk.

The only consolation, says a twentieth-century priest, echoing a sixteenth-century mystic, is that in the evening we shall be judged by love.

That hell has been, and indeed still is, a burning issue is the subject of the seventh chapter.

Hell is a pit full of fire, says the evangelist Mark; the fire is undying and unquenchable, says Basil of Caesarea; the whole thing is a veritable Vesuvius, says Minucius Felix.

These views from the first few centuries of the Christian era are corroborated by visions in the sixteenth and twentieth centuries.

It is a comfortable doctrine; it is an intolerable doctrine. The discussion continues. Fear of it is healthy; fear of it is neurotic. The debate never ends.

Two poets and a playwright from the fourteenth to the twentieth centuries have contributed, if not to man's knowledge, then to his appreciation of hell. And cartoonists have customized hells for people who have especially or notoriously offended.

Disquieting are the not-quite-after-death experiences of people who saw that as many people go to hell as to heaven: a corroboration of Jesus's parable of the five wise, five foolish virgins.

Will people throw parties in heaven?

Will people go to heaven by themselves, or will they arrive in chartered buses with rest rooms and picture windows?

These are the sort of questions we have long wanted to ask about heaven, subject of the eighth chapter, but we could not find a cleric with satisfactory answers.

What is God doing? is answered by a fourteenth-century Dominican.

What does God look like? is answered by a thirteenth-century Franciscan and a fifteenth-century cardinal.

Will we work in heaven or will we rest? A seventeenth-century clergyman counts nine kinds of rest.

Will we huddle like angels before the throne of God, or will we be able to peek about, see some family, say hello to friends? These are answered by a nineteenth-century Jesuit.

Will I have my pet in heaven?

Not many theologians in the history of Christian thought have given a good bow-wow about animals in the afterlife. Arnobius of Sicca did maintain that animals have souls. Aelred of Rievaulx did observe that animals can develop spiritual friendships. Even Augustine of Hippo was forced to concede that there is in the souls of beasts an undeniable force.

Ratiocination whose conclusion is that animals cannot possibly be in the afterlife proves with cogency only that animals cannot possibly be in this life. *Quod non potest demonstrari.* Reason alone is blind; it must be led gently by the imagination, the sort of imagination C. S. Lewis displayed when he answered "where will you put all the mosquitoes" with "combine a heaven for mosquitoes with a hell for humans."

Brimful of imagination too is the Mississippi of metaphor flowing blackfully through gospel song.

Knowing what endtime is and what the endthings are is not always helpful. Sometimes such knowledge causes anxiety; sometimes it paralyzes; sometimes it provokes violence. Living in endtime, therefore, subject of the ninth chapter, requires the special attention of all eschatologists.

The perfect endtime virtue is hope, which a Jesuit paleontologist assures us is the horizon before the sunrise.

The perfect endtime country, or so says a German theologian, is America, where life is a succession of trials and errors and the future is gracious to those who persevere.

The perfect endtime prayer is the one Jesus prayed to his Father. On its petitions twelve men and women from different centuries and different communions offer meditative comments.

One modern ascetical master suggests three ways to pray the Lord's Prayer.

Pictured praying it is the Lord himself as he is portrayed in various Jesus movies.

Lastly, the perfect endtime adverb—perfect grammatically as well as theologically—is *hopefully*.

Baptists and Methodists, Quakers and Catholics, Lutherans and Presbyterians, Conformists and Nonconformists, Liberals and Evangelicals, all can leap over the boundaries of church membership and become contemporaries in Christ. What they have in common is mere Christianity and when they share that commonality, the result is a blessed community, a holy fellowship. When they share it with regard to endthings, the happy result is *Endtime*: mere Christianity but with pictures and conversations.

WILLIAM GRIFFIN
*Macmillan Publishing Co., Inc.*
*August 19, 1979*

# END-TIME

I.

# DYING

# THE LONG HABIT OF LIVING

## Lewis Thomas

"THE LONG HABIT OF LIVING," said Thomas Browne, "indisposeth us to dying." These days, the habit has become an addiction: we are hooked on living; the tenacity of its grip on us, and ours on it, grows in intensity. We cannot think of giving it up, even when living loses its zest—even when we have lost the zest for zest.

We have come a long way in our technologic capacity to put death off, and it is imaginable that we might learn to stall it for even longer periods, perhaps matching the life spans of the Abkhazian Russians, who are said to go on, springily, for a century and a half. If we can rid ourselves of some of our chronic, degenerative diseases, and cancer, strokes, and coronaries, we might go on and on. It sounds attractive and reasonable, but it is no certainty. If we became free of disease, we would make a much better run of it for the last decade or so, but might still terminate on about the same schedule as now. We may be like the genetically different lines of mice, or like Hayflick's different tissue-culture lines, programmed to die after a predetermined number of days, clocked by their genomes. If this is the way it is, some of us will continue to wear out and come unhinged in the sixth decade, and some much later, depending on genetic timetables.

If we ever do achieve freedom from most of today's diseases, or even complete freedom from disease, we will perhaps terminate by drying out and blowing away on a light breeze, but we will still die.

Most of my friends do not like this way of looking at it. They prefer to take it for granted that we die only because we get sick, with one lethal ailment or another, and if we did not have our diseases we might go on indefinitely. Even biologists choose to think this about themselves, despite the evidences of the absolute inevitability of death that surround their professional lives. Everything dies, all around, trees, plankton, lichens, mice, whales, flies, mitochondria. In the simplest creatures it is sometimes difficult to see. it as death, since the strands of replicating DNA they leave behind are more conspicuously the living parts of themselves than with us (not that it is fundamentally any different, but it seems so). Flies do not develop a ward round of diseases that carry them off one by one. They simply age, and die, like flies.

We hanker to go on, even in the face of plain evidence that long, long lives are not necessarily pleasurable in the kind of society we have arranged thus far. We will be lucky if we can postpone the search for new technologies for a while, until we have discovered some satisfactory things to do with the extra time. Something will surely have to be found to take the place of sitting on the porch reexamining one's watch.

Perhaps we would not be so anxious to prolong life if we did not detest so much the sickness of withdrawal. It is astonishing how little information we have about this universal process, with all the other dazzling advances in biology. It is almost as though we wanted not to know about it. Even if we could imagine the act of death in isolation, without any preliminary stage of being struck down by disease, we would be fearful of it.

There are signs that medicine may be taking a new interest in the process, partly from curiosity, partly from an embarrassed realization that we have not been handling this aspect of disease with as much skill as physicians once displayed, back in the days before they became convinced that disease was their solitary and sometimes defeatable enemy. It used to be the hardest and most important of all the services of a good doctor to be on hand at the time of death and to provide comfort, usually in the home. Now it is done in hospitals, in secrecy (one of the reasons for the increased fear of death these days may be that so many people are totally unfamiliar with it; they never actually see it happen in real life). Some of our technology permits us to deny its existence, and we maintain flickers of life for long stretches in one community of cells or another, as though we were keeping a flag flying. Death is not a sudden-all-at-once affair; cells go down in sequence, one by one. You can, if you like, recover great numbers of them many hours after the lights have gone out and grow them in cultures. It takes hours, even days, before the irreversible word finally gets around to all the provinces.

We may be about to rediscover that dying is not such a bad thing to do after all. Sir William Osler took this view: he disapproved of people who spoke of the agony of death, maintaining that there was no such thing.

In a nineteenth-century memoir on an expedition in Africa, there is a story by David Livingstone about his own experience of near-death. He was caught by a lion, crushed across the chest in the animal's great jaws, and saved in the instant by a lucky shot from a friend. Later, he remembered the episode in clear detail. He was so amazed by the extraordinary sense of peace, calm, and total painlessness associated with being killed that he constructed a theory that all creatures are provided with a protective physiologic mechanism, switched on at the verge of death, carrying them through in a haze of tranquillity.

I have seen agony in death only once, in a patient with rabies; he remained acutely aware of every stage in the process of his own disintegration over a twenty-four-hour period, right up to his final moment. It was as though, in the special neuropathology of rabies, the switch had been prevented from turning.

We will be having new opportunities to learn more about the physiology of death at first hand, from the increasing numbers of cardiac patients who have been through the whole process and then back again. Judging from what has been found out thus far, from the first generation of people resuscitated from cardiac standstill (already termed the Lazarus syndrome), Osler seems to have been right. Those who remember parts or all of their episodes do not recall any fear, or anguish. Several people who remained conscious throughout, while appearing to have been quite dead, could only describe a remarkable sensation of detachment. One man underwent coronary occlusion with cessation of the heart and dropped for all practical purposes dead, in front of a hospital; within a few minutes his heart had been restarted by electrodes and he breathed his way back into life. According to his account, the strangest thing was that there were so many people around him, moving so urgently, handling his body with such excitement, while all his awareness was of quietude.

In a recent study of the reaction to dying in patients with obstructive disease of the lungs, it was concluded that the process was considerably more shattering for the professional observers than the observed. Most of the patients appeared to be preparing themselves with equanimity for death, as though intuitively familiar with the business. One elderly woman reported that the only painful and distressing part of the process was in being interrupted; on several occasions she was provided with conventional therapeutic measures to maintain oxygenation or restore fluids and electrolytes, and each time she found the experience of coming back harrowing; she deeply resented the interference with her dying.

I find myself surprised by the thought that dying is an alright thing to do, but perhaps it should not surprise. It is, after all, the most ancient and fundamental of biologic functions, with its mechanisms worked out with the same attention to detail, the same provision for the advantage of the organism, the same abundance of genetic information for guidance through the stages, that we have long since

## THE LAZARUS SYNDROME

### John the Evangelist (John 11:39–44)

JESUS SAID, Take ye away the stone. Martha, the sister of him that was dead, saith unto him, Lord, by this time he stinketh: for he hath been dead four days.

Jesus saith unto her, Said I not unto thee, that, if thou wouldest believe, thou shouldest see the glory of God?

Then they took away the stone from the place where the dead was laid. And Jesus lifted up his eyes, and said, Father, I thank thee that thou hast heard me.

And I knew that thou hearest me always: but because of the people which stand by I said it, that they may believe that thou hast sent me.

And when he thus had spoken, he cried with a loud voice, Lazarus, come forth.

And he that was dead came forth, bound hand and foot with graveclothes; and his face was bound about with a napkin. Jesus saith unto them, Loose him, and let him go.

become accustomed to finding in all the crucial acts of living.

Very well. But even so, if the transformation is a coordinated, integrated physiologic process in its initial, local stages, there is still that permanent vanishing of consciousness to be accounted for. Are we to be stuck forever with this problem? Where on earth does it go? Is it simply stopped dead in its tracks, lost in humus, wasted? Considering the tendency of nature to find uses for complex and intricate mechanisms, this seems to me unnatural. I prefer to think of it as somehow separated off at the filaments of its attachment, and then drawn like an easy breath back into the membrane of its origin, a fresh memory for a biospherical nervous system, but I have no data on the matter.

This is for another science, another day. It may turn out, as some scientists suggest, that we are forever precluded from investigating consciousness by a sort of indeterminacy principle that stipulates that the very act of looking will make it twitch and blur out of sight. If this is true, we will never learn. I envy some of my friends who are convinced about telepathy; oddly enough, it is my European scientist acquaintances who believe it most freely and take it most lightly. All their aunts have received communications, and there they sit, with proof of the motility of consciousness at their fingertips, and the making of a new science. It is discouraging to have had the wrong aunts, and never the ghost of a message.

# DIE WHEN YOU ARE ALIVE

## David Steindl-Rast

FACED WITH THE PROSPECT of death, we must say "I can't take it." After a life in which we take and take, we eventually come up against something which we can't take; death takes us. This is serious. One can go through life taking, and in the end all this will add up to having taken one's life, which is in a real sense suicide. But we can learn to give ourselves. It doesn't come easy, conditioned as we are to be fearful of giving ourselves, but it can be learned. In learning to give ourselves we learn both to live and to die—to die not only our final death, but those many deaths of daily living by which we become more alive.

This is precisely the point: whenever we give ourselves to whatever presents itself instead of grasping and holding it, we flow with it. We do not arrest the flow of reality, we do not try to possess, we do not try to hold back, but we let go, and everything is alive as long as we let it go. When we cut the flower it is no longer alive; when we take water out of the river it is just a bucketful of water, not the flowing river; when we take air and put it in a balloon it is no longer the wind. Everything that flows and is alive has to be taken and given at the same time—taken with a very, very light touch. Here again we are not playing off give against take, but learning to balance the two in a genuine response to living as well as to dying.

I remember a story told me by a young woman whose mother was close to death. She once asked her: "Mother, are you afraid of dying?" and her mother answered, "I am not afraid, but I don't know how to do it." The daughter, startled by that reply, lay down on the couch and wondered how she herself would do it if she had to; and she came back with the answer: "Mother, I think you have to give yourself to it." Her mother didn't say anything then but later she said, "Fix me a cup of tea and make it just the way I like it, with lots of cream and sugar, because it will be my last cup of tea. I know now how to die."

This inner gesture of giving yourself to it, of letting go from moment to moment, is what is so terribly difficult for us; but it can be applied to almost any area of experience. We mentioned time, for instance: there is the whole problem of "free time," as we call it, of leisure. We think of leisure as the privilege of those who can afford to take time (this endless taking!)—when in reality it isn't a privilege at all. Leisure is a virtue, and one that anyone can acquire. It is not a matter of taking but of giving time. Leisure is the virtue of those who give time to whatever it is that takes time—give as much time to it as it takes. That is the reason why leisure is almost inaccessible to us. We are so preoccupied with taking, with appropriating. Hence, there is more and more free time, and less and less leisure. In former centuries when there was much less free time for anybody, and vacations, for instance, were unheard of, people were leisurely while working; now they work hard at being leisurely. You find people who work from nine to five with this attitude of "Let's get it done, let's take things in hand," totally purpose-oriented, and when five o'clock comes they are exhausted and have no time for real leisure either. If you don't work leisurely, you won't be able to play leisurely. So they collapse, or else they pick up their tennis racket or their golf clubs and continue working, giving themselves a workout, as they say.

We can laugh about it, but it goes deep. The letting go is a real death, a real dying; it costs us an enormous amount of energy, the price, as it were, which life exacts from us over and over again for being truly alive. For this seems to be one of the basic laws of life; we have only what we give up. We all have had the experience of a friend admiring something we owned, when for a moment we had an impulse to give that thing away. If we follow this impulse—and something may be at stake that we really like, and it pains for a moment—then for ever and ever we will have this thing; it is really ours; in our memory it is something we have and can never lose.

It is all the more so with personal relationships. If we are truly friends with someone, we have to give up that friend all the time, we have to give freedom to that friend—like a mother who gives up her child continually. If the mother hangs onto the child, first of all it will never be born; it will die in the womb. But even after it is born physically it has to be set free and let go over and over again. So many difficulties that we have with our mothers, and that mothers have with their children, spring exactly from this, that they can't let go; and apparently it is

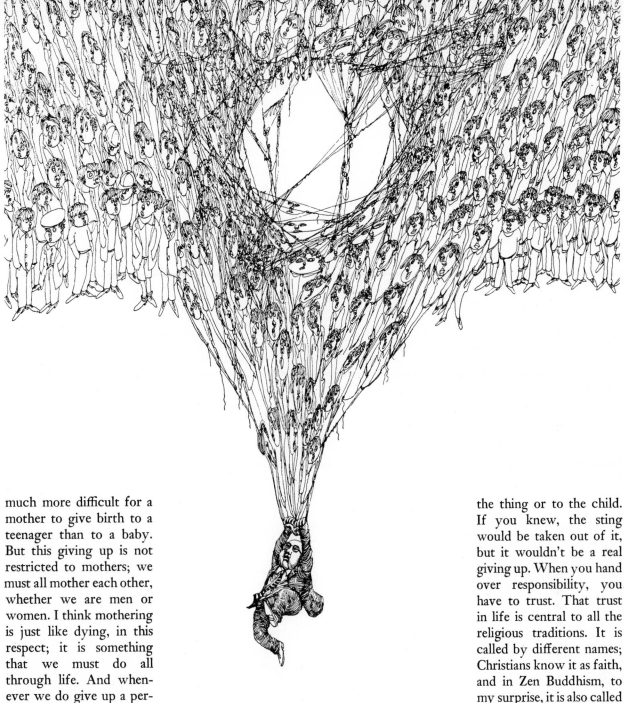

much more difficult for a mother to give birth to a teenager than to a baby. But this giving up is not restricted to mothers; we must all mother each other, whether we are men or women. I think mothering is just like dying, in this respect; it is something that we must do all through life. And whenever we do give up a person or a thing or a position, when we truly give it up, we die—yes, but we die into greater aliveness. We die into a real oneness with life. Not to die, not to give up, means to exclude ourselves from that free flow of life.

But giving up is very different from letting someone down; in fact, the two are exact opposites. It is an upward gesture, not a downward one. Giving up the child, the mother upholds and supports him, as friends must support one another. We cannot let down responsibilities that are given to us, but we must be ready to give them up, and this is the risk of living, the risk of the give and take. There is a tremendous risk involved, because when you really give up, you don't know what is going to happen to the thing or to the child. If you knew, the sting would be taken out of it, but it wouldn't be a real giving up. When you hand over responsibility, you have to trust. That trust in life is central to all the religious traditions. It is called by different names; Christians know it as faith, and in Zen Buddhism, to my surprise, it is also called faith, though with a connotation different from the one it has in the biblical tradition. It isn't faith in anything or anyone, but there is a lot of emphasis in Buddhist monasteries on the tension between faith and doubt, faith always being a nose's length ahead of doubt. The greater your doubt, the greater your faith will be—faith in ultimate reality, faith in yourself, if you wish, your true Self. But in the Buddhist as well as in the Christian tradition faith is courage—the courage to take upon yourself the risk of living, and dying, because the two are inseparable.

Thus, one could distinguish between two ways of dying: a mere giving in, which means you are being killed without really dying; and a vital way of dying, a giving up, which is this giving of yourself and so dying into deeper life. But that takes a great deal of courage, because it is always a risk, a step into something unknown. It also takes a great deal of vitality, and that is why I am a little reluctant to accept what Karl Rahner and Ladislas Boros have to say about death. They are two German Catholic theologians who have written with a great deal of insight on death, but both put much weight on their ideas of what happens in a person's last moments. I would much rather say: Die when you are alive, because you don't know how well you will be able to do something that takes all your energy when you are senile, weak, or very sick.

# WE ARE BORN DYING

*June Singer*

WHEN the late-winter sun burns the snow off tree branches and buds begin to swell, we anticipate that in due time there will be tiny yellow-green leaflets, then pale leaves greening as summer progresses, which will turn red or golden in autumn, and that before the winter returns they will become dry and brittle and subject to the merciless wind which tears them off and blows them away. Nor are we surprised, though, when some leaves drop before they are fully grown, nor when some are blown off or chewed up by insects when they are fully ripe and strong-looking, nor that there are always a few that, shriveled and brown, cling tightly to the twig in the face of autumn storms and winter winds, until the new buds gently nudge them aside.

I have observed in the course of my work [as a psychoanalyst], and also in the events in my personal life, that nature has an inexorable way of proceeding that is, at the same time, unpredictable as to details. We enter into life, but despite the actuarial tables and the learned doctors' prognoses there is no way of knowing whether we shall die in the spring or the summer of life or cling to our last breath in the icy cold of winter. Only one thing is certain, life proceeds onward toward its goal, which is death, and it is the knowledge of that fact which determines much that we do, and the choices that we make. I heard a television announcement the other day asking for contributions to aid research on a fatal children's disease. The sentence that caught my attention was, "Did you know that some children are born dying?" I started for a moment and then I knew why the words had stabbed me —I know that *all* children are born dying, *we are all born dying*! This is the central fact of life. . . .

# A HAPPY DEATH

## *Abigail McCarthy*

WE SEEM TO BE MADE SO as to find our own deaths unthinkable. Others die; it hardly seems credible that we ourselves will. This attitude is in part, I suppose, a protective device of nature. It is also a symptom of the Zeitgeist. Until recently, we averted our eyes at the mention of death. We spoke of it, if at all, in terms of the death rate, rather than of death, the end of us all.

But we are being persuaded these days to face the reality of death as the inevitable, ordinarily natural, end of life. We have been instructed by research in the psychology of the dying.

It began with Elisabeth Kubler Ross's compassionate study of the stages those who are dying go through. It has continued with the current Hospice movement, the effort to make death less dreaded by providing care in homelike places— places where friends and family may visit or stay and where medicine concentrates on comfort and the control of pain.

We have been instructed, too, by the emergence of the old from the retirement colonies and the ill-named "rest homes" to which society relegated them. Twenty million Americans are over sixty-five today. There is at least one estimate that there will be over forty million by the year 2000. The expected life span of both men and women has lengthened dramatically. The age of retirement has been forced upward. Those in the last years of life are once again active and visible among us, and will have to face the irony that they are not so much afraid of death as of dying.

In our effort to understand that death is the ultimate human act and attend it with humanity, it would almost seem that we have come full circle.

When I was a small girl, death was not a stranger. In our little town, people died at home, more often than not, and were buried from their homes, too. It was not unusual, on the way to school, to pass a house marked with the sign of death within—a spray of palm or fern, tied with purple for an adult, white for a child.

Our dying were not cut off from the living. They lay quite often in downstairs bedrooms with sliding

## DEATH OF A FRIEND

### Augustine of Hippo

IN THOSE YEARS when I first began to teach rhetoric in my native town, I had made a friend, but too dear to me, from a community of pursuits, of mine own age, and, as myself, in the first opening flower of youth. He had grown up of a child with me, and we had been both school-fellows and play fellows. . . .

For long, sore sick of a fever, he lay senseless in a death-sweat; and his recovery being despaired of, he was baptized, unknowing; myself meanwhile little regarding, and presuming that his soul would retain rather what it had received of me, not what was wrought on his unconscious body. But it proved far otherwise: for he was refreshed, and restored. Forthwith, as soon as I could speak with him (and I could, so soon as he was able, for I never left him, and we hung but too much upon each other), I essayed to jest with him, as though he would jest with me at that baptism which he had received, when utterly absent in mind and feeling, but had now understood that he had received. But he so shrank from me, as from an enemy; and with a wonderful and sudden freedom bade me, as I would continue his friend, forbear such language to him. I, all astonished and amazed, suppressed all my emotions till he should grow well, and his health were strong enough for me to deal with him as I would. But he was taken away from my frenzy, that with Thee he might be preserved for my comfort; a few days after in my absence, he was attacked again by the fever, and so departed.

At this grief my heart was utterly darkened; and whatever I beheld was death.

---

or folding doors slightly ajar so that they were aware of the household comings and goings, of the neighbors and friends who dropped by to make inquiries or to bring gifts of food and bunches of garden flowers. (The fragrance of peonies or of lilacs is still a sharp reminder of those times to me.)

The dying often confided their last wishes and took part in planning their funerals with the certainty that their requests would be honored. Thus, their separation from the living was, in prospect, less abrupt, less brutal. (In fact, it may have been sadly true that many a person felt uniquely important only at the time of death.) Dying confirmed a certain dignity on the whole house. Something grave, special, and universal centered there. A nurse moved in to join the family. The priest or minister came and went. Relatives came from afar.

Although we were of varied religions and nationalities in that little town, our rituals of grief were pretty much the same. Once death occurred the house was opened to all who came, the dead "viewed," wept, and prayed over, the mourning consoled, and the body watched over all night. If Protestants murmured about the tendency of Catholics to be less solemn, we, in our turn, were superior about their poverty of ceremony. But for both, and for the unbeliever, bells tolled, processions formed, and shovels full of earth rattled onto the coffin before those who had followed it turned away. Afterward we stayed mindful of our dead. We were at home in cemeteries, visited them often, and brought bouquets and plants on anniversaries.

Yet even then things were changing. The long period of mourning once observed had already disappeared. And, in what seems a remarkable short time, looking back, other things changed, too. The dying were taken to hospitals. The dead were taken to funeral homes. Cremation, the donation of organs and bodies, and memorial services began to take the place of processions and burials. And, in the process, the gap between those who were to die and those who would go on living widened to the breaking point. Dying began to seem shameful and unmentionable. The dying were left in dreadful isolation, and the bereft were not allowed to grieve.

Somehow the war on the causes of death gradually

became a war on the dying. For doctors and scientists—for all medical personnel—the dying came to seem their failures. With misplaced zeal, as we are coming to realize, they labor to keep the body alive at the expense of the person. Those doomed by age or disease lose all dignity and their suffering is needlessly prolonged.

In a simpler time, in pioneer days and in rural cultures, living and dying were part of a continuous process. But it was also possible to come to emotional terms with the fact that killing diseases cut short those in the prime of life and children, too. There was a time, for example, when tuberculosis was known in almost every family. A whole literature grew up around it. A common grief was recognized in tears shed over Mimi, over Camille, and over Beth in *Little Women*. Untimely death was accepted as a sad, even tragic, part of the general experience of humankind. And, although research

struggled with and eventually triumphed over consumption, as it was graphically and popularly called, most doctors dealt with it in terms of the sick person. "It was up to the doctor," as one authority put it, "to see to it that the end came as peacefully as possible for the patient, and to provide information and support for the patient's family."

That such care should be described as a phenomenon of the past is a measure of how far from the ideal we have strayed. But now we are beginning to see that advances against disease—especially against today's dreaded killer, cancer—can be concomitant with the practice of that older, more humane medicine. And there is today a new honesty that allows for, makes possible, shared thought and feeling between the dying and those around them. We used to speak of "a happy death." The phrase seems strange today, but we may come to use it once more.

# DEATH, THE RESULT OF LIFE

## *Paul Brand*

WHEN I LOOK at the world of nature, its most impressive feature as a closed system is the lavish expenditure of life at every level. Every time a whale takes a mouthful he swallows a million plankton. Every garden pond is a scene of constant sacrifice of life for the building up of other life. Death is not some evil intruder who has upset beautiful creation; it is woven into the very fabric and essence of the beautiful creation itself. Most of the higher animals are designed so that they depend for their survival on the death of lower levels of life. Having created this food pyramid, and placed man at its apex, the Creator instructed him to enjoy and to use it all responsibly. In modern, Western culture, we tend to see a certain ruthlessness and lack of love in nature, but I believe that viewpoint comes from a civilization whose main contact with animal life is through domestic pets and children's anthropomorphic animal stories. . . .

I feel reasonably sure that Adam felt pain, if his body was like mine. If there were sharp rocks on which he could have hurt himself, I hope he had a pain system to warn him. The pain network is so inextricably tied to the functions of the body—it tells you when to go to the bathroom, how close you may go to the fire, and carries feelings of pleasure as well as pain—that I could not imagine a worthwhile body in this world without it.

And, I believe physical death was present before the fall also. The very nature of the chain of life requires it. You cannot have soil without the death of bacteria; you couldn't have thrushes without the death of worms. The shape of a tiger's teeth are wholly inappropriate for eating plant matter (and even vegetarians thrive off the death of plants, part of the created order). A vulture would not survive unless something died. I don't see death as being a bad thing at all.

*Drawing by Koren;* © *1969*
THE NEW YORKER MAGAZINE, INC.

*"What's it like to be at the top of the food chain?"*

# DEATH, THE RESULT OF SIN

*C. S. Lewis*

HUMAN DEATH, according to the Christians, is a result of a human sin; man, as originally created, was immune from it: man, when redeemed, and recalled to a new life (which will, in some undefined sense, be a bodily life) in the midst of a more organic and more fully obedient nature, will be immune from it again. This doctrine is, of course, simply nonsense if a man is nothing but a natural organism. But if he were, then, as we have seen, all thoughts would be equally nonsensical, for all would have irrational causes. Man must therefore be a composite being—a natural organism tenanted by, or in a state of symbiosis with, a supernatural spirit. The Christian doctrine, startling as it must seem to those who have not fully cleared their minds of naturalism, states that the relations which we now observe between that spirit and that organism, are abnormal or pathological ones. At present spirit can retain its foothold against the incessant counterattacks of nature (both physiological and psychological) only by perpetual vigilance, and physiological nature always defeats it in the end. Sooner or later it becomes unable to resist the disintegrating processes at work in the body and death ensues. A little later the natural organism (for it does not long enjoy its triumph) is similarly conquered by merely physical nature and returns to the inorganic. But, in the Christian view, this was not always so. The spirit was once not a garrison, maintaining its post with difficulty in a hostile nature, but was fully "at home" with its organism, like a king in his own country or a rider on his own horse —or better still, as the human part of a centaur was "at home" with the equine part. Where spirit's power over the organism was complete and unresisted, death would never occur. No doubt, spirit's permanent triumph over natural forces which, if left to themselves, would kill the organism, would involve a continued miracle: but only the same sort of miracle which occurs every day—for whenever we think rationally we are, by direct spiritual power, forcing certain atoms in our brain and certain psychological tendencies in our natural soul to do what they would never have done if left to nature. The Christian doctrine would be fantastic only if the present frontier situation between spirit and nature in each human being were so intelligible and self-explanatory that we just "saw" it to be the only one that could ever have existed. But is it?

In reality the frontier situation is so odd that nothing but custom could make it seem natural, and nothing but the Christian doctrine can make it fully intelligible. There is certainly a state of war. But not a war of mutual destruction. Nature by dominating spirit wrecks all spiritual activities: spirit by dominating nature confirms and improves natural activities. The brain does not become less a brain by being used for rational thought. The emotions do not become weak or jaded by being organized in the service of a moral will—indeed they grow richer and stronger as a beard is strengthened by being shaved or a river is deepened by being banked. The body of the reasonable and virtuous man, other things being equal, is a better body than that of the fool or the debauchee, and his sensuous pleasures better simply as sensuous pleasures: for the slaves of the senses, after the first bait, are starved by their masters. Everything happens as if what we saw was not war but rebellion: that rebellion of the lower against the higher by which the lower destroys both the higher and itself. And if the present situation is one of rebellion, then reason cannot reject but will rather demand the belief that there was a time before the rebellion broke out and may be a time after it has

---

## SIN INHERITED

*Paul the Apostle*
*(Romans 5:12)*

WHEREFORE, as by one man sin entered into the world, and death by sin; and so death passed upon all men, for all that have sinned.

# THE FIRST MAN'S DISOBEDIENCE

## Theophilus of Antioch

FOR THE FIRST MAN disobedience procured his expulsion from Paradise. Not, therefore, as if there were any evil in the tree of knowledge, but from his disobedience did man draw, as from a fountain, labor, pain, grief, and at last fall a prey to death.

tion of either corpse or ghost. Because the thing ought not to be divided, each of the halves into which it falls by division is detestable. The explanations which naturalism gives both of bodily shame and of our feeling about the dead are not satisfactory. It refers us to primitive taboos and superstitions—as if these themselves were not obviously results of the thing to be explained. But once accept the Christian doctrine that man was originally a unity and that the present division is unnatural, and all the phenomena fall into place. It would be fantastic to suggest that the doctrine was devised to explain our enjoyment of a chapter in Rabelais, a good ghost story, or the *Tales* of Edgar Allan Poe. It does so nonetheless.

been settled. And if we thus see grounds for believing that the supernatural spirit and the natural organism in man have quarreled, we shall immediately find it confirmed from two quite unexpected quarters.

Almost the whole of Christian theology could perhaps be deduced from the two facts: (a) that men make coarse jokes, and (b) that they feel the dead to be uncanny. The coarse joke proclaims that we have here an animal which finds its own animality either objectionable or funny. Unless there had been a quarrel between the spirit and the organism, I do not see how this could be: it is the very mark of the two not being "at home" together. But it is very difficult to imagine such a state of affairs as original —to suppose a creature which from the very first was half shocked and half tickled to death at the mere fact of being the creature it is. I do not perceive that dogs see anything funny about being dogs; I suspect that angels see nothing about being angels. Our feeling about the dead is equally odd. It is idle to say that we dislike corpses because we are afraid of ghosts. You might say with equal truth that we fear ghosts and dislike corpses—for the ghost owes much of its horror to the associated ideas of pallor, decay, coffins, shrouds, and worms. In reality we hate the division which makes possible the concep-

# THE DEVIL'S ENVY

## Martin Luther

DEATH HAS BEEN introduced into the world through the devil's envy, and on this account the devil is called the author of death. For what else does Satan do than seduce from true religion, provoke sedition, cause wars, pestilence, etc., and bring about every evil?

# THINKING ABOUT DEATH

## *Thomas à Kempis*

YOUR TIME HERE is short, very short; take another look at the way in which you spend it. Here man is today; tomorrow, he is lost to view; and once a man is out of sight, it's not long before he passes out of mind. How dull they are, how obdurate, these hearts of ours, always occupied with the present, instead of looking ahead to what lies before us! Every action of yours, every thought, should be those of a man who expects to die before the day is out. Death would have no great terrors for you if you had a quiet conscience, would it? Then why not keep clear of sin, instead of running away from death? If you aren't fit to face death today, it's very unlikely you will be by tomorrow; besides, tomorrow is an uncertain quantity; you have no guarantee that there will be any tomorrow—for you.

What's the use of having a long life, if there's so little improvement to show for it? Improvement? Unfortunately it happens, only too often, that the longer we live the more we add to our guilt. If only we could point to one day in our life here that was really well spent! Years have passed by since we turned to God; and how little can we show, many of us, in the way of solid results! Fear death if you will, but don't forget that long life may have greater dangers for you.

Well for you, if you keep an eye on your deathbed all the time, and put yourself in the right dispositions for death as each day passes. Perhaps, before now, you've seen a man die? Remember, then, that you have got the same road to travel.

Each morning, imagine to yourself that you won't last till evening; and when night comes, don't make bold to promise yourself a new day. Be ready for it all the time; so live, that death cannot take you unawares.

Plenty of people die quite suddenly, without any warning; the Son of Man will appear just when we are not expecting him. And when that last hour comes, you'll find yourself taking a completely different view of the life that lies behind you. How bitterly you will regret all that carelessness, all that slackening of effort!

If you hope to live well and wisely, try to be, here and now, the man you would want to be on your deathbed. What will give you confidence then—the confidence which ensures a happy death? To have despised the world utterly; to have longed earnestly for advancement in holiness; to have loved discipline, to have taken penance seriously, to have obeyed readily, to have renounced self, to have put up with everything that was uncongenial to you for the love of Christ.

You see, there is so much you can undertake while you are still in health—what will you be able to manage, when illness comes? Illness doesn't often change people for the better, any more than going on pilgrimage makes saints of them.

You will have friends and relations to pray for you? Don't, for that reason, leave the business of your soul to be settled later on. You will be forgotten sooner than you imagine; better make provision now, by opening a credit account for yourself,

# OUT OF MY SOUL'S DEPTH

*Thomas Campion*

*Out of my soul's depth to thee my*
*cries have sounded:*
*Let thine ears my plaints receive,*
*on just fear grounded.*
*Lord, should'st thou weigh our*
*faults, who's not confounded?*

*But with grace thou censur'st thine*
*when they have errèd,*
*Therefore shall thy blessed name*
*be loved and fearèd.*
*E'en to thy throne my thoughts and*
*eyes are rearèd.*

*Thee alone my hopes attend, on*
*thee relying;*
*In thy sacred word I'll trust, to thee*
*fast flying,*
*Long ere the watch shall break, the*
*morn descrying.*

*In the mercies of our God who live*
*securèd,*
*May of full redemption rest in him*
*assurèd,*
*Their sin-sick souls by him shall*
*be recurèd.*

My friend, my very dear friend, only think what dangers you can avoid, what anxieties you can escape, if you will be anxious now, sensitive now to the thought of death! Make it your business so to live, today, that you can meet death with a smile, not with a shudder, when it comes. If that moment is to be the beginning of a life with Christ, you must learn, now, to die to the world; if you are to find free access to Christ then, you must learn now to despise everything else. A body chastened by mortification means a soul that can face death with sure confidence.

Poor fool, what makes you promise yourself a long life, when there is not a day of it that goes by in security? Again and again, people who looked forward for a long life have been caught out over it, called away quite unexpectedly from this bodily existence. Nothing commoner than to be told, in the course of conversation, how such a man was stabbed, such a man was drowned; how one fell from a height and broke his neck, another never rose from table, another never finished his game of dice. Fire and sword, plague and murderous attack, it is always the same thing—death is the common end that awaits us all, and life can pass suddenly, like a shadow when the sun goes in.

Once you are dead, how many people will remember you, or say prayers for you? To work, friend, to work, as best you may, since there is no saying when death will come, or what will be the issue of it. Hoard up, while there is still time, the riches that will last eternally; never a thought but for your soul's welfare, never a care but for God's honor. Make yourself friends now, by reverencing God's saints and following their example; when your tenancy of this life is up, it is they who can give you the freehold of eternity. Live in this world like some stranger from abroad, dismissing its affairs as no concern of yours; keep your heart free, and trained up toward God in heaven—you have no lasting citizenship here. Heaven must be the home you long for daily, with prayers and sighs and tears, if your soul, after death, is to find a happy passage to its Master's presence.

than trust to the good offices of other people. You, so unconcerned about yourself today—why should other people concern themselves about you tomorrow? No, here is the time of pardon; the day of salvation has come already. The more pity you should make so little use of it, your opportunity for winning a title to eternal life. Sometime, you'll know what it is to wish you had another day, even another hour, to put your life straight; and will you get it? There's no saying.

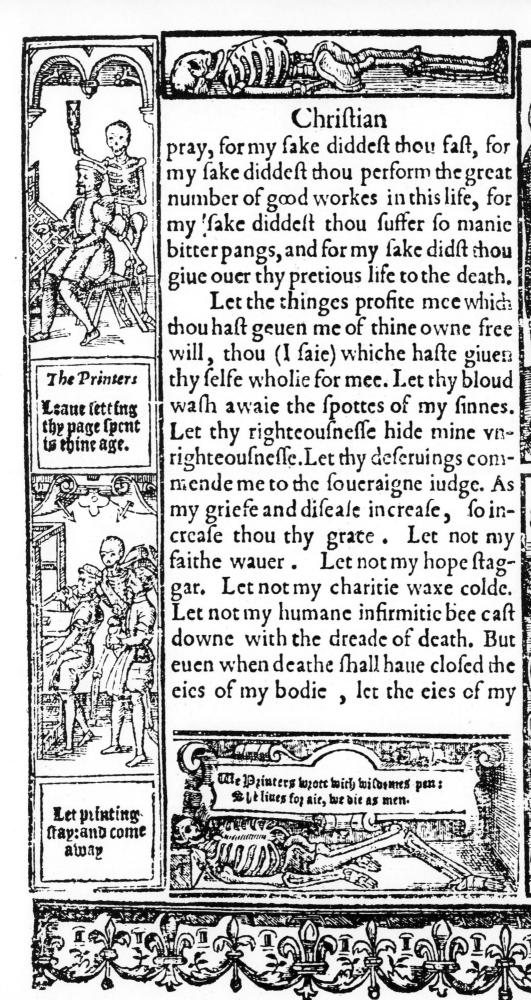

# Chriſtian

pray, for my ſake diddeſt thou faſt, for my ſake diddeſt thou perform the great number of good workes in this life, for my ſake diddeſt thou ſuffer ſo manie bitter pangs, and for my ſake didſt thou giue ouer thy pretious life to the death.

Let the thinges profite mee which thou haſt geuen me of thine owne free will, thou (I ſaie) whiche haſte giuen thy ſelfe wholie for mee. Let thy bloud waſh awaie the ſpottes of my ſinnes. Let thy righteouſneſſe hide mine vnrighteouſneſſe. Let thy deſeruings commende me to the ſoueraigne iudge. As my griefe and diſeaſe increaſe, ſo increaſe thou thy grace. Let not my faithe wauer. Let not my hope ſtaggar. Let not my charitie waxe colde. Let not my humane infirmitie bee caſt downe with the dreade of death. But euen when deathe ſhall haue cloſed the eies of my bodie , let the eies of my

# THE FIVE STAGES OF DYING

## Elisabeth Kubler Ross

### DENIAL

Among the over two hundred dying patients we have interviewed, most reacted to the awareness of a terminal illness at first with the statement, "No, not me, it cannot be true." This *initial* denial was as true for those patients who were told outright at the beginning of their illness as it was true for those who were not told explicitly and who came to this conclusion on their own a bit later on. . . .

### ANGER

When the first stage of denial cannot be maintained any longer, it is replaced by feelings of anger, rage, envy, and resentment. The logical next question becomes: "Why me?" . . .

### BARGAINING

The third stage, the stage of bargaining, is less well-known but equally helpful to the patient, though only for brief periods of time. If we have been unable to face the sad facts in the first period and have been angry at people and God in the second phase, maybe we can succeed in entering into some sort of an agreement which may postpone the inevitable happening: "If God has decided to take us from this earth and he did not respond to my angry pleas, he may be more favorable if I ask nicely." . . .

### DEPRESSION

When the terminally ill patient can no longer deny his illness, when he is forced to undergo more surgery or hospitalization, when he begins to have more symptoms or becomes weaker and thinner, he cannot smile it off anymore. His numbness or stoicism, his anger and rage will soon be replaced with a sense of great loss. . . .

### ACCEPTANCE

If a patient has had enough time (i.e., not a sudden, unexpected death) and has been given some help in working through the previously described stages, he will reach a stage during which he is neither depressed nor angry about his "fate." He will have been able to express his previous feelings, his envy for the living and the healthy, his anger at those who do not have to face their end so soon. He will have mourned the impending loss of so many meaningful people and places and he will contemplate his coming end with a certain degree of quiet expectation.

# THE FIRST FIVE MINUTES AFTER DEATH

*H. P. Liddon*

AN INDIAN OFFICER, who in his time had seen a great deal of service, and had taken part in more than one of those decisive struggles by which the British authority was finally established in the East Indies, had returned to end his days in this country, and was talking with his friends about the most striking experiences of his professional career. They led him, by their sympathy and their questions, to travel in memory through a long series of years; and as he described skirmishes, battles, sieges, personal encounters, hairbreadth escapes, the outbreak of the mutiny and its suppression, reverses, victories—all the swift alterations of anxiety and hope which a man must know who is entrusted with command, and is before the enemy—their interest in his story, as was natural, became keener and more exacting. At last he paused with the observation, "I expect to see something much more remarkable than anything I have been describing." As he was some seventy years of age, and was understood to have retired from service, his listeners failed to catch his meaning. There was a pause; and then he said in an undertone, "I mean in the first five minutes after death."

"The first five minutes after death!" Surely the expression is worth remembering, if only as that of

a man to whom the life to come was evidently a great and solemn reality. "The first five minutes." If we may employ for the moment when speaking of eternity standards of measurement which belong to time, it is at least conceivable that, after the lapse of some thousands or tens of thousands of years, we shall have lost all sense of a succession in events; that existence will have come to seem to be only a never-ceasing present; an unbegun and unending now. It is, I say, at least conceivable that this will be so; but can we suppose that at the moment of our entrance on that new and wonderful world we shall already think and feel as if we had always been there, or had been there, at least, for ages?

There is, no doubt, an impression sometimes to be met with that death is followed by a state of unconsciousness.

> *If sleep and death be truly one,*
> *And every spirit's folded bloom,*
> *Through all its intervital gloom,*
> *In some long trance should slumber on,*
>
> *Unconscious of the sliding hour,*
> *Bare of the body, might it last,*
> *And all the traces of the past*
> *Be all the color of the flower.*

But that is a supposition which is less due to the exigencies of reason than to the sensitiveness of imagination. The imagination recoils from the task of anticipating a moment so full of awe and wonder as must be that of the introduction of a conscious spirit to the invisible world. And, according, the reason essays to persuade itself, if it can, that life after death will not be conscious life, although it is difficult to recognize a single reason why, if life, properly speaking, survives at all, it should forfeit consciousness.

Certainly the life of the souls under the heavenly altar, who intercede perpetually with God for the approach of the Last Judgment, is not an unconscious life. Certainly the paradise which our Lord promised to the dying thief cannot be reasonably imagined to have been a moral and mental slumber, any more than can those unembodied ministers of God who do His pleasure, who are sent forth to minister to them that are the heirs of salvation, be supposed to reach a condition no higher than that which is produced by chloroform. No, this supposition of an unconscious state after death is a discovery, not of Revelation, not of reason, but of desire; of a strong desire on the one hand to keep a hold on immortality, and on the other to escape the risks which immortality may involve. It cannot be doubted that consciousness—if not retained to the last in the act of dying, if suspended by sleep, or by physical disease, or by derangement—must be recovered as soon as the act of death is completed, with the removal of the cause which suspended it. Should this be the case, the soul will enter upon another life with the habits of thought which belong to time still clinging to it; they will be unlearned gradually, if at all, in the after-ages of existence. And, assuredly, the first sense of being in another world must be overwhelming.

Imagination can, indeed, form no worthy estimate of it; but we may do well to try to think of it as best we can, since it is at least one of the approaches to the great and awful subject which should be before our thoughts at this time of the year, namely, the second coming of Jesus Christ to judgment. And here the apostle comes to our assistance with his anticipation of the future life, as a life of enormously enhanced knowledge: "Then shall I know, even as also I am known." He is thinking, no doubt, of that life as a whole, and not of the first entrance on it, immediately after death. No doubt, also, he is thinking of the high privileges of the blessed, whose knowledge, we may presume to say, with some great teachers of the church, will be thus vast and comprehensive because they will see all things in God, as in the ocean of truth. But it cannot be supposed that an increase of knowledge after death will be altogether confined to the blessed. The change itself must bring with it the experience which is inseparable from a new mode of existence: it must unveil secrets; it must discover vast tracts of fact and thought for every one of the sons of men.

# FUNERAL SERVICE

## Roman Ritual

MAY THE ANGELS lead thee into paradise. May the martyrs receive thee at thy coming and take thee to Jerusalem, the holy city. May the choirs of the angels receive thee, and mayest thou with the once poor Lazarus have rest everlasting.

# DEPARTURE OR ARRIVAL

## J. B. Phillips

I HAVE TAKEN over five thousand funerals. Though, of course, many of the mourners on such occasions have a very sketchy faith, even in the case of those who are convinced Christians of some years' standing, I find a strange inability to grasp the transitory nature of our present life and the breath-taking magnificence of the life which is to come.

I have, for instance, frequently suggested that it would be more appropriate to refer to the one whose physical body has died as the "arrived" rather than as the "departed."

No doubt there is nothing particularly original about this, but the significance lies in the fact that to many Christian people this is quite a new thought! They simply have not considered, or so it appears, that we are living this painful and difficult life against a background of unimaginable splendor.

Most of them hold desperately to a belief of some kind of survival, but that "the sufferings of this present time are not worthy to be compared with the glory that shall be revealed in us" seems hardly to have entered their hearts and minds.

# DEATH AS FULFILLMENT

## *Ignace Lepp*

WE NEED NOT be afraid of death, but it is difficult not to think about it. Whether we admit it or not, it would seem (so far as I am able to judge by the confidences I have received) that after a certain age, generally around sixty, it is impossible not to think about death at least at certain times. The death of friends is a common occurrence at that age. When an older man makes plans for the future he knows that little time remains to carry them out. In rural areas where the consciousness of familial continuity is greater, this kind of inhibition probably plays a lesser role. An old farmer continues to plant trees and care for his crops in the knowledge that his son or grandson will profit by his efforts. But in cities we are more conscious of our individuality and take little consolation in the knowledge that our descendants will benefit by what death prevents us from enjoying ourselves. This state of mind explains why governments, even in communist countries, find it increasingly difficult to persuade citizens to make sacrifices for future generations. This is why there is a decrease in long-range savings and investments and a constant increase of expenditures on goods for immediate consumption. . . .

The ancient Greeks thought that to die young, in the full flush of our powers, was an exceptionally good piece of luck, a blessing from the gods. Latter-day romantics like Byron and Charles Péguy proclaim the same thing. They, too, believed that long life without glory was not to be envied. Only the greedy and those without the courage to take chances would prefer such a life to a heroic death. I am personally inclined to think that it is better to live intensely for thirty or forty years than to vegetate for a hundred. But a long life that is well lived is desirable. We express admiration for a Mozart, who wrote such magnificent music in a brief lifetime, but Beethoven wrote many of his finest works in old age. Blaise Pascal, Sören Kierkegaard, Franz Kafka, and Emmanuel Mounier died young but their accomplishments were considerable. On the other hand, Goethe, Bergson, Blondel, and Jung wrote some of their most important books in the last periods of long lifetimes. These examples show that it is altogether pointless to say when a man's creative output is ended. The important thing is to live well. It is a sure mark of decadence in a civilization when a large percentage of men are willing to sell their souls, their bodies, and their honor for a few more years of life, especially when they have no idea how life should be lived.

From time immemorial, men have admired those who faced death fearlessly. The heroes of history and all mythology are as distinguished by the way they died as by the nobility of their lives. Quite rightly, we consider courage in the face of death the sign *par excellence* of the soul's strength. It is irrefutable proof that there are values which are more important than life itself, that the finest flower of life is its transcendent dimension. But only those who are deeply aware of total humanity can appreciate life's transcendence. Without this awareness, we would normally consider our individual lives the most precious of values. Those who argue that the fear of death is the direct and inevitable consequence of man's consciousness of his individuality are not altogether right. Fear of death existed in primitive societies and seems to be at the origin of the diverse magical rites intended to exorcise this fear. And, as we have noted earlier, even animals are not exempt from a certain "physical" fear of death. Resistance to death is one of the normal reactions of the life instinct. What distinguishes the excessive individualism of modern Western society is the paralyzing fear of death that prevents many from living deeply. We are so conscious of being an *individual* that we have totally lost the consciousness of our appurtenance to the *whole*. . . .

What made the deaths of early Christian martyrs such joyful events, so much so that even torture failed to frighten them, was not, as is often believed, the hope of individual reward. It was the firm conviction of belonging to a community of brothers and the belief that their martyrdom would be singular proof of their love for that community. The blood of the martyrs was in fact looked upon by the Church as the seed of holiness. Those who die for reasons of patriotism, freedom, and justice are perhaps less conscious of the ties that bind them to the community, but this sentiment must be operative at least unconsciously or they would not be able to renounce their lives. Whether or not they believed in personal survival, none of them could believe that he was destroying himself in dying for a transcendent cause. . . .

Man questions himself on the meaning of his life precisely because he knows that he is mortal. If we believed that we were immortal we would no longer question the meaning of our lives. . . . Life and death are so intimately related that it is impossible to establish the sense of one without being confronted with the meaning of the other. Plato, who defined life as an apprenticeship for death, emphatically recommended meditation on death in order to discover the meaning of life. I personally would be more inclined to adopt Spinoza's point of view. He advised meditation on life in order to grasp the meaning of death. However, properly understood, both forms of meditation have the same result. Modern man, it is true, is more familiar with Freud and Heidegger than with Plato. Thus he has subjective reasons for fearing that meditation on death will only lead to a depreciation of life. In any case, there is little doubt that if our experience of life is intense and dramatic, if we are convinced that we do not have the right to waste the little time allotted to us, it is because we know that we are mortal. If we did not know what we would die one day, life would be little more than a boring routine.

# THE STING OF DEATH

## Paul the Apostle
## (1 Corinthians 15:54–57)

So WHEN this corruptible shall have put on incorruption, and this mortal shall have put on immortality, then shall be brought to pass the saying that is written, Death is swallowed up in victory.

O death, where is thy sting? O grave, where is thy victory?

The sting of death is sin; and the strength of sin is the law.

But thanks be to God, which giveth us the victory through Our Lord Jesus Christ.

# DEATHDAY AS BIRTHDAY

## from the Martyrdom of St. Polycarp

WHEN THE CENTURION noticed the contentiousness of [those standing about], he declared the body [of the just-martyred Polycarp] public property and, according to their custom, burned it. And thus it came about that we afterward took up his bones, more precious than costly stones and more excellent than gold, and interred them in a decent place. There the Lord will permit us, as far as possible, to assemble in rapturous joy and celebrate his martyrdom—his birthday—both in order to commemorate the heroes that have gone before, and to train and prepare the heroes yet to come.

Oct. 3, 1788

# WELL IS THE HOUR OF DEATH

*John Henry Newman*

WELL IS THE HOUR of death described as the evening. There is something in the evening especially calm and solemn, fitly representing the hour of death. How peculiar, how unlike anything else, is a summer evening, when after the fever and heat of the day, after walking, or after working, after any toil, we cease from it, and for a few minutes enjoy the grateful feeling of rest! Especially is it so in the country, where evening tends to fill us with peace and tranquillity. The decreasing light, the hushing of all sounds, the sweet smell, perhaps, of the woods or the herbs which are all about us, the mere act of resting, and the consciousness that night is coming, all tend to tranquilize us and make us serious.

Alas, I know that in persons of irreligious mind it has a very different effect, and while other men are raised to the love of God and Christ and the thought of heaven by the calm evening, they are but led to the thought of evil and deeds of sin. But I am speaking of those who live toward God and train their hearts heavenward, and I say that such persons find in the calm evening but an incitement to greater devotion, greater renunciation of the world. It does but bring before them the coming down of death, and leads them with the apostle to die daily.

Evening is the time for divine visitations. The Lord God visited Adam after he had sinned in the garden, in the cool of the evening. In the evening the patriarch Isaac went out to meditate in the field. In the evening our Lord discovered Himself to the two disciples who went to Emmaus. In the same evening He appeared to the eleven, breathed on them, gave them the Holy Ghost, and invested them with the power of remitting and retaining sins.

Nay, even in a town the evening is a soothing time. It is soothing to be at the end of the week, having completed the week's work, with the day of rest before us. It is soothing, even after the day of rest, though labor is in store for us against the morrow, to find ourselves in the evening of the day. It is a feeling that almost all must be able to bear witness to, as something peculiar, as something fitly prefiguring that awful time when our work will be done, and we shall rest from our labors.

That indeed will be emphatically our evening, when the long day of life is over and eternity is at hand. Man goeth forth to his work and to his labor until the evening, and then the night cometh when no man can work. There is something inexpressibly solemn and subduing in that time, when work is done and judgment is coming. O my brethren, we must each of us in his turn, sooner or later, arrive at that hour. Each of us must come to the evening of life. Each of us must enter on eternity. Each of us must come to that quiet, awful time, when we appear before the Lord of the vineyard, and answer for the deeds done in the body, whether they be good or bad.

That, my dear brethren, you will have to undergo. Every one of you must undergo the particular judgment, and it will be the stillest, awfullest time which you ever can experience. It will be the dread moment of expectation, when your fate for eternity is in the balance, and when you are about to be sent forth the companion of saints or devils without possibility of change. There can be no change, there can be no reversal. As that judgment decides it, so it will be for ever and ever. Such is the particular judgment.

The general judgment at the end of the world will be a time of dreadful publicity, and will be full of the terrible brightness of the Judge. The trump of the archangel will sound, and the Lord will descend from heaven in lightning. The graves will open. The sun and the moon will be darkened and this earth will pass away. This is not the time of evening, but rather it will be a tempest in the midst of the night. But the parable in the Gospel speaks of the time of evening, and by the evening is meant, not the end of the world, but the time of death. And really perhaps it will be as awful, though very different, that solitary judgment, when the soul stands before its Maker, to answer for itself.

O who can tell which judgment is the more terrible, the silent secret judgment, or the open glorious coming of the Judge. It will be most terrible certainly, and it comes first, to find ourselves by ourselves, one by one, in His presence, and to have brought before us most vividly all the thoughts, words, and deeds of this past life. Who will be able to bear the sight of himself? And yet we shall be obliged steadily to confront ourselves and to see ourselves. In this life we shrink from knowing our real selves. We do not like to know how sinful we are. We love those who prophesy smooth things to us, and we are angry with those who tell us of our faults. But then, not one fault only, but all the secret, as well as evident, defects of our character will be clearly brought out. We shall see what we feared to see here, and much more. And then, when the full sight of ourselves comes to us, who will not wish that he had known more of himself here, rather than leaving it for the inevitable day to reveal it all to him!

## EASY AT THE HOUR OF DEATH

*William Law*

THE BEST WAY for anyone to know how much he ought to aspire after holiness is to consider not how much will make his present life easy, but to ask himself how much he thinks will make him easy at the hour of death.

Now any man that dares be so serious as to put this question to himself will be forced to answer that at death everyone will wish that he had been as perfect as human nature can be.

Is not this therefore sufficient to put us not only upon wishing but also laboring after all that perfection, which we shall then lament the want of? Is it not excessive folly to be content with such a course of piety as we already know cannot content us, at a time when we shall so want it as to have nothing else to comfort us? How can we carry a severer condemnation against ourselves than to believe that at the hour of death we shall want virtues of the saints and wish that we had been among the first servants of God, and yet take no methods of arriving at their height of piety while we are yet alive?

# PARTICULAR JUDGMENT

*Fulton J. Sheen*

[PARTICULAR JUDGMENT] is a recognition on the part of God. Imagine two souls appearing before the sight of God, one in the state of grace, the other in the state of sin. Grace is a participation in the nature and life of God. Just as a man participates in the nature and life of his parents, so too a man who is born of the Spirit of God by baptism participates in the nature of God—the life of God, as it were, flows through his veins, imprinting an unseen but genuine likeness. When, therefore, God looks upon a soul in the state of grace, He sees in it a likeness of His own nature. Just as a father recognizes his own son because of likeness of nature, so too Christ recognizes the soul in the state of grace in virtue of resemblance to Him, and says to the soul: "Come ye blessed of My Father: I am the natural Son, you are the adopted son. Come into the Kingdom prepared for you from all eternity."

God looks into the other soul that is in the state of sin and has not that likeness, and just as a father knows his neighbor's son is not his own, so too God, looking at the sinful soul and failing to see therein the likeness of His own flesh and blood, does not recognize it as His own kind, and says to it as He said in the parable of the bridegroom "I know you not"—and it is a terrible thing not to be known by God.

Not only is sin a recognition from God's point of view, but it is also a recognition from man's point of view. Just suppose that while cleaning your car, or your house, a very distinguished person was announced at the door. You would probably act differently than if you were thoroughly clean, well dressed, and presentable. In such an unclean condition you would ask to be excused, saying you were not fit to appear in the sight of such a person. When a soul is before the sight of God, it acts in much the same manner. Standing before the tremendous majestic presence of Almighty God, it does not plead, it does not argue, it does not entreat, it does not demand a second hearing, it does not protest the judgment, for it sees itself as it really is. In a certain sense, it judges itself, God merely sealing the judgment. If it sees itself clean and alive with the life of God, it runs to the embrace of Love, which is heaven, just as a bird released from its cage soars into the skies. If it sees itself slightly stained and the robes of its baptism remediably soiled, it protests that it is not to enter into the sight of Purity, and hence throws itself into the purifying flames of purgatory. If it sees itself irremediably vitiated, having no likeness whatever to the Purity and Holiness of God; if it has lost all affection for the things of spirit, then it could no more endure the Presence of God than a man who abhors beauty could endure the pleasure of music, art, and poetry. Why, heaven would be hell to such a soul, for it would be as much out of place in the holiness of heaven as a fish out of water. Hence, recognizing its own unworthiness, its own unholiness, its own ungodliness, its own distaste for the Purity of God, it casts itself into hell in the same way that a stone, released from the hand, fall to the ground. Only three states, therefore, are possible after the particular judgment: heaven, purgatory, and hell. Heaven is love without pain; purgatory is pain with love; hell is pain without love.

Such is judgment! And oh! how much better the present age would be if it lived in the habitual temper of men who remembered that they had an account to give! How much more justice would reign in our economic and social life if all men walked in fear of the judgment that is to come! How much happier life would be if each realized that there are only two beings in all the world, our soul and the God who made it. Our emphasis on the group and on the nation and on the masses has made us oblivious to the great truth lying behind the judgment—that we are all individual souls responsible to God. We find ourselves talking of society as if it were a permanent thing, forgetting that it is really the passing of separate immortal persons into an unseen state, that while some slip away and others steal in, the flux and influx is the going of individual personal existences, each of which is worthy of redemption. We talk of masses of human beings as of a counter which was cleared from time to time, all the while forgetting the pathetic truth that all is not over with those whom history describes.

# THE HARROWING OF HELL

*Medieval Mystery Play*

*The region of Hell. First there is total darkness except for the glow of sultry fires. But suddenly Hell is mysteriously filled with a growing light.*

ADAM. O sovereign Savior,
Comfort and Counsellor,
Of this great light Thou are the author—
I know this well;
This is a sign that thou wilt succor us
And of the devil be conqueror.
Me thou madest, Lord, of clay,
And gavest Paradise for play;
But through my sin, to say the truth,
From thy goodly garden I was put away,
And here have longed, the truth to say,
In thirstiness both day and night.
Now by this light that I can see,
Joy is coming, Lord, through Thee!
Surely it may none other be,
But that thou hast brought me mercy!

ISAIAH. Yea, surely, this same light
I foretold aright:
The people, I did say express,
That went about in darkness
Should see a great lightness.

SIMEON. And I too, I Simeon, truth to say;
For when Christ a child was, in good fay,
I already felt without a doubt
Joy to the people of Israel:
Now is it won, that very weal!

JOHN THE BAPTIST. Ah. Lord, I am that prophet John
That dipped thee in Jordan's flood to baptize thee in,
And preached to everyone of thy coming.
With my finger I showed express
Thy mercy concluding righteousness.

SETH. And I, Seth, Adam's son, did pray
That he would grant an angel to me
With the oil of mercy
To anoint my father in his sorrowing
When in old sickness he lay.
To me appeared the angel Michael,
For me to tell
That of this oil I might have none,
Made I never so much moan,
Till five thousand years have gone,
And five hundred more.

DAVID. Ah, high God, and king of bliss,
I hope that time now comen is,
To take out thy folk every one,
For the years all have come and gone.

(*Then* SATAN, *sitting on his throne, speaks to his demons.*)

SATAN. Hell-hounds all, all that be here,
Make your bow to this fellowship without fear:
Jesus, that is God's son, dear,
Comes he hither with us to dwell?
On him now wreak your hell,
For a *man* he is fully, in fay,
Since greatly death he feared today,
And these words I heard him say,
"My soul is thirsty unto death."
Such as I made halt and blind,
He has healed them to their kind,
Therefore this boaster look that you bind
In bale of hell-breath.

SECOND DEMON. Sir Sathanas, what man is he,
That should deprive thee of thy power?
How dare he do against thee.
Greater than thou he seems to be,
And degraded of thy degree
Thou must be soon,—this well I see.

THIRD DEMON. Who is he so bold and strong
That masterly comes us among?
He shall sing a sorry song!

SATAN. Against this shrew that cometh here
I tempted the folk in foulest manner,
To give gall for his dinner
And hang him on a tree;
Now he is dead through me,
And to hell, as you shall see,
He comes anon in fear.

SECOND DEMON. Sir Sathanas, is not this that seer
That raised Lazarus out of here?

SATAN. Yea, this is he that did conspire
Anon to deprive us all.

THIRD DEMON. Out, out! alas! by fire
I conjure thee, Sathanas,
Thou suffer him not to come near!

SECOND DEMON. Yea, verily, if he comes here,
Vanished is our power,
Over all this fellowship of fear.

(JESUS *enters, and the dead
raise a great shout.*)

JESUS. Open up hell gates anon,
You princes of pain every one,
That the son of God may enter in!

SECOND DEMON. Hence, hypocrite, out from this
place,
Or thous shalt have but sorry grace!

(JESUS *arrives on the scene.*)

SATAN. Out, alas! what is this?
Saw I never so much bliss,
Since I was warden here!
My masterdom fares amiss.

THIRD DEMON. Yea, Sathanas, thy sovereignty
Fails clean, and therefore must thou flee;
Go forth and fight for thy degree,
Or henceforth our prince thou mayst not be.

(SATAN *rises from his throne.*)

SATAN. My might fails verament,
This prince that is now present
Will soon take from me my prey.
Adam's brood through me were galled,
But now they hence shall all be called
And only I left in hell for aye.

## OPENING THE GATES OF DEATH

### Rufinus

CHRIST'S SUFFERING in His flesh entailed no loss or injury to His Deity. It was in order to accomplish salvation through the weakness of flesh that His divine nature went down to death in the flesh. The intention was, not that He might be held fast by death according to the law governing mortals, but that, assured of rising again by His own power, He might open the gates of death. It was as if a king were to go to a dungeon and, entering it, were to fling open its doors, loosen the fetters, break the chains, bolts, and bars in pieces, conduct the captives forth to freedom, and restore *such as sat in darkness and in the shadow of death* to light and life. In a case like this the king is, of course, said to have been in the dungeon, but not under the same circumstances as the prisoners confined within it. They were there to discharge their penalties, but he to secure their discharge from punishment.

That in body meet us as I see,
That dead came not to hell as we?
When I trespassed, God told me
That this place closed should be
To earthly men, to have no entry;
And yet I find you here.

ENOCH. Sir, I am Enoch, the truth to say,
And here have lived since aye;
And my fellow here
Is Elijah the prophet, as see you may.

ELIJAH. Yea, bodily death, never suffered we
But here ordained we are to be
Till Antichrist arise.
To fight against us shall he,
And slay us in our holy city;
But surely in days three
And a half we shall rise.

ADAM. And who is that comes here?

THIEF (*bearing a cross on his shoulder*).
I am that thief
That hung on the rood tree.
Because I had belief
That he was God's son dear,
To him devoutly did I pray
That he would think on me alway;
And he answered and said, "This day
In Paradise thou shalt with me me";
Then he told me,
This cross upon my back hanging
To the Angel Michael to bring,
That I might have entry.

ADAM. Now go we to bliss both old and young,
To worship God all-willing;
And thitherward let us sing.

   (*They all go out singing, "Te Deum laudamus,
   te Dominum confitemur."*)

DAVID THE KING. I David, now may say
My prophecy fulfilled is, in fay.

JESUS. Open ye hell gates, I say,
And let the king of glory enter this way,
That he may fulfill his intent.

   (*At this the gates of hell
   burst open, and* JESUS *enters.*)

Peace to thee, Adam, my darling,
And all the righteous once on earth living!
To bliss I will you bring,
To live without ending.

MICHAEL. Come, Adam, come forth with me:
Our Lord upon the tree
Your sins has all forbought;
Now shall you have liking and lee,
And be restored to degree.

   (MICHAEL *leads forth* ADAM *and the saints
   to paradise, and there they are met by* ENOCH
   *and* ELIJAH *and the saved* THIEF.)
   ADAM (*speaks to* ENOCH *and* ELIJAH). Sirs,
   what manner of men be ye,

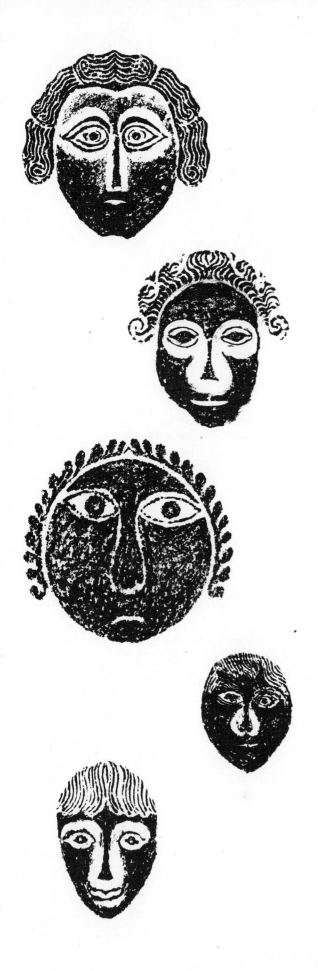

# POOR SOULS

## Romano Guardini

SIMPLE, NATURALLY RELIGIOUS PEOPLE, whose roots have not been loosened by the restless activity of mind and will, know themselves to be closely united to the dead. The term "poor souls" expresses their sense of nearness to them and their solicitude for them. This solicitude occupies a large place in their devotions, and it would be a pity for it to disappear. It would be somewhat like separating the farmer from the soil and transplanting him to the city. The educated man (here the word carries no contempt which would be as foolish as contempt for *the people*, for the educated man is a reality who has, in a sense, a special destiny) has lost touch with that particular concern for the dead. Therefore many customs and ideas associated with the feast have become foreign to him. Such an attitude does not imply loss of faith. Solicitude for the dead, prayers and sacrifices popularly offered for the poor souls, need not signify faith in the Christian sense. Such solicitude arises from that primitive sense of nearness felt by the man of the soil for the kingdom of the dead. It need not mean continued attachment of the heart to those who have been dear to us. It has, indeed, nothing to do with intensity of feeling, or personal loyalty, but arises, rather, from man's association with the passage from light into darkness, from pulsating earthly life into the realm of death. And this association is dependent not upon the will of the individual, but upon the extent to which he still lives in the primitive form of existence.

We must not forget that while this sense gives great depth to existence, it can also be dangerous. There have been times in man's consciousness when the dead have been more powerful than the living— let us recall for a moment the early Greeks and their domination by the kingdom of the dead, the overcoming of which by the Olympian religion constituted a brilliant achievement of the Homeric world. It is this connection with the kingdom of the dead which underlies the popular feeling for the poor souls, and gives it such keenness. The educated man, as we have said, has lost this sense, hence the dead are not real to him as a matter of course. He feels no immediate response to their existence. His relation to them is determined by his mind and heart rather than by the depths of his being. Dying, for him, has become a biological process, a purely personal matter, which has lost its mystery. Thus his relation to the dead is no longer primarily religious, but intellectual-moral in character. The thought of the poor souls makes no direct appeal to him. Solicitude for them together with the usages attached to it are alien to him.

There is something else which belongs here. The relation to the dead has always been a sphere in which instinctive urges, at times of a dark order, have played a prominent part. For death is not only somber and exalted, but destructive as well. Hence death appeals not only to what is serious and noble in man, but also to what is shady, and the sympathy aroused by tales of the sufferings of the departed have not infrequently been mixed with cruelty. Something of this cruelty has crept into the representations of the poor souls, and the feelings which they arouse.

This is apparent when we compare the way in which the early Christians spoke of the dead with that common in the Middle Ages and later. The earliest ideas were much more intellectual and spiritual; the dominating images were those of light and peace, of birth into eternal life, of Christ's victory over hell and death, and of the judgment of the righteous God. Later, pictures of suffering force their way in. Clerical eloquence and pious writing are increasingly concerned with suffering, and portray it by every device of imagination. Pity is thus aroused. But pity brings into play all the contradictions in man—his tendency to the dubious as well as to the pure. Thus into the representations of the poor souls has crept a good deal that is offensive, sentimental, and sensational. And to the educated man who lacks that immediate sense of union with the dead, the whole business seems disreputable.

Nevertheless, solicitude for the departed is an important element in liturgical life—we have only to recall the Memorial of the Dead in the Mass, and the Office of the Dead. We cannot, then, be indifferent to the matter, or reject it. We must try to understand why it has a claim on us, and what lies at the root of it. Perhaps we may find a way which will teach us better to understand that mysterious realm which has become so profoundly strange to us, and the meaning of that word "purgatory" which is used to designate the condition of the dead who are in need of our help. And it may be that this understanding will give us a deeper insight into human existence generally.

Revelation promises that man will one day enter

into the eternal presence of God. Through contact with Christ, through sanctifying grace and faith, the new life has been born in him. As long as he is a pilgrim in time, that life is hidden, but at the moment of death it breaks through. From the first it was eternal in the sense that it was God's life. Now it is eternal in actuality for him, that is to say, free from time, purely present. An important moment has been reached in the believer's life when he perceives that what was to follow in the future is actually present, when his consciousness reaches out beyond death.

However, no evil thing can enter God's presence, for God is the Holy One, the Pure One, the Righteous One. Not merely pure and just, He is also the source of all good, and He hates everything evil, low, impure, corrupt, and thrusts it from Him. The believer must ask himself, then, whether there is any way which leads from himself, as he is, to God. The one who is about to enter eternal life is I, myself, but how things stand with me I know only in part, and if I have advanced so far as to reject the superficial appeal to God's goodness which is not more than saying, "Oh, I'm sure everything is going to be all right," then I must realize the impossibility of my attaining to God's presence as I am. But does not the faith teach that I attain to that presence, not through my own efforts, but through grace? That I shall be forgiven because of Christ's redemptive act? That I shall share in His righteousness? Yes, but I shall share in it, not through magic, but in reality. Christ's righteousness will be not merely imputed to me, not hung about me like a cloak, but it will be part of my very self. So again the question comes up: Is this righteousness truly my own, and has my life, through grace, become an entirely new life?

What, in the long run, determines the worthiness or unworthiness of a man? His inner disposition, his intention. This disposition issues freely from that mysterious mobility which enables him to strike out in a mental direction. The inner disposition is the man's inner direction, his "intention." It might be called the directing will itself, from which freedom derives. It is the intention in which that beginning which is called freedom starts—whether in good or evil, whether from God or from one's own self, whether directed toward God or away from Him. When a man's inner disposition is toward the good, he belongs to God.

## SOULS OF DEPARTED SAINTS

### Augustine of Hippo

THE SOULS of departed saints make light of the death by which they are separated from their bodies. This is because their "flesh rests in hope," whatever the humiliations it may seem to have suffered, which it is now unable to feel. For they do not (as Plato supposed) long to receive bodies through forgetfulness: but because they remember the promise given them by one who always keeps his word, who gave them assurance of the preservation of the hairs of their head, they look forward with patient yearning to the resurrection of the bodies in which they endured many hardships, but in which they will never feel any further pain. If they did not "hate their own flesh" when they constrained it by the law of the spirit because through its weakness it opposed their will, how much more do they love it when it is itself destined to be spiritual. The spirit when subservient to the flesh is not inappropriately called carnal: so the flesh in subservience to the spirit is rightly called spiritual, not because it is converted into spirit, as some infer from the scriptural text, "It is sown as a natural body, it will rise as a spiritual body," but because it will be subdued to the spirit, readily offering complete and wonderful obedience. And this will lead to the fulfillment of their desire, with the secure attainment of secure immortality, with the removal of all feeling of discomfort, all corruptibility and reluctance.

# THE FIRE OF PURGATORY

## *Carlo Carretto*

IF THE MASTER should knock on my door tonight and tell me that my earthly pilgrimage is at an end, I feel that on balance I should not be consigned to hell.

Why?

Because neither God nor my self wishes it, He for love of me, I for love of Him. Despite immense evil in me, I feel, in the strength of His love, the desire to be with Him, and this seems to me to be quite normal between friends. I know sin as ignorance and even more so as weakness, but I have never felt opposed to God. I cannot even visualize —thanks to His grace—the sin against the Holy Spirit; I cannot imagine how someone could impugn the known truth. Theologians discuss it at length, but their subtleties do not impress me.

I was saying, then, that if I died today, I should not on balance be condemned to an eternity of torment. But then neither should I be admitted to heaven! I am not ready for it. I felt that very, very keenly under the rock when I had denied Kada my blanket, and I still feel it today, Good Friday, as I meditate on our Lord's passion. Yes, I am afraid to suffer for others, I tremble before the cold blade of charity.

And so? If I am not to go to hell and heaven is too good for me, where shall I go?

I must stay here, I cannot pass beyond, and purgatory is certainly this side of the eternal watershed.

I am not a theologian, but even theologians know little about purgatory. It is a passing place or state or condition in which those not yet ready for the kingdom of perfect love pray and suffer and so prepare themselves for the day when they will be admitted to the eternal banquet.

I imagine purgatory to be like the large cupboard where my grandmother put medlars to ripen. Please forgive this curious comparison. When I was young, I occasionally stayed at my grandmother's house, which was a farm in the Langhe hills of Piedmont,

and I remember my grandmother puttting the medlars which were still not ripe by the autumn into this cupboard, among the straw. "Everything comes to him who waits." A spiritual fruit that has failed to ripen under the sun of God's charity will ripen in the cupboard.

The comparison is perhaps a good one because the cupboard is part of the house.

I should not like to offend anyone's sensibilities, and so I say this from a purely personal point of view, but I think of purgatory as being this side of eternity and therefore still tied to my home. I think of the souls of the dead completing their period of expiation near where they lived, perhaps even in their homes themselves. If I can make a request at the moment of death, I know what I shall ask: "Send me to the stretch of desert between Tit and Silet," where I had the deepest insight into the need for perfect love at the earliest possible moment.

And the fire? Ah, I thought that question would come.

Well, I think there is fire but not of a material kind. Many times as a boy, especially in the sacristies of mountain churches, I have seen the souls in purgatory wrapped in flames—real flames—with fiery tongues higher than the highest heads there. It is natural for artists to think and paint in this way: how else could one depict the spiritual fire of purgatory? In the Middle Ages, and since, the flames are always shown as real ones, simply because it is easier that way.

Everyone, however, knows that real fire would damage the body . . . and the body is not in purgatory but in the cemetery, like a piece of cast-off clothing.

To touch my soul another type of fire is necessary: charity, which I rejected on earth, or at least did not fully accept. Now that I have my back to the wall, I cannot escape it any longer, I must accept it. I cannot put it off anymore.

The first of charity, that is, this supernatural kind of love, will attack my soul as flames attack wood. My soul will writhe, sizzle, and smoke like green wood, but it will burn in the end. Not a single fiber will escape, all must be consumed by that divine love.

How long will this take? It will go on until the work is done. Some people will need no more than a few days, others thousands of years; the important thing is that the purification must be completed. All this will take place while a sort of film of our lives is screened before our eyes.

There is more than enough there. When I think that I shall have to relive in slow motion certain episodes in my life which I did not subject to the

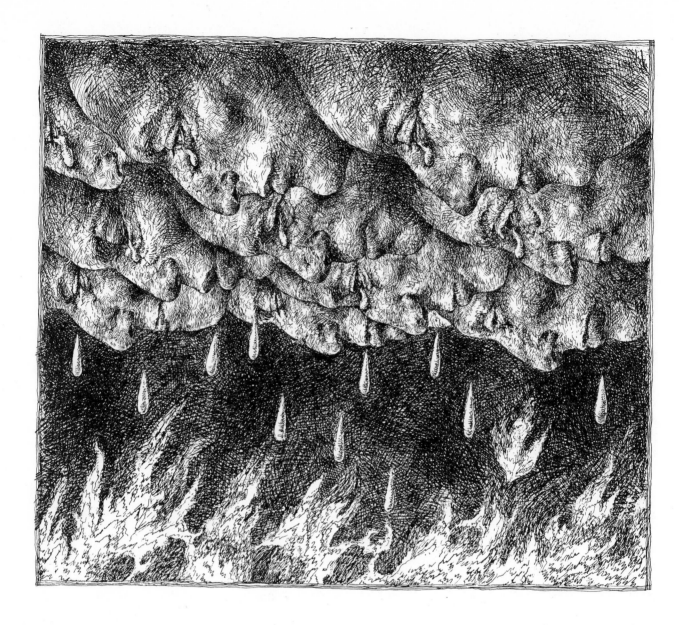

flames of love but constructed on egoism, falsehood, cowardice, and pride, and all the time with the fire of charity in my veins, I can assure you that it comes home to me what a serious, deadly serious, business it will be. Imagine me arriving in purgatory wearing a mask put together with years of patience and skill which I have never dared or been able to remove for fear of revealing myself as I really am to God and men.

When the fire of love licks up at it, gets beneath it, and burns it off my soul, it will, I have no doubt, prove an agonizing experience. And what will happen when the fire starts to burn the property to which I was clinging so firmly: a blanket perhaps, or a piece of meat I took first from the plate when Jesus would have wanted me to be last?

No, there is no need for a coal fire to burn my soul: the fire of failed responsibility, of injustices, of thefts, of lies, of help denied to someone who needed me, of love not lived with those who were my brothers, is more than sufficient.

Not very much, you say? Well, that is only a part of it, the part we can imagine by the standards of earthly justice. True justice, measured on God's justice, on the Transcendence of the Absolute, appalled St. John of the Cross when he was undergoing the terrors of the dark night of the soul.

Yes, the fire of purgatory is charity, that is, the highest degree of love in its supernatural state.

It is the fire which consumed Jesus's sacrifice on Calvary, the fire which burned the saints with inextinguishable love, the fire which led the martyrs to martyrdom and baptized them if they were not already baptized, giving them access to the Kingdom. We shall not escape this fire, nothing we do can avert it.

On the other hand I should not wish to escape it. I know it will hurt, but I also know that I have to go through it.

I have no desire to continue for all eternity the ups and downs of my sensibility, the perennial resistance to the fire of love. I am green wood, and I do not wish to enter paradise still green. I want to burn in purgatory and then be finished with it.

I want to go where Jesus went, to feel what He felt in His divine heart. I shall suffer, I know, but there is no other way, and in any case God's power will be there beside me to bring me assistance.

Here and now I accept that fire which will smelt from me and my earthly slag the hidden metal of my person, willed by God but obscured by sin.

I shall be given a new face, the face that God saw when He drew me from the primeval chaos and that Satan sullied with his slaver.

I shall emerge a child, God's child for ever.

And since purgatory is this side of the eternal watershed, the only appropriate course for me is to combine it with my life on earth, pretend I am already there, apply the fire of charity to myself a little at a time but courageously, start to burn out the clinkers, at least the biggest and most obvious ones.

What I do here I shall not need to do hereafter: I have therefore gained. I must accept the asceticism my life imposes on me, the sufferings and trials I experience on the road, the tedium and troubles of human society, the inconveniences and inevitable illnesses as precious and providential opportunities for advance payment.

I say *opportunities*, because there is more to paying than suffering. One must suffer with love, with patience, otherwise it is useless. We were saved not by the scourges on Jesus's flesh but by the love with which He accepted them.

We were redeemed not by His road to Calvary but by the patience, mercy, obedience with which He trod it.

In short, the redemption renewed the world by Jesus's charity. Charity is the essence of Christianity. Yes, we can state with absolute certainty that *love is for living*.

And if we can transform every moment of our existence into an act of love, all our problems will be resolved. The fire of purgatory is love, and if we wish to avoid purgatory, we must accept its fire on earth.

## PURGATORY IN SCRIPTURE

### Franz Seibel

IN BOTH the Old and the New Testaments there are no biblical texts which speak specifically about purgatory. However, there are texts which seem to suggest the idea.

In 2 Maccabees 12:40–46 we read that some Jewish soldiers—wearing pagan amulets—died fighting for God's cause. In order to make atonement for this idolatry, Judas Maccabeus collected two thousand silver drachmas to provide a sin offering. "Therefore he made atonement for the dead, that they might be freed from their sin" (2 Mac-

cabees 12:45). The author of 2 Maccabees appears not only to believe in the resurrection of the dead (2 Maccabees 12:44) but also in a possible cleansing from sin after death. Thus there is at least some indication that around 100 B.C. prayer and sacrifice for the dead were known among the Israelites.

In the New Testament the passage which speaks of the sin against the Holy Spirit which cannot "be forgiven, either in this age or in the age to come" (Matthew 12:32) suggests that other sins are forgiven after death. But this argumentation can hardly be seen as dogmatic proof for the existence of purgatory; it is hardly more than conjecture.

1 Corinthians 3:11–15 speaks of a fire which on that day "will test the quality of each man's work." But this passage, too, cannot, with no further ado, be interpreted as proof for the existence of purgatory.

## JOYFUL FIRE

*Catherine of Genoa*

I DO NOT believe it would be possible to find any joy comparable to that of a soul in purgatory, except the joy of the blessed in paradise—a joy which goes on increasing day by day, as God more and more flows in upon the soul, which He does abundantly in proportion as every hindrance to His entrance is consumed away. The hindrance is the rust of sin; the fire consumes the rust, and thus the soul goes on laying itself open to the divine inflowing.

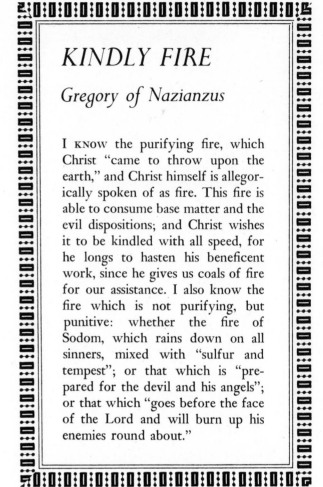

## KINDLY FIRE

*Gregory of Nazianzus*

I KNOW the purifying fire, which Christ "came to throw upon the earth," and Christ himself is allegorically spoken of as fire. This fire is able to consume base matter and the evil dispositions; and Christ wishes it to be kindled with all speed, for he longs to hasten his beneficent work, since he gives us coals of fire for our assistance. I also know the fire which is not purifying, but punitive: whether the fire of Sodom, which rains down on all sinners, mixed with "sulfur and tempest"; or that which is "prepared for the devil and his angels"; or that which "goes before the face of the Lord and will burn up his enemies round about."

## ANTISEPTIC FIRE

*C. S. Lewis*

OUR SOULS *demand* purgatory, don't they? Would it not break the heart if God said to us, "It is true, my son, that your breath smells and your rags drip with mud and slime, but we are charitable here and no one will upbraid you with these things, nor draw away from you. Enter into the joy"? Should we not reply, "With submission, sir, and if there is no objection, I'd *rather* be cleaned first." "It may hurt, you know"— "Even so, sir."

I assume that the process of purification will normally involve suffering. Partly from tradition; partly because most real good that has been done me in this life has involved it. But I don't think suffering is the purpose of the purgation. I can well believe that people neither much worse nor much better than I will suffer less than I or more. "No nonsense about merit." The treatment given will be the one required, whether it hurts little or much.

My favorite image on this matter comes from the dentist's chair. I hope that when the tooth of life is drawn and I am "coming around," a voice will say, "Rinse your mouth out with this." This will be a purgatory.

The newspaper headline reads:

CHATSBURG HERALD

MILLIONS FLEE FROM CITIES!
END OF THE WORLD

# II.

# WAITING

# TWILIGHT OF THE DAY, THE LIFE, THE WORLD

## *Helmut Thielicke*

A DROWNING MAN sees his whole life pass before him. Is he not likely to see the several events with even greater accuracy than in the moment when he first experienced them? There is a colorful kaleidoscope of memories: how his mother used to kiss him goodnight, how he brought home the first money he earned himself, how he got married, and perhaps how he later spent cold and lonely hours on guard duty in far-off fields of service. It is as though everything that once happened to him by chance and without apparent meaning is now arranged in perfect order, hung up and stretched out like a string of beads, suspended from the anchor point of the end to which it all led.

The passage which constitutes our text [Matthew 24:1–14] points to a somewhat similar process. Almost as by a shock treatment the disciples are suddenly confronted with a vision of the absolute end. As in the dream of a man who is being sucked under for the last time, the film of world history unrolls before them, and everything suddenly makes sense: wars and the horrors of war, earthquakes, terror, and persecution take on new meaning and become signs and signals that point to something. They are the agonies of a world coming to an end; they are the birth pangs of a new life surpassing human imagination.

It would pay us to think about this last "dream" of those who were drawn into the end. We should reflect on the visions that these words of the Lord waked in them.

It is indeed peculiar how some incidental remark will suddenly cause an ominous certainty to pop into our heads. That happened to me once when I was a little boy. I wanted a truck more than anything in the world. Finally they gave it to me. I thought I would burst with joy. I must have acted quite silly, almost as if I were out of my head. When my father then grabbed it away and carried it into the house, I broke into tears. He took me to task for this sudden outburst and scolded me for my ungratefulness, to which I replied—as he later told me—"It's going to fall apart anyway some day." All of a sudden, in the moment of fulfillment, the evanescence of beauty became clear to me and I experienced the shock of finitude. When Troy was still in full flower, Homer sounded the same note: "The day will come when holy Ilion will fall."

Our text describes a similar situation. People stroll past the temple and then look back from the Mount of Olives to let the solid monumental walls take full effect. They stand as a symbol of durability, a citadel that endures the ravages of time. Ancient proverbs foretold that when the temple fell the world would end. And then Jesus says, "Not a stone will remain on another." He sees bizarre ruins and charred rafters where a copy of the heavenly Jerusalem now rises like a fortress of eternity.

Of course, people already knew that everything is hastening toward oblivion. The leaves fall in autumn, youth fades, and the good old days—they had them then too—give way to a changed world. We too, as we came back to our homes after the war and walked through devastated streets we no longer recognized—we too sensed something of the ultimate oblivion. In the autobiography of Carl Zuckmayer there are the lines he wrote during that war while he was an emigrant on a foreign shore:

*I know I'll see it all again
and yet find nothing I once left.*

This eternal oscillation between becoming and perishing, however, seems to take place against a fixed background: these walls will stand, and the hymns continue to be sung; these prayers will never cease, and the regularity with which the church's "Amen" follows will be a sort of prototype for whatever events are to occur with absolute regularity. If all this too should cease and desist what an abyss would open beneath us!

Secular man too is not immune to such thoughts. He too has the feeling that something will remain, safe from all change. Even if the Chinese take over, the lakes will continue to sparkle, Bach's B Minor Mass will still resound somewhere, and the audacious dome of Michelangelo above St. Peter's will go on being a testament in stone. It would be simply unthinkable that a nuclear war could destroy it all. If that happened, what would be the sense of thoughtful men having sought the truth for thousands of years, of artists having given form to beauty, of people having loved and laughed and searched for happiness? What an abyss, what an absurdity that would be!

Yet, despite its eeriness, the question of the disciples—"When will this [absolute] end come?"—is overshadowed by a peculiar peace. They tie the question about the fall of the temple and of the world to the question of the Lord's return. Thus, the triumph of God stands at the end of all endings. And therefore, the dissolution of everything that exists or counts in the world is not totally without a note of comfort.

Of course, that is also true elsewhere. Our greatest anxieties do not stem from the intensity of our pain. They arise when we cannot see any point or sense to the pain. Job had probably endured bodily and spiritual attacks much more severe than those we read about. What finally threw him was not the pain itself, but the abyss of emptiness that opened before him. Weren't the deaths of his children, the disastrous fire, and the loathsome sores that befouled his body a monstrous contradiction of everything

he had formerly held to and believed? Didn't this completely nonsensical punishment of a righteous man refute any divine governance of the world, any "higher thoughts"? Wasn't it all so terribly senseless that there was no point in living any longer? Didn't this make a mockery out of all holy writ and truths of faith? Hadn't the holy phrase "I am the Lord your God" been replaced by the cynical conclusion "You never know . . ."?

*That* was Job's suffering! It was not simply a matter of physical pain. Think for a moment of what it would mean if everything that the folk-singers and recording artists sing about—love, death, parting, longing, fulfillment—were simply wiped out without a trace! What if the silence of an absolute end would spread like a godforsaken desert across an earth that was once the home of Plato, Lao-tze, Albrecht Dürer, and Beethoven? Then the abyss of total meaninglessness would open before us also. This is probably the seat of that secret fear which is kindled deep within us at the thought of

---

# THE OLIVET DISCOURSE

*Matthew the Evangelist*
*(Matthew 24:1–14)*

AND JESUS went out, and departed from the temple: and his disciples came to him for to show him the building of the temple.

And Jesus said unto them, See ye not all these things? verily I say unto you, There shall not be left here one stone upon another, that shall not be thrown down.

And as he sat upon the mount of Olives, the disciples came unto him privately, saying, Tell us, when shall these things be? and what shall be the sign of thy coming, and of the end of the world?

And Jesus answered and said unto them, Take heed that no man deceive you.

For many shall come in my name, saying, I am Christ; and shall deceive many.

And ye shall hear of wars and rumors of wars: see that ye be not troubled: for all these things must come to pass, but the end is not yet.

For nation shall rise against nation, and kingdom against kingdom: and there shall be famines, and pestilences, and earthquakes, in divers places.

All these are the beginning of sorrows.

Then shall they deliver you up to be afflicted, and shall kill you: and ye shall be hated of all nations for my name's sake.

And then shall many be offended, and shall betray one another, and shall hate one another.

And many false prophets shall rise, and shall deceive many.

And because iniquity shall abound, the love of many shall wax cold.

But he that shall endure unto the end, the same shall be saved.

And this gospel of the kingdom shall be preached in all the world for a witness unto all nations; and then shall the end come.

the world's atomic self-destruction. The fact that you and I could be killed in such a holocaust is surely not sufficient to explain this fear. After all, we can't be deader than dead, and we could be just as dead from falling off a ladder or being hit by a car. No, the fearfulness lies in the snuffing out of everything that exists or matters and of every meaningful principle and truth for which anyone has ever lived.

The disciples, however, can no longer be carried away by this ultimate fear, since it is the Lord himself who uses the destruction of the temple as a symbol for the total end of the world. They know that someone is standing beyond the end who will receive them when they emerge from the fires of destruction. They know that someone is there beside them always, even to the end of the world, and that he awaits them on the other side of the great abyss.

For them this is far more than a mere forecast of the distant future. Mere hints of the future leave us just as cold as mere reports of a past when God supposedly performed miracles and was on friendly terms with Moses and other figures of ancient times. How distant "once-upon-a-time" is! And how distant the future is! That's why it leaves us cold. Therefore it is not the mere prophecy of the end that bothers us here and now. If the astronomers tell us that our earth will meet its death by fire or ice in a few million years that doesn't spoil the taste of our steak one bit. Intellectually it may be very interesting, but existentially it is irrelevant. It doesn't affect my life in the least. My loves, my hates, and my scale of values remain untouched.

The whole situation changes radically, however, as soon as Jesus tells us that *he* is the one whose work is being carried out in the tumults of the end, and that he will come again in a new and apocalyptic repetition of Christmas. News like that changes the present too. Such a future reshapes the now. It becomes so decisive for the present moment that many contemporary theologians, taking proper note of it, allow themselves to be led astray. Stressing the present relevance, they conclude that the message doesn't really refer to the Lord's future and his impending return at all, but is merely a cryptic, futuristically phrased statement about the present. The future tense is supposed to be a disguised way of saying that every moment of our lives is the end of the line, lived as a "moment before God."

No matter how mistaken this conclusion may be, one thing is sure. If the Lord is coming again, if all the floods and fires that cleanse the world will subside before his throne, if at the Last Day those who have been saved need not look back into a world-wide grave wherein lie buried—according to the

## FIRE AND ICE

*Robert Frost*

*Some say the world will end in fire,*
*Some say in ice.*
*From what I've tasted of desire*
*I hold with those who favor fire.*
*But if it had to perish twice,*
*I think I know enough of hate*
*To say that for destruction ice*
*Is also great*
*And would suffice.*

famous vision of Jean Paul—also their ideas of God and their dreams of a heavenly Father, if instead they are able to sing, "God has brought us to this place"—I say, if all that is so, then the present moment of my life is also radically changed. Then my death is not merely a departure, but a going home. Then war and terror, plane crashes and mine disasters, marital difficulties and stays in the hospital are no longer simply impersonal results of natural processes; they cease to be "visitations" and become "visits." Someone is there. His heart is both the source and the goal of it all. . . .

That is not to say that we understand the plan of God. How often it remains obscure and puzzling to us! We humans often see no difference between God's plan and a sphinxlike fate. Yet, we trust him who makes the plan. We trust him because we know Jesus Christ.

No one has expressed this transformation of the moment and its terror more profoundly than Christ himself as quoted in John's gospel (John 16:20–21): ". . . you will weep and lament . . . you will be sorrowful, but your sorrow will turn into joy. When a woman is in travail she has sorrow, because her hour has come; but when she is delivered of the child, she no longer remembers the anguish, for joy that a child is born into the world."

In the same way we look at life differently when the Son of Man comes again and is once more "brought into the world"—this time openly and in majesty. Then our pains become birth pangs. They are the very opposite of those toothaches and turned ankles which make me ask in irritation or despair, "Why did this have to happen to me, of all people?" To be sure, birth pangs lead to that difficult time when "her hour is come," but they are filled with joy and anticipation of the great event ahead. And so, even the "hour" is lived under the brightness of Advent. This is why images of motherhood always stand at the crucial points of salvation history. There is the Virgin Mary in the stable of Bethlehem at the first coming of the Lord, and there is the woman in travail (Revelation 12:1–2)—the symbol for believing mankind—whose pain and sorrow are mysteriously transformed and hallowed because they press toward a great fulfillment: the Lord is about to come. The hand of the clock moves a little closer to twelve.

I cannot rest on this greatly comforting certainty as though it were a pillow, however. It is not a secure possession, but must be won anew every day. It must be achieved through the "nevertheless" of faith. The Lord depicts what terrors lie ahead in order to show that one does not possess this certainty with the black-and-white assurance of a mathematical rule, but must snatch it again and again from the fire of doubt and temptation. These terrors are already in the offing. They rise up in consecutive

waves even as the earth quakes before the destruction of the temple. In Nero's time entire cities in southern Italy and Asia Minor are reduced to ashes and rubble. Imperial coups bring war, bloodshed, and political upheavals. In Caesarea there is a Syrian-Jewish conflict that results in the massacre of thousands of Jews. And yet all this is only a sample of history as a whole with its ever-recurring destruction and terror. World history, in fact, is a dreadful parallel to the cruelty of nature. Nations eat and are eaten. The sequence repeats itself with the rhythm of all natural processes. In earlier days people feared the Huns, then it was the Turks, then the French, then the Germans. Today people fear the communists or Black Power or the Yellow Peril. It's always the same. However, that is not to say that faith remains untouched by this struggle and that believers have a metaphysical inside track that lets them slip through or nonchalantly stand above it. That certainly is not the intention of Erich Kästner's phrase, "The believer knows more."

No, says the Lord, when unrighteousness gets the upper hand, the love of many will grow cold. No wonder it turns out that way! People can get by for a while with the idea that God directs the woes of history toward his great fulfillment. Then when the going gets tough, luck runs out, and burdens

"Does this mean it's all over between us, Harvey?"

hang heavy upon us, we can still comfort ourselves by saying that God is purifying us in this fire and preparing us for better things. Only he'd better not pile it on too thick! For there are two instances where this sort of comfort breaks down.

First, when the pain becomes too great, when a person is suffering the torments of hell—perhaps in the agony of a heart attack—he is so racked with pain that he can no longer ask about its meaning, to say nothing of growing in maturity because of it. He cries only for relief, for a tiny pause to catch his breath.

The second case in which complications arise occurs when the pain lasts too long and just won't let up. I can take it for a year or two. I can tell myself, "God is permitting you to pass through this school of suffering." I even realize that I needed something of the sort—"needed," for now I have gotten beyond that stage, I have learned my lesson. After this, any further torment would be absurd. Nevertheless, the pain continues. In this case Erich Kästner's phrase, "The believer knows more," becomes out-and-out irony. Faith has to face the fact that a man is not only run through the wringer, but stuck between the rollers. This is the point at which I encounter meaninglessness. At least I am not able to discern any meaning. And for me, meaninglessness invariably becomes a refutation of God. . . .

In his fine book *Behind the Forest* Gerhard Nebel tells of a nurse who is wrapped up in her work, knowing nothing of the joy of playboys and playgirls and not looking for it either. But in the poverty of her simple life she is brimful of joy, passing it on to the patients in her care. Then he says the only effective means of combating neuroses and depression is self-sacrifice, not the game rooms of Las Vegas, or pampered lap dogs, or cocktail parties—only self-sacrifice will do. For it is the Lord whom we meet in our neighbor. When we hold him here, then he holds us. When we serve here, then our loins are girt and our lamps burning. Those who call upon his presence here learn to know his inexhaustible riches —and to await still more. The longer they believe, the more insatiable is their hope; the greater the fulfillments they anticipate, the less importance they put upon themselves. It is this shifting relationship between small and great, important and unimportant, which must thus be properly arranged if it is not to produce neuroses and perplexities in my life.

Jesus Christ reveals these last things to his followers, for he can scan the horizon from beginning to end. He sees the twilight of the day, the twilight of life, and the twilight of the world. And in the all-consuming desire of his love he says, "Would that even today you knew the things that make for peace!"

# THE NINE LAST THINGS

## David W. Lotz

IN THE CHURCH's eschatology as it developed during the classical period, these Last Things came to include the following components: (1) *temporal death*, understood as the separation of body and soul; (2) the *particular judgment* whereby God passes immediate sentence on the soul at the time of death, assigning it to heaven, purgatory, or hell; (3) the so-called *intermediate state* which, consequent upon the particular judgment, pertains to the state or condition of the disembodied souls between death and the resurrection at the Last Day; (4) the *Parousia* or Second Advent of Christ, when he will return in glory as the world's visible King and as the agent of God's general judgment on the living and the dead; (5) the *universal resurrection* of the dead when their souls will be reunited with their bodies; (6) the *general judgment*, or Last Day, or Great Assize, when God's ultimate sentence of acceptance or rejection will be delivered on humanity as a whole, as well as on the body and soul of each individual;

(7) the *End of the World*, usually understood as a cosmic conflagration; (8) *eternal damnation*, or Hell; and (9) *eternal life*, or Heaven.

In speaking of a "traditional" eschatology—and specifically of a "traditional" doctrine of heaven and hell—I mean that teaching which was almost universally held in the Christian churches of the West (and, for that matter, in the Eastern Orthodox churches) from the early Middle Ages until the modern period. To be sure, significant disagreements existed even during this classical period, particularly as a result of the Reformation. Furthermore, the traditional doctrine by no means passed away with the advent of modern "enlightened" Christianity. Heaven and hell, indeed Christian eschatology in general, were fiercely debated topics in the nineteenth century, most notably in Great Britain. In the earlier part of the twentieth century they also figured prominently in the fundamentalist-modernist controversy in the United States. And the widespread popular reception accorded the books of C. S. Lewis—especially *The Weight of Glory*, *The Screwtape Letters*, and *The Great Divorce*—shows that a modified form of the old doctrine of heaven and hell continues to have a powerful hold on contemporary religious consciousness.

The overall picture, therefore, is exceedingly complex, and one must beware of sweeping generalizations and oversimplified assertions. But the main lines of development and the salient details can, I believe, be fairly sketched in brief compass. . . .

ETERNAL JUDGMENT, HELL, DEATH, SEPARATION...

THAT KIND OF RELIGIOUS TALK SCARES ME...

LETS TALK ABOUT SANTA CLAUS, THE EASTER BUNNY...

# ESCHATOLOGY, REALIZED AND UNREALIZED

## J. B. Phillips

"ESCHATOLOGY" IS THE DOCTRINE or teaching about "the last things"—death, judgment, heaven, and hell. Much of today's Christianity is almost completely earthbound, and the words of Jesus about what follows this life are scarcely studied at all. This, I believe, is partly due to man's enormous technical successes, which make him feel master of the human situation. But it is also partly due to our scholars and experts. By the time they have finished with their dissection of the New Testament and with their explaining away as "myth" all that they find disquieting or unacceptable to the modern mind, the Christian way of life is little more than humanism with a slight tinge of religion. For it is not only advertisers who attempt to deaden our critical faculties by clever words, there are New Testament scholars who, whether consciously or not, do the same thing. Thus, if you are to be thought up-to-date and "with it," you are expected to believe in current phrases.

One of these is "realized eschatology," which means that all those things which Jesus foretold have happened, either at the destruction of Jerusalem in A.D. 70 or in the persecutions of the church. In other words, the prophetic element in the teaching of Jesus is of no value at all to us in the twentieth century. Such a judgment makes Jesus less of a prophet than Amos, Isaiah, Micah, Jeremiah, and the rest. I find myself quite unable to accept this. There *is* an element of the prophecy of Jerusalem's terrible downfall and of the desecration of the temple—the horror of which we who are not Jews find hard to appreciate. But the prophetic vision goes far beyond this. It envisages the end of the life of humanity on this planet, when, so to speak, eternity erupts into time. There is no time scale: there is rarely such an earthbound factor in prophetic vision. The prophet sees the truth in compelling terms, but he cannot tell the day or the hour of any event, still less the time of the final end of the whole human affair.

We are ourselves somewhere in the vast world-wide vision which Jesus foresaw, and for all we know, we may be near the end of all things. You simply cannot read the New Testament fairly and come to the conclusion that the world is going to become better and better, happier and happier, until at last God congratulates mankind on the splendid job they have made of it! Quite the contrary is true; not only Jesus but Paul, Peter, John, and the rest never seriously considered human perfectibility in the short span of earthly life. This is the preparation, the training ground, the place where God begins His work of making us into what He wants us to be. But it is not our home.

We are warned again and again not to value this world as a permanency. Neither our security nor our true wealth are rooted in this passing life. We are strangers and pilgrims, and while we are under the pressure of love to do all that we can to help our fellows, we should not expect a world which is largely God resisting to become some earthly paradise. All this may sound unbearably old-fashioned, but this is the view of the New Testament as a whole.

In a true and real sense the Kingdom of God was already established upon earth, but none of the New Testament writers expects the vast work of redeeming the whole world to take place either easily or quickly.

Some, at least, of the early Christians apparently expected the return of their risen Lord in power in a very short time, and both Peter and Paul had to remind their converts that the "time" was entirely a matter of God's choosing. Meanwhile the Christian life must be led with patience and courage, the true gospel must be proclaimed, and Christian worship continued. The light must shine in a dark and cruel world.

## ESCHATOLOGY IN A NUTSHELL
### Karl Rahner

BECAUSE of man's very nature . . . Christian anthropology is Christian futurology and Christian eschatology.

# ESCHATOLOGY, APOCALYPTIC AND PROPHETIC

*Frederick C. Grant*

IT IS NOW generally recognized that an "eschatological" outlook dominated the early church, not only in the New Testament period but for some time after. The beginning of the Gospel, in the days of John the Baptist, was Jesus's proclamation, "The time is fulfilled, and the kingdom of God is at hand; repent, and believe in the gospel," i.e., believe in this good news (Mark 1:15). At the other end of the New Testament period, it is true, there were those whose love had begun to grow cold (Matthew 24:12), while some complained, "Where is the promise of his coming? For since the fathers fell asleep, all things have continued as they were from the beginning of the creation" (2 Peter 3:4). 2 Peter probably dates from c. A.D. 150; a half-century later Clement of Alexandria and Origen marked the complete abandonment of any expectation of the immediate coming of the Kingdom. But in between the days of John the Baptist and the latest New Testament book, the eschatological outlook and emphasis was all but universal.

Jesus certainly expected the immediate coming—in fact, as we have seen, He believed that the "signs of the times" all pointed to the Kingdom as already on its way, and He expected that it would soon be fully manifested. The apostles certainly held this view, and also the conviction that Jesus was the one who had fully realized the promises of God (2 Corinthians 1:20), and was now in heaven, seated at God's right hand (Ephesians 1:20), from whence He would soon come and hold the Last Judgment of all mankind. Various conceptions of the age to come, and of the events to precede the end, were set forth in the New Testament writings; they exhibit much the same variety as that which is found in the Jewish apocalyptic writings of the same period, i.e., beginning with the Book of Daniel (c.

165 B.C.) and ending with 2 Esdras ( = 4 Ezra) and 2 Baruch (c. A.D. 100). Moreover, the conception of the heavenly Son of Man, found in the "Parables" of 1 Enoch, is also taken for granted in parts of the New Testament. . . . As Professor Ethelbert Stauffer and others maintain, "apocalyptic eschatology" was the closest and most natural background anywhere to be found in contemporary Judaism as the setting for the rise of Christian belief.

There are many who hold that Jesus Himself was an apocalyptist, and identified Himself the heavenly Son of Man. Others believe that He was an eschatological prophet, but not an apocalyptist, and that the identification of the risen and glorified Jesus with the exalted Son of Man reflects the faith of the church, not Jesus's own conviction. Whichever view is correct, one fact is certain: the "eschatological" outlook, as distinct from the "apocalyptic," characterizes not only the New Testament but also the Old. As contrasted with the old Oriental religions, e.g., with Hinduism, and also with Graeco-Roman religion, the religion of the Hebrews and the Jews looked forward, not backward, to a golden age. It took for granted God's absolute sovereignty, His ability to control all events in heaven and earth and bend them to His purposes—He could make even "the wrath of man" to praise Him (Psalms 76:10). Accordingly, the course of history *must* finally lead to the realization of the divine plan. The Bible does

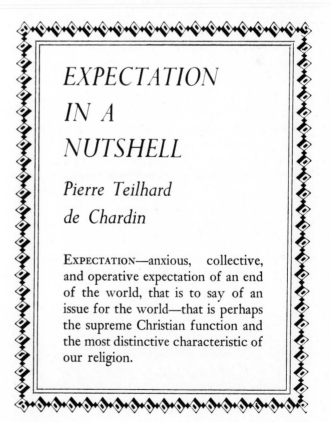

## EXPECTATION IN A NUTSHELL

*Pierre Teilhard de Chardin*

EXPECTATION—anxious, collective, and operative expectation of an end of the world, that is to say of an issue for the world—that is perhaps the supreme Christian function and the most distinctive characteristic of our religion.

not say that "all things" by their very nature "work together for good," but that "in everything *God works* for good with those who love him" (Romans 8:28, R.S.V.).

It is this Hebrew and Jewish "eschatological" idea, this linear rather than circular view of history, which is also presupposed in the New Testament. The ancient prophetic conviction is still strong, namely that God is in absolute control of events, and nothing escapes Him; that nothing can frustrate His purposes; and that nothing can fail to serve its appointed end, in the final realization upon earth of the divine Reign which exists—and has always existed—everywhere else in the universe. God's Kingdom is "everlasting" (Psalms 145:13), and yet by a paradox it must "come" here on earth. It will come, as Jesus said, when God's will is done "on earth as it is in heaven" (Matthew 6:10).

The difference between "apocalyptic" eschatology and "prophetic" is to be seen partly in the intensity of its conviction of the nearness of the end of history, the great turning point soon to be reached, and partly in the methodical calculation of "times and seasons" (which Jesus repudiated; Acts 1:7) and the working out of a rigid timetable or schedule for coming events—chiefly the unfulfilled prophecies of the Old Testament. There was also a stronger strain of dualism in apocalyptic thought, and much more use was made of angels, demons, and other celestial *dramatis personae*; and there was a whole set of machinery, consisting of supernatural "signs, wonders, and portents" which the apocalyptists used in describing the approach of the end. By the very nature of the case, this additional apocalyptic element or emphasis added nothing to the religious meaning or exigency of the Gospel, but only made its acceptance burdensome for those who held a nonapocalyptic view of the world. It was only a temporary phase of thought, and in course of time it was left behind, its flaming manifestos thereafter being read as poetry, not prose, and certainly not as sober prediction of the future. It is curious that the Book of Revelation—the chief example of apocalyptic thought in the New Testament—was finally admitted to the New Testament canon, i.e., included in the authoritative list of generally accepted contents, because it was understood to contain a preview of the future history of the church.

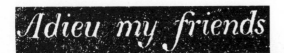
*Adieu my friends*

# ESCHATOLOGY AND HISTORY

*John L. McKenzie*

IN THE NEW TESTAMENT there is what has often been called a tension between history and eschatology. This tension corresponds to two other terms which have become common in recent theological literature, the eschatological character of the church and the incarnational character of the church. In the first of these terms the church is conceived as tending to a fulfillment which will be reached only in the eschatological process; in the second term it is conceived as having a function and mission in the world. Despite the apparent paradox, both characters must be retained; for both are solidly founded in the New Testament idea of the church. The emphasis at times falls on one rather than another; in critical moments of history theology turns to the eschatological idea as the only solution of the crises of history. In more tranquil times the church can be more aware of her mission in the world. The tension in the New Testament is reflected in the life of the church, which has a fulfillment in the world yet at the same time knows that its fulfillment in the world is not complete and final.

I have observed above that if New Testament eschatological terms are taken too rigidly we find ourselves in a posteschatological era. Yet the theme recurs in the New Testament that the Reign is initiated by the coming of Jesus. We must understand that the Reign has a dimension after him which it did not have before him. He is an eschatological figure in the sense that he is final; and he is final in the sense that he will not happen again. He is not only the word of God, he is God's last word. The New Testament speaks with conviction of the fullness of revelation in Jesus Christ; and the church has always understood that there cannot be another gospel. He begins the last age; and when this is understood, one feels that the tension between history and eschatology has become more acute.

The entire course of biblical thinking, in both Old and New Testaments, demands an eschatological term at least in the minimum sense in which I have defined it. In ancient Near Eastern mythology and in Greek philosophical and historical thinking the course of events is an endless chain, a treadmill, or a revolving circle. Ultimately the course of events becomes meaningless as a whole, for it leads to nothing and accomplishes nothing. In this view the individual person becomes if possible even more meaningless. Man lives in history and makes it; and if the story of the race as a whole is a pursuit of nothing, how can the individual person achieve anything? The tone of despair which is heard so often in the literature of Greece and Rome is deep; and if the gospel had nothing to say to this despair, it could not rise above the level of philosophy or the mystery cults. For the men of the Hellenistic age human life was ruled by fate or fortune; human life did not make sense and was not supposed to, for fate and fortune are personifications of the irrational.

In biblical faith, if God did not rule history, then history is greater than God—which is to say that man is greater than God, and this is to say that there really is no God. God can rule history only if he rules it purposefully; otherwise his rule would not differ from the caprice of the gods of ancient religion or from the irrationality of fate. His purpose in both Old Testament and New Testament is salvation and judgment. This purpose is executed in each turn of history; in the Bible God is always savior and always judge. But the Reign of God must mean more than the exercise of the will to save and to judge in particular cases; if it does not, then God is engaged in a perpetual struggle with hostile forces which he never wins and never loses. History relapses into the mythological pattern of the cyclic struggle between good and evil, light and darkness, order and chaos. It is a very reasonable view of history, but it is not the biblical view.

The biblical view of God's power and righteousness demands that the powers which resist him must be finally overcome. We observe that the Bible does not attend to the problem implicit in the temporary conflict between God and hostile powers; the assurance of a final victory made further consideration of this problem unnecessary for them. We may be driven to further examination of the problem by our speculative curiosity; but we are here engaged with the New Testament, and we can see that the New Testament faith in God is not satisfied with a partial victory of God. Eschatology is the answer of the Bible to dualism; and it is impossible to conceive an answer to dualism which does not accept some kind of eschatology.

The New Testament idea of man leads with a like necessity to eschatology. No ancient religious or philosophical system arrived at the ideal of human unity which is seen in the New Testament. Modern individualism is not a part of its thought. The New Testament does indeed reveal in an entirely new fashion the dignity and importance of the individual person, and, as we have noticed, it calls for a personal decision; but the individual person does not live in solitary grandeur. He is one of the company of mankind, one of the children of one Father, a member of one body. The New Testament is well aware of the actions of man in society—which is one definition of history. Man must proceed to his destiny as a society; history must reach its fulfillment as history. The New Testament does not view mankind as a stream of isolated atoms falling through a void; and without eschatology, does not human destiny issue in such an atomic stream? The system of Teilhard de Chardin is a new statement of eschatology, although not all of his readers have recognized it. Teilhard sees not only mankind but all of nature converging toward a single eschatological fulfillment. And he means a fulfillment; the process of evolution which never reaches a term is a purposeless evolution; and a purposeless process cannot be incorporated into a theistic view of the world. What I point to here is his vision of nature and of man as one great unity whose fulfillment is found in the perfection of unity. This is exactly the element in biblical thinking which I wish to emphasize here.

For biblical eschatology is not only concerned with man. In a striking passage Paul sees the whole creation longing for its liberation; for it too has been

## THE WORLD IS NOT CONCLUSION

*Emily Dickinson*

*This world is not conclusion;*
  *A sequel stands beyond,*
*Invisible, as music,*
  *But positive, as sound.*
*It beckons and it baffles;*
  *Philosophies don't know,*
*And through a riddle, at the last,*
  *Sagacity must go.*
*To guess it puzzles scholars;*
  *To gain it, men have shown*
*Contempt of generations,*
  *And crucifixion known.*

**"It has to do with eschatology!"**

in bondage because of man's sin (Romans 8:19–23). The Apocalypse sees a new heaven and a new earth; the author echoes Isaiah 66:22. The eschatological process is more than once described, explicitly or implicitly, as a new creation. For God is Lord of nature as well as of history. He must reassert his dominion over nature, which man has attempted to usurp. The conception is indeed mythological, but it expresses a profound truth. Teilhard has expressed this truth in scientific language which is itself mythological in character. A regeneration of God's creation must include the scene of history as well as the actors. Nature, like man, has not reached its potential fulfillment in the present age; and it remains frustrated unless it shares in man's destiny, as it has shared in his history.

We turn to the problem posed by the New Testament that the last age begins with the coming of Jesus. Here we do well to recall a biblical conception of history which, as I expressed it in an earlier work, sees the present both as recapitulating the entire past and as implicitly containing the entire future. One may call this way of thinking mythological rather than historical or philosophical, and I have no quarrel with the word. With the coming of Jesus the power which will establish the Reign has made itself known, and its activity has begun. The Reign of God is effectively present. With Jesus fulfillment begins, and history will never be the same. It is at this point that we realize that our categories of eschatology are too rigid for the flexibility of New Testament thought; and we should loosen the categories rather than harden New Testament thought.

We have observed that the purely eschatological church is not a faithful summary of New Testament teaching. The church is in the world and for the world, as Jesus himself was in the world and for the world. Its concern, like his, cannot be with the eschatological solely. Jesus proclaimed how men ought to live; and he had no intention that this proclamation should have no effect in the world of men. He was conscious of the dynamism of his person and message. A church which would live withdrawn in eschatological expectation is hardly a continuation of the life and work of Jesus of Nazareth, who was in the world and of the world as much as a man could be. He illustrated perfectly the principle that one does not win people by refusing to associate with them; and the Gospels relate that in the opinion of the Pharisees he was not selective enough in his associations—in fact, they charged, he liked low company. I remarked above that the primitive church could understand what it was only when it understood what he was. Possibly

it took the community some time to realize that its life was too withdrawn for the followers of Jesus of Nazareth. Whether the Parousia was near or far, they had to do what he did, which was to go to people and proclaim the coming of the Reign. The tension between history and eschatology could not be speculatively resolved. Practically it was resolved by doing what Jesus did, and that was to engage oneself in history. The hour of the Parousia, Jesus had said, was unknown even to the Son—by whom he meant himself. He certainly meant at least that the hour of the Parousia was of no concern and no importance to the church; and this left the church no alternative but engagement in history.

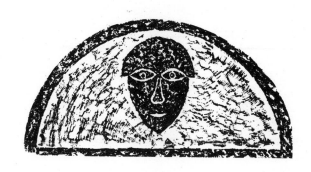

# THE WORLD'S LAST NIGHT

## *John Donne*

*What if this present were the world's last night?*
*Mark in my heart, O soul, where thou dost dwell,*
*The picture of Christ crucified, and tell*
*Whether that countenance can thee affright,*
*Tears in his eyes quench the amazing light,*
*Blood fills his frowns, which from his pierced head*
  *fell.*
*And can that tongue adjudge thee unto hell,*
*Which prayed forgiveness for his foes' fierce spite?*
*No, no; but as in my idolatry*
*I said to all my profane mistresses,*
*Beauty, of pity, foulness only is*
*A sign of rigor: so I say to thee,*
*To wicked spirits are horrid shapes assigned,*
*This beauteous form assures a piteous mind.*

# FOR WHOM THE END
# DID NOT COME

## PHRYGIA, A.D. 150

### Jacques Lacarrière

IN PHRYGIA in the second century, a certain
Montanus, in the company of two women, Priscilla
and Maximilla, for seven years in succession prophesied the imminent descent of the New Jerusalem
upon the earth, without the slightest waning of public enthusiasm and credulity. He even specified the
exact spot where the Holy City was to come down,
viz. the plain of Pepuza, in Phrygia, and everyone
waited patiently in the plain for the descent of the
celestial city, while listening to Montanus's prophecies.

> Man sleeps, while I keep watch.
> And now the Lord takes away
>   the heart of each man,
> To replace it with another.
>
> (Montanus, ORACLE V)

Long after Montanus's death, his prophecies continued to shake the multitudes they collected, since
very many Montanistic churches were formed
throughout the Christian East and some of them
were still in existence at the end of the fourth
century.

## CARTHAGE, A.D. 250

### Cyprian of Carthage

## CARTHAGE, A.D. 200

### Tertullian

THE HOLY CITY of Jerusalem appeared during the
course of the Eastern expedition, which took place
in recent years. Even pagans, who were in Judea at
the time, declared that every morning for forty days
a town which seemed to come from the sky took
shape in the air. It was equipped with walls which
vanished in the full light of day. It is in that city
that the saints will live in spiritual bliss after the
Resurrection.

WHO CANNOT SEE that the world is already in its
decline and no longer has the strength and vigor of
former times? There is no need to invoke scriptural
authority to prove it. The world tells its own tale
and in its general decadence bears adequate witness
that it is approaching its end. There is less rain in
winter to encourage the growth of seeds; springtime
is not now so enjoyable or autumn so fruitful; the
quarries, as if from weariness, give less stone and
marble and the gold and silver mines are already
worked out; the land remains untilled, the seas lack
pilots and the armies are without men; there is less
innocence in the courts, less justice in the judges, less
concord between friends, less artistic sincerity, less
moral strictness. Do you think that anything which

is in a decline can be as vigorous as it was originally? Everything which is approaching its end must of necessity wither away. We see children who are already quite white; their hair dies before it can grow and they are stricken with old age at the beginning of their lives. Thus, everything in these days is rushing to its doom and is affected by the general debility.

## SCOTLAND, A.D. 700

### Adamnan of Iona

THESE ARE THE TIDINGS which Elias declared continually unto the souls of the righteous, under the Tree of Life, which is in paradise. As soon as Elias opens his book in order to instruct the spirits, the

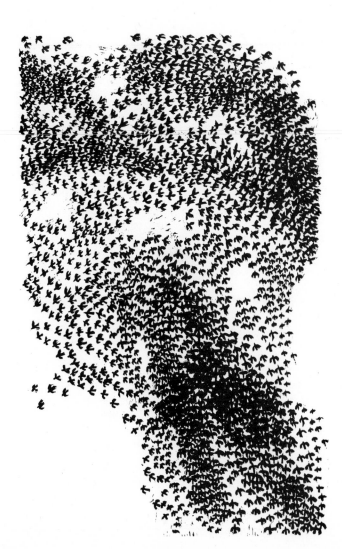

souls of the righteous, in the form of bright white birds, repair to him from every side. Then he tells them, first, of the wages of the righteous, the joys and delights of the Heavenly Realm, and right glad thereat are all the throng. After that he tells them of the pains and torments of hell and the woes of doomsday. . . . Then Elias shuts his book, and thereupon the birds make exceeding great lamentation. . . .

## ITALY, 1260

### Marjorie Reeves

AS THE 1250S APPROACHED, attention focused more and more sharply on the date of impending disaster. It was no new thing to proclaim the advent of Antichrist, but the notable concentration of hopes and fears on the decade 1250–60, and especially on the year 1260, can hardly be dissociated from Joachim, [abbot of the Franciscan monastery at Fiore]. This is almost ironical, for the abbot in his writings took care to emphasize the uncertainty of all calculations of Last Things and hardly committed himself to the *year* 1260, though he did to the *number* 1260. He did, however, declare that the two generations after 1200 were crucial, and, in words which communicated suspense and excitement and were therefore often quoted, he summoned the next generation to watch:

"Tempus autem quando haec erunt dico manifeste quia prope est: diem autem et horam Dominus ipse novit. Quantum tamen secundum adaptationem concordie extimare queo, si pax conceditur ab his malis usque ad annum millesimum ducentesimum incarnationis dominice: exinde ne subito ista fiant suspecta mihi sunt omnimodis et tempora et momenta." (*Lib. Conc.*, f. 41ᵛ)

## HOLLAND, 1533

### Ronald A. Knox

ONE INFLUENCE . . . played a great part in the Anabaptism of Holland and of the Rhine countries. This was chiliasm—the conviction that the existing

## NEW ENGLAND, 1843

### William Miller

I AM SATISFIED that the end of the world is at hand. The evidence flows in from every quarter. . . . Soon, very soon God will arise in his anger and the vine of the earth will be reaped. *See! See!*—the angel with his sharp sickle is about to take the field! See yonder trembling victims fall before his pestilential breath! High and low, rich and poor, trembling and falling before the appalling grave, the dreadful cholera. . . . Behold, the heavens grow black with clouds; the sun has veiled himself; the moon, pale and forsaken, hangs in middle air; the hail descends; the seven thunders utter loud their voices; the lightnings send their vivid gleams and sulfurous flames abroad; and the great city of the nations falls to rise no more forever and forever! At this dread moment, look! The clouds have burst asunder; the heavens appear; the great white throne is in sight! Amazement fills the universe with awe! He comes!—He comes!—Behold the Savior comes!—Lift up your heads, ye saints—He comes! He comes! He comes!

world order was about to come to an end, and that an earthly millennium, during which the "saints" would reign, was to succeed it. The impulse to this conviction seems to have been given entirely by that remarkable missionary spirit Melchior Hofmann. He announced the second coming for the year 1533, and suspended baptisms for two years in order to prepare for it. The choice of date was an obvious one: it is probable that such views have had their vogue at and around each centenary of the Crucifixion. Nicholas of Cusa, giving his readers some three centuries' grace, held that the world would not outlast 1734; and in recent years apocalyptic warnings have not been wanting. (Arthur E. Ware, interviewed in the *Daily Express* of 4 May 1933, foretold that 12 June of that year would be the beginning of a great tribulation, ushering in the millennium.) Hofmann, more fortunate than other prophets in the opportunity of his death, ended his life in prison at Strasbourg before the day to which he looked forward.

## LONDON, 1934

### J. B. Phillips

I REMEMBER A MAN in 1934 hiring the Queen's Hall in London solemnly to warn the British Empire that Jesus Christ would return in person on, I think, the 24th of June of that year. So convinced was he of his calculations that he stated at the time that if he were wrong he would "sink into well-merited obscurity." He left himself no loophole for later revision of the timetable as others have done, and I presume he still lives in his obscurity. This example is only one of hundreds of misguided people who have thought they could calculate what, on Jesus's own admission, was known only to the Father (Mark 13:32). But I really don't see why, because this important New Testament hope has been the stamping ground of the fanatical, we should be cheated altogether of what was essentially a part of early Christian teaching. . . .

## ARKANSAS, 1976

### Associated Press

GRANNIS, ARK., June 30, 1976 (AP)—The world didn't end Tuesday, but a spokesman for the twenty-four persons awaiting its demise says the group still has faith in their mission.

"Everything is in the hands of God. We know He will provide," said Elizabeth Nance Bard. "We are not worried, we are just as sure as ever that He will come. We just know it."

She had said Monday the end of the world could occur the following day because that was the nine-month anniversary of the beginning of the vigil to await the Second Coming of Christ. "From conception to birth is nine months," she noted. . . .

But she also said Monday that the world might not end for everyone at the same time. . . .

## NEW YORK, 1914

### Barbara Grizzuti Harrison

[Pastor Charles Taize] Russell preached that the six thousand years of man's existence on earth had ended in 1872—Victoria Woodhull also foresaw an end to "man's" rule in 1872, but she meant by that something quite different—and that the seventh millennium had begun in 1873. The glorified Christ became invisibly present in 1874. Shortly after 1874 had begun the "antitypical Jubilee," an event "foreshadowed" by the ancient jubilees observed under the Mosaic Law. For forty years, the "saints," God's consecrated ones, would be "harvested," until, on October 1, 1914, the Gentile Times would end. On October 1, 1914, the evil worldly system would collapse, God would have His everlasting day, and there would be a general "Restitution" for all mankind—but not before the "living saints" (Russell and his followers) could be suddenly and miraculously caught away bodily to be with their Lord, 1878.

# FEAR OF COLLECTIVE DEATH

*Ignace Lepp*

CERTAIN RELIGIOUS SECTS periodically announce the end of the world by direct divine intervention. The first great religious expectation of the end of the world, in which all of Christendom seems to have believed, took place just before the year 1000. But there is no evidence that this expectation generated universal terror. Of course, preachers profited by the circumstances to incite repentance and a change of life and stressed the more terrifying aspects of the last judgment. But joyful hope in the immediate return of the Savior seems to have been the dominant attitude. An extraordinary number of beautiful churches and cathedrals were built, for Christians wanted the world to be worthy to receive the Master. But Christ's return and the consequent end of the world did not take place in 1000. Since then, every dramatic age has had its prophets and "illuminati" who have predicted the precise date of the world's end, usually with biblical evidence to support their claims. And there have always been those who believed the prophecies. In modern times the Adventists and other Pentecostal sects specialize in the discernment of signs and prophecies of the apocalyptic end of the world. They have already set several dates in the twentieth century. Each time, the credulous are seized with fear and give away their worldly goods in the hope that they will be numbered among the elect while all others go to eternal punishment. It is remarkable that despite so many disillusionments each prophet of doom continues to find followers. It may be concluded from this that mankind's expectation of a collective death has its roots in the collective unconscious. This seems to correspond to one of the archetypes of Jungian psychology. This is not unique to Christianity; it is the spiritual patrimony of other civilizations as well.

"Civilizations now know that they are mortal," wrote Paul Valéry. But since the fifties, the fear of collective death has taken on an entirely new form which is no longer related to the expectation of a last judgment, the possible collision of the stars, or the future cooling of the earth. Since the beginning of the insane race for nuclear superiority, the fate of mankind is in the hands of men themselves. What took place on a relatively modest scale in 1945 at Hiroshima and Nagasaki furnishes us with a very concrete image of how the destruction of the earth and its inhabitants could come about. The bombs stockpiled by the Americans and Russians could end life on our planet in a few hours. Nor is the production of nuclear energy for industrial and peaceful uses entirely without danger. Like Prometheus, men today have succeeded in unleashing forces they cannot totally master.

## THE GREATEST PHANTASMAGORIA

*John A. T. Robinson*

WITH THE second coming of Christ we reach what perhaps to most people seems the greatest phantasmagoria in the whole collection of mumbo-jumbo that goes under the name of Christian doctrine.

For people really suppose that the church teaches that one afternoon—this year, next year, sometime—Telstar will pick up a picture of Christ, descending from the skies with thousands of angels in train, returning to earth to judge the world.

But I certainly don't believe that. Nor does any intelligent Christian I know.

For the second coming is not something that can be caught by radar or seen on a screen. It's not a truth like that at all.

It stands for the conviction that—however long it takes—*Christ must come into everything*. There's no part of life from which he can or will be left out.

Thus the fear of collective death is far more justified than ever before. Some optimists trust in the wisdom of heads of state, hoping that the famous "balance of terror" will prevent not only a final cataclysm but also the "classic" type of war. But the pessimists have a point when they say that an accident, an error in calculation, or a Nero-type madness in one of those who control the button could unleash a universal holocaust. The hot line linking Moscow and the White House is a feeble guarantee, especially in view of the fact that a monopoly on nuclear arms will not long remain in the hands of the two great powers. And who can guarantee that men far less scrupulous than our present leaders, men like Hitler and Stalin, will not accede to power at some future date?

In most of the countries of Western Europe, men are rationally convinced of the great danger represented by nuclear weapons. But most of them don't seem to be especially disturbed. Perhaps they lack imagination. Yet, on the other hand, I have heard people in West Germany say, "Why should we work so hard to erect permanent buildings and save for the future when the chances for a future are so slim?" Some of my patients have refused to marry or have children since, they argue, it is clear that their offspring would suffer the horrors of a thermonuclear war. This is a modern version of the fear that neurotics of all times have experienced when confronted with the risks and responsibilities of life. Still, it seems that more normal people today are affected by this fear of collective death, at least unconsciously. This is at least a partial explanation of the disarray of our time, which is expressed in gratuitous crime, vandalism, eroticism, and the accelerated pace of life. Even modern music and dances seem to express the despair of a humanity that no longer believes in its own future. Unlike the Adventists and other phophets who expect the end of the world through divine intervention, most men today are not inclined to await, in prayer and penance, the nuclear destruction of life. They are not about to change their hearts but rather are intent upon enjoying whatever passing pleasure life affords them. They hope, more or less consciously, to repress their fear in distractions.

It is psychologically significant that the fear of death by thermonuclear war or accident is greatest in those countries that for the moment have a quasi-monopoly on this frightful weapon. Our knowledge of Russia is admittedly indirect. But from what we are able to garner, it appears that the Soviet leaders are bad psychologists because they fail to realize that the immediate effect of their boasting is necessarily to increase fear.

## UNBRIDLED INEBRIATION

### C. S. Lewis

I HATE and distrust reactions not only in religion but in everything. Luther surely spoke very good sense when he compared humanity to a drunkard who, after falling off his horse on the right, falls off it next time on the left. I am convinced that those who find in Christ's apocalyptic the whole of his message are mistaken. But a thing does not vanish—it is not even discredited—because someone has spoken of it with exaggeration. It remains exactly where it was. The only difference is that if it has recently been exaggerated, we must now take special care not to overlook it; for that is the side on which the drunk man is now most likely to fall off.

In the United States the fear of collective death is often overtly neurotic in character. This explains much of the recent absurd behavior of this fundamentally democratic and pacific nation. The witch hunts of the McCarthy period, the propaganda for a preventive nuclear war against Russia and, more recently, against China, and the millions of dollars spent to assure hypothetical protection against an atomic attack are so many expressions of the fear affecting a whole people. Bomb shelters, for example, are constructed at great expense, although it is obvious that they would be useless in case of war. Incidents of criminality, eroticism, abuse of alcohol and drugs seem more rampant in the United States than elsewhere. Today the stronger and richer a nation is, the greater is its insecurity.

# MILLENNIAL MADNESS

*Alice Felt Tyler*

As THE EXCITEMENT mounted, men began to demand a date—a definite day for the great event of the Lord's coming. Miller was reluctant to make any such statement. The year 1843 was to him the last sure "year of time"; whether the advent would occur during 1843 or shortly thereafter, he could not say. Even if his estimate should prove slightly inaccurate, he pleaded, his followers should have faith that their deliverance would come soon, in God's appointed time. Many of the Millerite preachers, however, were far less cautious. Their radicalism distressed Miller, and even Himes, more and more as 1843 wore on. A certain John Starkweather encouraged the most violent physical manifestations of conversion among his followers, and hallucinations and catalyptic and epileptic attacks were considered evidences of extreme piety. Mesmerism was one of his accomplishments, and his camp meetings were orgies of exhibitionism that were heartily condemned by the leaders of the movement. Miller himself was always opposed to fanaticism, perversion of his ideas, and all "excess of zeal"—little realizing that the dynamite of his original thesis was far too dangerous a weapon to place in the hands of his followers.

As 1843 drew to its close, the dangers of such religious excitement and delusion became apparent. Suicides were attributed to despair over the necessity of facing the day of judgment. The state insane asylums reported the admission of several who had been crazed by fear of the end of the world. In Portsmouth, New Hampshire, a Millerite in voluminous white robes climbed a tree, tried to fly when he thought the fatal hour was near, fell, and broke his neck. A Massachusetts farmer cut his wife's throat because she refused to be converted to Millerism, and a despairing mother poisoned herself and all her children. The editor of a New Bedford paper described the somewhat amusing anguish of a mechanic whom he had seen kneeling in the snow with a Millerite pamphlet in each hand, praying and blaspheming alternately in a "most piteous manner." In Wilkes-Barre, Pennsylvania, a storekeeper requested the sheriff to give all his goods to anyone who would take them away, and in New York another merchant offered to give a pair of shoes to anyone who needed them, since "he had no further use for them."

# THE NINE BILLION NAMES OF GOD

*Arthur C. Clarke*

"THIS IS A SLIGHTLY unusual request," said Dr. Wagner, with what he hoped was commendable restraint. "As far as I know, it's the first time anyone's been asked to supply a Tibetan monastery with an Automatic Sequence Computer. I don't wish to be inquisitive, but I should hardly have thought that your—ah—establishment had much use for such a machine. Could you explain just what you intend to do with it?"

"Gladly," replied the lama, readjusting his silk robes and carefully putting away the slide rule he had been using for currency conversions. "Your Mark V Computer can carry out any routine mathematical operation involving up to ten digits. However, for our work we are interested in *letters*, not numbers. As we wish you to modify the output circuits, the machine will be printing words, not columns of figures."

"I don't quite understand. . . ."

"This is a project on which we have been working for the last three centuries—since the lamasery was founded, in fact. It is somewhat alien to your way of thought, so I hope you will listen with an open mind while I explain it."

"Naturally."

"It is really quite simple. We have been compiling a list which shall contain all the possible names of God."

"I beg your pardon?"

"We have reason to believe," continued the lama imperturbably, "that all such names can be written with not more than nine letters in an alphabet we have devised."

"And you have been doing this for three centuries?"

"Yes: we expected it would take us about fifteen thousand years to complete the task."

"Oh." Dr. Wagner looked a little dazed. "Now I see why you wanted to hire one of our machines. But exactly what is the *purpose* of this project?"

The lama hesitated for a fraction of a second, and Wagner wondered if he had offended him. If so, there was no trace of annoyance in the reply.

"Call it ritual, if you like, but it's a fundamental part of our belief. All the many names of the Supreme Being—God, Jehovah, Allah, and so on—they are only man-made labels. There is a philosophical problem of some difficulty here, which I do not propose to discuss, but somewhere among all the possible combinations of letters that can occur are what one may call the *real* names of God. By systematic permutation of letters, we have been trying to list them all."

"I see. You've been starting at AAAAAAA . . . and working up to ZZZZZZZ. . . ."

"Exactly—though we use a special alphabet of our own. Modifying the electronic typewriters to deal with this is, of course, trivial. A rather more interesting problem is that of devising suitable circuits to eliminate ridiculous combinations. For example, no letter must occur more than three times in succession."

"Three? Surely you mean two."

"Three is correct: I am afraid it would take too long to explain why, even if you understood our language."

"I'm sure it would," said Wagner hastily. "Go on."

"Luckily, it will be a simple matter to adapt your Automatic Sequence Computer for this work, since once it has been programmed properly it will permute each letter in turn and print the result. What would have taken us fifteen thousand years it will be able to do in a hundred days."

Dr. Wagner was scarcely conscious of the faint sounds from the Manhattan streets far below. He was in a different world, a world of natural, not man-made, mountains. High up in their remote aeries these monks had been patiently at work, generation after generation, compiling their lists of meaningless words. Was there any limit to the follies of mankind? Still, he must give no hint of his inner thoughts. The customer was always right. . . .

"There's no doubt," replied the doctor, "that we can modify the Mark V to print lists of this nature. I'm much more worried about the problem of installation and maintenance. Getting out to Tibet, in these days, is not going to be easy."

"We can arrange that. The components are small enough to travel by air—that is one reason why we chose your machine. If you can get them to India, we will provide transport from there."

"And you want to hire two of our engineers?"

"Yes, for the three months that the project should occupy."

"I've no doubt that Personnel can manage that." Dr. Wagner scribbled a note on his desk pad. "There are just two other points—"

Before he could finish the sentence the lama had produced a small slip of paper.

"This is my certified credit balance at the Asiatic Bank."

"Thank you. It appears to be—ah—adequate. The second matter is so trivial that I hesitate to mention it—but it's surprising how often the obvious gets overlooked. What source of electrical energy have you?"

"A diesel generator providing fifty kilowatts at a hundred and ten volts. It was installed about five years ago and is quite reliable. It's made life at the lamasery much more comfortable, but of course it was really installed to provide power for the motors driving the prayer wheels."

"Of course," echoed Dr. Wagner. "I should have thought of that."

The view from the parapet was vertiginous, but in time one gets used to anything. After three months, George Hanley was not impressed by the two-thousand-foot swoop into the abyss or the remote checkerboard of fields in the valley below. He was leaning against the wind-smoothed stones and staring morosely at the distant mountains whose names he had never bothered to discover.

This, thought George, was the craziest thing that had ever happened to him. "Project Shangri-La," some wit back at the labs had christened it. For weeks now the Mark V had been churning out acres of sheets covered with gibberish. Patiently, inexorably, the computer had been rearranging letters in all their possible combinations, exhausting each class before going on to the next. As the sheets had emerged from the electromatic typewriters, the monks had carefully cut them up and pasted them into enormous books. In another week, heaven be praised, they would have finished. Just what obscure calculations had convinced the monks that they needn't bother to go on to words of ten, twenty, or a hundred letters, George didn't know. One of his recurring nightmares was that there would be some

change of plan, and that the high lama (whom they'd naturally called Sam Jaffe, though he didn't look a bit like him) would suddenly announce that the project would be extended to approximately A.D. 2060. They were quite capable of it.

George heard the heavy wooden door slam in the wind as Chuck came out onto the parapet beside him. As usual, Chuck was smoking one of the cigars that made him so popular with the monks—who, it seemed, were quite willing to embrace all the minor and most of the major pleasures of life. That was one thing in their favor: they might be crazy, but they weren't bluenoses. Those frequent trips they took down to the village, for instance . . .

"Listen, George," said Chuck urgently. "I've learned something that means trouble."

"What's wrong? Isn't the machine behaving?" That was the worst contingency George could imagine. It might delay his return, and nothing could be more horrible. The way he felt now, even the

sight of a TV commercial would seem like manna from heaven. At least it would be some link with home.

"No—it's nothing like that." Chuck settled himself on the parapet, which was unusual because normally he was scared of the drop. "I've just found what all this is about."

"What d'ya mean? I thought we knew."

"Sure—we know what the monks are trying to do. But we didn't know why. It's the craziest thing—"

"Tell me something new," growled George.

"—but old Sam's just come clean with me. You know the way he drops in every afternoon to watch the sheets roll out. Well, this time he seemed rather excited, or at least as near as he'll ever get to it. When I told him that we were on the last cycle he asked me, in that cute English accent of his, if I'd ever wondered what they were trying to do. I said, 'Sure'—and he told me."

"Go on: I'll buy it."

"Well, they believe that when they have listed all His names—and they reckon that there are about nine billion of them—God's purpose will be achieved. The human race will have finished what it was created to do, and there won't be any point in carrying on. Indeed, the very idea is something like blasphemy."

"Then what do they expect us to do? Commit suicide?"

"There's no need for that. When the list's completed, God steps in and simply winds things up . . . bingo!"

"Oh, I get it. When we finished our job, it will be the end of the world."

Chuck gave a nervous little laugh.

"That's just what I said to Sam. And do you know what happened? He looked at me in a very queer way, like I'd been stupid in class, and said, 'It's nothing as trivial as *that*.'"

George thought this over for a moment.

"That's what I call taking the Wide View," he said presently. "But what d'you suppose we should do about it? I don't see that it makes the slightest difference to us. After all, we already knew that they were crazy."

"Yes—but don't you see what may happen? When the list's complete and the Last Trump doesn't blow —or whatever it is they expect—*we* may get the blame. It's our machine they've been using. I don't like the situation one little bit."

"I see," said George slowly. "You've got a point there. But this sort of thing's happened before, you know. When I was a kid down in Louisiana we had a crackpot preacher who once said the world was going to end next Sunday. Hundreds of people believed him—even sold their homes. Yet when nothing happened, they didn't turn nasty, as you'd expect. They just decided that he'd made a mistake in his calculations and went right on believing. I guess some of them still do."

"Well, this isn't Louisiana, in case you hadn't noticed. There are just two of us and hundreds of these monks. I like them, and I'll be sorry for old Sam when his lifework backfires on him. But all the same, I wish I was somewhere else."

"I've been wishing that for weeks. But there's nothing we can do until the contract's finished and the transport arrives to fly us out."

"Of course," said Chuck thoughtfully, "we could always try a bit of sabotage."

"Like hell we could! That would make things worse."

"Not the way I meant. Look at it like this. The

machine will finish its run four days from now, on the present twenty-hours-a-day basis. The transport calls in a week. OK—then all we need to do is to find something that needs replacing during one of the overhaul periods—something that will hold up the works for a couple of days. We'll fix it, of course, but not too quickly. If we time matters properly, we can be down at the airfield when the last name pops out of the register. They won't be able to catch us then."

"I don't like it," said George. "It will be the first time I ever walked out on a job. Besides, it would make them suspicious. No, I'll sit tight and take what comes."

"I *still* don't like it," he said, seven days later, as the tough little mountain ponies carried them down the winding road. "And don't you think I'm running away because I'm afraid. I'm just sorry for those poor old guys up there, and I don't want to be around they find what suckers they've been. Wonder how Sam will take it?"

"It's funny," replied Chuck, "but when I said goodbye I got the idea he knew we were walking out on him—and that he didn't care because he knew the machine was running smoothly and that the job would soon be finished. After that—well, of course, for him there just isn't any After That. . . ."

George turned in his saddle and stared back up the mountain road. This was the last place from which one could get a clear view of the lamasery. The squat, angular buildings were silhouetted against

the afterglow of the sunset: here and there, lights gleamed like portholes in the side of an ocean liner. Electric lights, of course, sharing the same circuit as the Mark V. How much longer would they share it? wondered George. Would the monks smash up the computer in their rage and disappointment? Or would they just sit down quietly and begin their calculations all over again?

He knew exactly what was happening up on the mountain at this very moment. The high lama and his assistants would be sitting in their silk robes, inspecting the sheets as the junior monks carried them away from the typewriters and pasted them into the great volumes. No one would be saying anything. The only sound would be the incessant patter, the never-ending rainstorm of the keys hitting the paper, for the Mark V itself was utterly silent as it flashed through its thousands of calculation a second. Three months of this, thought George, was enough to start anyone climbing up the wall.

"There she is!" called Chuck, pointing down into the valley. "Ain't she beautiful!"

She certainly was, thought George. The battered old DC-3 lay at the end of the runway like a tiny silver cross. In two hours she would be bearing them away to freedom and sanity. It was a thought worth savoring like a fine liqueur. George let it roll around his mind as the pony trudged patiently down the slope.

The swift night of the high Himalayas was now almost upon them. Fortunately, the road was very good, as roads went in that region, and they were both carrying torches. There was not the slightest danger, only a certain discomfort from the bitter cold. The sky overhead was perfectly clear, and ablaze with the familiar, friendly stars. At least there would be no risk, thought George, of the pilot being unable to take off because of weather conditions. That had been his only remaining worry.

He began to sing, but gave it up after a while. This vast arena of mountains, gleaming like whitely hooded ghosts on every side, did not encourage such ebullience. Presently George glanced at his watch.

"Should be there in an hour," he called back over his shoulder to Chuck. Then he added, in an afterthought: "Wonder if the computer's finished its run. It was due about now."

Chuck didn't reply, so George swung around in his saddle. He could just see Chuck's face, a white oval turned toward the sky.

"Look," whispered Chuck, and George lifted his eyes to heaven. (There is always a last time for everything.)

Overhead, without any fuss, the stars were going out.

# THE LAST THINGS HAVE ALREADY BEGUN

## Jean Daniélou

[There] are a number of apparently sound conclusions, leading to an integral view of the manifold and complex teaching of the New Testament on the subject of the judgment, without minimizing any of its aspects. But this is not all. Certain necessary consequences follow, which have a bearing on our ideas about life. We do not have to elaborate a theory of the eschatological significance of nuclear weapons; all we have to do is to read the New Testament, as interpreted by any normal professor of biblical exegesis, and then to work out what it means.

First of all, it means that the last things have already begun. The resurrection of Christ is presented as the first and decisive act of the last day. The Word of God took humanity to himself in the Incarnation, and cleansed it through his precious blood, and brought it into his Father's house forever at his ascension. The work of salvation has been substantially done, everything essential has been secured already. It is incompatible with an evolutionary theory looking forward to any future event of comparable importance, or any future development transcending Christ.

On the other hand, this work of judgment which Christ has substantially completed has not yet produced its due consequences throughout mankind and throughout creation. For many people this is a principal stumbling block. Nothing seems to have been changed: before and after Christ, men are equally enslaved; history is still dictated by the will to power and the greed of gold. There is little sign of the arrival of that time when, as Isaias foretold, "they will melt down their swords into plowshares." And turning to even more essential matters, mankind is still a prey to suffering and death. "The whole of nature, as we know, groans in a common

travail all the while" until "nature in its turn will be set free from the tyranny of corruption." We are still waiting for that judgment that will destroy the world of corruption and establish a kingdom of saints.

This twofold relationship to something achieved and to something awaited specifies the current phase of time, which is the epoch of the church. It is the period of grace allowed to mankind for the acceptation of the judgment which Christ has substantially won, and so escape the judgment to come. The church's preaching is eschatological in character, consisting in an announcement of the danger that threatens the human race, with notice of the way of salvation, the ark of the church, affording the only safe passage through the deep waters of the judgment.

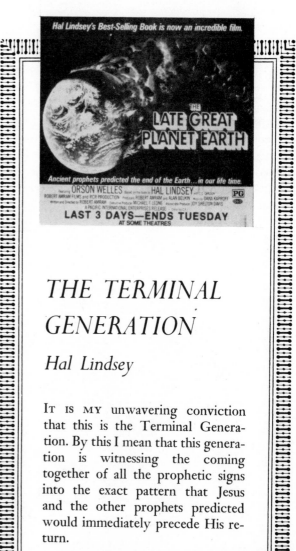

## THE TERMINAL GENERATION

### Hal Lindsey

IT IS MY unwavering conviction that this is the Terminal Generation. By this I mean that this generation is witnessing the coming together of all the prophetic signs into the exact pattern that Jesus and the other prophets predicted would immediately precede His return.

# ANTICIPATING THE END

## Tim LaHaye

THERE IS NO QUESTION that we are living in the last days. The Bible passages we have examined make that very clear. It is fascinating to us who have preached this for years to hear the growing chorus of voices that declare the same thing.

The president of the World Bank [Robert S. McNamara] has been calling attention to the population explosion that is alarming world economists. Pointing out that 1,600 years were required to double the first-century population from 125 million to 250 million, he stated, "Today, the more than three billions on earth will double in thirty-five years. To project the totals beyond the year 2000 becomes so demanding on the imagination as to make the statistics almost incomprehensible."

Economists make it clear that technology is not keeping pace with population, and we are rapidly approaching the time when we will not be able to feed the people on earth. Already some parts of the world have malnourished masses who are reproducing more hungry millions, with no solution in sight.

Pollution experts warn that if something drastic is not done soon, we will smother earth life. Pollution has plagued large cities for years, but in recent times it has reached dangerous proportions. Can you imagine the pollution if the present population doubled in thirty-five years?

China now has nuclear weapons and is working for a delivery system. No thinking person wishes to predict the frightening possibilities that await this world when that happens. One political scientist on a TV interview, when asked his view of life in the twenty-first century, said, "Pardon my pessimism, but when I think of China's nuclear development in the light of their past, I see no future for the known world beyond the year 2000."

We could cite other trends in the field of travel, knowledge, technology, dope addiction, and family breakdown—mankind is on a runaway course that portends the end of this age. Just such an end has been prophesied by God.

Most people don't heed warnings. The people of Noah's day disregarded his warnings for 120 years—then they were swept away in the Flood. Jesus warned our generation, "Therefore, be ye also ready; for in such an hour as ye think not the Son of man cometh" (Matthew 24:44). That challenge is for our generation!

The fact that we are the generation that will be on earth when our Lord comes certainly should not depress us. In fact, the depressing conditions presently ensnaring our society should not make us despondent. Instead, we should anticipate the Lord's coming every day.

Shortly after the death of Dr. M. R. DeHaan, the much-loved radio Bible teacher and capable prophecy student, I visited his study. Behind his desk was a framed wall sign that read, "Perhaps Today!" That mental attitude should characterize every believer.

## BIBLICAL CLIMAX
### Billy Graham

I BELIEVE that this world, as we know it, will come to an end. When, I do not know, but all history is pointing forward to a climactic event when everything now seen will be purified by fire. This is not fanciful imagination but the clear and repeated testimony of the Bible. In both the Old and New Testaments we have this climax foretold. Our Lord Himself said such would take place. A study of this universe, in which this world is but an infinitesimal speck, shows that any one of a number of factors could bring about this physical cataclysm.

The Bible says: "But the day of the Lord will come as a thief in the night; in the which the heavens shall pass away with a great noise, and the elements shall melt with fervent heat, the earth also, and the works that are therein shall be burned up." This same Bible says: "Believe on the Lord Jesus Christ, and thou shalt be saved, and thy house."

# WHEN AND HOW WILL THE END COME?

*Malcolm W. Browne*

THE DOOMSDAY QUESTION—When and how will the human race die out?—has assumed a new perspective as scientific knowledge has advanced in several areas.

The subject is a matter of heated controversy on campuses and in laboratories across the nation. Interviews with astronomers, geophysicists, biologists, and health experts disclose that they believe total human extinction is not necessarily as distant a possibility as many of us would choose to think.

While most scientists regard as remote the likelihood of human extinction in the near future, it is real enough, some assert, that governments should start seeking ways to limit the risks. As the earth hurtles through space at 1.3 million miles an hour, there is the chance of catastrophe from both cosmic and terrestrial causes, but the damage might be reduced by timely precautions.

Scientists have, for example, redoubled their efforts to learn why the dinosaurs suddenly died out 65 million years ago after having flourished for 140 million years. Implicit in such scholarly studies is a practical question: Could the same thing happen to us?

Among the potential catastrophes seen by scientists as possible threats to human survival are these:

• A collision. Earth may collide with one or more fairly large objects—asteroids or comets, for example—and if the object in such a collision were more than a few miles in diameter life on earth could be extinguished. A collision of that sort could come at anytime, with as little as six months' warning.

• A nearby supernova. A supernova is the explosion of an extraordinarily massive star, producing in one year the same amount of energy that our sun takes a billion years to radiate. If a supernova occurred appreciably less than sixty light-years from earth, life here could be ended in a matter of minutes with no warning.

• Solar radiation. Earth's magnetic field normally shields life from much of the harmful radiation generated by the sun. But if earth's geomagnetic field were to approach zero and stay there for several thousand years, the effect on terrestrial life could be critical, according to some experts.

• Carbon dioxide. Some scientists believe that the extinction of a number of animal species, including the dinosaurs, is related to changing amounts of carbon dioxide in the atmosphere and the seas and resulting thermal and ecological changes. A similar change, one activated by man himself, may threaten human survival by destroying the environment on which man depends.

• Disease. No existing disease, however deadly, appears to have the potential for wiping out the entire human species. But epidemiologists do not discount the possibility that there could appear some new organism capable of destroying either the human race or the life forms on which man depends for food.

• The depletion of the earth's resources. Some biologists see an analogy between mankind on earth and a colony of microbes in a culture dish in which the supply of nutrients is limited. As resources dwindle, the bacterial colony must decline, sustaining itself for a time by cannibalism before dying out. Something similar must happen to humanity, according to this view, and even by migrating to other planets man will inevitably face at some point the depletion of all the habitable places he can reach.

Just how serious are these hazards?

A few of the scientists canvassed shrugged off all speculation about man's extinction. Among them was Dr. Alexander P. Langmuir, an epidemiologist at Harvard University, who said: "Despite all the beatings he's taken, man is still around today. Humanity is resilient and resourceful, with tremendous powers of survival."

But most scientists agreed that man is doomed and only the time and manner of his demise are in question. In any case, life here cannot outlast the sun, which will begin to expand to scorch the earth in about 4.5 billion years.

Surprisingly, none of those interviewed regarded war as likely to end the human race.

"In the future," one scientist said, "bloody wars could actually give mankind a new lease on life. Even thermonuclear holocausts would never kill everyone, and by reducing population pressures on shrinking global resources, wars could prolong the existence of the human race by thousands of years."

Some government scientists are studying natural hazards to human survival, among them Dr. George C. Reid of the Aeronomy Laboratory of the National Oceanic and Atmospheric Administration.

Dr. Reid and his colleagues are examining two scenarios in particular: a solar outburst occurring while earth's protective magnetic field is reduced, and the explosion of a nearby supernova. Either event could threaten human survival.

Probably because of the iron that makes up a large part of the earth's core, the earth behaves like a bar magnet enveloped in a magnetic field. This field, well outside earth's atmosphere, normally blocks the blast of charged particles reaching us from the sun.

But if the magnetic field were to falter, charged particles from the sun would hit the atmosphere and a blaze of ultraviolet radiation would reach us. Such radiation can cause gross genetic mutations and cancer, change the climate, and kill outright. It would be particularly lethal during a violent solar flare.

Scientists believe that the geomagnetic field has decayed before and will do so again. It is deteriorating rapidly now, but could reverse itself within a few hundred years.

An even greater catastrophe could be caused by a nearby supernova, Dr. Reid said. "We know that there's at least one supernova in our galaxy every fifty to one hundred years," he explained. "We can assume that such an explosion any closer to us than somewhere between thirty and sixty light-years would be critical for terrestrial life.

"The probability is," Dr. Reid said, "that a supernova should explode in this region roughly once every hundred million years. Since it apparently has not done so in the last five hundred or six hundred million years, the statistical inference would seem to be that we're overdue for a nearby supernova."

Should a supernova explode very nearby, earth would be vaporized.

Another threat from outer space is posed by asteroids and comets.

According to Dr. Clark R. Chapman, an astronomer at the Planetary Science Institute in Tucson, Arizona, an object only a kilometer in diameter that struck earth would cause widespread devastation and loss of life, possibly endangering the survival of many species. It could cause vast, global earthquakes and tidal waves large enough to devastate all land in the vicinity of oceans.

Furthermore, something much bigger than one kilometer could hit earth.

"There are almost certainly comets beyond the outer planets that are unknown to us," Dr. Chapman said. "Some may be quite massive, and could someday intersect our orbit. A large one would certainly destroy all life here.

"Earth could also be struck by an asteroid," one of the thousands of planetoids orbiting the sun, Dr. Chapman said. "We pretty well know the current orbits of the largest ones, but these orbits will change with the passage of time in ways we cannot predict mathematically. I am thinking particularly of Eros."

Eros is the largest of the asteroids that periodically approach earth. Once every forty-four years, it comes within 13.8 million miles, but earth strongly affects its orbit, and with the passage of tens of thousands of years, Eros could be pulled into collision with us.

Dewey M. McLean, a geologist at Virginia Polytechnic Institute, believes that a more immediate danger is carbon dioxide, an invisible gas that acts in some respects like a one-way mirror.

As a component of the atmosphere, carbon dioxide allows the sun's radiation to reach the earth, but prevents heat reflected from the earth's surface from escaping. Consequently, the atmosphere heats up as the level of carbon dioxide rises.

Dr. McLean warned that a greenhouse mechanism may already be at work on earth, with incalculable effects on life. The carbon dioxide that man pours into the atmosphere by burning fossil fuels could soon start a chain of environmental effects similar to those that led to the extinction of many species of the Mesozoic era, including all the dinosaurs.

"A panel of the National Academy of Sciences has reported," Dr. McLean said in an interview, "that at the rate carbon dioxide is increasing in the atmosphere it will produce a six-degree increase in global temperature in the next century or so.

"This is more than enough to cause enormous effects on life, including a collapse of the ecosystem through loss of essential food animals. The potential for global-scale extinctions is great."

Such a period of intense and destructive warming would very likely be followed by a new ice age, he said, which would greatly complicate survival problems.

# WITHOUT WARNING

## C. S. Lewis

IN *King Lear* (III:vii) there is a man who is such a minor character that Shakespeare has not given him even a name: he is merely "First Servant." All the characters around him—Regan, Cornwall, and Edmund—have fine long-term plans. They think they know how the story is going to end, and they are quite wrong. The servant has no such delusions. He has no notion how the play is going to go. But he understands the present scene. He sees an abomination (the blinding of old Gloucester) taking place. He will not stand it. His sword is out and pointed at his master's breast in a moment: then Regan stabs him dead from behind. That is his whole part: eight lines all told. But if it were real life and not a play, that is the part it would be best to have acted.

The doctrine of the Second Coming teaches us that we do not and cannot know when the world drama will end. The curtain may be rung down at any moment: say, before you have finished reading this paragraph. This seems to some people intolerably frustrating. So many things would be interrupted. Perhaps you were going to get married next month, perhaps you were going to get a raise next week: you may be on the verge of a great scientific discovery; you may be maturing great social and political reforms. Surely no good and wise God would be so very unreasonable as to cut all this short? Not *now*, of all moments!

But we think thus because we keep on assuming that we know the play. We do not know the play. We do not even know whether we are in Act I or Act V. We do not know who are the major and who the minor characters. The Author knows. The audience, if there is an audience (if angels and archangels and all the company of heaven fill the pit and the stalls), may have an inkling. But we, never seeing the play from the outside, never meeting any characters except the tiny minority who are "on" in the same scenes as ourselves, wholly ignorant of the future and very imperfectly informed about the past, cannot tell at what moment the end ought to come. That it will come when it ought, we may be sure; but we waste our time in guessing when that will be. That it has a meaning we may be sure, but we cannot see it. When it is over, we may be told. We are led to expect that the Author will have something to say to each of us on the part that each of us has played. The playing it well is what matters infinitely.

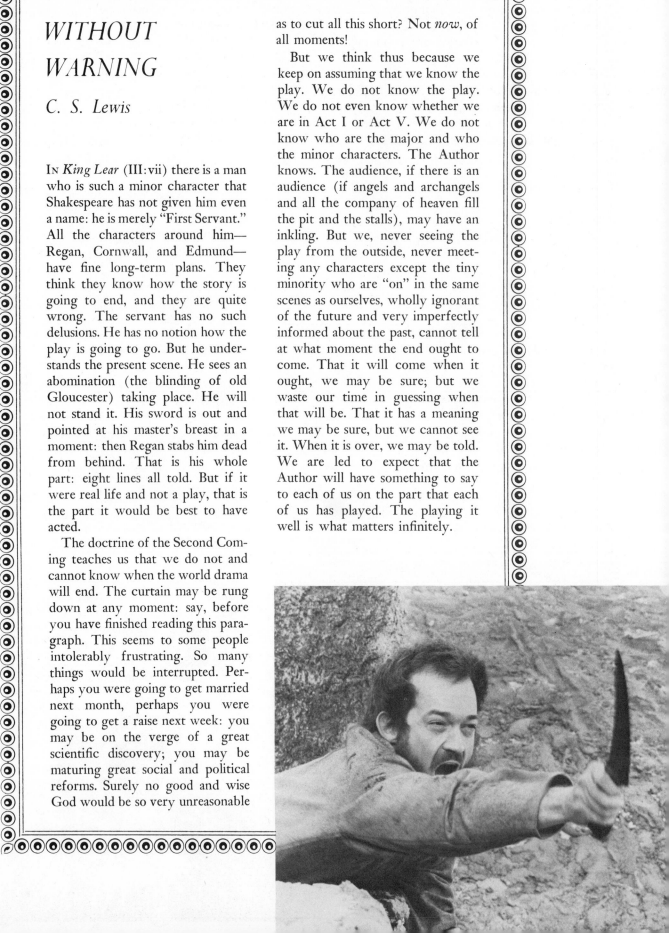

# WITH A BANG

## Robert Jastrow

Now THAT astronomers are generally agreed on how the universe began, what do they have to say about how it will end? At first thought, it would seem that the universe must continue to expand forever, with space becoming emptier and emptier. As the old stars burn out, one by one, the stage grows dark, and eventually all life ceases.

But many astronomers believe that the expansion cannot continue because gravity, pulling back on the outward-moving galaxies, must slow their retreat and bring them to a halt. Then, after the briefest instant, they begin to move toward one another. Slowly at first, and then with increasing speed, the universe collapses under the relentless pull of gravity. After a time, the universe returns to the conditions of searing heat and chaos from which it emerged billions of years earlier.

What will happen then? No one knows. Some astronomers say the universe, now a cosmic black hole, can never recover from this collapsed state. Others speculate that the universe will rebound from the collapse in a new explosion, and experience a new moment of Creation. According to this view, our universe will be melted down and remade in the caldron of the second Creation. It will become an entirely new world, in which no trace of the existing universe remains.

In the reborn world, once again the hot, dense materials will expand rapidly outward in a cosmic fireball. Later, gravity will slow down the expansion and turn it into a collapse, followed again by still another Creation; and after that, another expansion, and another collapse. . . .

This theory is particularly attractive to astronomers because it combines the scientific evidence for an explosive moment of Creation with the concept of an eternal universe. Unfortunately, the latest measurements indicate that the expansion of the universe will continue forever, because the amount of matter in the universe has turned out to be ten times too little to exert the gravitational pull that would be needed to halt the outward movement of the galaxies.

We still come across pieces of mass here and there in the universe, and someday we may find the missing matter, but the consensus at the moment is that it will not be found; it appears that there was only one beginning, and there will be only one end. However, astronomers are inclined to keep an open mind on the latter question.

# III.

# RAPTURE

# THE GLORIOUS INBREAKING OF GOD

## Margaret MacDonald

IT WAS FIRST the awful state of the land that was pressed upon me. I saw the blindness and infatuation of the people to be very great. I felt the cry of Liberty just to be the hiss of the serpent, to drown them in perdition. It was just "no God." I repeated the words, Now there is distress of nations, with perplexity, the seas and the waves roaring, men's hearts failing them for fear—now look out for the sign of the Son of man. Here I was made to stop and cry out, Oh, it is not known what the sign of the Son of man is; the people of God think they are waiting, but they know not what it is. I felt this needed to be revealed, and that there was great darkness and error about it; but suddenly what it was burst upon me with a glorious light. I saw it was just the Lord himself descending from Heaven with a shout, just the glorified man, even Jesus; but that all must, as Stephen was, be filled with the Holy Ghost, that they might look up, see the brightness of the Father's glory. I saw the error to be, that men think that it will be something seen by the natural eye; but 'tis spiritual discernment that is needed, the eye of God in his people. Many passages were revealed, in a light in which I had not before seen them. I repeated, "Now is the kingdom of Heaven like unto ten virgins, who went forth to meet the Bridegroom, five wise and five foolish; they that were foolish took their lamps, but took no oil with them; but they that were wise took oil in their vessels with their lamps." "But be ye not unwise, but understanding what the will of the Lord is; and be not drunk with wine wherein is excess, but be filled with the Spirit." This was the oil the wise virgins took in their vessels—this is the light to be kept burning—the light of God—that we may discern that which cometh not with observation to the natural eye. Only those who have the light of God within them will see the sign of his appearance. No need to follow them who say, see here, or see there, for his day shall be as the lightning to those in whom the living Christ is. 'Tis Christ in us that will lift us up—he is the light—'tis only those that are alive in him that will be caught up to meet him in the air. I saw that we must be in the Spirit, that we might see spiritual things. John was in the Spirit, when he saw a throne set in heaven.—But I saw that the glory of the ministration of the Spirit had not been known. I repeated frequently, but the spiritual temple must and shall be reared, and the fullness of Christ be poured into his body, and then shall we be caught up to meet him. Oh, none will be counted worthy of this calling but his body, which is the church, and which must be a candlestick all of gold. I often said, Oh, the glorious inbreaking of God which is now about to burst on this earth; oh, the glorious temple which is now about to be reared, the bride adorned for her husband; and Oh, what a holy, holy bride she must be, to be prepared for such a glorious bridegroom. I said, Now shall the people of God have to do with realities—now shall the glorious mystery of God in our nature be known—now shall it be known what it is for man to be glorified. I felt that the revelation of Jesus Christ had yet to be opened up—it is not knowledge about God that it contains, but it is an entering into God—I saw that there was a glorious breaking in of God to be. I felt as Elijah, surrounded with chariots of fire. I saw as it were, the spiritual temple reared, and the Head Stone brought forth with shoutings of grace, grace, unto it. It was a glorious light above the brightness of the sun, that shone around about me. I felt that those who were filled with the Spirit could see spiritual things, and feel walking in the midst of them, while those who had not the Spirit could see nothing—so that two shall be in one bed, the one taken and the other left, because the one has the light of God within while the other cannot see the Kingdom of Heaven. I saw the people of God in an awfully dangerous situation, surrounded by nets and entanglements, about to be tried, and many about to be deceived and fall. Now will THE WICKED be revealed, with all power and signs and lying wonders, so that if it were possible the very elect will be deceived.—This is the fiery trial which is to try us. —It will be for the purging and purifying of the real members of the body of Jesus; but Oh, it will be a fiery trial. Every soul will be shaken to the very center. The enemy will try to shake in everything we have believed—but the trial of real faith will be found to honor and praise and glory. Nothing but what is of God will stand. The stony-ground hearers will be made manifest—the love of many

# CAUGHT UP TOGETHER

*Paul the Apostle*

*(1 Thessalonians 4:16–18)*

FOR THE LORD himself shall descend from heaven with a shout, with the voice of the archangel, and with the trump of God: and the dead in Christ shall rise first:

Then we which are alive and remain shall be caught up together with them in the clouds, to meet the Lord in the air: and so shall we ever be with the Lord.

Wherefore comfort one another with these words.

will wax cold. I frequently said that night, and often since, now shall the awful sight of a false Christ be seen on this earth, and nothing but the living Christ in us can detect this awful attempt of the enemy to deceive—for it is with all deceivableness of unrighteousness he will work—he will have a counterpart for every part of God's truth, and an imitation for every work of the Spirit. The Spirit must and will be poured out on the church, that she may be purified and filled with God—and just in proportion as the Spirit of God works, so will he—when our Lord anoints men with power, so will he. This is particularly the nature of the trial, through which those are to pass who will be counted worthy to stand before the Son of man. There will be outward trial too, but 'tis principally temptation. It is

brought on by the outpouring of the Spirit, and will just increase in proportion as the Spirit is poured out. The trial of the church is from Antichrist. It is by being filled with the Spirit that we shall be kept. I frequently said, Oh, be filled with the Spirit—have the light of God in you, that you may detect Satan —be full of eyes within—be clay in the hands of the potter—submit to be filled, filled with God. This will build the temple. It is not by might nor by power, but by my Spirit, saith the Lord. This will fit us to enter into the marriage supper of the Lamb. I saw it to be the will of God that all should be filled. But what hindered the real life of God from being received by his people, was their turning from Jesus, who is the way to the Father. They were not entering in by the door. For he is faithful who hath

## NOT A FICKLE KAZOO

*Arthur D. Katterjohn
with Mark Fackler*

THE "TRUMP OF GOD" (1 Thessalonians 4:16) is not a fickle kazoo beamed at church-age saints to alert them to a secret rapture, so faint that its frequency escapes the ears of mockers and rebels. The trump is a noise, a blast, a fearful booming fanfare to the arrival of the King of love and judgment. It is the "last trump" mentioned by Paul in 1 Corinthians 15:42, the "great sound of a trumpet" prophesied by Christ in Matthew 24:31, and the final trumpet of the seventh angel in Revelation 11:15. Trumpets herald the triumphal procession of a person of high office; the trump can announce nothing other than the *parousia* of the Lord.

---

said, By me if any man enter in he shall find pasture. They were passing the cross, through which every drop of the Spirit of God flows to us. All power that comes not through the blood of Christ is not of God. When I say, they are looking from the cross, I feel that there is much in it—they turn from the blood of the Lamb, by which we overcome, and in which our robes are washed and made white. There are low views of God's holiness, and a ceasing to condemn sin in the flesh, and a looking from him who humbled himself, and made himself of no reputation. Oh! it is needed, much needed at present, a leading back to the cross. I saw that night, and often since, that there will be an outpouring of the Spirit on the body, such as has not been, a baptism of fire, that all the dross may be put away. Oh, there must and will be such an indwelling of the living God as has not been—the servants of God sealed in their foreheads—great conformity to Jesus—his holy image seen in his people—just the bride made comely, by his comeliness put upon her. This is what we are at present made to pray much for, that speedily we may all be made ready to meet our Lord in the air—and it will be. Jesus wants his bride. His desire is toward us. He that shall come, will come, and will not tarry. Amen and Amen. Even so come Lord Jesus.

## BUT A SONIC BOOM

*John Wesley White*

WHAT WILL PROPEL glorified man aloft? In 1 Thessalonians 4:16, we read that "the Lord Himself will come down from heaven, with a loud command, with the voice of the archangel and with the trumpet call of God." There is a threefold sound: Christ's personal "loud command," "the voice of the archangel," and "the trumpet call of God" (1 Thessalonians 4:16). It is now demonstrable in several laboratories of the world that by a sonic boom, a steel ball a foot in diameter can be lifted and held aloft indefinitely. Whether there is any relationship between these two points is not very important. It is of paramount importance, however, that we realize that God has any number of laws at His command to enact His will, and He could very well use the sonic boom or some similar phenomenon as a part of His resurrection and rapturing home of His own. Even so, it should be remembered that God is not bound by present laws of nature. The ascension of Christ was surely not associated with any loud sound.

# RAPTURE IN SCRIPTURE

## *Leon J. Wood*

IN KEEPING with its importance, the rapture is mentioned frequently in Scripture. It is well to note some of the more significant passages as a beginning point in the discussion. Jesus spoke of it as He began His closing message to His disciples, just before the crucifixion, saying, "I will come again, and receive you unto myself; that where I am, there ye may be also" (John 14:3). The scene was the upper room, with the Lord's Supper having just been instituted. Jesus spoke of leaving His disciples shortly and of going to prepare a place for them, meaning heaven. Then He voiced these important words, that He would come to get them that they might be with Him in that place so prepared. The passage reveals several things regarding the rapture.

One is that it is a planned event; at the time of His departure Christ anticipated returning for the disciples. Another is that it concerns Christ's own, His followers. Christ was speaking only to the disciples when He gave the promise. Third, Christ's return for His own will be personal. He Himself will come for them, not sending some angel, for instance, nor merely giving a general permission for the church finally to come to Him. Fourth, the rapture results in the church being taken out of the world. Jesus said that He would come and "receive" the disciples, that there where He had made the preparations, they might be also. The church will not remain here on earth, then, merely in some improved status, but will be taken away from the earth to heaven.

Another important passage is 1 Corinthians 1:7, where Paul refers to the rapture with the words, "Waiting for the coming of our Lord Jesus Christ." He uses that thought as a basis for urging the Corinthian Christians to "come behind in no gift," as they seek to live for and serve God. Paul thus says that the expectancy of the rapture provides a reason for the Christian's total life being dedicated to God. Paul's main thought is to urge this kind of dedication. His reference to the rapture shows that it should motivate the Christian to this end.

In Philippians 3:20 Paul writes of the rapture as the time when Christians will be taken to the place of their true citizenship. This passage reads, "For our conversation citizenship is in heaven; from whence also we look for the Savior, the Lord Jesus Christ." The thought is that, since the Christian's final home is heaven and not this troubled world, he looks forward to going there. Since the rapture is the occasion when he will be taken there, it is made the more important to him.

The writer of Hebrews mentions the rapture as he contrasts the purpose of Christ's second coming with that of His first coming. He states, "So Christ was once offered to bear the sins of men; and unto them that look for him shall he appear the second time without sin unto salvation" (Hebrews 9:28). The thought is that Christ came the first time to pay the penalty of man's sin, but the second time He will come to effect man's deliverance from the world. The phrase "without sin" does not imply that Christ had sin in His first coming, of course; but in the second He will not be involved with sin in any way, as He was the first time in bearing man's sin. The rapture, then, will be the time when Christ delivers the Christian out of the world unto Himself.

The same writer refers to the rapture again as a reason for hope on the part of suffering Christians. He states, "For yet a little while, and he that shall come will come, and will not tarry" (Hebrews 10:37). The rapture is a source of true comfort for every child of God, knowing that, no matter the degree or kind of suffering one may experience here on earth, Christ is coming to bring deliverance.

# PAROUSIA, EPIPHANY, APOCALYPSE

## J. Barton Payne

THE TERMS USED by the Greek New Testament to identify the second advent of Christ also have relevance in determining the components of the church's anticipation. Her reunion with Him is said to be at the *parousia*, the "coming" of the Lord (1 Thessalonians 4:15). The stress of *parousia*, however, falls not so much upon the coming as upon the arrival and resultant presence. Reese has indeed cast doubt upon the whole dispensational reconstruction by defining *parousia* as a triumphant arrival: "An overpowering manifestation of divine power and glory . . . full of terror for the impenitent and the ungodly, and opening up a new era for the world." It is true that *parousia* may also be used to indicate an unspectacular sort of coming (1 Corinthians 16:17), but even in secular settings this is not true when a king is the subject. Some dispensationalists seek to make a distinction between the *parousia*, or coming, of "the Son of man," to bring in the period of Christ's wrath against His enemies, and the *parousia* of "the Lord Jesus Christ," to rapture the church. New Testament usage hardly warrants such a fine line of demarcation; but, since both are said to occur at the same time and to constitute but one *parousia*, or coming, the point raises no real problem. Most dispensationalists simply identify the "coming" with "the bright and blessed hope of the believer, which may be realized at any moment," but then go to contrast it with His "appearing" in judgment upon the world, an event which is not imminent. The Greek word for appearing is *epiphaneia*, "epiphany," closely related to which is *apokalupsis*, "unveiling," or "revelation." The latter is the word used in 2 Thessalonians 1:7-8: "the revelation of the Lord Jesus from heaven with the angels of his power in flaming fire, rendering vengeance to them that know not God." The emphasis of both of these terms is upon visible manifestation; and, while some dispensationalists have at certain points sought to apply them to the pretribulation rapture, when the church (but nobody else) would "see the glory of Christ," the appearance of either of these names would ordinarily be embarrassing to the defense of a coming of Christ distinguished by its "secrecy."

Even in reference to the term *parousia* older dispensationalists have attempted to justify exceptions, claiming that in a limited number of passages Christ's *parousia* means something other than His "coming." *Parousia* does indeed have an alternate translation of "presence" (cf. Philippians 2:12 and 1 Thessalonians 4:15, margin), but the idea of "presence," if divorced from the idea of "arrival," would not fit the passages that are concerned with Christ's appearing. For example, Matthew 24:27, "As the lightning cometh forth from the east, and is seen even unto the west; so shall be the *parousia* of the Son of man." Elsewhere in the chapter, *parousia* is admitted to mean "coming, arrival"; but it has been claimed that, though in verses 37 and 39 it means "arrival," still in verse 27 it must be understood as the subsequent "presence." But the passage itself forbids this, for the *parousia* is compared with the coming forth of a bolt of lightning, a thing which

is an event, a "coming," and not a condition, a "presence," that exists as a continuation of some previous coming. Again, 2 Thessalonians 2:8, "The Lord Jesus shall . . . bring [the Antichrist] to naught by the manifestation of his *parousia*." Here again it has been claimed that the Antichrist is destroyed, not by Christ's coming, but by the manifestation of His "presence," a presence that has existed as a continuation of His "coming" seven years previously. But that the years of tribulation should take place after Christ has "come" and during His subsequent "presence," even if it be His "veiled" presence, would require considerable credulity. Christ's *parousia* does mean His coming.

# ONE TWINKLING BUT SEVEN MOMENTS

*Tim LaHaye*

We FIND seven distinct steps taking place in the "twinkling of an eye" at the Rapture. . . .

1. "For the Lord himself shall descend. . . ." The Lord is not sending the archangel Michael, but our Savior himself is coming for us.

2. ". . . with a shout . . ." The shout for the believer is going to be from the Lord himself, whose voice has already proved its authority to raise the dead. One day, standing at the tomb of Lazarus, who had been dead for four days, Jesus shouted, "Lazarus, come forth," and before the eyes of many witnesses Lazarus "came forth." Just as dead Lazarus responded, so all those that sleep in Jesus will respond when he calls.

3. ". . . the voice of the archangel . . ." will lead the Jews through the Tribulation period or the "time of Jacob's trouble."

4. ". . . the trump of God . . ." will single imminent judgment upon the earth for its gross wickedness. The Tribulation that follows the Rapture is an unparalleled visitation of plagues.

5. ". . . and the dead in Christ shall rise first . . ." is the same as "the dead shall be made incorruptible." All dead Christians will be given a glorified body which will unite with their soul and spirit. This is called the resurrection of the believer.

6. ". . . then we which are alive and remain shall be caught up together with them in the clouds. . . ." We who happen to be living at the Rapture will be "made incorruptible." Our soul and spirit never leave the body, but suddenly our body becomes "like unto his glorified body," referring to our Lord's resurrection body, and we will immediately leave this earth. No matter what we are doing we will suddenly be taken out of the world.

The Rapture of the church will be an event of such startling proportions that the entire world will be conscious of our leaving. Some have suggested that there will be airplane, bus, and train wrecks throughout the world when Christian operators are suddenly taken out of the world. Who can imagine the chaos on the freeways when automobile drivers are snatched out of their cars!

One cannot help but surmise that many strangers will be in churches the first Sunday after the Rapture. A gospel-preaching church will probably have a few unsaved members anxiously gathering to tremble together over their destiny. Liberal churches, where heretics in clerical garb have not preached the Word of God and the need for a new-birth experience, may be filled to capacity with wondering and frantic church members. Many a minister will have to "explain it away" in some fantastic manner or seriously alter his theology.

7. ". . . to meet the Lord in the air . . ." It seems that our Lord permits us to meet one another in the clouds before we gather together unto him. What a blessed reunion we will have renewing fellowship with other saints and with loved ones who have passed away before our Lord's coming! Then we will meet our blessed Lord face to face, fulfilling the scriptures that we will "see him as he is."

---

## IN A TWINKLING

*Paul the Apostle*
*(1 Corinthians 15:51–53)*

BEHOLD, I show you a mystery; We shall not all sleep, but we shall all be changed,

In a moment, in the twinkling of an eye, at the last trump: for the trumpet shall sound, and the dead shall be raised incorruptible, and we shall be changed.

For this corruptible must put on incorruption, and this mortal must put on immortality.

"And so shall we ever be with the Lord." What exhilarating words these are, promising that after the Rapture of the church we will forever enjoy the presence of our Lord. A little girl was asked by a scoffer of the Second Coming of Christ, "How can you enjoy heaven? Christ is supposed to come down to earth!" The scoffer's question bothered her only a moment before she replied, "It really doesn't matter, because wherever he goes I'll go with him!"

"Wherefore, comfort one another with these words" (1 Thessalonians 4:18). There is much comfort to be found and shared with other Christians through this anticipation. The Christians' future is not just bright—it's dazzling!

# THE ESCHATOLOGICAL RESURRECTION

*George Eldon Ladd*

THE RESURRECTION OF JESUS was itself an eschatological event. By this we mean to say that the resurrection of Jesus was not an isolated event in the midst of history; it was itself the beginning of the eschatological resurrection.

This can be established by numerous passages. Jesus is called the "firstborn from the dead" (Colossians 1:18). This means not only that Jesus was the first to rise from the dead (Acts 26:23), but as such, he stands at the head of a new order of existence—resurrection life.

This fact can also be seen in the experience of the early church. Acts tells us that the Sadducees were "annoyed because they the disciples of Jesus were teaching the people and proclaiming in Jesus the resurrection from the dead" (Acts 4:2). This at first is puzzling. It is a historical commonplace that of the Jews, the Pharisees believed in the resurrection of the dead, while the Sadducees denied this doctrine (see Acts 23:7–8). However, they lived together and did not quarrel over points of doctrine like the resurrection of the dead. The fact is, there was a wide variety of views in Judaism about the resurrection (see Ladd, *I Believe in the Resurrection of Jesus*). Why then should it trouble the Sadducees that these disciples of Jesus—this new messianic sect —were preaching resurrection?

The answer is found in the fact that the disciples were not preaching a doctrine, a mere *hope* for the future. They were proclaiming an event in the present which *guaranteed* the future. They were preaching *in Jesus* the resurrection from the dead. Now resurrection was no longer merely a future event, a doctrine, a hope; it had happened in their very midst. If their proclamation was true, it provided an unanswerable denial of the Sadducees' doctrine.

The eschatological character of Jesus's resurrection is most clearly seen in Paul's affirmation that his resurrection was "the first fruits of those who have fallen asleep" (1 Corinthians 15:20). "First fruits" means very little to the American city dweller. However, in ancient Palestine it carried a vivid meaning. The first fruits was the actual beginning of the harvest which was offered in sacrifice to God for granting a new harvest. It was not hope; it was not promise; it was the actual beginning of the harvest, which immediately followed by the full harvest.

So Jesus's resurrection bears the character of first fruits. Although it was not *immediately* followed by the resurrection of the saints, it still bears the character of an eschatological event. If we may speak inelegantly, God has split off a portion to the eschatological resurrection and planted it in the midst of history.

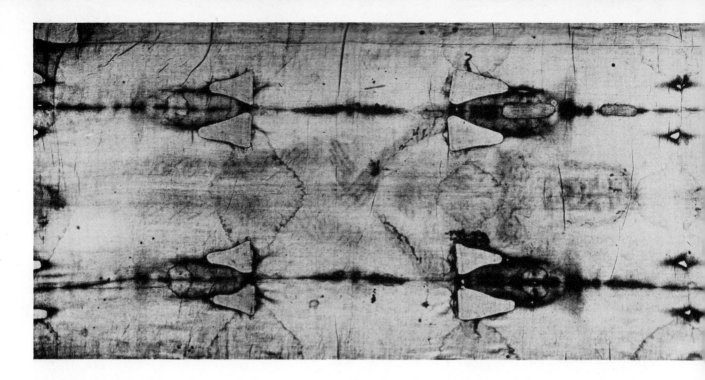

# WHEN
# JESUS ROSE

*Robert K. Wilcox*

THE TOMB, a rocky chamber carved out of a hillside, a stone rolled against the door, is dark and silent. Lying on a slab is a long, rectangular cocoon, the hills and valleys clearly being the contours of a human body. Jesus lay there, face up, a ribbon around the head and chin to keep the mouth closed, bags of spices packed along the sides of his dead body.

At some unknown moment in the dead of the night, the air in the tomb becomes electric.

Minute vibrations at first, the sort that could be detected by sensitive twentieth-century instruments; then they dramatically increase until they shake the ground and blow the boulder from the door.

A glow, faint at first, emanating from the shroud suddenly intensifies until rays of light shoot through the threads, star-filled golden rays filling the tomb and pouring out the door.

For thirty seconds—no more—the blinding, pulsating movement continues.

The source of the activity is the corpse, the body,

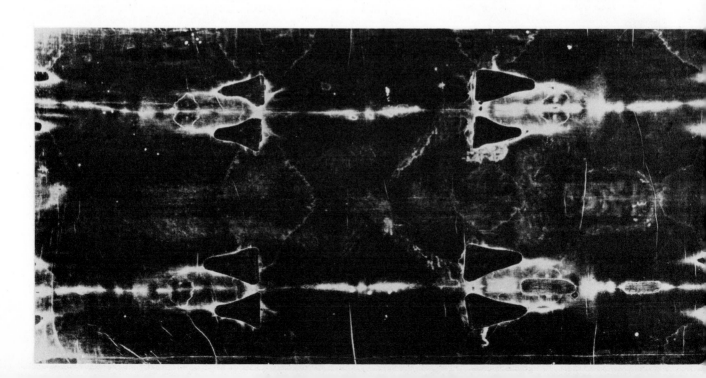

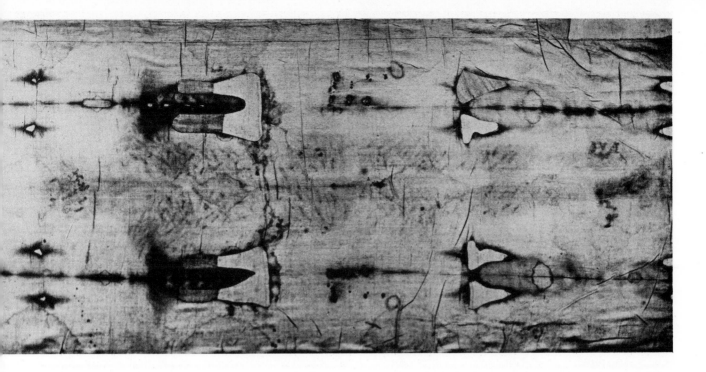

somehow being revitalized, dematerialized, its mass being converted into energy, pure energy, which in the material world is radiant white light.

The body rises from the slab through the cloth, hovers for a moment in midair, then disappears.

The cocoon collapses. Darkness returns. Shouts of "Earthquake! Earthquake!" diminish as the two guards run for their lives. And in the air, the distinct odor of scorched linen.

When dawn comes, the women in Jesus's life draw tentatively toward the tomb, look in the opening, and see the shroud unopened, still wrapped, but definitely deflated. The body is gone. At sunrise the disciples come. John enters the tomb, puts his hand on the cloth, and presses it to the slab. Jesus is there no longer. The disciples and the women quickly gather up the burial garments—the chin band is still inside the shroud—and the spice bags and leave before the Romans can return.

At another time, in another place, when they have a chance to gather their wits, they will discover the figure of their master imprinted on the inside of the shroud. The images would be faint, probably not as dark as the passage of time and exposure to air have made them; and the images would be negative ones, a phenomenon that would also become clearer with the passage of time. They would pay more attention to the images of the shroud, the disciples would, if they weren't already waiting, with the greatest anticipation, for Jesus himself, who, before his death had promised to visit them after he rose from the dead.

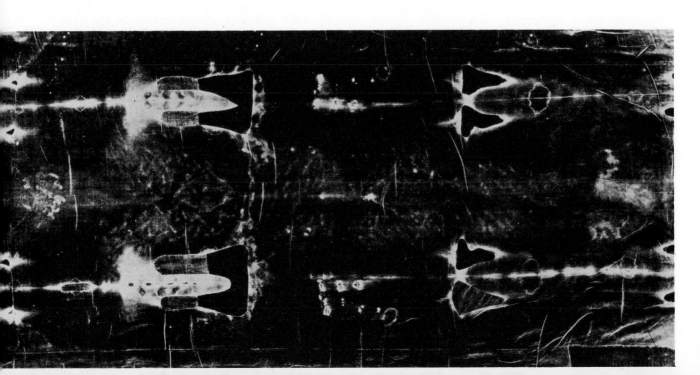

# THE RESURRECTED BODY

## *Romano Guardini*

THE NATURAL BODY is not only a fixed, spatial form, but it has had a history. From its origin to its decay it goes through an endless number of forms. Which of these is properly its own? Is it the child's, the mature man's, the elderly man's? The answer can only be: All are essential. The individual form does not exist only that the next should take its place, and so on, one after the other, in order that the last one, death, might appear. Each phase is the man, and each is indispensable to his life as a whole. That endless series of configurations which is the human body must be included in the resurrected body. It must have a new dimension, that of time, but time raised to the power of eternity with the result that its history included in its present, and all the successive moments of its past exist in an absolute now.

Besides man's history, in the sense of successive developments, in the sense of what he has done or what has happened to him, there must be present also his joys, sorrows, frustrations, liberations, victories, defeats, his love and his hatred. All the unending experiences of the soul were expressed in and by the body and have become part of it, contributing either to its development or to its crippling and destruction—all are present and retained in the risen body. The pattern of the life is there with all that befell the man, for the resurrection of the body means the resurrection of the life that has been lived, with all its good and all its evil.

And what are the limits of a man's body? Surely his clothes belong to it since they performed the double function of protection and expression. What of his work tools, the articles he kept about him, his house, his much-loved garden; what of the whole sphere of his life? Let us not be too fanciful, yet it is certain that the body goes beyond its mere anatomical limits. Fundamentally it is limitless. It is the essence of man's earthly existence in visible form. In the resurrection, form, substance, life, all will rise. Nothing that has been is annihilated. Man's deeds and his destiny are part of him, and, set free from the restrictions of history, will remain for eternity, not by any power of his own, not as a final phase of an inner development, but at the summons of the Lord Almighty, and in the strength of His Spirit.

Man will rise to his salvation, or to his eternal perdition. The body will be blessed or accursed.

But how will it stand with the body of the man in need of purification? . . . If man, after his death, is in need of purification, that is true also of his body. But how shall that body be purified if it rises only at the end of time when blessedness and accursedness are the only alternatives? Though there is no explicit answer, we can at least indicate the direction in which the answer may be found.

Soul and body are not clearly separable entities. The body is continuously informed by the spiritual soul; indeed, what we call body is at every point, in every act, one with the soul. Could the soul be completely removed, there would be no body, but only a biological substance, perhaps of mutually destructive chemical particles. The soul, on its side, does not live on its own account, but in effect in and through the body, to the point that it seems doubtful whether a single purely spiritual act is possible in human life. Throughout, it is spirit-body that is human. The soul, as we say, is "in" the body, meaning that it is the principle of its life, the content of its appearance, the purpose behind its activity. But we might as well say that the body is "in" the soul, and mean that the soul embraces the body as its means of operation, as the revelation of its hidden nature, as material for its historical existence, as form and act; for the fate of the body is conferred upon it by the quickening soul. When at death the soul leaves the body, it does not leave the bodily sphere altogether. It does not become an angel. It remains a *human* soul. As such it bears the body within itself. The soul was the premise of the body and the expression of its life, and that fact is unforgotten. The soul, as the scholastics said, is the body's form, and not a form in general, but the form of a particular body. It is not its blueprint only, but contains its whole experience, not as an agent of the body's activity alone, but also as effecting its own development, taking up bodily happenings into itself. This falls in with the resurrection of the dead, for in the resurrection God has given the soul with its body-forming power the opportunity to build up the body entrusted to it as it was meant to be.

If this is true, and the soul undergoes the purification we spoke of, then, if we may put it so, the latent body will be equally cleansed, so that when the dead man rises, his new body has been made fit for a soul purified and made absolute.

# RESURRECTION OF CHURCH SAINTS

*Leon J. Wood*

THE RESURRECTION at the Rapture . . . is one aspect in this series of resurrections. At this time those raised will be the church saints, that is, all who have been saved during the period of the church, from its beginning on the day of Pentecost until the moment of Rapture. The number of people involved will be very large, much larger, for instance, than the number of living saints at the time, who will be translated without dying. The latter group will include only the one generation then alive, while the resurrected saints will include all the many generations since the early first century. This time of resurrection is an occasion every Christian can anticipate with joy, for at that time he will see departed loved ones again as well as the great saints of past days.

# RESURRECTION OF THE SENSES

*C. S. Lewis*

IN . . . DRAWING you had only plain white paper for sun and cloud, snow, water, and human flesh. In one sense, how miserably inadequate! Yet in another, how perfect. If the shadows are properly done that patch of white paper will, in some curious way be very like blazing sunshine: we shall almost feel cold while we look at the paper snow and almost warm our hands at the paper fire. May we not, by a reasonable analogy, suppose likewise that there is no experience of the spirit so transcendent and supernatural, no vision of Deity Himself so close and so far beyond all images and emotions, that to it also there cannot be an appropriate correspondence on the sensory level? Not by a new sense but by the incredible flooding of those very sensations we now have with a meaning, a transvaluation, of which we have here no faintest guess?

# "GLORIFIED BODIES"

*Leon J. Wood*

PERHAPS THE GREATEST HELP in understanding the nature of glorified bodies comes from Paul's statement that God will "change our vile body, that it may be fashioned like unto his glorious body" (Philippians 3:21; cf. 1 John 3:2). Glorified bodies, then, will be like Christ's resurrected body. In that body, Christ could enter a room when the door was shut (John 20:19, 26); vanish from sight while talking with others (Luke 24:30, 31); remain unknown to others until special perception was granted (Luke 24:15, 16, 31; John 20:15, 16); and defy gravity in ascending from the earth to disappear in the clouds (Acts 1:9). At the same time, His body was real, for it could be touched (John 20:27), was capable of speaking (Luke 24:17–32), and quite clearly could consume food (Luke 24:30; John 21:12–15). Glorified bodies, then, will be real and physical, but will not be subject to death and decay; they will not become weary or sick; they will not need food for sustenance, though being capable of eating on occasion; and they will not be limited by either ordinary physical matter or natural laws, being able to vanish and appear at will and to defy gravity for upward movement. Since Christ at His ascension apparently moved from earth to heaven with the speed of thought, this too will no doubt be possible for glorified saints. The saints of the church will be endowed with such bodies at the rapture, moving up in them to meet Christ in the air.

# DR. ALFORD'S BIBLICAL CHART of MAN.

**LAW OF THE SENSES. SPECIAL SENSES.** | **THROUGH SIN THE SENSES MUST DIE.** | Man's Primitive Attributes and their Derivatives. | THE ATTRIBUTES ARE OF GOD, And Cannot Cease to Exist. | **SPECIAL ATTRIBUTES, Law of Attributes.**

1st. Thou shalt not make or worship idols.

2d. Thou shalt not take the name of the Lord God in vain, or Lie or Swear.

3d. Thou shalt not labor on the Sabbath Day.

4th. Thou shalt not dishonor thy father or mother.

5th. Thou shalt not kill or murder.

6th. Thou shalt not violate chastity or become lewd.

7th. Thou shalt not steal or covet anything.—*Deut. 5: 7–21.*

The Law of the Senses is negative, because the senses are totally depraved.

## SEEING
## HEARING
## SMELLING
## TASTING
CEREBRAL CENTERS.

## BODY

From LIGHT, comes, Knowledge, Intelligence, Perception.
From MERCY, comes Pity, Forbearance, Faith, Charity.
From HOLINESS, comes Innocence, Purity, Piety.
From JUSTICE, Equity, Honor, Righteousness.
From TRUTH, Decision, Infallibility, Unchangeableness, Authority.
From LOVE, comes Affection, Peace, Joy, Hope, Veneration, Reverence.
From LIFE, comes Power, Majesty, Purpose, Independence.
From all these Attributes combined, comes Wisdom.
God alone possesses these Attributes in perfection. See "Mystic Numbers of the Word."

**SIGHT, HEARING, SMELLING, TASTING.** | **LIGHT, MERCY, HOLINESS, JUSTICE.**

"I will praise thee, for I am fearfully and wonderfully made; marvelous are thy works, and that my soul knoweth right well."—*Ps. 139: 14.*

## SOUL

## LIGHT
## MERCY
## HOLINESS
## JUSTICE
CEREBRAL CENTERS.

Thou shalt love the Lord thy God with all thy soul, and with all thy mind, and with all thy strength, and thy neighbor as thyself. On these two Commandments hang all the law and the prophets.—*Mat. 22: 37–40.*

The heart of the soul when renewed is called a new heart—a clean heart, a pure heart. When unrenewed, it is called a hard heart, a wicked heart, a deceitful heart. When God's love vitalizes our love attributes, it greatly affects the Judgment Sense.

The Law of the Attributes is POSITIVE, because they have the power of access to the Holy Spirit.

## COMMON SENSES—VITAL CENTERS.

## TALKING
## JUDGING
## FEELING

**MAN, OF EARTHLY ORIGIN.**

"The first man is of the earth earthy."—*I. Cor.*, 15: 47.

"In Adam all die."—*I. Cor.*, 15: 22.

"The Lord God formed Man out of the dust of the ground."—*Gen.*, 2: 7.

### OUR SAVIOR, A MAN.

"The man Christ Jesus."—*I. Tim.*, 2: 5.

"By man came death; by man also came the resurrection of the dead."—*I. Cor.*, 15: 21.

"A man of sorrows and acquainted with grief."—*Isa.*, 53: 3.

"My Father is greater than I."—*John*, 14: 28.

"Jesus increased in wisdom and stature."—*Luke*, 2: 52.

### Passages of Scripture referring to our Depraved Senses

"The heart is deceitful above all things, and desperately wicked; who can know it?"—*Jer.*, 17: 46.

"Out of the heart proceeds evil thoughts, murders, adulteries, thefts false witness, blasphemies."—*Matt.*, 15: 19.

"I know that in me (that is in my flesh) dwelleth no good thing."—*Rom.*, 7: 18.

"There is none that doeth good; no, not one."—*Rom.*, 3: 10–12.

"If we say we have no sin we deceive ourselves."—*I. John*, 1: 8–10.

"These are murmurers, complainers, walking after their own lusts, and their mouths speaketh great swelling words."—*Jude*, 1: 16.

### SEPARATE USE OF EACH OF THE SENSES.

**SIGHT.**—This Sense is developed by the optic nerve and light, and conveys to the judgment sense colors and shapes.

**HEARING.**—This Sense, by the aid of the organs and the atmosphere, convey to the judgment the harmonies, and the meaning of sounds in music, language, devotion and religion.

**SMELLING.**—Reveals God's marvelous work in odors, fragrance and perfumes.

**TASTING.**—By this Sense man discovers stimulating medicines, and condiments and relishes wholesome cooked diet, flavorings and fruits. This Sense is peculiarly predisposed to depravity, and the Judgment Sense often fails to control it.

### THE SENSES of JESUS.

The Seven Senses of Jesus were as holy in Him throughout His life and death, as they were in Adam before his transgression; hence, His senses could not die only as he laid them down in death, and thereby became the second Adam. "The seven eyes of the Lord," sometimes called the "Seven Spirits of God," also the Holy Spirit, united in the person of Jesus with his Seven Senses, making Him "God manifest in the flesh," from Eternity to Eternity. Man is now a four-fold being. The Attributes, as a life-power, in the man; the soul-form is truly the man. The Senses die, and when the body is raised from the dead we shall be the triune children of God, celestial beings.

The Beasts have no spirit-form or attributes, and only five Senses, so they can snort and neigh, or cipher; plead law, practice medicine, preach or pray. Education and religion are to them worthless institutions.

## Common Attributes—Vital Centers.

## TRUTH
## LOVE
## LIFE

**MAN, A SPIRITUAL BEING.**

"God created man in his own image, in the image of God created he him." — *God is a spirit.—Gen.*, 1: 27.

"And man became a living soul.—*Gen.*, 2: 7.

"God is my witness whom I serve with my spirit."—*Rom.*, 1: 9.

"For as the body without the spirit is dead."—*Jas.*, 2: 26.

"Receive my spirit."—*Acts*, 7: 59.

### THE DEITY OF OUR SAVIOUR'S ATTRIBUTES.

"I and my Father are one."—*John*, 10: 30.

"He that hath seen me hath seen the Father."—*John*, 14: 9–10.

"Jesus being full of the Holy Ghost."—*Luke*, 4: 1.

"The Word was with God and the Word was God."—*John*, 1: 1.

"God was manifest in the flesh."—*I. Tim.*, 3: 16.

"In Him dwelleth all the fullness of the Godhead bodily."—*Col.*, 2: 9.

"Saith He that hath the Seven Spirits of God."—*Rev.*, 3: 1.

### Biblical Allusions to our Spiritual Senses, or Attributes.

"And if Christ be in you the body is dead because of sin, but the spirit is life because of righteousness."—*Rom.*, 8: 10.

"For ye are the temple of the living God.—*II. Cor.*, 6: 16.

"So then, with the mind I myself serve the law of God."—*Rom.*, 7: 25.

"They are not of the world even as I am not of the world."—*John*, 17: 16.

"Locked up steadfastly into heaven and saw the glory of God.—*Acts*, 7: 55.

"But are not able to kill the soul."—*Mat.*, 10: 28.

"Lifted up his eyes in hell, being in torments."—*Luke*, 16: 23.

"I was in the Spirit on the Lord's day."—*Rev.*, 1: 10.

"Whosoever liveth and believeth in me shall never die."—*John*, 11: 26.

### SEPARATE USE OF EACH OF THE SENSES.

**TALKING.**—This sense pervades the entire man. He talks with his tongue and organs of speech; with his lips, with his eyes, his gait, his face, his head, his hands, his gestures, his feet. By grammar, by chirography, typography, telegraphy and symbols. He talks with himself, his fellow-men and with God; by language and song.

**JUDGING.**—By this sense we count, combine, add, subtract, multiply and divide; originate currency, place values on commodities of traffic, weigh, invent machinery, compound medicines, frame laws, govern armies and nations, secure wealth, build stately mansions, measure time and distances, inches and magnitudes. This sense reserves and retains insult, jealousy and revenge.

**FEELING.**—This sense connects the organism with the outer world, and through it flows pleasure and protection. In many things it obviates the necessity of sight.

---

## ☞ Explanatory Key to Dr. L. A. Alford's Biblical Chart of Man, ☜
### SHOWING THE RELATION OF THE SOUL TO THE BODY, THE SENSES TO THE ATTRIBUTES, MORTALITY TO IMMORTALITY.

**Man** is in possession of two forms and two natures—mortal and spiritual. The senses and attributes, like the veins and arteries unite; and make man a moral being.

The senses are the life centers of the human body and are destitute of form, and must die. When one sense dies, we are "struck with death," and the rest soon follow.

The attributes are life centres of the soul, and cannot cease to exist. They too, are without form, and are destitute of the senses, which cloud their vision. The dissolution of the relation of senses and attributes is death; and as soon as this dissolution occurs, ordinarily, decomposition of the body commences. The attributes of our spirit partake of the eternity of God, and were breathed by Him into life-centers of the soul, and after the death of the senses, will see God and Angels.

Everything we do, is done by and through the *Senses*, and they are responsible for our acts; they only *use* the body.

In morality and religion, the *Attributes* do all that is done, and are responsible to God and to man; they not only use the soul, but *also through the Senses, the body.*

Grace so far pervades our infantile nature, as to harmonize the attributes and save us, if we die before actual transgression. Sin, or actual transgression, is the limit to this grace; still the attributes are under the covenant and conditions of salvation, but cannot be regenerated without the Holy Spirit. "Ye must be born again."

By Sin, the condition of the soul is like the body, in eminent peril with the five animal senses paralyzed, and only the judgment sense and sense of language at our command, we can positively judge of our condition and ask God for help.

God commands us to ask his aid, and is ready to help. In this condition, the soul is under the curse of the law, "dead in trespasses and sins." When we cry to God for help, His attribute, Love, touches ours, and this is *regeneration.* Then all our attributes are in harmony, and we are in Christ, and He in us—born again.

The *Baptism of the Holy Ghost*, is the union of all God's attributes with ours, in positive and direct connection. "Spake as the Holy Ghost gave them utterance."

The *sin against the Holy Ghost*, is the angry rejection and blasphemy against God's seven attributes, viz: *Light, Mercy, Holiness, Justice, Truth, Life and Love.*

Each of these attributes the human soul possesses; but without God's light, the eye of the soul can no more see than the eye of the body, without natural light; and so with all the attributes.

The attributes, by their connection, make the senses moral. Hence, if by disease one attribute fails to connect with one sense, we are *Monomaniacs.* If three or four, we are *Crazy.* If all, we are *totally Insane*, and are not responsible to moral law, however atrocious the act may be, or otherwise horrible the crime.

The Senses have a memory as well as the attributes. The memory of all transgression of the senses, is by the application of the archetypal blood of Christ forever blotted out of our memory, and heaven becomes our happy, blessed home throughout eternity; while those who reject salvation, will carry the memory of their sins and crimes forever and ever.

All our Christian devotion and labors for our fellow-men and the world's redemption, as well as our associations in the love of God, will be photographed through the senses upon the attributes, and their memory will last forever and ever.

When we are turned around, or lost, the senses and attributes (as seen by the compass) are all variance, and we cannot possibly harmonize the difficulty or make the points of compass correspond to our opinion. So we are, without Christ, lost.

"If our gospel be hid, it is hid to them that are lost."

Published by Rev. L. A. ALFORD, Prof. of Anthropology, Chicago, Ill.

# JUMBLING SEEDS AND SOWING THEM

## Rufinus

IMAGINE A MAN jumbling seeds of different sorts together and sowing them indiscriminately, scattering them at random on the field. Is it not the case that, wherever all these various seeds have been scattered, each of them will develop into the appropriate shoot of its species at the proper season, exactly reproducing its own shape and structure? It is the same with the substance of each individual's flesh: however strangely and widely it has been dispersed, it possesses within it the principle of immortality, for it is the flesh of an immortal soul. Hence, at the precise moment which, when the bodies were planted like seed in the earth, seemed suitable to the will of the true God, this principle gathers the several particles from the earth and unites them with their own substance, restoring the identical structure which death previously destroyed. The result is that each soul has restored to it, not a composite or alien body, but the actual one it formerly possessed. That is why it becomes possible, in recompense for the struggles of the present life, for the flesh which has lived morally to be crowned along with its soul, and for the immoral flesh to be punished.

# PUTTING THE BODY BACK TOGETHER

## Augustine of Hippo

SUPPOSE . . . THAT a statue made of some soluble metal were melted down by fire or crushed into powder or reduced to a shapeless mass, and an artist wished to restore the statue from the mass of its original material, it would make no difference to its completeness what particular particles of the material would be returned to any one part of the statue, as long as the restored statue recovered all the materials of which it was originally composed. In like manner God, the Artist of marvelous and ineffable power, will with marvelous and ineffable speed restore our body from the totality of matter of which it originally consisted. Nor will it be of any importance for its restoration whether hairs return to hairs and nails to nails, or whether that portion of them which was lost be changed into flesh and taken back into other parts of the body: in His Providence the Artist sees to it that nothing unseemly results.

# MISSING LIMBS

## Hal Lindsey

A NURSE CAME UP to me after I'd just spoken on the signs of Christ's return and said, "Hal, will you please come and meet a soldier I brought over from the veterans' hospital? He accepted Christ as His Savior and Lord as a result of my reading *The Late Great Planet Earth* to him. It really took courage for him to come here tonight—he's in great pain because both arms and legs have been amputated. He lost them in Vietnam."

When I walked up to the wheeled stretcher on which he was lying, the young man looked up with a radiant face and said, "Tell me, Hal, will my new body have arms and legs?"

While choking back tears I turned to Philippians 3:20 and 21 and read:

" 'But our citizenship is in heaven. And we eagerly await a Savior from there, the Lord Jesus Christ, who, by the power that enables him to bring everything under his control, will transform our lowly bodies so that they will be like his glorious body' " (Philippians 3:20–21, N.I.V.)

"Jim," I said, "your body will be like Jesus Christ's glorious body. We know that His resurrection body is perfect, so we know that yours will be, too."

His face flooded with beautiful joy as this promise of God gave birth to hope in him.

You may have an aching, aging, or a badly damaged body. Lay hold of this hope and press on with new strength.

This hope was the basis of the great apostle Paul's strength in enduring all kinds of physical deprivation and torture. Right after speaking of being "hard pressed on every side . . . perplexed . . . persecuted . . . struck down," Paul says, "Therefore we do not lose heart. Though outwardly we are wasting away, yet inwardly we are being renewed day by day. For our light and momentary troubles are achieving for us an eternal glory that far outweighs them all. So we fix our eyes not on what is seen, but on what is unseen. For what is seen is temporary, but what is unseen is eternal" (2 Corinthians 4:8–9, 16–18, N.I.V.).

Let's also fix our eyes on what is unseen and eternal. This refers to the things we will experience in our new forever bodies with Christ.

I believe persecution is coming for most believers in this generation. So these promises and the hope they inspire will be worth more than gold then, if not now. Let this hope inspire us ". . . to throw off everything that hinders and the sin that so easily entangles, and let us run with perseverance the race marked out for us" (Hebrews 12:1, N.I.V.).

# RESURRECTION OF THE BODY, NOT THE FLESH

*Frederick C. Grant*

PAUL SPEAKS of the resurrection of "the body," not the flesh (for Paul, "flesh" was more or less abhorrent, as it was the seat of sin with its hopeless infection and corruption); but he does not mean the body that is buried in the grave. Instead, "the body which is to be" is given by God (1 Corinthians 15:35–38), and will be incorruptible, powerful, glorious, and imperishable—for "flesh and blood cannot inherit the kingdom of God, nor does the perishable inherit the imperishable" (1 Corinthians 15:40–50). This new and glorified body must be "put on" at the resurrection. Paul shudders at the thought of a bare, naked, purely "spiritual" (as we would say, but he would say "psychic") existence, that of a disembodied soul : "not that we would be unclothed, but that we would be further clothed [or reclothed], so that what is mortal may be swallowed up by life. . . ." And yet he goes on to say that "we would rather be away from the body and at home with the Lord" (2 Corinthians 5:1–10;

cf. Philippians 1:19–26). Of course Paul is not writing a treatise on Systematic Theology—his letters are more like sermons. But the occasional chance phrase is as clearly an expression of his real convictions as are the formal statements. For example in 1 Corinthians 5:3–5, he directs his readers to hold a church court and try the man who is guilty of incest (so the case was viewed in both Jewish and Roman law): "you are to deliver this man to Satan for the destruction of the flesh, that his *spirit* may be saved in the day of the Lord Jesus." In this passage there is no reference to any resurrection of the body; though Paul certainly expected the man to die (by Satan's action) after he was excommunicated—the words provided a terrible text for the later Inquisition! Evidently Paul was concerned for the saving of the man's "spirit," not the resurrection of his "body." And there are other passages which likewise indicate that Paul, instead of championing the traditional Palestinian-Pharisaic doctrine of resurrection against the Hellenistic-philosophical view of immortality, in effect combines the two—as he often does, and as all powerful, creative religious thinkers tend to do—bringing forth out of their treasures "what is new and what is old" (Matthew 13:52). Immortality and resurrection are not identical . . . and both ideas are required if justice is to be done the New Testament conception of the "spiritual body."

## COME ALIVE WITH PEPSI    Campus Life

# WILL THE TALL BE SHORT AND THE THIN FAT?

## Augustine of Hippo

IT DOES NOT FOLLOW that because individuals differed in stature during life, that they will also differ in stature when they are brought back to life; nor that those who were thin will be thin, and those who were fat will return to life with their former obesity. But if it is in the Creator's plan that each should preserve in his new features his individuality and a recognizable likeness to his former self, while in the remaining physical endowment all should be equal, then all matter will be so disposed of in each that none of it will be lost; and what may have been wanting in some, will be supplied by Him who, as He willed it, was able to create even out of nothing.

# OUR SECOND BODY

## J. V. Langmead Casserley

THE EARLY CHRISTIANS had no illusions about death. They knew quite well what happens to the bodies which we bury in graves. They were as familiar with the phenomenon of physical corruption as we are, but they had a robust faith in what we may call, with reverence, the divine common sense. God has not created embodied souls in order to frustrate for all eternity their physical needs and nature. He who provides us with the type of body suited to our present sphere of existence will no doubt replace it with the probably quite different kind of body requisite for life in that world for which this world is a preparation. St. Paul likens the burial of the old worn-out flesh and the reembodying of the bereaved soul with its new spiritual body to the process of the sowing of the seed and the reaping of the harvest. The fruit and the flower do not particularly resemble the seed which is buried in the ground, but they are continuous with it and the one must vanish before the other can appear. St. Paul's analogy is illuminating, but it must not be regarded as more than an illustration. We do not know how we shall get our second body, but then we do not really understand how we acquired our first one. What we have yet to experience is not, and indeed could not be, more mysterious and inscrutable than the familar yet quite incomprehensible phenomenon which we have experienced already.

# THAT NATURE IS A HERACLITEAN FIRE AND OF THE COMFORT OF THE RESURRECTION

## *Gerard Manley Hopkins*

Cloud-puffball, torn tufts, tossed pillows flaunt
   forth, then chevy on an air-
built thoroughfare: heaven-roysterers, in gay-gangs
   they throng; they glitter in marches.
Down roughcast, down dazzling whitewash,
   wherever an elm arches
Shivelights and shadowtackle in long lashes lace,
   lance, and pair.
Delightfully the bright wind boisterous ropes,
   wrestles, beats earth bare
Of yestertempest's creases; in pool and rut peel
   parches
Squandering ooze to squeezed dough, crust, dust;
   stanches, starches
Squadroned masks and manmarks treadmire toil
   there
Footfretted in it. Million-fueled, nature's bonfire
   burns on.
But quench her bonniest, dearest to her, her
   clearest-selved spark
Man, how fast his firedint, his mark on mind, is
   gone!

Both are in an unfathomable, all is in an enormous
   dark
Drowned. O pity and indignation! Manshape, that
   shone
Sheer off, disseveral, a star, death blots black out;
   nor mark
     Is any of him at all so stark
But vastness blurs and time beats level. Enough! the
   Resurrection,
A heart's-clarion! Away grief's gasping, joyless days,
   dejection.
     Across my foundering deck shone
A beacon, an eternal beam. Flesh fade, and mortal
   trash
Fall to the residuary worm; world's wildfire, leave
   but ash:
     In a flash, at a trumpet crash,
I am all at once what Christ is, since he was what I
   am, and
This Jack, joke, poor potsherd, patch, matchwood,
   immortal diamond,
     Is immortal diamond.

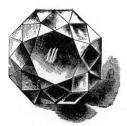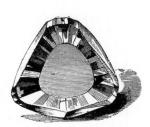

# DAY OF THE LORD, DAY OF CHRIST

*James Montgomery Boice*

To PAINT THE prophetic picture for end times in clearer detail and to have a basis for understanding some of the most important New Testament prophecies, we must distinguish between them.

"The day of the Lord" . . . is quite prominent in the Old Testament, but it occurs frequently in the New Testament too, even in the context of some of the verses I have been quoting. This phrase is a technical phrase used initially by the Old Testament prophets to designate a future period of catastrophic judgment. Literally, it is the day of Jehovah, the day in which Jehovah will break silence and intervene in history to judge Israel and the Gentile nations. The characteristics of this day can be seen in the following quotations.

"For the day of the Lord of hosts shall be upon every one who is proud and lofty, and upon every one who is lifted up; and he shall be brought low" (Isaiah 2:12).

"Howl ye; for the day of the Lord is at hand; it shall come as a destruction from the Almighty. . . . Behold, the day of the Lord cometh, cruel both with wrath and fierce anger, to lay the land desolate: and he shall destroy the sinners thereof out of it. For the stars of heaven and the constellations thereof shall not give their light; the sun shall be darkened in its going forth, and the moon shall not cause its light to shine" (Isaiah 13:6, 9, 10).

"Woe unto you that desire the day of the Lord! To what end is it for you? The day of the Lord is darkness, and not light, as if a man did flee from the lion, and a bear met him; or went into the house, and leaned his hand on the wall, and a serpent bit him. Shall not the day of the Lord be darkness, and not light? Even very dark, and no brightness in it?" (Amos 5:18-20).

It is obvious from the reference to the darkening of the sun, moon, and stars that this is the event referred to by Jesus in Matthew 24, where Jesus taught that He would exercise judgment. It is also the event of which Peter spoke when he wrote:

"But the day of the Lord will come as a thief in the night, in which the heavens shall pass away with a great noise, and the elements shall melt with fervent heat; the earth also, and the works that are in it, shall be burned up" (2 Peter 3:10).

In the liturgy of the church this is expressed by the *Dies Irae*, which means the day of the wrath of God.

From an examination of these and other texts (Jeremiah 46:10; Lamentations 2:22; Ezekiel 30:3ff.: Joel 1:15; 2-1-11; 3-14-16; Zephaniah 1:7-2:3; Zechariah 14:1-7; Malachi 4:5) several things are clear. First, the day of the Lord is the day of God's judgment. Second, the day is still future. Third, it is preceded by a time of great trouble on earth. Fourth, it is followed by the earthly rule of the Messiah. . . . Fifth, it has nothing to do with the church of Jesus Christ, for the church is not in view in these prophecies and was, in fact, completely unknown to the Old Testament writers who composed them.

To be sure, as Kenneth S. Wuest, who summarized much of this data in his collection of *Word Studies in the Greek New Testament*, observed, "Some of the references to the day of the Lord in the Old Testament have a fulfillment in the past, and are precursors of the day of the Lord to follow." But that does not alter the fact that the strict fulfillment of most of these prophecies awaits a future day.

That day is coming. The disasters of this life— pestilence, famine, wars, natural catastrophes—are only little judgments which come in the most part from man's own activities. When the day of God's wrath is revealed, these things will pale by comparison, and no one who is not united to Christ by faith will be able to stand against Him.

No one can be sure of defending himself even from man-made destruction. For instance, there is an extensive military radar network called the DEW line (Distant Early Warning), which stretches across the North American continent. This line of defense has cost the United States billions of dollars. It was designed to limit to a minimum the breakthrough of Soviet long-range bombers coming to wreak nuclear destruction on the United States; but today it is outmoded by missiles. Man can never defend himself adequately against the possibility of future destruction.

Thus, too, does he stand before God. Man has run away from God, and God has pursued him. God came to die for him in Jesus Christ.

The second major idea is associated with the phrase "the day of Jesus Christ." That is not the same as "the day of the Lord." The day of Jesus Christ is a happy day rather than a day of judgment.

Moreover, far from warning men to fear it, the New Testament actually speaks of it as an event to be warmly anticipated. Christians are to be ready and watching, and they are to encourage one another because of it.

What is the nature of this day? The clearest answer to this question is in the verses . . . from Paul's first letter to the Christians at Thessalonica. They were in sorrow over certain of their number who had died, and Paul wrote to them to comfort them with the thought that they would see their departed friends once again at the day of Jesus Christ. He describes it thus: "For the Lord himself shall descend from heaven with a shout, with the voice of the archangel, and with the trump of God: and the dead in Christ shall rise first: Then we who are alive and remain shall be caught up together with them in the clouds, to meet the Lord in the air; and so shall we ever be with the Lord" (1 Thessalonians 4:16–17). Quite obviously, this day does not concern Christ's earthly rule. It is an aspect of His coming to draw believers out of this world to Himself. He will come in the air and gather His church up to meet Him, first those who have died and then—almost in the same instant—those who are living.

Jesus described this event, also stressing its unexpected and selective nature: "Then shall two be in the field; the one shall be taken, and the other left. Two women shall be grinding at the mill; the one shall be taken, and the other left. Watch, therefore; for ye know not what hour your Lord doth come" (Matthew 24:40–42). In biblical theology this event is generally called the rapture. It is the first in the whole series of events prophesied for the end times.

It is possible that at this point some of this teaching has become confusing. So let me elaborate upon the distinction between the day of Jesus Christ and the day of the Lord by looking at the way the apostle Paul dealt with a similar confusion in his day.

Wherever he went, Paul apparently preached the full body of Christian doctrine as it had been revealed to him. And that included, quite naturally, the doctrine of the Lord's imminent return to be followed, after certain events, by God's judgment. These events included persecution and great tribulation. We know that this doctrine had been accepted by the church at Thessalonica, for Paul alluded to it in his first letter, reminding the Christians there that they were to be comforted by the doctrine of the Lord's return in face of the death of their friends. Some time after he had written this letter, however, a time of persecution broke out in the church at Thessalonica. Because the persecution seemed terrible and intense, someone began to teach that the persecutions were those leading up to the day of the Lord, with its ultimate judgments, and that the Christians of Thessalonica, therefore, had missed the rapture. The Thessalonians may actually have received a letter purporting to be from Paul which affirmed this idea (2 Thessalonians 2:2).

News of their distress reached Paul, and he immediately wrote to the Thessalonians again, attempting to explain the meaning of their present persecution and assuring them that they had not missed the coming again of the Lord Jesus Christ for those who believe on Him. First, he dealt with the meaning of present persecution. This occupies the first chapter. Then, in the second chapter, he began to deal with the view that the Christians

## THIEF IN THE NIGHT

*Peter the Apostle
(2 Peter 3:10–13)*

BUT THE DAY of the Lord will come as a thief in the night; in which the heavens shall pass away with a great noise, and the elements shall melt with fervent heat, the earth also and the works that are therein shall be burned up.

Seeing then that all these things shall be dissolved, what manner of persons ought ye to be in all holy conversation and godliness.

Looking for and hasting unto the coming of the day of God, wherein the heavens being on fire shall be dissolved, and the elements shall melt with fervent heat?

Nevertheless we, according to his promise, look for new heavens and a new earth, wherein dwelleth righteousness.

might already be going through the days of tribulation.

"Now we beseech you, brethren, by the coming of our Lord Jesus Christ, and by our gathering together unto him this is a reference to the rapture which he had described in the earlier letter, that ye be not soon shaken in mind, or be troubled, neither by spirit, nor by word, nor by letter as from us, as that the day of the Lord is present. Let no man deceive you by any means; for that day shall not come, except there come the falling away first, and that man of sin be revealed, the son of perdition, who opposeth and exalteth himself above all that is called God, or that is worshiped, so that he, as God, sitteth in the temple of God, showing himself that he is God. Remember ye not that, when I was yet with you, I told you these things?" (2 Thessalonians 2:1–5).

Paul's main points clearly were that the present suffering of the Christians at Thessalonica was not the tribulation prophesied in the Old Testament and taught by himself, that the final tribulation would not come until after the Christians were caught up to meet the Lord Jesus Christ in the air, and, therefore, that the coming of Christ rather than the final judgment should be uppermost in the minds of believers. . . .

It is worth pointing out that precisely the same order of events is presented in 1 Thessalonians. Once again the two different days—the day of the Lord

# FIRST RAPTURE, THEN WRATH

## Arthur D. Katterjohn
## with Mark Fackler

"As it was in the days of Noah, so shall it be also in the days of the Son of man" (Luke 17:26). Much of this important passage already has been discussed in our chapter on the Olivet Discourse, but some points brought out by Luke warrant further emphasis.

Normal activities during the days of Noah are the same ones we experience today—eating, drinking, and marrying. All of these continued "until the day Noah entered into the ark," when "the flood came and destroyed them all." Both God's rescue of His people and judgment on the wicked happened in quick succession. The time interval between Noah's entering the ark and the first signs of flooding was short indeed. In fact, Genesis 7:7 states that Noah went into the ark "because of [or driven by] the waters of the flood." We can expect therefore that the coming of Christ and the judgment of wickedness will occur in almost spontaneous succession.

Likewise, people pursued their regular daily activities during the "days of Lot" (Luke 17:28). But on the same day that Lot hiked out of Sodom, fire and sulfur rained from the sky and devastated the city. On the same day that God delivers His people, judgment will fall on the wicked.

Since the same day brings both rapture and wrath, the question arises: "What is the order? Will believers be raptured before God pours out wrath, or must Christians also endure this final, worldwide judgment?"

It is extremely important to understand that saints will never suffer the wrath of God. Christ Himself suffered in our place and tasted death for us that we should live forever (Hebrews 2:9). "We are not appointed unto wrath, but to salvation" (1 Thessalonians 5:9). Noah was first shut in the ark, then the flood waters fell. When Christ comes at the close of the age, He will first gather the saints to Himself, then dispense the judgment of God on the wicked. Matthew's account gives the same order—first the coming of Christ for the elect (Matthew 24:30–32), then the judgment (Matthew 25:31–46). First rapture, then wrath.

and the day of Jesus Christ—are in view, as well as two distinct classes of people. The day of the Lord is a day that should concern unbelievers. Paul speaks of this group as "they" and "them." The day of Jesus Christ is for believers only. Paul speaks of this class as "us" and "you."

"For yourselves [the Christians at Thessalonica] know perfectly that the day of the Lord so cometh as a thief in the night. For when they [the unbelievers] shall say, Peace and safety; then sudden destruction cometh upon them, as travail upon a woman with child, and they [the unbelievers] shall not escape. But ye, brethren [the Christians], are not in darkness, that that day should overtake [the word means "seize" or "affect"] you as a thief. Therefore, let us [i.e., we who are Christians] not sleep, as do others [unbelievers]; but let us watch and be sober. For God hath not appointed us to wrath [that is, Christians will not undergo the day of the Lord], but to obtain salvation by our Lord Jesus Christ [that is, our final salvation in the day when Jesus will call us out of this world to be with Himself]" (1 Thessalonians 5:2–4, 6, 9).

Paul's teaching clearly indicates that the rapture, "the day of Jesus Christ," must come first. Then will come the unfolding of the other events of prophecy, beginning with a period of great tribulation and continuing through Christ's return to earth to judge Israel and the nations, the millennium, the final judgment, and a complete transition from the life of this world to the life of eternity.

These are the two greatest days of future world history—the day of Jesus Christ and the day of the Lord. Every man who has ever lived must stand before the Lord Jesus Christ on one of these days. . . . If you are a believer in Christ, let me encourage you to look up and be faithful to Him.

# BULATION

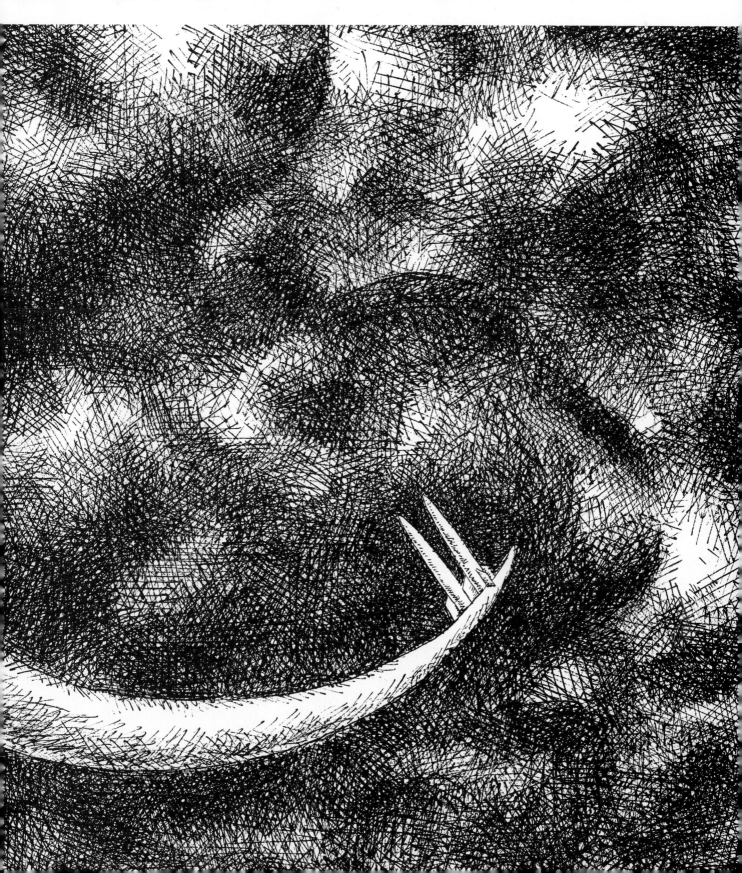

# APOCALYPTICAL SIGNS

## *John Wesley White*

ON JULY 14, 1976, CBS was covering the Democratic Convention in which Jimmy Carter was chosen as the Democratic candidate for the presidency of the United States. During the roll-call vote, Walter Cronkite suddenly interjected a quotation from the gospel song "When the Roll Is Called Up Yonder":

> *When the trumpet of the Lord shall sound*
> *And time shall be no more,*
> *And the morning breaks eternal, bright,*
>    *and fair;*
> *When the saved of earth shall gather*
> *To their home beyond the skies,*
> *And the roll is called up yonder,*
>    *I'll be there.*

There was a ring of nostalgia in Cronkite's allusion, harking back twelve and a half years to the funeral of John F. Kennedy—a predecessor of President Carter: Cardinal Cushing was reciting from the apostle Paul to a billion people on all continents: "For the Lord Himself with cry of command, with voice of archangel, and with trumpet of God, will descend from heaven; and the dead in Christ will rise up first. Then we who live, who survive, shall be caught up together with them in the clouds to meet the Lord in the air, and so we shall ever be with the Lord! Wherefore comfort one another with these words" (1 Thessalonians 4:13–18, *Douay Version*). But for those who are left behind, there will be the horrors of wars and a final war, which will be the worst in human history.

"You will hear of wars and rumors of wars. . . . Nation will rise against nation, and kingdom against kingdom." So Jesus replied to His disciples' question: "What will be the sign of your coming and of the end of the age?" (Matthew 24:3, 6, 7). Continuing His answer to the apostle John a half century later, Jesus enlarged on how human warmongering would escalate into worldwide war incited by the "spirits of demons performing miraculous signs," driving blindly the heads of state "of the whole world, to gather them for the battle on the great day of God Almighty . . . to the place that in Hebrew is called Armageddon" (Revelation 16:14, 16). That will indeed be World War III. WW I was fought in Western Europe. WW II enveloped three of the world's five continents and three of its five oceans. Armageddon will involve the nations "of the whole world," and as such will indeed be WW III. Its inciter and villain will be the Son of Perdition from hell, the Antichrist; its Savior and Victor will be the Son of God from heaven, Jesus Christ.

China's operational head, as spokesman for the most populous nation in history, said recently to the president of the United States, the most powerful nation in history, that mankind indisputably is headed for world war. "This is independent of man's will." Surely that has to be one of the most amazing statements in the annals of political atheism: that world war is "independent of man's will." It is precisely what Jesus assured John: that mankind would bottom out by falling into the hands of demonized rulers, who, with minds drugged and bewitched by Satan, would march him down the road to Armageddon. " It is too late to avoid the third World War," reckons Aleksandr Solzhenitsyn, as he witnesses the gladiatorial beating of war drums and immolational battle cries from Moscow to Washington, to Southeast Asia, to the Middle East, to Angola, to Rhodesia. The editor of Canada's leading news magazine was asked what is his chief worry. His reply: "Just what every other news magazine editor worries about—World War III being declared."

As we read chapters 38 and 39 of Ezekiel's prophecy, we cannot escape feeling that the prime mover of a major war en route to Armageddon is to be Soviet Russia. Leonid Brezhnev himself departs far enough from his usual chronic détente propaganda to launch into the final quarter of our century with an allusion to universal man's "return to the Cold War and to an ever more risky balance on the brink of a hot war. . . . It is important for all to understand this well." One who believes he understands it well, exceedingly well, is British Tory Winston Churchill II, who replies wryly to Brezhnev:

> *There is a nation whose armies—wherever they face the West—are always in attack formation. They are backed by an armaments industry consuming the same percentage of national wealth that Adolf Hitler spent one year before he plunged humanity into World War II. The nation is Soviet Russia. . . . Their whole economy is geared to a war footing. . . . If they are tempted by the total apathy and demonstrated feebleness of the West in the past few weeks, if we go down this slope for many more months, it won't be a question of the independence of a few African countries . . . it will be a question of peace, global peace.*

Clare Booth Luce called herself "an optimist who thinks good things can happen but probably won't." She further states, "There is a great likelihood of nuclear war in the next twenty-five years."

United States Senator Robert Griffin, appearing on "Meet the Press," stated that the world is sitting on a tinderbox with annihilation beckoning, while Senator Peter Dominick bemoans the fact that the only international agency that for a full generation has been in a position to negotiate peace is now in a state of strangulation: "We must frankly face the fact that the U.N., dominated by the General Assembly, no longer offers any hope or promise of peace," a fact that was especially evident in July 1976 when the Israelis went into Uganda to rescue their hijacked hostages, only to incur yet another United Nations condemnation from the antipeace propagandists.

Perhaps the most patrician premier on the planet is President Valéry Giscard d'Estaing of France who reckons, "The world is unhappy. It is unhappy because it doesn't know where it is going and because it senses that, if it knew, it would discover that it was heading for disaster." Henry Kissinger burst into tears before a television camera, as he stood in the Armageddon-bound Middle East, which had hanging over it an unmistakable thermonuclear sword-of-Damocles. Kissinger grieved, "One has to live with a sense of the inevitability of tragedy."

Abba Eban, Israel's urbane foreign minister, reflects how "a fluke or a miscalculation" with one of the intractable nuclear warheads that with ever-increasing indiscrimination are being distributed around the world could cause mankind to be destroyed in a universal crematorium. The late Albert Schweitzer analyzed humanity's proclivity for self-destruction: "Man has lost the capacity to foresee and to forestall. He will end by destroying the earth."

H. G. Wells lived only one year into the nuclear age, but it was long enough for him to press the alarm buzzer: "For man and his world, there is no way out." The late Arnold Toynbee foresaw how, as man enters the final quarter of this century, "people are going to find themselves in a permanent state of siege. . . . The future austerity will be perennial and it will become progressively more severe. What then?" And it is with this "What then?" that man senses apocalypse. *Time* points out that George Orwell's ominous prognostications a quarter of a century ago have made him today an uncanny "cliché for apocalypse." Or, as Clive Cooking wrote in 1976, "We are currently entering the zone of 'Way stations of the Apocalypse.'" Best-seller books currently carry such titles as *Ultimatus* and *Doomsday*, an ubiquitous number engaging the catchword "Armageddon," such as *Armageddon, The Voice of Armageddon,* and *The Road to Armageddon.*

## WARS AND RUMORS OF WARS

*Mark the Evangelist*

*(Mark 13:1–8)*

AND AS HE WENT out of the temple, one of his disciples saith unto him, Master, see what manner of stones and what buildings are here!

And Jesus answering said unto him, Seest thou these great buildings? there shall not be left one stone upon another, that shall not be thrown down.

And as he sat upon the mount of Olives over against the temple, Peter and James and John and Andrew asked him privately,

Tell us, when shall these things be? and what shall be the sign when all these things shall be fulfilled?

And Jesus answering them began to say, Take heed lest any man deceive you:

For many shall come in my name, saying, I am Christ; and shall deceive many.

And when ye shall hear of wars and rumors of wars, be ye not troubled: for such things must needs be; but the end shall not be yet.

For nation shall rise against nation, and kingdom against kingdom: and there shall be earthquakes in divers places, and there shall be famines and troubles: these are the beginnings of sorrows.

# SATAN IN THE NEW TESTAMENT

*John L. McKenzie*

THERE IS NO APPRECIABLE difference in meaning between the New Testament titles *satanas* and *diabolos*. Satan is also called the strong one (Matthew 12:29; Mark 3:27; Luke 11:21), the evil one (Matthew 13:19), the prince of this world (John 12:31). Satan is a tempter who even tempts Jesus (Matthew 4:1; Mark 1:13; Luke 4:2). When Peter attempts to dissuade Jesus from His passion, Jesus calls him Satan; his thoughts are human, not divine (Matthew 16:23; Mark 8:33). Satan takes the seed of the word from the mouth of those who receive it (Matthew 13:19; Mark 4:15; Luke 8:12). Satan put the betrayal of Jesus into the heart of Judas (John 13:2), and then entered Judas for the consummation of the deed (Luke 22:3; John 13:27). Satan tries to sift the disciples like wheat (Luke 22:31). He filled the heart of Ananias with deceit (Acts 5:3). He tempts with designs (1 Corinthians 7:5; 2 Corinthians 2:11) and with wiles (Ephesians 6:11) and with snares (1 Timothy 3:7; 2 Timothy 2:26). He disguises himself as an angel of light (2 Corinthians 11:14). He seduces some of the faithful (1 Timothy 5:15). He is the enemy who sows cockle in the field of the Lord's wheat (Matthew 13:39; Luke 8:12). He is like a roaring lion seeking prey (1 Peter 5:8). Christians should give him no room to work (Ephesians 4:27).

Satan also has power to do bodily harm. He has a house and a kingdom (Matthew 12:26; Mark 3:23, 26; Luke 11:18). He claims that all the kingdoms of the world are in his power (Luke 4:6). Luke so constructs the temptation narrative as to show that the power of Satan, which is frustrated in the temptation "until an opportunity" (Luke 4:13), finds its opportunity in the passion of Jesus, the hour of the power of darkness (Luke 22:53). The power of Satan is the power of darkness opposed to the power of light also in Acts 26:18. Satan bound a paralyzed woman for eighteen years (Luke 13:16), and his angel is the "thorn in the flesh" from which Paul suffered (2 Corinthians 12:7). It is to

Satan as the agent of bodily harm that sinners and adversaries of the apostles are delivered (1 Corinthians 5:5; 1 Timothy 1:20). Satan hindered Paul from making a journey to Thessalonica (1 Thessalonians 2:18). The Antichrist comes with the active power of Satan (2 Thessalonians 2:9). In the millennium Satan is bound in the pit (Revelation 20:2); he is then released and permitted to work destruction in the final world period (Revelation 20:7). But the time granted to the devil is short (Revelation 12:12). He has the power to kill (Hebrews 2:14).

## WHEN HE REIGNS, IT'S HELL

*Daniel Defoe*

*Wherever God erects a house of prayer,*
*The Devil always builds a chapel there:*
*And 'twill be found upon examination*
*The latter has the largest congregation:*
*For ever since he first debauched the mind,*
*He made a perfect conquest of mankind.*
*With uniformity of service, he*
*Reigns with a general aristocracy.*
*No nonconforming sects disturb his reign,*
*For of his yoke, there's very few complain.*
*He knows the genius and inclination,*
*And matches proper sins for every Nation,*
*He needs no standing army government;*
*He always rules us by our own consent. . . .*

(FROM *The True-Born Englishman*)

# ANTICHRIST IN THE NEW TESTAMENT

## L. L. Morris

The expression *antichristos* is found in the Bible only in the Johannine Epistles (1 John 2:18, 4:3; 2 John 7), but the idea behind it is widespread. We should probably understand the force of *anti* as indicating opposition, rather than a false claim, i.e. the antichrist is one who opposes Christ rather than one who claims to be the Christ. If this is so, then we should include under the heading "antichrist" such Old Testament passages as Daniel 7, and those in 2 Thessalonians 2 and Revelation which deal with the strong opposition that the forces of evil are to offer Christ in the last days.

The concept is introduced in John as already well-known ("ye have heard that antichrist shall come," 1 John 2:18). But though he does not dispute the fact that at the end of this age there will appear an evil being, called "antichrist," John insists that there is a temper, an attitude, characteristic of antichrist, and that already exists. Indeed, he can speak of "many antichrists" as already in the world (1 John 2:18). He gives something in the nature of a definition of antichrist when he says, "He is antichrist, that denieth the Father and the Son" (1 John 2:22). This becomes a little more explicit when the criterion is made the denial that "Jesus Christ is come in the flesh" (1 John 4:3, 2 John 7). For John it is basic that in Jesus Christ we see God acting for man's salvation (1 John 4). When a man denies this he is not simply guilty of doctrinal error. He is undercutting the very foundation of the Christian faith. He is doing the work of Satan in opposing the things of God. At the end of the age this will characterize the work of the supreme embodiment by evil. And those who in a smaller way do the same thing now demonstrate by that very fact that they are his henchmen.

Paul does not use the term "antichrist," but the "man of sin" of whom he writes in 2 Thessalonians 2 clearly refers to the same being. The characteristic of this individual is that he "opposeth and exalteth himself above all that is called God, or that is wor-shipped" (2:4). He claims to be God (2:4). He is not Satan, but his coming "is after the working of Satan" (2:9). It cannot be said that all the difficulties of this passage have been cleared up, and, in particular, the identification of the man of sin is still hotly debated. But for our present purpose the main points are clear enough. Paul thinks of the supreme effort of Satan as not in the past, but in the future. He does not think of the world as gradually evolving into a perfect state, but of evil as continuing right up till the last time. Then evil will make its greatest challenge to good, and this challenge will be led by the mysterious figure who owes his power to Satan, and who is the instrument of Satan's culminating challenge to the things of God. Paul is sure of the outcome. Christ will consume the man of sin "with the spirit of his mouth" (2:8). The last, supreme challenge of Satan will be defeated.

That is surely the meaning of some, at least, of the imagery of the book of Revelation. Biblical students are far from unanimous about the right way to interpret this book, but nearly all are agreed that some of the visions refer to the final struggle of the forces of evil with Christ. Sometimes the symbolism refers plainly to Satan. Thus the "great red dragon" of Reverend 12:3 is expressly identified with Satan (12:9). But the "beast" of Reverend 11:7 is not. He is closely related to Satan, as his works show. Other similar figures appear (Reverend 13:11, etc.). It is not our purpose here to identify any particular one with the antichrist, but simply to point to the fact that this book too knows of one empowered by Satan who will oppose Christ in the last days. This may fairly be said to be characteristic of the Christian view of the last days.

# WHO IS THE ANTICHRIST?

*Arthur D. Katterjohn*
*with Mark Fackler*

THESE . . . are the names given to this terrifying figure: a horn, a beast (even *the* beast), the man of sin or perdition, and Antichrist. We must not think, however, just because these names are used, that Antichrist when he appears will be repulsive. Some commentators have taken the word "Antichrist" in this sense, that is, as one who is *the opposite* of Christ, and have therefore made the mistake of identifying him with the worst tyrants of history—Nero, Hitler, Mussolini. It is true that the prefix "anti" can mean "against" or "opposite to." But it also can mean "instead of," and this is the meaning here. Antichrist will be a substitute for Christ, as much like Christ as is possible for a tool of Satan. He will talk about justice and love, peace and prosperity. He will be brilliant and eloquent. In short, he will appear as an angel of light, as Satan himself often does, and will be hailed by millions as a superman who will save mankind.

To make this precise we may say that the Antichrist is far more likely to appear as someone like Dr. Albert Schweitzer—who did not believe in the full divinity of Jesus Christ or accept the authority of Scripture and yet went as an angel of light to Africa —than as someone like Adolf Hitler, who rose to power in Germany at about the same time.

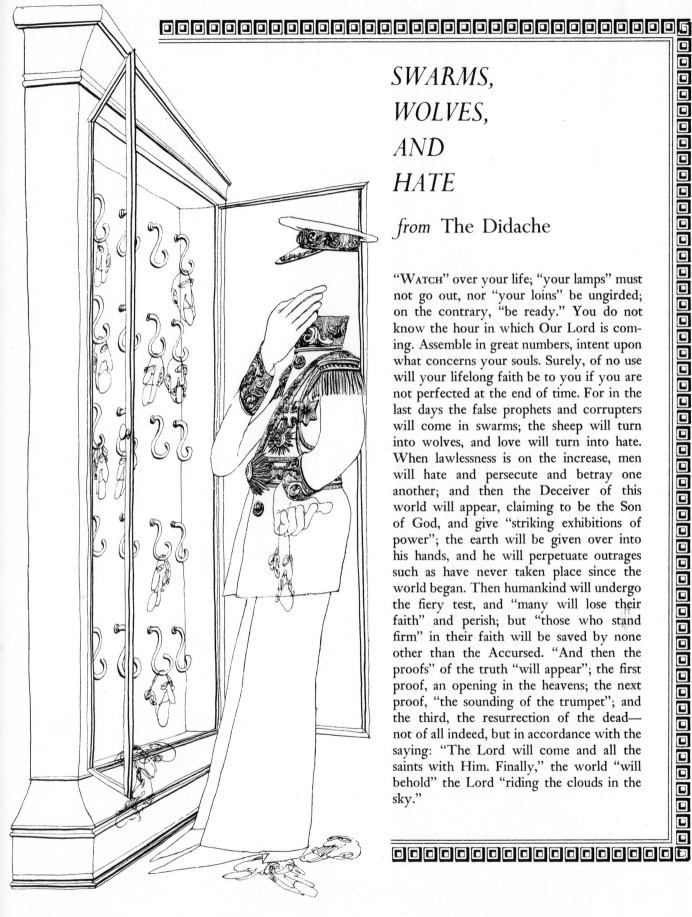

# SWARMS, WOLVES, AND HATE

## *from* The Didache

"WATCH" over your life; "your lamps" must not go out, nor "your loins" be ungirded; on the contrary, "be ready." You do not know the hour in which Our Lord is coming. Assemble in great numbers, intent upon what concerns your souls. Surely, of no use will your lifelong faith be to you if you are not perfected at the end of time. For in the last days the false prophets and corrupters will come in swarms; the sheep will turn into wolves, and love will turn into hate. When lawlessness is on the increase, men will hate and persecute and betray one another; and then the Deceiver of this world will appear, claiming to be the Son of God, and give "striking exhibitions of power"; the earth will be given over into his hands, and he will perpetuate outrages such as have never taken place since the world began. Then humankind will undergo the fiery test, and "many will lose their faith" and perish; but "those who stand firm" in their faith will be saved by none other than the Accursed. "And then the proofs" of the truth "will appear"; the first proof, an opening in the heavens; the next proof, "the sounding of the trumpet"; and the third, the resurrection of the dead—not of all indeed, but in accordance with the saying: "The Lord will come and all the saints with Him. Finally," the world "will behold" the Lord "riding the clouds in the sky."

# FALSE PROPHET

## John the Divine
## (Revelation 13:11–18)

AND I BEHELD another beast coming up out of the earth; and he had two horns like a lamb, and he spake as a dragon.

And he exerciseth all the power of the first beast before him, and causeth the earth and them which dwell therein to worship the first beast, whose deadly wound was healed.

And he doeth great wonders, so that he maketh fire come down from heaven on the earth in the sight of men,

And deceiveth them that dwell on the earth by the means of those miracles which he had power to do in the sight of the beast; saying to them that dwell on the earth, that they should make an image to the beast, which had the wound by a sword, and did live.

And he had power to give life unto the image of the beast, that the image of the beast should both speak, and cause that as many as would not worship the image of the beast should be killed.

And he causeth all, both small and great, rich and poor, free and bond, to receive a mark in their right hand, or in their foreheads.

And that no man might buy or sell, save he that had the mark, or the name of the beast, or the number of his name.

Here is wisdom. Let him that hath understanding count the number of the beast: for it is the number of a man; and his number is Six hundred threescore and six.

## WHO IS THE THE FALSE PROPHET?

### Arthur D. Katterjohn
### with Mark Fackler

THE THIRD FIGURE of the Satanic substitute for the Trinity is called the False Prophet. This designation is given to him twice in the Book of Revelation, in Revelation 19:20 and 20:10. Both verses describe his end. Earlier in Revelation he is described as "another beast" (that is, in addition to Antichrist) who is able to do "great wonders" (13:11, 13).

It is rather difficult to determine from the account in Revelation exactly what these wonders are. The False Prophet is said to be able to call down fire from heaven and to make an image of the Antichrist speak, but the exact nature of these so-called wonders probably will not be known until they actually happen. There is one exception to this, however. Apparently an accident will take place in which Antichrist will almost be killed (Revelation 13:3, 14), but he seemingly will be brought back to life by the False Prophet. This may describe an attempted assassination, for the phrase used in one of the verses often indicates an assassination. Probably this will not be an actual murder and true assassination, for in each case the verses say either "*as though* it were wounded to death" or merely "the wound by a sword." However, Antichrist will seem to die and then rise again.

Here is the final indication of Satan's desire to ape God. For Satan's attempt at a duplication of the Trinity will be accompanied by an attempt through the False Prophet to duplicate Christ's resurrection.

# THE WHORE OF BABYLON

## John the Divine
## (Revelation 17:1–18)

AND THERE CAME one of the seven angels which had the seven vials, and talked with me, saying unto me, Come hither; I will show unto thee the judgment of the great whore that sitteth upon many waters:

With whom the kings of the earth have committed fornication, and the inhabitants of the earth have been made drunk with the wine of her fornication.

So he carried me away in the spirit into the wilderness: and I saw a woman sit upon a scarlet-colored beast, full of names of blasphemy, having seven heads and ten horns.

And the woman was arrayed in purple and scarlet color, and decked with gold and precious stones and pearls, having a golden cup in her hand full of abominations and filthiness of her fornication:

And upon her forehead was a name written, MYSTERY, BABYLON THE GREAT, THE MOTHER OF HARLOTS AND ABOMINATIONS OF THE EARTH.

And I saw the woman drunken with the blood of the saints, and with the blood of the martyrs of Jesus: and when I saw her, I wondered with great admiration.

And the angel said unto me, Wherefore didst thou marvel? I will tell thee the mystery of the woman, and of the beast that carrieth her, which hath the seven heads and ten horns.

The beast that thou sawest was, and is not; and shall ascend out of the bottomless pit, and go into perdition: and they that dwell on the earth shall wonder, whose names were not written in the book of life from the foundation of the world, when they behold the beast that was, and is not, and yet is.

And here is the mind which hath wisdom. The seven heads are seven mountains, on which the woman sitteth.

And there are seven kings: five are fallen, and one is, and the other is not yet come; and when he cometh, he must continue a short space.

And the beast that was, and is not, even he is the eighth, and is of the seven, and goeth into perdition.

And the ten horns which thou sawest are ten kings, which have received no kingdoms as yet; but receive power as kings one hour with the beast.

These have one mind, and shall give their power and strength unto the beast.

These shall make war with the Lamb, and the Lamb shall overcome them: for he is Lord of lords, and King of kings: and they that are with him are called, and chosen, and faithful.

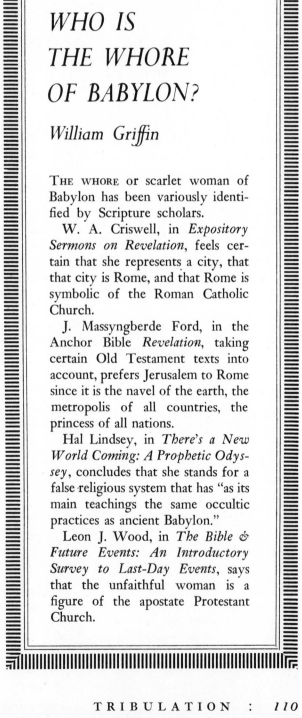

## WHO IS THE WHORE OF BABYLON?

### William Griffin

THE WHORE or scarlet woman of Babylon has been variously identified by Scripture scholars.

W. A. Criswell, in *Expository Sermons on Revelation*, feels certain that she represents a city, that that city is Rome, and that Rome is symbolic of the Roman Catholic Church.

J. Massyngberde Ford, in the Anchor Bible *Revelation*, taking certain Old Testament texts into account, prefers Jerusalem to Rome since it is the navel of the earth, the metropolis of all countries, the princess of all nations.

Hal Lindsey, in *There's a New World Coming: A Prophetic Odyssey*, concludes that she stands for a false religious system that has "as its main teachings the same occultic practices as ancient Babylon."

Leon J. Wood, in *The Bible & Future Events: An Introductory Survey to Last-Day Events*, says that the unfaithful woman is a figure of the apostate Protestant Church.

# SEALS, TRUMPETS, BOWLS

*W. A. Criswell*

THE ACTION of the Book of Revelation begins . . . in Chapter 6. Here begins the word of our goal, our kinsman-redeemer, in whose hands God Almighty has placed the authority of this universe. This is the act of that great, sovereign Lord who takes our forfeited inheritance out of the hands of the usurper, the interloper, the intruder, the stranger, and the alien. This is the act by which, in the judicial proceedings of God, our Lord and Savior takes back out of the hands of Satan our rightful inheritance. This is the casting out of the dynasties of evil. This is the destruction of the powers of darkness and the bringing in of light, life, liberty, and everlasting righteousness. These seven seals encompass all of the story of God from the rapture until the return.

These seven seals include the whole proceedings of the Almightly after God's people are taken out of the earth until they come back with their reigning Lord, given the possession of God's inheritance. The seventh seal is the seven trumpets, and the seventh trumpet is the seven bowls of the seven vials of the wrath and plagues of Almighty God. When they are finished, the seventh seal and the seventh trumpet and the seventh bowl, then is finished the judgment of God upon iniquity, then is the cleansing of this earth, then is the binding of Satan, then is the establishment of the millennium kingdom in which God's children shall reign with Him in the earth.

# THE SEVEN SEALS

## John the Divine (Revelation 5:1)

AND I SAW in the right hand of him that sat on the throne a book written within and on the backside, sealed with seven seals. . . .

## THE SCROLL, THE BOOK, WHAT IS IT?

### Jacques Ellul

WE ARE HERE before the scroll, rolled up, sealed with seven seals, in the hand of God, written on the interior and exterior, and destined for men. In the hand of God, which means that it refers to his action, and since God is "the one seated upon the throne," it is the expression of his sovereignty. Written on the exterior and the interior, which means first of all that it is complete, finished, that nothing can be added, but also that there is a possible exterior reading (relative, and unimportant) but that the interior reading, the meaning of the text, is itself hidden, impossible to obtain without opening the book. It is held out to man. Which means that it is intended for him. This then is not an act of God directed to himself, nor a secret that God wishes to keep; on the contrary, it is a revelation for the one who is Son of God, image of God. The latter addresses himself to his whole creation. The seven seals are probably the seven spirits. In any case they express a radical closure. How can we know what this book is? We proceed by elimination.

On the one hand it is certainly not the Bible (which would be held out to the church, and which, on the other hand, is not a closed book; on the contrary, there is no esoteric comprehension of the Bible: this goes counter to all that the biblical text affirms to us). This is not "the book of creation" (there is no doublet of Genesis here), nor the book of destiny where the life and lot of each would be written: here we encounter a deep-rooted error. Biblically and through the God of Jesus Christ there is no destiny. Precisely, the work of the liberator is to abolish destiny. Further, this is not a book that concerns Jesus Christ himself: we do not have in this part of the Apocalypse a doublet of the gospels. Finally, this is not the book of the church (the question of the church has been raised in the preceding part) or the book where the names of the saved are written: we are told not that we are in the presence of a list of names, but of a text. And moreover, that would not correspond at all to the events launched by the breaking of the seals. It can only be the book of that which man is called by his Father to be, to do, and to become (this is why it is held out to all men). But there is also an action of man which launches and provokes an action of God, a work of God. This man is both the heir of God and engaged in a process by which he becomes himself, which is to say, a history. This book appears then as both the book of man and of the history of man.

# THE
# FIRST SEAL

*John the Divine*
*(Revelation 6:1–2)*

AND I SAW in the right hand of him that sat on the throne a book written within and on the backside, sealed with seven seals. . . .

And I saw when the Lamb opened one of the seals, and I heard, as it were the noise of thunder, one of the four beasts saying, Come and see.

And I saw, and behold a white horse: and he that sat on him had a bow; and a crown was given unto him: and he went forth conquering, and to conquer.

# THE
# SECOND SEAL

*John the Divine*
*(Revelation 6:3–4)*

AND WHEN he had opened the second seal, I heard the second beast say, Come and see.

And there went out another horse that was red: and power was given to him that sat thereon to take peace from the earth, and that they should kill one another: and there was given unto him a great sword.

# THE THIRD SEAL

*John the Divine
(Revelation 6:5–6)*

AND WHEN he had opened the third seal, I heard the third beast say, Come and see. And I beheld, and lo a black horse; and he that sat on him had a pair of balances in his hand.

And I heard a voice in the midst of the four beasts say, A measure of wheat for a penny, and three measures of barley for a penny; and see thou hurt not the oil and the wine.

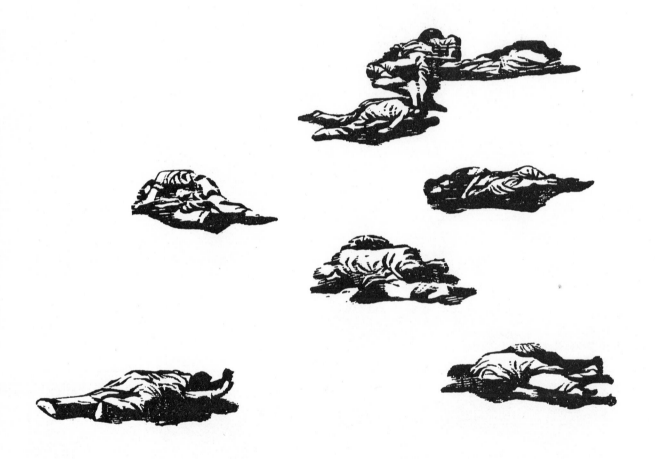

# THE FOURTH SEAL

*John the Divine
(Revelation 6:7–8)*

AND WHEN he had opened the fourth seal, I heard the voice of the fourth beast say, Come and see.

And I looked, and behold a pale horse: and his name that sat on him was Death, and Hell followed with him. And power was given unto them over the fourth part of the earth, to kill with sword, and with hunger, and with death, and with the beasts of the earth.

# THE FIFTH SEAL

*John the Divine*
*(Revelation 6:9–11)*

AND WHEN he had opened the fifth seal, I saw under the altar the souls of them that were slain for the word of God, and for the testimony which they held:

And they cried with a loud voice, saying, How long, O Lord, holy and true, dost thou not judge and avenge our blood on them that dwell on the earth?

And white robes were given unto every one of them; and it was said unto them, that they should rest yet for a little season, until their fellow servants also and their brethren, that should be killed as they were, should be fulfilled.

## THEIR MURDERERS STILL LIVE

*W. A. Criswell*

WHO ARE these martyrs whose souls John sees under the altar of heaven? As they cry to God they say, "O Lord, how long dost thou not judge and avenge our blood on them that dwell on the earth?" So, these martyrs are a special group and their murderers still live on the earth. . . . These are the martyrs who have lost their lives under those first four seals, in the first half of the Tribulation. The other martyrs of the Tribulation, in the last half, are referred to when God says to these, "You rest for a while until these other martyrs that are to be slain are slain," that is, those who are to be slain in the last half of the Tribulation. At the end of the Tribulation and at the beginning of the millennium, in Revelation 20:4, we shall find all of the martyrs standing in the presence of God and preparing to enter that millennium kingdom where they reign with the Lord for a thousand years. So, these are they who have lost their lives under those terrible blood baths of the opening of the first four seals.

# THE INTERMEDIATE STATE

## John Henry Newman

SOME MEN WILL SAY that this is all figurative, and means merely that the blood of the martyrs, crying now for vengeance, will be requited on their murderers at the last day. I cannot persuade myself thus to dismiss so solemn a passage. It seems a presumption to say of dim notices about the unseen world, "they only mean this or that," as if one had ascended into the third heaven, or had stood before the throne of God. No; I see herein a deep mystery, a hidden truth, which I cannot handle or define, shining "as jewels at the bottom of the great deep," darkly and tremulously, yet really there. And for this very reason, while it is neither pious nor thankful to explain away the words which convey it, while it is a duty to use them, not less a duty is it to use them humbly, diffidently, and teachably, with the thought of God before us, and of our own nothingness. . . .

Now first in this passage [Revelation 6:9–11] we are told that the saints are *at rest*. "White robes were given unto every one of them." "It was said unto them that they should *rest* yet for a little season." This is expressed still more strongly in a later passage of the same book: "Blessed are the dead which die in the Lord *from henceforth*. Yea, saith the Spirit, that they *may rest from their labours*." Again, St. Paul had a desire "to depart and *to be with Christ*, which (he adds) is far better." And our Lord told the penitent robber, "Today shalt thou be with Me in *paradise*." And in the parable He represents Lazarus as being "*in Abraham's bosom*"; a place of rest surely, if words can describe one. . . .

Next, in this description is implied, what I have in fact already deduced from it, that departed saints, though at rest, have not yet received their actual reward. "Their works do follow with them," not yet given in to their Savior and Judge. They are in an incomplete state in every way, and will be so till the Day of Judgment, which will introduce them to the joy of their Lord. . . .

Lastly, it is the manner of Scripture to imply that all saints make up but one body, Christ being the Head, and no real distinction existing between dead and living; as if the church's territory were a vast field, only with a veil stretched across it, hiding part from us. This at least, I think, will be the impression left on the mind after a careful study of the inspired writers. St. Paul says, "I bow my knees unto the Father of our Lord Jesus Christ, of whom the *whole* family in heaven and earth is named," where "heaven" would seem to include paradise. Presently he declares that there is but "one body," not two, as there is but one Spirit. In another epistle he speaks of Christians in the flesh being "come to the heavenly Jerusalem, and the spirits of just men made perfect." Agreeably to this doctrine, the collect for All Saints' Day teaches us that "Almighty God has knit together His elect" (that is, both living and dead), "in *one* communion and fellowship in the mystical body of His Son."

This, then, on the whole, we may humbly believe to be the condition of the saints before the Resurrection, a state of repose, rest, security; but again a state more like paradise than heaven—that is, a state which comes short of the glory which shall be revealed in us after the Resurrection, a state of waiting, meditation, hope, in which what has been sown on earth may be matured and completed.

---

# SOULS UNDER THE ALTAR

## J. Massyngberde Ford

THE IDEA of souls under the altar is . . . a Jewish, not a Christian, concept. Rabbi Akiba is reputed to have said that whoever was buried in the land of Israel was considered as if he were buried under the altar, and "whoever was buried under the altar was just as if he were buried under the throne of glory" (*Aboth, Rabbi Nathan,* 26).

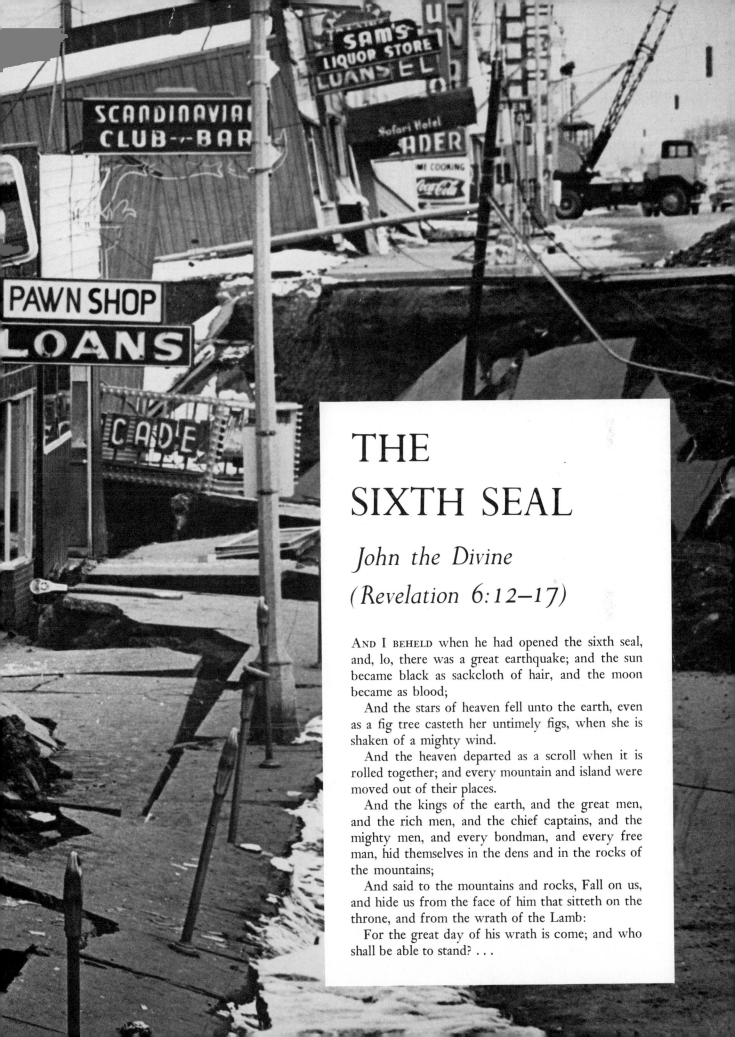

# THE SIXTH SEAL

## John the Divine
## (Revelation 6:12–17)

AND I BEHELD when he had opened the sixth seal, and, lo, there was a great earthquake; and the sun became black as sackcloth of hair, and the moon became as blood;

And the stars of heaven fell unto the earth, even as a fig tree casteth her untimely figs, when she is shaken of a mighty wind.

And the heaven departed as a scroll when it is rolled together; and every mountain and island were moved out of their places.

And the kings of the earth, and the great men, and the rich men, and the chief captains, and the mighty men, and every bondman, and every free man, hid themselves in the dens and in the rocks of the mountains;

And said to the mountains and rocks, Fall on us, and hide us from the face of him that sitteth on the throne, and from the wrath of the Lamb:

For the great day of his wrath is come; and who shall be able to stand? . . .

# THE SEVENTH SEAL

## *John the Divine (Revelation 8:1)*

AND WHEN he had opened the seventh seal, there
was silence in heaven about the space of half an
hour.

# HALF AN HOUR'S SILENCE IN HEAVEN

*Andrew Murray*

THERE WAS *silence in heaven about the space of half an hour*—to bring the prayers of the saints before God, before the first angel sounded his trumpet. And so ten thousands of God's children have felt the absolute need of silence and retirement from the things of earth for half an hour, to present their prayers before God, and in fellowship with Him be strengthened for their daily work.

How often the complaint is heard that there is not time for prayer. And often the confession is made that, even if time could be found, one feels unable to spend the time in real conversation with God. No one need ask what it is that hinders growth in the spiritual life. *The secret of strength can be found only in living contact with God.*

If you would only obey Christ when He says: "When thou hast shut thy door, pray to thy Father which is in secret," and have the courage to be alone with God for half an hour. Do not think, I will not know how to spend the time. Just believe that if you begin and are faithful and bow in silence before God, He will reveal himself to you.

If you need help, read some passage of Scripture, and let God's Word speak to you. Then bow in deepest humility before God and wait on Him. *He will work within you.* Read Psalm 61, 62, or 63, and speak the words out before God. Then begin to pray.

God longs to bless you. Is it not worth the trouble to take half an hour alone with God? In heaven itself there was need for half an hour's silence to present the prayers of the saints before God. If you persevere, you may find that the half hour that seems the most difficult in the whole day may at length become the most blessed in your whole life.

"My soul is silent unto God. . . . My soul, be thou silent unto God; for my expectation is from him" (Psalm 62:1,5).

# AWE AND EXPECTANCY

*W. A. Criswell*

WHY THIS SILENCE in heaven? It is, first, the silence of awe and of intense expectancy. This is the last drama of the ultimate mystery of Almighty God. This is the ultimate seal. We can almost hear the unspoken intensity and expectancy of the hosts of heaven as they say to themselves, "What now will God do and what will be the final disposition of His judicial administration in this rebellious and blasphem-ing world?" It is an intense silence of expectancy. We are told in Chapter 22 of the Book of Acts that Paul stood on the steps of the Tower of Antonio and before a maddening mob clamoring for his life, he raised his hand and spoke unto them in the Hebrew tongue. When he did so, the Bible says, ". . . and there followed a great silence." When Numa was crowned king of Rome, and they came to that august moment when they were to look for the birds by which the gods would foreshow his destiny, the priest put his hand devoutly on the head of the crowned king, and the historian says, "And there reigned among the people an incredible silence." So here, all heaven was mute and motionless with awe.

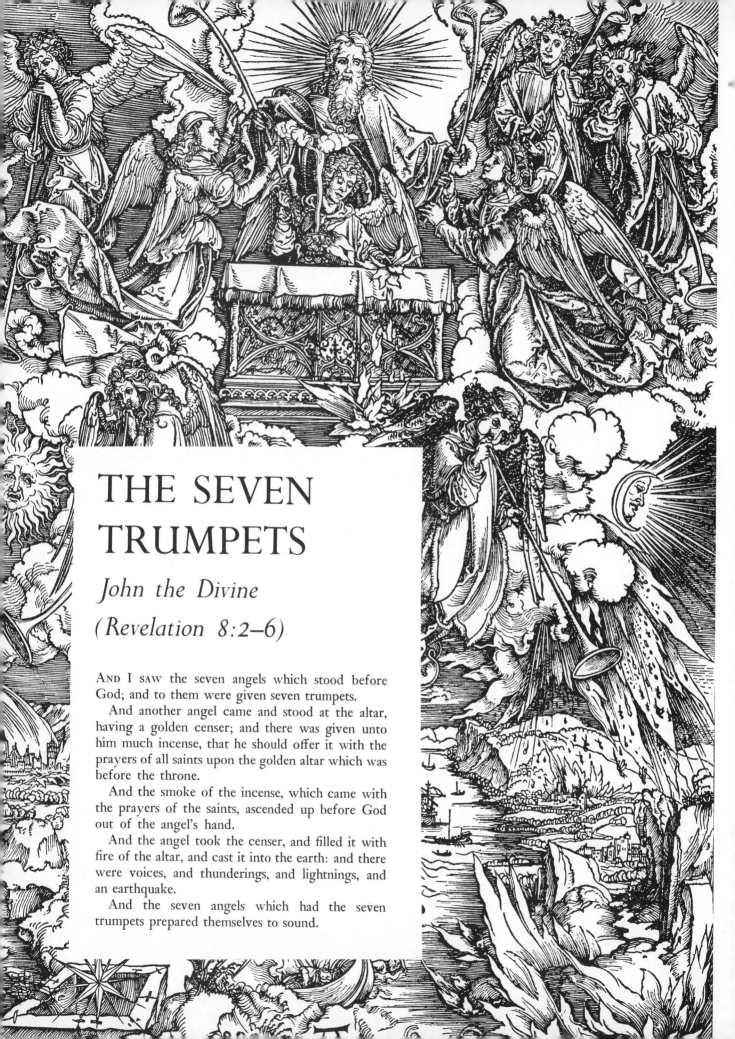

# THE SEVEN TRUMPETS

*John the Divine*

*(Revelation 8:2–6)*

AND I SAW the seven angels which stood before God; and to them were given seven trumpets.

And another angel came and stood at the altar, having a golden censer; and there was given unto him much incense, that he should offer it with the prayers of all saints upon the golden altar which was before the throne.

And the smoke of the incense, which came with the prayers of the saints, ascended up before God out of the angel's hand.

And the angel took the censer, and filled it with fire of the altar, and cast it into the earth: and there were voices, and thunderings, and lightnings, and an earthquake.

And the seven angels which had the seven trumpets prepared themselves to sound.

# THE FIRST
# TRUMPET

*John the Divine*
*(Revelation 8:7)*

THE FIRST ANGEL sounded, and there followed hail and fire mingled with blood, and they were cast upon the earth: and the third part of trees was burnt up, and all green grass was burnt up.

# THE SECOND TRUMPET

## John the Divine
## (Revelation 8:8–9)

AND THE SECOND ANGEL sounded, and as it were a
great mountain burning with fire was cast into the
sea: and the third part of the sea became blood;

And the third part of the creatures which were
in the sea, and had life, died; and the third part of
the ships were destroyed.

# THE THIRD TRUMPET

*John the Divine*
*(Revelation 8:10–11)*

AND THE THIRD ANGEL sounded, and there fell a great
star from heaven, burning as it were a lamp, and it
fell upon the third part of the rivers, and upon the
fountains of waters;

And the name of the star is called Wormwood:
and the third part of the waters became wormwood;
and many men died of the waters, because they
were made bitter.

# THE FOURTH TRUMPET

## *John the Divine (Revelation 8:12)*

AND THE FOURTH ANGEL sounded, and the third part of the sun was smitten, and the third part of the moon, and the third part of the stars; so as the third part of them was darkened, and the day shone not for a third part of it, and night likewise.

And I beheld, and heard an angel flying through the midst of heaven, saying with a loud voice, Woe, woe, woe, to the inhabiters of the earth by reason of the other voices of the trumpet of the three angels, which are yet to sound!

# THE FIFTH TRUMPET

## *John the Divine (Revelation 9:1-3, 9-10)*

AND THE FIFTH ANGEL sounded, and I saw a star fall from heaven unto the earth: and to him was given the key of the bottomless pit.

And he opened the bottomless pit; and there arose a smoke out of the pit, as the smoke of a great furnace; and the sun and the air were darkened by reason of the smoke of the pit.

And there came out of the smoke locusts upon the earth: and unto them was given power, as the scorpions of the earth have power.

And it was commanded them that they should not hurt the grass of the earth, neither any green thing, neither any tree; but only those men which have not the seal of God in their foreheads.

And to them it was given that they should not kill them, but that they should be tormented five months: and their torment was as the torment of a scorpion, when he striketh a man.

And in those days shall men seek death, and shall not find it; and shall desire to die, and death shall flee from them.

And the shapes of the locusts were like unto horses prepared unto battle; and on their heads were as it were crowns like gold, and their faces were as the faces of men.

And they had hair as the hair of women, and their teeth were as the teeth of lions.

And they had breastplates, as it were breastplates of iron; and the sound of their wings was as the sound of chariots of many horses running to battle.

And they had tails like unto scorpions, and there were stings in their tails: and their power was to hurt men five months.

And they had a king over them, which is the angel of the bottomless pit, whose name in the Hebrew is Abaddon, but in the Greek tongue hath his name Apollyon.

One woe is past; and, behold, there come two woes more hereafter.

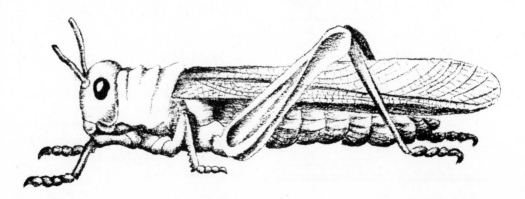

# THE SIXTH TRUMPET

## John the Divine
## (Revelation 9:13–11:14)

AND THE SIXTH ANGEL sounded, and I heard a voice from the four horns of the golden altar which is before God,

Saying to the sixth angel which had the trumpet, Loose the four angels which are bound in the great Euphrates.

And the four angels were loosed, which were prepared for an hour, and a day, and a month, and a year, for to slay the third part of men.

And the number of the army of the horsemen were two hundred thousand thousand: and I heard the number of them.

And thus I saw the horses in the vision, and them that sat on them, having breastplates of fire, and of jacinth, and brimstone: and the heads of the horses were as the heads of lions; and out of their mouths issued fire and smoke and brimstone.

By these three was the third part of men killed, by the fire, and by the smoke, and by the brimstone, which issued out of their mouths.

For their power is in their mouth, and in their tails: for their tails *were* like unto serpents, and had heads, and with them they do hurt.

And the rest of the men which were not killed by these plagues yet repented not of the works of their hands, that they should not worship devils, and idols of gold, and silver, and brass, and stone, and of wood: which neither can see, nor hear, nor walk:

Neither repented they of their murderers, nor of their sorceries, nor of their fornication, nor of their thefts.

And I saw another almighty angel come down from heaven, clothed with a cloud: and a rainbow was upon his head, and his face was as it were the sun, and his feet as pillars of fire:

And he had in his hand a little book open: and he set his right foot upon the sea, and his left foot on the earth.

And cried with a loud voice, as when a lion roareth: and when he had cried, seven thunders uttered their voices.

And when the seven thunders had uttered their voices, I was about to write: and I heard a voice from heaven saying unto me, Seal up those things which the seven thunders uttered, and write them not.

And the angel which I saw stand upon the sea and upon the earth lifted up his hand to heaven,

And sware by him that liveth for ever and ever, who created heaven and the things that therein are, and the earth, and the things that therein are, and the sea, and the things which are therein, that there should be time no longer:

But in the days of the voice of the seventh angel, when he shall begin to sound, the mystery of God should be finished, as he hath declared to his servants the prophets.

And the voice which I heard from heaven spake unto me again, and said, Go and take the little book which is open in the hand of the angel which standeth upon the sea and upon the earth.

And I went unto the angel, and said unto him, Give me the little book. And he said unto me, Take it, and eat it up; and it shall make thy belly bitter, but it shall be in thy mouth sweet as honey.

And I took the little book out of the angel's hand, and ate it up; and it was in my mouth sweet as honey: and as soon as I had eaten it, my belly was bitter.

And he said unto me, Thou must prophesy again before many peoples, and nations, and tongues, and kings.

And there was given me a reed like unto a rod: and the angel stood, saying, Rise, and measure the temple of God, and the altar, and them that worship therein.

But the court which is without the temple leave out, and measure it not; for it is given unto the Gentiles: and the holy city shall they tread under foot forty and two months.

And I will give power unto my witnesses, and they shall prophesy a thousand two hundred and three-score days, clothed in sackcloth.

These are the two olive trees, and the two candlesticks standing before the God of the earth.

And if any man will hurt them, fire proceedeth out of their mouth, and devoureth their enemies: and if any man will hurt them, he must in this manner be killed.

These have power to shut heaven, that it rain not in the days of their prophecy: and have power over waters to turn them to blood, and to smite the earth with all plagues, as often as they will.

And when they shall have finished their testimony, the beast that ascendeth out of the bottomless pit shall make war against them, and shall overcome them, and kill them.

And their dead bodies shall lie in the street of the great city, which spiritually is called Sodom and Egypt, where also our Lord was crucified.

And they of the people and kindreds and tongues and nations shall see their dead bodies three days and a half, and shall not suffer their dead bodies to be put in graves.

And they that dwell upon the earth shall rejoice over them, and make merry, and shall send gifts one to another; because these two prophets tormented them that dwelt on the earth.

And after three days and a half the Spirit of life from God entered into them, and they stood upon their feet; and great fear fell upon them which saw them.

And they heard a great voice from heaven saying unto them, Come up hither. And they ascended up to heaven in a cloud; and their enemies beheld them.

And the same hour was there a great earthquake, and the tenth part of the city fell, and in the earthquake were slain of men seven thousand: and the remnants were affrighted, and gave glory to the God of heaven.

The second woe is past; *and*, behold, the third woe cometh quickly.

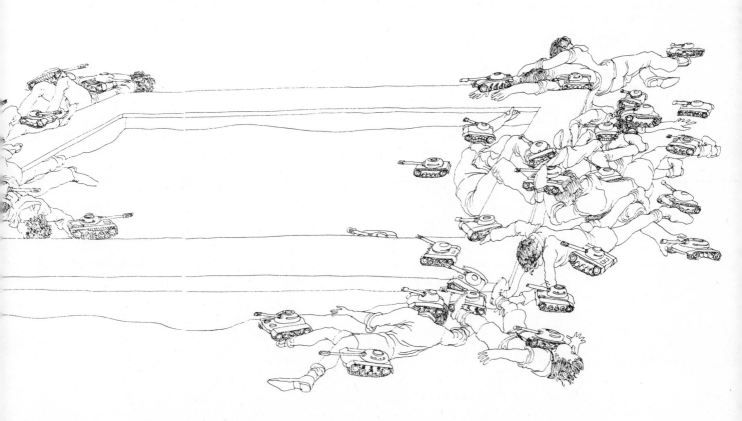

# THE SEVENTH TRUMPET

## *John the Divine*
## *(Revelation 11:15–19)*

AND THE SEVENTH ANGEL sounded; and there were great voices in heaven saying, The kingdoms of this world are become the kingdoms of our Lord, and of his Christ; and he shall reign for ever and ever.

And the four and twenty elders, which sat before God on their seats, fell upon their faces, and worshiped God,

Saying, We give thee thanks, O Lord God Almighty, which art, and wast, and art to come; because thou hast taken to thee thy great power, and hast reigned.

And the nations were angry, and thy wrath is come, and the time of the dead, that they should be judged, and that thou shouldest give reward unto thy servants the prophets, and to the saints, and them that fear thy name, small and great; and shouldest destroy them which destroy the earth.

And the temple of God was open in heaven, and there was seen in his temple the ark of his testament: and there were lightnings, and voices, and thunderings, and an earthquake, and great hail.

# THE SEVEN
# VIALS OF WRATH

## *John the Divine*
## *(Revelation 16:1)*

AND I HEARD a great voice out of the temple saying
to the seven angels, Go your ways, and pour out the
vials of the wrath of God upon the earth.

## *ENIGMAS OR SYMBOLS*

### *Jacques Ellul*

IT IS UNNECESSARY to say, on the one hand, that the seer does not at all claim to describe thereby, photographically, what will be, nor, on the other hand, is it necessary to study plague by plague "what it is" (what does he mean when he speaks of "hail-stones"? etc.): rather, we must recall that the Apocalypse does not proceed by enigmas but by symbols. He does not propose to use either riddles or charades. It matters little if the sore is cancer or leprosy, if the scorching that is greater than the sun is the atomic bomb, and if the frogs are venomous or if they represent modern music. This kind of research has no meaning. By contrast, we must repeat that the evident allusion to the plagues of Egypt is essential (there are here six plagues out of ten that are identical to those that had struck

Egypt): the meaning is the same; it is the "putting against the wall" before the liberation, the harsh appeal to listen, spoken by God in order that man be converted, and the refusal to be converted, which provokes the annihilation of that which chains, shackles, enslaves, alienates, and reifies the elect people: but now the elect people is all of humanity. Therefore the issue has changed: in Egypt God threatened Pharaoh and his people in order to win the liberation of Israel. In this first time of judgment God drives humanity into a corner in order that the latter might herself be set free from that which alienates (since the people of God is humanity). And both times there is failure; which is to say that the call of God addressed to man by means of threats and plagues, by misery and suffering, in order that man act of himself and freely, make his decision in the presence of the decision of God, understand that it is surely a matter of a decision of God and enter by himself into this design, make himself the final decision—then for Pharaoh the free and autonomous decision to let the Hebrew people depart—this decision is not made and the call of God is not heard.

# THE FIRST VIAL

*John the Divine*
*(Revelation 16:2)*

AND THE FIRST WENT, and poured out his vial upon the earth; and there fell a noisome and grievous sore upon the men which had the mark of the beast, and upon them which worshiped his image.

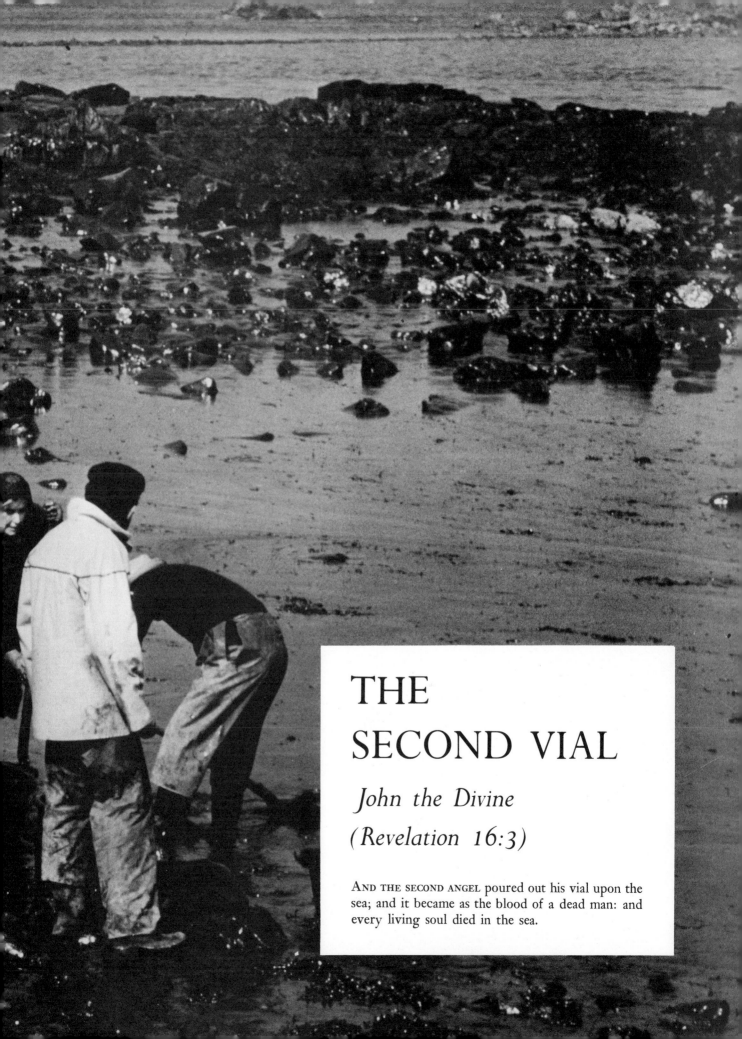

# THE
# SECOND VIAL

*John the Divine
(Revelation 16:3)*

AND THE SECOND ANGEL poured out his vial upon the
sea; and it became as the blood of a dead man: and
every living soul died in the sea.

# THE THIRD VIAL

*John the Divine*

*(Revelation 16:4–7)*

AND THE THIRD ANGEL poured out his vial upon the rivers and fountains of waters; and they became blood.

And I heard the angel of the waters say, Thou art righteous, O Lord, which art, wast, and shalt be, because thou hast judged thus.

For they have shed the blood of saints and prophets, and thou hast given them blood to drink; for they are worthy.

And I heard another out of the altar say, Even so, Lord God Almighty, true and righteous are thy judgments.

# THE FOURTH VIAL

*John the Divine*

*(Revelation 16:8–9)*

AND THE FOURTH ANGEL poured out his vial upon the sun; and power was given unto him to scorch men with fire.

And men were scorched with great heat, and blasphemed the name of God, which hath power over these plagues: and they repented not to give him glory.

# THE FIFTH VIAL

## John the Divine (Revelation 16:10–11)

AND THE FIFTH ANGEL poured out his vial upon the seat of the beast; and his kingdom was full of darkness; and they gnawed their tongues for pain,

And blasphemed the God of heaven because of their pains and their sores, and repented not of their deeds.

# THE SIXTH VIAL

## John the Divine (Revelation 16:12–16)

AND THE SIXTH ANGEL poured out his vial upon the great river Euphrates; and the water thereof was dried up, that the way of the kings of the east might be prepared.

And I saw three unclean spirits like frogs come out of the mouth of the dragon, and out of the mouth of the beast, and out of the mouth of the false prophet.

For they are the spirits of devils, working miracles, which go forth unto the kings of the earth and of the whole world, to gather them to the battle of that great day of God Almighty.

Behold, I come as a thief. Blessed is he that watcheth, and keepeth his garments, lest he walk naked, and they see his shame.

And he gathered them together into a place called in the Hebrew tongue Armageddon.

## BLOODBATH AT ARMAGEDDON

### David Wilkerson

THE SIXTH JUDGMENT describes how the blood will flow in Armageddon. This planet's last and most devastating battle will cause death and destruction so complete that the blood from dead armies will flow bridle-deep in an area two hundred miles long. Although soldiers on horseback may seem strangely archaic in this age of tanks and jeeps, we can still assume a literal cavalry force (Revelation 9:15–16, *The Living Bible*), similar to those shown in recent films released by Chinese Communists. Israel, the Arab nations, and the Soviet Union also have large horse cavalry units (Revelation 14:18–20, *The Living Bible*), which may be employed during the battle or Armageddon. One thing is certain. The Bible predicts a bloodbath at Armageddon.

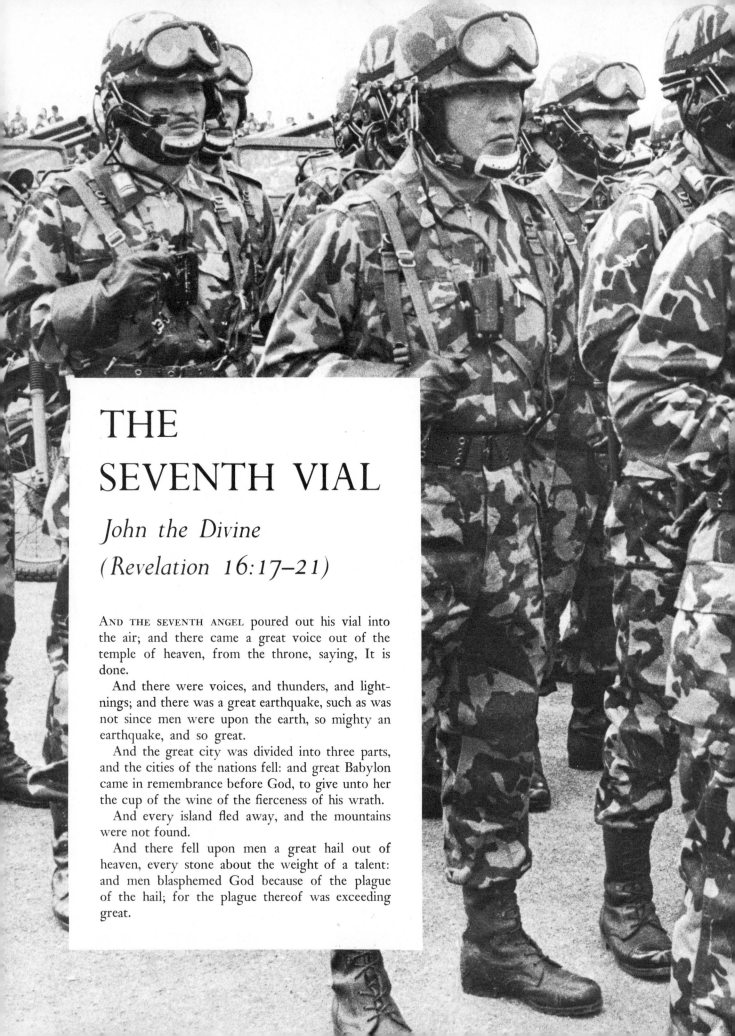

# THE SEVENTH VIAL

*John the Divine
(Revelation 16:17–21)*

AND THE SEVENTH ANGEL poured out his vial into the air; and there came a great voice out of the temple of heaven, from the throne, saying, It is done.

And there were voices, and thunders, and lightnings; and there was a great earthquake, such as was not since men were upon the earth, so mighty an earthquake, and so great.

And the great city was divided into three parts, and the cities of the nations fell: and great Babylon came in remembrance before God, to give unto her the cup of the wine of the fierceness of his wrath.

And every island fled away, and the mountains were not found.

And there fell upon men a great hail out of heaven, every stone about the weight of a talent: and men blasphemed God because of the plague of the hail; for the plague thereof was exceeding great.

# ARMAGEDDON I
# IS WORLD WAR III

## John Wesley White

"YOU WILL HEAR of wars and rumors of wars. . . . Nation will rise against nation, and kingdom against kingdom." So Jesus replied to His disciples' question: "What will be the sign of your coming and of the end of the age?" (Matthew 24:3, 6–7). Continuing His answer to the apostle John a half-century later, Jesus enlarged on how human warmongering would escalate into worldwide war incited by the "spirits of demons performing miraculous signs," driving blindly the heads of state "of the whole world, to gather them for the battle on the great day of God Almighty . . . to the place that in Hebrew is called Armageddon" (Revelation 16:14, 16). That will indeed be World War III. World War I was fought in Western Europe. World War II enveloped three of the world's five continents and three of its five oceans. Armageddon will involve the nations "of the whole world," and as such will indeed be World War III. Its inciter and villain will be the Son of Perdition from hell, the Antichrist; its Savior and Victor will be the Son of God from heaven, Jesus Christ.

# V.

# MILLEN

NIUM

# THE KINGDOM SOCIETY

*Billy Graham*

PRESIDENT JOHNSON'S ADDRESS to the students at the University of Kentucky some time ago is still being quoted. The president warned the young people that to build a Great Society will take years of sacrifice.

He said, "If you wish a sheltered and uneventful life, you are living in the wrong generation. No one can promise you calm or ease or undisturbed comfort. But we can promise you this: we can promise enormous challenge and arduous struggle, hard labor and great danger."

During the last few years various presidents have had slogans to dramatize their philosophy of government. Franklin Roosevelt had the New Deal, Harry Truman had the Fair Deal, John Kennedy had the New Frontier, and now President Johnson has the Great Society.

Jesus Christ also had slogans. For example, He said, "Blessed are the poor in spirit: for theirs is the kingdom of heaven" (Matthew 5:3). This was one of the many slogans that He used to announce His "great society," which is the Kingdom Society.

A society has been defined as "a group living together under the same environment and regarded as constituting a homogeneous unit or entity." Though our American society possibly more nearly approximates this definition than any group of people in the world, we in America are still racked at this hour with painful divisions, deep hatreds, gross misunderstandings, and great social injustices.

Though the Great Society may be a noble objective, we have a great distance to go before we even come close to living up to that name.

The Great Society ideal is not new. Plato formulated his *Republic*, Sir Thomas More his *Utopia*, Karl Marx devised his Classless Society, and many others have made attempts to form the ideal society. But while the motivation may have been good, past attempts to create the "great society" have failed miserably.

Clouding the development of the Great Society today are such specters as Vietnam, the Congo, China—not to mention our own trouble spots of internal anguish in North and South.

President Johnson's goal of the Great Society is certainly an admirable one. We all long for a better world, for a better kind of man, for a lasting peace. But history does not offer much hope. Human nature has always stood in the way.

All previous efforts have failed; and there is no valid reason to believe that this effort will succeed, in spite of good intentions. Historians are already speaking of our time as the post-Christian era. Many of our Western leaders go along with the Communists in believing that Christ and the church are irrelevant to these times.

Every year there is a wider gap between our national ideals and Christian morality. In talking of equality we have forgotten the importance of quality, and no nation can rise higher than the average moral quality of its individual citizens.

When Jesus was upon the earth He talked not of a "great society" but of the Kingdom Society. Rome, when Jesus lived on earth, was a prosperous, growing empire. It possessed a military, artistic, and ethical superiority over other nations and was equipped intellectually and militarily to hold the place as the world's number-one power.

But Jesus saw the whole structure of the Roman Empire as something fleeting and temporary. He looked at the great buildings in Jerusalem and said, "Seest thou these great buildings? there shall not be left one stone upon another, that shall not be thrown down" (Mark 13:2).

He talked of the world He lived in, with its armed might, its great edifices and institutions—the world that the Romans doubtless thought of as the "great society"—as something soon to crumble. He spoke of the seeds of war—hate, lust, and greed. He talked of the end of the existing world of that day.

The Roman world did end, the empire did fall, and Caesar's "great society" disintegrated. But Christ's Kingdom Society will endure forever. It will endure because the Kingdom Society is not built on a false promise.

How does the Kingdom Society differ from all other societies that men devise today?

*First*, conversion is a requirement of citizenship. The kingdoms of this world do not require spiritual conversion. Any religion will do; the philosophy of this world is, "It doesn't matter what you believe just so you are sincere." But Jesus Christ said, "Except ye be converted . . . ye shall not enter the kingdom of heaven" (Matthew 18:3).

The world says that all we need to do is be

decent, respectable, and reasonable. True, that is all one needs to do to be a member of the Great Society, but to be a member of the Kingdom of God there must be an inner change.

A Communist in Hyde Park, London, pointed to a tramp and said, "Communism will put a new suit on that man."

A Christian standing nearby said, "Yes, but Christ will put a new man in that suit!"

In the Kingdom Society, men are transformed from the inside out by the power of God. Paul said, "If any man be in Christ, he is a new creature: old things are passed away; behold, all things are become new" (2 Corinthians 5:17).

The Kingdom Society will endure because it is composed of men who have enduring character. "[God] hath delivered us from the power of darkness, and hath translated us into the kingdom of his dear Son: in whom we have redemption through his blood, even the forgiveness of sins," wrote the apostle Paul to the Colossians (1:13, 14).

God demands a righteousness which is apart from the law and apart from our own efforts. Jesus said, "Except your righteousness shall exceed the righteousness of the scribes and Pharisees, ye shall

in no case enter into the kingdom of heaven" (Matthew 5:20).

Fallible men cannot create an infallible society. You can't produce a Great Society with men who hate, connive, take advantage, pillage, and overrun, with self-interest as the motivation. National greed and selfishness are the corporate expression of self-interest, and Jesus predicted that it would still exist in the last agonizing days of man's world.

He said, "For nation shall rise against nation, and kingdom against kingdom . . . and then shall many be offended, and shall betray one another, and shall hate one another" (Matthew 24:7, 10).

This self-interest must be eliminated by the transforming power of Christ if we are to be a part of the Kingdom Society. And Jesus made it an inescapable imperative when He said to Nicodemus, "Except a man be born again, he cannot see the kingdom of God" (John 3:3).

Yes, conversion is a requirement for membership in the Kingdom Society that Jesus talked about.

*Second*, the Kingdom Society is built upon love rather than hate. Hate is necessary in a world of war. Millions of dollars are spent generating sufficient hate to keep the world in a mood of war.

The way of the world is tyranny, war, and chaos.

But in the Kingdom Society, love is the dominant ethic. It was love which sent Christ to the cross. "The good shepherd giveth his life for the sheep" (John 10:11).

It was love which inspired these words of Jesus: "Ye have heard that it hath been said, Thou shalt love thy neighbor, and hate thine enemy. But I say unto you, Love your enemies, bless them that curse you, do good to them that hate you, and pray for them which despitefully use you and persecute you; that ye may be the children of your Father which is in heaven" (Matthew 5:43-45). He instilled the spirit of Christian love in His followers so that they lived without malice and died without rancor.

When H. G. Wells summed up the influence of Jesus in history, he said, "Is it any wonder that this Galilean is too much for our small hearts?" And yet the heart of man, though small, is big enough for Christ to live in if man will only make room for Him.

The love that Christ talked about can only be given to us by God. It is one of the fruits of the Spirit (Galatians 5:22). When you come to Jesus Christ and accept Him as your Lord and Savior, He gives you a supernatural love that allows you to love your enemy whom you normally would not love. This is the answer to the race problem. This is the answer to the many other problems that face the world today.

When you come to Jesus Christ, He transforms you. Your past is forgiven. You receive a power to love men, beyond your natural ability to love.

*Third*, the Kingdom Society is not built on the profit motive. The verb of the world is "get." The verb of the Christian is "give." Self-interest is basic in the Great Society. Everyone asks, "What's in it for me?" In a world founded on materialism this is natural and normal.

But in the Kingdom Society, self-interest is not basic—selflessness is. The Founder, Jesus Christ, was rich, and yet He became poor that we "through his poverty might be rich" (2 Corinthians 8:9). His disciples followed Him, and it was said of them, "Neither said any of them that aught of the things which he possessed was his own" (Acts 4:32). Peter, rich in heavenly goods but poor in worldly goods, said to the lame man on the temple steps, "Silver and gold have I none; but such as I have give I thee" (Acts 3:6). The apostles realized that there is no permanent value in worldly goods, and cherished the abiding values of the Spirit. They lived with eternity in view.

Today in what we call the society of the world, we hold spiritual things in contempt and lust after the things of this world. Little wonder that the world is in a state of turmoil! Mammon is worshiped, and God is disdained. Pleasure takes precedence over purity, and gain has priority over God.

But in the Kingdom Society he that is greatest among you is the servant of all (see Matthew 23:11). Service to God and mankind are put above self-interest. Jesus said, "Greater love hath no man than this, that a man lay down his life for his friends" (John 15:13). These are the ideals of the Kingdom Society.

*Fourth*, the form of government in the Kingdom Society is unique. It is not a democracy where the people govern, but a Christocracy where Christ is the supreme Authority. In a government of unredeemed men, democracy is the only fair and equitable system. But no democracy can ever be better than the people who make it up. When men are selfishly motivated, the government will be inequitable. When men are dishonest, the government will be rigged and contrived. When everyone wants his own way, someone is going to get hurt.

But in the Kingdom Society, Christ is King. He is compassionate, fair, merciful, and just. When He is sovereign in men's hearts, anguish turns to peace, hatred is transformed into love, and misunderstanding into understanding.

And *fifth*, the Kingdom Society is lasting. The history of man has been a continuous series of half successes and total failures. Prosperity exists for a time, only to be followed by war and depression. Twenty-six civilizations have come and gone, and man still battles with the same problems, over and over again.

But the Kingdom Society will abide forever. The fluctuations of time, the swinging of the pendulum from war to peace, from starvation to plenty, from chaos to order, will end forever. The Bible says, "And of his kingdom there shall be no end" (Luke 1:33). And Christ's subjects will be transformed into His image and they shall be like Him. "Beloved, now are we the sons of God, and it doth not yet appear what we shall be: but we know that, when he shall appear, we shall be like him for we shall see him as he is" (1 John 3:2).

How do you get into the Kingdom Society? Jesus said, "You must be born again" (John 3:7). "Not of blood, nor of the will of the flesh, nor of the will of man, but of God" (John 1:13). And, "As many as received him, to them gave he power to become the sons of God, even to them that believe on his name" (John 1:12).

Christ is saying to those who are on the outside, "Him that cometh to me I will in no wise cast out" (John 6:37). His hand, His heart, is extended to all

who will repent of their sins and accept Him as Savior.

"What if I don't?" you ask. The alternatives are fearful. "And many of them that sleep in the dust of the earth shall awake, some to everlasting life, and some to shame and everlasting contempt," said Daniel (12:2).

Great societies have come and gone. That is what is wrong with them—they are transient. But you may be a member of the Kingdom Society—the Kingdom of the redeemed. God is our Father; Jesus Christ is our older Brother; the Holy Spirit is our abiding, guiding Comforter and Teacher; and the devil is no relation at all.

Today you may join the aristocracy of heaven. You may be a legal, loyal son through Jesus Christ. And I bear this news to you upon the authority and under the seal of the King Himself.

Receive Christ as your Savior. Be converted today and join the Kingdom Society. March under the flag of Jesus Christ. Sing His song. Commit your life to Him, and find fulfillment in Jesus Christ.

# MILLENNIAL MANAGEMENT POSITIONS AVAILABLE

## George Otis

THERE WILL BE high "management" openings for can-do Christians during millennial civilization. Jesus is now silently recruiting those demonstrating capability as overcomers. He needs saints who develop success patterns in this present real-life testing ground, through their application of his spiritual principles. The Lord has published a valuable "how-to" manual. It's called the Bible! By practicing its spiritual formulas, we can be converted from chronic losers into consistent winners. "That ye would walk worthy of God, who hath called you unto His Kingdom and Glory" (1 Thessalonians 2:12).

Many leaders will be needed to reign over cities, nations, territories, and millennium projects. We are now training for these Kingdom Age assignments. "Let a man so account of us as . . . stewards of the mysteries of God. Moreover, it is required of stewards *that a man be found faithful*" (1 Corinthians 4:1–2).

And don't be surprised when, during the Kingdom Age, we find some little-known Christians reigning in positions of great honor and scope. We may remember some as a "little" people who labored quietly for the Lord.

God marks those who learn to wield spiritual victory weapons. The Bible says, "The weapons of our warfare are not carnal but mighty through God to the pulling down of strongholds." Jesus paid a price that we who believe might be potent on this planet. "They overcame him by the blood of the Lamb, and by the word of their testimony." Neither heavenly prizes nor millennial positions will be given to the fearful and unbelieving. We are designed for such power that the "gates of hell" shall not prevail against us. We are being groomed to assume leadership roles in His universe by learning spiritual disciplines.

Olympic champions must not only have talent but discipline in order to become winners. The prizes for disciplined believers are dazzling. In Revelation is showcased a display of those glittering spiritual trophies. They will soon be awarded to Christians who purpose, during this lifetime, to let the Holy Spirit develop them into overcomers. Here is a partial array of God's prizes for the overcomer:

- "He that overcomes will I give to *eat of the tree of life*, which is in the midst of the paradise of God."

- "He that overcomes will I give to eat of the *hidden manna*."

- "He that overcomes will I give *power over the nations* . . . and I will give him *the morning star*."

- "He that overcomes shall be clothed in *white raiment*."

- "He that overcomes I will *confess his name* before my Father and before His angels."

- "He that overcomes will I *make a pillar* in the temple of My God."

- "He that overcomes will I grant to *sit with me in my throne*, even as I also overcame."

Yes, God is now training His children for victory under the tutelage of the Holy Spirit. Developing overcoming skills requires spiritual understanding and great discipline. It also takes practice in real life situations. We are in mortal combat with unseen forces, and the stakes in this battle are eternal. "We wrestle not against flesh and blood, but against principalities, against the rulers of the darkness of this world, against spiritual wickedness in high places" (Ephesians 6:12).

# SIGNS OF THE KINGDOM

*William Barclay*

THERE ARE SIGNS that the Kingdom is on the way and that the King comes. Let us once again remember our definition—the Kingdom of God is a society upon earth where God's will is as perfectly done as it is in heaven. That is to say, the nearer the world is to doing God's will the nearer is the coming of the King. Sometimes people argue as to whether the world is getting better or worse. There is only one answer to that question. When Oliver Cromwell was arranging his son Richard's education, he said, "I would have him know a little history." And to anyone who knows history the world is getting better. Let us take some examples. More people know, and can know, about Jesus now than ever before. In the first six centuries of the history of the church the New Testament was translated into six different languages; by the end of the first sixteen centuries it had only reached thirty different languages; but in our own day the New Testament exists in whole or in part in no fewer than one thousand one hundred and twenty different languages. The message of Jesus is spreading farther and farther abroad. The way in which people treat each other has improved beyond all knowledge. Seneca was the highest of all the Roman thinkers. He said things so wise and so noble that they would not be out of place in any Christian book. He lived at exactly the same time as Paul. Seneca writes in one of his letters: "We strangle a mad dog; we slaughter a fierce ox; we plunge the knife into a sickly cattle lest they taint the herd; *children who are born weakly and deformed we drown*." In his day that was the natural thing to do; nobody looked on it even as out of place, let alone cruel. We cannot conceive of that happening nowadays. Why? Not because the world is a fully Christian place yet, but because the influence of Jesus has so permeated society that that cannot happen. We have a letter written from a husband who is away on business to his wife. The letter was written in A.D. I. It was dug up in the sands of Egypt and it can still be read just as it was written. It goes like this:

"Hilarion to Alis, his wife, heartiest of greetings, and to my dear Berous and Apollonarion. Know that we are still even now in Alexandria. Do not worry if when all the others return I remain in Alexandria. I beg and beseech you to take care of the little child, and as soon as we receive wages I will send them to you. If—good luck to you—you bear a child, if it is a boy, let it live, *if it is a girl, throw it out*. You told Aphrodisias, Do not forget me. How can I forget you? I beg you therefore not to worry."

It is a queer mixture of tender affection and utter callousness. In Roman times it was the regular thing to expose—that is, to throw away—unwanted children, especially girls. Even a Roman senator could say in the senate, "There is scarcely one of us here who has not ordered one or more of his infant children to be exposed to death." In Rome, when a child was born, the child was laid at the father's feet. If the father picked up the child that meant that he acknowledged the child and the child would be kept; if he refused to pick up the child, the child was exposed and thrown away to die. Once again, we cannot conceive of that happening today. Why? Again, not because the world is wholly Christian, but because the influence of Christianity has so permeated society that these things cannot happen. In Roman times a slave was classed as a living tool. He was a thing and had no rights whatever. Once a slave was carrying a precious goblet of wine to his master; he slipped and the goblet fell and broke. Immediately the master ordered him to be flung living into the fishpond in the centre of the courtyard, where the savage lampreys tore him to pieces. It is impossible to imagine a master treating a servant like that nowadays. Even morally the world is getting better. Demosthenes, one of the great Greeks, wrote this: "We keep prostitutes for pleasure; we keep mistresses for the day-to-day needs of the body; we keep wives for the begetting of children and for the faithful guardianship of our homes." Lax as moral standards are today, we cannot conceive of any man in a public position, as Demosthenes was, laying down a principle like that as the ordinary accepted standard of morality. How can you say that the world is getting better, when so many thousands of people are still refugees with little hope of a real purpose in life or a country in which to live? The answer is simply this—that two thousand years ago the refugee problem would have produced no special reaction, and certainly no feeling of shock. The very fact that the conscience of the nations has been stirred is the proof that they have begun to judge things by the standards and in the light of Christ. The dawn does not break like a lightning flash or a clap of thunder; the flower does not emerge full grown the minute the seed is planted; the harvest does not ripen in a day. It all takes time, for God's ways are not usually the sensational ways. The signs of the Kingdom are there; and for each one of them we should thank God, for each one of them brings the final consummation nearer.

# INTERPRETATIONS OF THE KINGDOM

## Herman A. Hoyt

BECAUSE THEOLOGIANS have approached the subject of the kingdom with differing principles of interpretation, a variety of interpretations have arisen. A survey of nine of these views will be helpful in reaching the biblical view.

1. Before Christ, there were Jews who believed that this kingdom was limited to Israel. Even the apostles were of this mind. This led them to raise the question about the restoration of the kingdom to Israel (Acts 1:6).

2. The phrase "the kingdom of heaven" has caused some to identify the kingdom with heaven, insisting that it concerns the reign of God in heaven. A passage like Matthew 19:23–24 is explained to mean going to heaven now, while Matthew 25:34 refers to the future.

3. By spiritualizing Scripture the church has been understood to be the totality of the kingdom. Passages such as Colossians 1:13 have been used to support this view. Roman Catholicism interpreted the visible hierarchy to be the kingdom, while Reformation theologians pointed to the invisible church.

4. Some theologians were so dominated by the spiritualization principle that they interpreted the rule of God in the heart to be the kingdom. Inasmuch as the new birth results in the impartation of new life, Luke 17:20–21 was cited in proof of this view.

5. To escape the sheer materialistic and carnal explanation of the kingdom, some men gravitated toward high morality and spiritual purpose, and found in Romans 14:17 a text that in their estimation supported this view of the kingdom.

6. Within recent years social organization and overall improvement of mankind offered a welcome explanation of a present kingdom as over against a future eschatological kingdom. The whole ecumenical movement is conditioned by this pattern of reasoning.

7. Some men have dared to charge the Bible writers, and even the Lord Jesus Christ, with delusions of grandeur. They took the text of the Bible literally but asserted that it was absolutely wrong, thus disposing of the whole eschatological system.

8. Barth and Brunner brought to the attention of the Christian public a most fantastic view of the kingdom. They lifted it out of the cycle of time-space events of history and placed it in the realm of eternity which belongs alone to God.

9. The biblical view, taking the Scriptures at face value, is a kingdom established on the earth at the Second Coming of Christ. This was the view of the early church, a view which persisted for the first two and one-half centuries. Not until the time of Augustine did any opposing view gain a proponent of sufficient stature to turn men aside from premillennialism.

# MILLENNIALISM

## *George Eldon Ladd*

THE ONLY PLACE in the Bible that speaks of an actual millennium is the passage in Revelation 20:1–6. Any millennial doctrine must be based upon the most natural exegesis of this passage.

The book of Revelation belongs to the genre of literature called apocalyptic. The first apocalyptic book was the canonical Daniel. This was followed by a large group of imitative apocalypses between 200 B.C. and A.D. 100 such as Enoch, Assumption of Moses, 4 Ezra, and the Apocalypse of Baruch. Two facts emerge from the study of apocalyptic: the apocalypses use highly symbolic language to describe a series of events in history; and the main concern of apocalyptic is the end of the age and the establishment of God's kingdom. Sometimes there is a Messiah, but not always. In the Assumption of Moses, it is God himself who establishes his kingdom. To illustrate: Daniel sees four beasts rise out of the sea which represent a succession of four worldwide empires. Then he sees one like a son of man come to the throne of God, receive a kingdom which he brings to earth to the saints of the Most High (Daniel 2). This is Daniel's way of describing the end of the age and the establishment of God's kingdom.

In the Revelation of John the beast of Chapter 13 is both the Rome of ancient history and an eschatological Antichrist. The first thing to note is that the events of Revelation 20 follow the vision of the Second Coming of Christ, which is pictured in 19:11–16. In this vision the emphasis is altogether on the coming of Christ as the Conqueror. He is pictured as riding on a white horse like a warrior, accompanied by the armies of heaven. He comes as "King of kings and Lord of lords" (Revelation 19:16). He comes to do battle with Antichrist, who has been pictured in Chapters 13 and 17. It is noteworthy that the only weapon mentioned is the sword that proceeds from his mouth. With it he smites the nations (Revelation 19:15). Here is a marvel indeed. He wins his victories by his word alone, which is "living and active, sharper than any two-edged sword" (Hebrews 4:12). He will not win his victory by the use of the military weapons of the world but with his bare word. He will speak and the victory will be his.

# PREMILLENNIALISM

## Herman A. Hoyt

THE LITERAL METHOD of approach to the teaching of the premillennial, dispensational doctrine of the kingdom is absolutely basic. Both friends and enemies of this doctrine freely admit that this is foundational to the doctrine. Walvoord, a clear exponent of premillennialism, asserts,

"Premillennialism is founded principally on interpretation of the Old Testament. If interpreted literally, the Old Testament gives a clear picture of the prophetic expectation of Israel. They confidently anticipated the coming of a Savior and Deliverer, a Messiah who would be Prophet, Priest, and King. They expected that He would deliver them from their enemies and usher in a kingdom of righteousness, peace, and prosperity upon a redeemed earth. . . . The premillennial interpretation offers the only literal fulfillment for the hundreds of verses of prophetic testimony."

Determined foes of this method of interpretation are just as clear in their admissions of the importance of the literal approach to the Scriptures to establish the doctrine of premillennialism. Allis unequivocally admits, "The Old Testament prophecies if literally interpreted cannot be regarded as having been fulfilled or as being capable of fulfillment in this present age." Floyd Hamilton, equally opposed to premillennialism, regretfully concedes the same point:

"Now we must frankly admit that a literal interpretation of the Old Testament prophecies gives us just such a picture of an earthly reign of the Messiah as the premillennialist pictures. That was the kind of a Messianic kingdom that the Jews of the time of Christ were looking for, on the basis of a literal interpretation of the Old Testament."

Where premillennialism prevails it will be observed that it is not only founded on the literal

interpretation of the Scriptures, but that from this point on it proceeds to erect an entire system of theology that incorporates the entire Bible. Beginning with the infallibility of the Scriptures, it reaches out and touches every facet of Christian doctrine. In fact it is the unifying principle that enables the believer to see every aspect of the Christian faith in its proper relation to the whole. Contrary to the charges that have been leveled against premillennialism, it is not based upon a few isolated texts nor even on an arbitrary selection of texts. It is a system of theology comprising the Bible, confronting the problems of the Bible, confining itself to the Bible, and commending hope to a world miserably failing and seized with fear.

Above all, premillennialism provides a philosophy of history that is the best and brightest of all philosophies. It takes into consideration every aspect of reality. It gives consideration to the life that now is and that which is to come (1 Timothy 4:8). It is concerned with the natural and also the spiritual (1 Corinthians 15:46). It recognizes the place of the earthly and also the heavenly (1 Corinthians 15:48). It places a value on life in the present and on the earthly level as well as regarding life on the heavenly plane as worthwhile. It sees the importance of history (Romans 15:4; 1 Corinthians 10:11), and suggests

that we can learn something reliable for application to the present and for expectation in the future.

Premillennialism points to the fact that God is progressively moving through history and directing the course of events to some good end. It is true that through sin humanity has failed. But in spite of that fact the movement of history is forward and upward, and will at last come to a grand consummation in the future under the power of God. We have failed because we turned our faces from God. But we succeed by the power of God in the conquering of disease, the prevention of some wars, the adding of years to the span of life, the elimination of some social and political ills, the conquering of space, and the increase of productiveness of the soil. All this points to that day when within the context of the power and grace of God, and on the earthly level, there will be ushered in the golden age of all civilization.

This sort of philosophy makes sense. It gives meaning to human effort. It provides an atmosphere of optimism to history. It provides the incentive for the exercise of all the aspirations and efforts of mankind to strive for that which is better, realizing that all the true values of life will be preserved and will reach their complete fulfillment in that coming kingdom of our Lord and Savior Jesus Christ.

# AMILLENNIALISM

## Anthony A. Hoekema

A COMMON CRITICISM of amillennial eschatology is that it is too negative, spending its strength primarily in opposing and refuting eschatological systems with which it does not agree. Leaving aside the question of whether this criticism is true or false, I would like at this point to counteract the negativism of some amillennial eschatologies by sketching briefly some positive affirmations made by amillennialist theologians. In this way we shall be able to see amillennial eschatology in its totality, rather than just as a certain interpretation of the millennium of Revelation 20.

This sketch will cover two areas: first, what amillennial eschatology teaches with regard to *inaugurated eschatology*, and, second, what it teaches with reference to *future eschatology*. By *inaugurated eschatology* I mean that aspect of eschatology which is already present now, during the gospel era. The term *inaugurated eschatology* is preferred to *realized eschatology* because, while the former term does full justice to the fact that the great eschatological incision into history has already been made, it does not rule out a further development and final consummation of eschatology in the future. When we speak of "inaugurated eschatology" we are saying that for the New Testament believer significant eschatological events have already begun to happen while other eschatological occurrences still lie in the future.

As regards *inaugurated eschatology*, then, amillennialism affirms the following:

1. *Christ has won the decisive victory over sin, death, and Satan.* By living a sinless life and by dying on the cross as the sacrifice of atonement for our sin, Christ defeated sin. By undergoing death, and then victoriously rising from the grave, Christ defeated death. By resisting the devil's temptations, by perfectly obeying God, and by his death and resurrection, Christ delivered a deathblow to Satan and his evil hosts. This victory of Christ's was decisive and final. The most important day in history, therefore, is not the Second Coming of Christ, which is still future, but the first coming, which lies in the past. Because of the victory of Christ, the ultimate issues of history have already been decided. It is now only a question of time until that victory is brought to its final consummation.

2. *The kingdom of God is both present and future.* Amillennialists do not believe that the kingdom of God is primarily a Jewish kingdom which involves the literal restoration of the throne of David. Nor do they believe that because of the unbelief of the Jews of his day Christ postponed the establishment of the kingdom to the time of his future earthly millennial reign. Amillennialists believe that the kingdom of God was founded by Christ at the time of his sojourn on earth, is operative in history now, and is destined to be revealed in its fullness in the life to come. They understand the kingdom of God to be the reign of God dynamically active in human history through Jesus Christ. Its purpose is to redeem God's people from sin and from demonic powers, and finally to establish the new heavens and the new earth. The kingdom of God means nothing less than the reign of God in Christ over his entire created universe.

The kingdom of God is therefore both a present reality and a future hope. Jesus clearly taught that the kingdom was already present during his earthly ministry: "But if I drive out demons by the Spirit of God, then the kingdom of God has come upon you" (Matthew 12:28, N.I.V.). When the Pharisees asked Jesus when the kingdom of God was coming, he replied, "The kingdom of God is not coming with signs to be observed; nor will they say, 'Lo, here it is!' or 'There!' for behold, the kingdom of God is in the midst of you" (Luke 17:20–21). But Jesus also taught that there was a sense in which the kingdom of God was still future, both in specific sayings (Matthew 7:21–23; 8:11–12) and in eschatological parables (such as those of the Marriage Feast, the Tares, the Talents, the Wise and Foolish Virgins). Paul also makes statements describing the kingdom as both present (Romans 14:17; 1 Corinthians 4:19–20; Colossians 1:13–14) and future (1 Corinthians 6:9; Galatians 5:21; Ephesians 5:5; 2 Timothy 4:18).

The fact that the kingdom of God is present in one sense and future in another implies that we who are the subjects of that kingdom live in a kind of tension between the "already" and the "not yet." We are already in the kingdom, and yet we look forward to the full manifestation of that kingdom; we already share its blessings, and yet we await its total victory. Because the exact time when Christ will return is not known, the church must live with a sense of urgency, realizing that the end of history may be very near. At the same time, however, the church must continue to plan and work for a future on this present earth, which may still last a long time.

Meanwhile, the kingdom of God demands of us all total commitment to Christ and his cause. We must see all of life and all of reality in the light of the goal of the redemption not just of individuals but of the entire universe. This implies, as Abraham Kuyper, the renowned Dutch theologian and statesman, once said, that there is not a thumb-breadth of the universe about which Christ does not say, "It is mine."

This total commitment further implies a Christian philosophy of history: all of history must be seen as the working of God's eternal purpose. This kingdom vision includes a Christian philosophy of culture: art and science, reflecting as they do the glory of God, are to be pursued for his praise. The vision of the kingdom also includes a Christian view of vocation: all callings are from God, and all that we do in everyday life is to be done to God's praise, whether this be study, teaching, preaching, business, industry or housework.

A common source of tension among evangelicals today is the question of whether the church should be primarily concerned with evangelism or social and political action. A proper kingdom vision, it seems to me, will help us to keep our balance on this question. Needless to say, evangelism—bringing people into the kingdom of God—is one of the essential tasks of the church. But since the kingdom of God demands total commitment, the church must also be vitally concerned about the implementation of Christian principles in every area of life, including the political and the social. Evangelism and social concern, therefore, must never be thought of as options between which Christians may make a choice; both are essential to full-orbed kingdom obedience.

3. *Though the last day is still future, we are in the last days now.* This aspect of eschatology, which is often neglected in evangelical circles, is an essential part of the New Testament message. When I say, "we are in the last days now," I understand the expression "the last days" not merely as referring to the time just before Christ's return, but as a description of the entire era between Christ's first and second comings. New Testament writers were conscious of the fact that they were already living

in the last days at the time they were speaking or writing. This was specifically stated by Peter in his sermon on the day of Pentecost when he quoted Joel's prophecy about the pouring out of the Spirit upon all flesh in the last days (Acts 2:16–17). He was thus saying in effect, "We are now in the last days predicted by the prophet Joel." Paul made the same point when he described believers of his day as those "upon whom the end of the ages has come" (1 Corinthians 10:11). And the apostle John told his readers that they were already living in "the last hour" (1 John 2:18). In the light of these New Testament teachings, we may indeed speak of an inaugurated eschatology, while remembering that the Bible also speaks of a final consummation of eschatological events in what John commonly calls "the last day" (John 6:39–40, 44, 54; 11:24; 12:48).

The fact that we are living in the last days now implies that we are already tasting the beginnings of eschatological blessings—that, as Paul says, we

already have "the first fruits of the Spirit" (Romans 8:23). This means that we who are believers are to see ourselves not as impotent sinners who are helpless in the face of temptation but as new creatures in Christ (2 Corinthians 5:17), as temples of the Holy Spirit (1 Corinthians 6:19), and as those who have decisively crucified the flesh (Galatians 5:24), put off the old self, and put on the new (Colossians 3:9–10). All this involves having an image of ourselves which is primarily positive rather than negative. It also involves seeing fellow Christians as those who are in Christ with us and for whom we should therefore thank God.

4. *As far as the thousand years of Revelation 20 are concerned, we are in the millennium now.* Earlier in the chapter, evidence was given for the position that the thousand years of Revelation 20 extended from the first coming of Christ to just before his Second Coming, when Satan will be loosed for a short time. The amillennial position on the thousand

great apostasy, the great tribulation, and the coming of the Antichrist. These signs, however, must not be thought of as referring exclusively to the time just preceding Christ's return. They have been present in some sense from the very beginning of the Christian era and are present now. This means that we must always be ready for the Lord's return and that we may never in our thoughts push the return of Christ off into the far-distant future.

Amillennialists also believe, however, that these "signs of the times" will have a climactic final fulfillment just before Christ returns. This fulfillment will not take the form of phenomena which are totally new but will rather be an intensification of signs which have been present all along.

2. *The Second Coming of Christ will be a single event.* Amillennialists find no scriptural basis for the dispensationalist division of the Second Coming into two phases (sometimes called the *parousia* and the *revelation*), with a seven-year period in between. We understand Christ's return as being a single event.

3. *At the time of Christ's return, there will be a general resurrection, both of believers and unbelievers.* Amillennialists reject the common premillennial teaching that the resurrection of believers and that of unbelievers will be separated by a thousand years. They also reject the view of many dispensationalists that there will be as many as three or four resurrections (since, in addition to the two resurrections just mentioned, dispensationalists also teach that there will be a resurrection of tribulation saints and a resurrection of believers who died dur-

years of Revelation 20 implies that Christians who are now living are enjoying the benefits of this millennium, since Satan has been bound for the duration of this period. As we saw, the fact that Satan is now bound does not mean that he is not active in the world today but that during this period he cannot deceive the nations—that is, cannot prevent the spread of the gospel. The binding of Satan during this era, in other words, makes missions and evangelism possible. This fact should certainly be a source of encouragement to the church on earth.

Amillennials also teach that during this same thousand-year period the souls of believers who have died are now living and reigning with Christ in heaven while they await the resurrection of the body. Their state is therefore a state of blessedness and happiness, though their joy will not be complete until their bodies have been raised. This teaching should certainly bring comfort to those whose dear ones have died in the Lord.

As regards *future eschatology*, amillennialism affirms the following:

1. *The "signs of the times" have both present and future relevance.* Amillennialists believe that the return of Christ will be preceded by certain signs: for example, the preaching of the gospel to all the nations, the conversion of the fullness of Israel, the

ing the millennium). We see no scriptural evidence for such multiple resurrections.

4. *After the resurrection, believers who are then still alive shall suddenly be transformed and glorified.* The basis for this teaching is what Paul says in 1 Corinthians 15:51–52: "Listen, I tell you a mystery: We shall not all sleep, but we shall all be changed—in a flash, in the twinkling of an eye, at the last trumpet. For the trumpet will sound, the dead will be raised imperishable, and we shall be changed" (N.I.V.).

5. *The "rapture" of all believers now takes place.* Believers who have just been raised from the dead, together with living believers who have just been transformed, are now caught up in the clouds to meet the Lord in the air (1 Thessalonians 4:17). That there will be such a "rapture" the Bible clearly teaches. But I have put the word *rapture* between quotation marks in order to distinguish the amillennial conception of the rapture from the dispensa-

tionalist view. Dispensationalists teach that after the rapture the entire church will be taken up to heaven for a period of seven years while those still on earth are undergoing the great tribulation.

Amillennialists see no scriptural evidence for such a seven-year period or for a transference of the church from earth to heaven during that period. Risen and glorified bodies of believers do not belong in heaven but on the earth. The word translated "to meet" in 1 Thessalonians 4:17 (*apantēsis*) is a technical term used in the days of the New Testament to describe a public welcome given by a city to a visiting dignitary. People would ordinarily leave the city to meet the distinguished visitor and then go back with him into the city. On the basis of the analogy conveyed by this word, all Paul is saying here is that raised and transformed believers are caught up in the clouds to meet the descending Lord, implying that after this meeting they will go back with him to the earth.

6. *Now follows the final judgment.* Whereas dispensationalists commonly teach that there will be at least three separate judgments, amillennialists do not agree. The latter see scriptural evidence for only one Day of Judgment which will occur at the time of Christ's return. All men must then appear before the judgment seat of Christ.

The purpose of the final judgment is not primarily to determine the final destiny of men, since by that time that final destiny has already been determined for all men except those still living at the time of Christ's return. Rather, the judgment will have a threefold purpose: first, it will reveal the glorification of God in the final destiny assigned to each person; second, it will indicate finally and publicly the great antithesis of history between the people of God and the enemies of God; and third, it will reveal the degree of reward or the degree of punishment which each shall receive.

7. *After the judgment the final state is ushered in.* Unbelievers and all those who have rejected Christ shall spend eternity in hell, whereas believers will enter into everlasting glory on the new earth. The concept of the new earth is so important for biblical eschatology that we should give it more than a passing thought. Many Christians think of themselves as spending eternity in some ethereal heaven, while the Bible plainly teaches us that there will be a new earth. When the book of Revelation tells us that the holy city, the new Jerusalem, will come down from heaven to the new earth (21:2), that God will now have his dwelling with men (21:3), and that the throne of God and of the Lamb will be in the new Jerusalem (22:3), it is teaching us in figurative language that in the life to come heaven

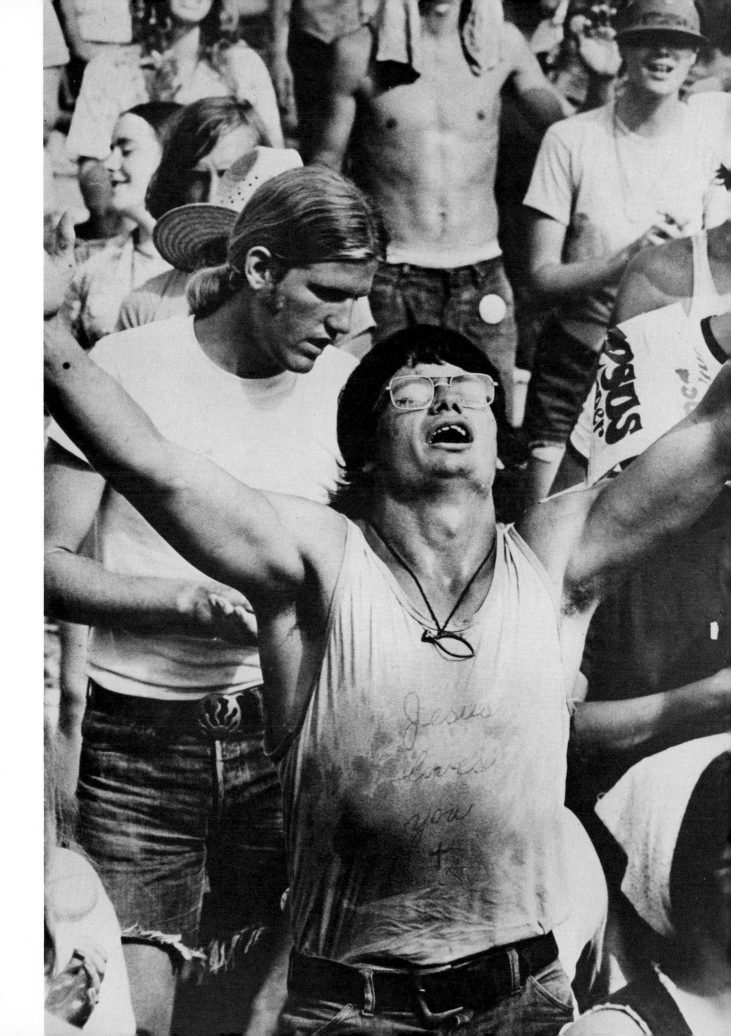

and earth will no longer be separated but will have merged. In the final state, therefore, glorified believers will be both in heaven and on the new earth, since the two shall then be one.

When one keeps the vision of the new earth clearly in mind, many biblical teachings begin to form a significant pattern. As we have seen, the resurrection of the body calls for a new earth. The cosmic significance of the work of Christ implies that the curse which came upon creation because of man's sin (Genesis 3:17–19) shall someday be removed (Romans 8:19–22); this renewal of creation means that there will indeed be a new earth. The Bible also contains specific promises about the new earth. We have already looked at Isaiah's prediction of the new earth in 65:17 (see 66:22). Jesus promised that the meek shall inherit the earth (Matthew 5:5). Peter speaks of new heavens and a new earth in which righteousness shall dwell (2 Peter 3:13). And the elders and living creatures whom John sees in the heavenly vision recorded in Revelation 5 sing a song of praise to the victorious Lamb which includes these words: "You have made them [those whom you purchased with your blood] to be a kingdom and priests to serve our God, and they will reign on the earth" (Revelation 5:10, N.I.V.).

In the light of biblical teaching about the new earth, many Old Testament prophecies about the land of Canaan and about the future of the people of God fall into place. From the fourth chapter of the book of Hebrews we learn that Canaan was a type of the Sabbath-rest of the people of God in the life to come. From Paul's letter to the Galatians we learn that all those who are in Christ are included in the seed of Abraham (Galatians 3:29). When we read Genesis 17:8 ("And I will give unto thee, and to thy seed after thee, the land of thy sojournings, all the land of Canaan, for an everlasting possession; and I will be their God" [A.S.V.]) with this understanding of the New Testament broadening of these concepts, we see in it a promise of the new earth as the everlasting possession of all the people of God, not just of the physical descendants of Abraham. And when, in the light of this New Testament teaching, we now read Amos 9:15 ("And I will plant them upon their land, and they shall no more be plucked up out of their land which I have given them, saith Jehovah thy God" [A.S.V.]), we do not feel compelled to restrict the meaning of these words to national Israel and the land of Palestine. We understand them to be a prediction of the eternal dwelling of all God's people, Gentiles as well as Jews, on the new earth of which Canaan was a type. Amillennialists therefore feel no need for positing an earthly millennium to provide for the fulfillment of prophecies of this sort; they see such prophecies as pointing to the glorious eternal future which awaits all the people of God.

# POSTMILLENNIALISM

## Loraine Boettner

POSTMILLENNIALISM IS THAT VIEW of the last things which holds that the kingdom of God is now being extended in the world through the preaching of the gospel and the saving work of the Holy Spirit in the hearts of individuals, that the world eventually is to be Christianized, and that the return of Christ is to occur at the close of a long period of righteousness and peace commonly called the millennium. It should be added that on postmillennial principles the Second Coming of Christ will be followed immediately by the general resurrection, the general judgment, and the introduction of heaven and hell in their fullness.

The millennium to which the postmillennialist looks forward is thus a golden age of spiritual prosperity during this present dispensation, that is, during the Church Age. This is to be brought about through forces now active in the world. It is to last an indefinitely long period of time, perhaps much longer than a literal one thousand years. The changed character of individuals will be reflected in an uplifted social, economic, political, and cultural life of mankind. The world at large will then enjoy a state of righteousness which up until now has been seen only in relatively small and isolated groups: for example, some family circles, and some local church groups and kindred organizations.

This does not mean that there will be a time on this earth when every person will be a Christian or that all sin will be abolished. But it does mean that evil in all its many forms eventually will be reduced to negligible proportions, that Christian principles will be the rule, not the exception, and that Christ will return to a truly Christianized world.

Postmillennialism further holds that the universal proclamation of the gospel and the ultimate conversion of the large majority of men in all nations during the present dispensation was the express command, meaning, and promise of the Great Commission given by Christ himself when he said, "All authority in heaven and on earth has been given to me. Go therefore and make disciples of all nations, baptizing them in the name of the Father and of the Son and of the Holy Spirit, teaching them to observe all that I have commanded you; and lo, I am with you always, to the close of the age" (Matthew 28:18–20).

We believe that the Great Commission includes not merely the formal and external announcement of the gospel preached as a "witness" to the nations, as the premillennialists and amillennialists hold, but the true and effectual evangelization of all the nations so that the hearts and lives of the people are transformed by it. That seems quite clear from the fact that all authority in heaven and on earth and an endless sweep or conquest has been given to Christ, and through him to his disciples specifically for that purpose. They were commanded not merely

to preach but to make disciples of all the nations. It was no doubtful experiment to which they were called, but to a sure triumph. The preaching of the gospel under the direction of the Holy Spirit during this dispensation is, therefore, the all-sufficient means for accomplishing that purpose.

We must acknowledge that the church during the past nineteen centuries has been extremely negligent in her duty and that the crying need of our time is for her to take seriously the task assigned to her. Instead of discussions of social, economic, and political problems, book reviews, and entertaining platitudes from the pulpit, the need is for sermons with real gospel content, designed to change lives and to save souls. The charge of negligence applies, of course, not only to ministers but equally to the laity. Every individual Christian is called to give his witness and to show his faith by personal testimony, through the distribution of the printed word, or through the generous and effective use of his time and money for Christian purposes. Christ commanded the evangelization of the world. That is our task. Surely

# LIKE THE COMING OF SUMMER

*Loraine Boettner*

THE COMING of the millennium is like the coming of summer, although ever so much more slowly and on a much grander scale. In the struggle between the seasons there are many advances and many apparent setbacks. Time and again the first harbingers of spring appear only to be overcome by the winter winds. It often seems that the struggle has been lost and that the cold of winter will never be broken. But gradually the moderate spring breezes take over, and after a time we find ourselves in the glorious summer season.

Trying to pinpoint the date on which the millennium begins is like trying to distinguish the day or year when medieval

history ended and modern history began. The discovery of America by Columbus usually is taken as the landmark dividing the two. At least for Americans that is where medievalism ends and where the story of America begins. But that discovery made no immediate changes in the life of the world, and in fact Columbus himself died without ever knowing that he had discovered a new world. In retrospect and for convenience we arbitrarily choose a date as the division point between two eras. But in reality one such age blends into another so slowly and so imperceptibly that no change is recognizable at the time. Only from the perspective of history can we look back and set an approximate date, perhaps within a century or two, as to when one era ceased and another began. So it is with the coming of the millennium. Undoubtedly it will follow the law of all the other great periods in the history of the church, being gradual and uncertain in its approach.

he will not, and in fact cannot, come back and say to his church, "Well done, good and faithful servant," until that task has been accomplished. The Rev. J. Marcellus Kik has said: "That there is still a remnant of paganism and papalism in the world is chiefly the fault of the church. The Word of God is just as powerful in our generation as it was during the early history of the church. The power of the Gospel is just as strong in this century as in the days of the Reformation. These enemies could be completely vanquished if the Christians of this day and age were as vigorous, as bold, as earnest, as prayerful, and as faithful as Christians were in the first several centuries and in the time of the Reformation."

It should be remembered, however, that while post-, and a-, and premillennialists differ in regard to the manner and time of Christ's return, that is, in regard to the events that are to precede or follow his return, they agree that he will return personally, visibly, and in great glory. Each alike looks for the "blessed hope, the appearing of the glory of our great God and our Savior Jesus Christ" (Titus 2:13). Each acknowledges Paul's statements that "the Lord himself will descend from heaven, with a cry of command, with the archangel's call, and with the sound of the trumpet of God" (1 Thessalonians 4:16). Christ's return is taught so clearly and so repeatedly in Scripture that there can be no question in this regard for those who accept the Bible as the Word of God. They also agree that at his coming he will raise the dead, execute judgment, and eventually institute the eternal state. No one of these views has an inherent liberalizing tendency. Hence the matters on which they agree are much more important than those on which they differ. This should enable them to cooperate as evangelicals and to present united front against modernists and liberals who more or less consistently deny the supernatural throughout the whole range of Bible truth.

# THE ALPHA AND THE OMEGA

## Documents of Vatican II

WHILE HELPING THE WORLD and receiving many benefits from it, the church has a single intention: that God's kingdom may come, and that the salvation of the whole human race may come to pass. For every benefit which the People of God during its earthly pilgrimage can offer to the human family stems from the fact that the church is "the universal sacrament of salvation," simultaneously manifesting and exercising the mystery of God's love for man.

For God's Word, by whom all things were made, was Himself made flesh so that as perfect man He might save all men and sum up all things in Himself. The Lord is the goal of human history, the focal point of the longings of history and of civilization, the center of the human race, the joy of every heart, and the answer to all its yearnings. He it is whom the Father raised from the dead, lifted on high, and stationed at His right hand, making Him Judge of the living and the dead. Enlivened and united in His Spirit, we journey toward the consummation of human history, one which fully accords with the counsel of God's love: "To reestablish all things in Christ, both those in the heavens and those on the earth" (Ephesians 1:10).

The Lord Himself speaks: "Behold, I come quickly! And my reward is with me, to render to each one according to his works. I am the Alpha and the Omega, the first and the last, the beginning and end" (Revelation 22:12-13).

# MARRIAGE SUPPER

## John the Divine
## (Revelation 19:6–9)

AND I HEARD as it were the voice of a great multitude, and as the voice of many waters, and as the voice of mighty thunderings, saying, Alleluia: for the Lord God reigneth.

Let us be glad and rejoice, and give honor to him: for the marriage of the Lamb is come, and his wife hath made her ready.

And to her was granted that she should be arrayed in fine linen, clean and white: for the fine linen is the righteousness of saints.

And he saith to me, Write, Blessed are they which are called unto the marriage supper of the Lamb. And he saith unto me, These are the true sayings of God.

## 𝕸𝖊𝖉𝖉𝖎𝖓𝖌 𝕴𝖓𝖛𝖎𝖙𝖆𝖙𝖎𝖔𝖓

*You are cordially invited, by God Almighty, the Creator of the Universe, to be in the Wedding of his only begotten son, Jesus Christ, to take place in the near future. The wedding will take place in the Ballroom of Heaven, in the presence of Arch-Angel's, Cherubims and Seraphims. Music will be furnished by the Angelic Heavenly Host of over 100,000,000 Angels.*

The bride will be the Christians of all ages, who have sincerely believed in the Lord Jesus Christ as their Lord and Saviour; who have given their hearts and lives to Him, and have lived and suffered for Him here on earth. Christians who are now dead will be resurrected from their graves, but those who are living will be caught up together with them in the clouds, to meet the Lord in the air; and so shall they ever be with the Lord!

The Marriage Supper will last for 3½ years, while the wrath of God is being poured out upon the earth, — upon all sinners and unbelievers.

The Honeymoon trip will extend back to earth, on white horses. The bridegroom (Jesus Christ) will slay the armies of the world that will have gathered to fight against Him, (the battle of Armageddon) with the sword of His mouth, for He is "King of Kings and Lord of Lords."

The bridegroom (Jesus Christ) will then take possession of the whole earth and rule with a rod of iron, in peace and righteousness, with His bride, for a thousand years, after which there will be a new heaven and a new earth. The Bridegroom has prepared a city for His bride (New Jerusalem) which will come down from heaven. It will be 1500 miles square, and 1500 miles high, with gates of pearl and streets of gold. "There shall in no wise enter into it any thing that defileth, neither worketh abomination, or maketh a lie: but they which are written in the Lamb's Book of Life." (Bible)

**WOULD YOU LIKE TO BE PART OF THE BRIDE OF JESUS CHRIST**

YOU can be, if YOU will only repent of YOUR sins and believe in Him as YOUR Saviour, as YOUR Lord, as YOUR Redeemer, as YOUR soon-coming Bridegroom! He came down from Heaven to Earth over 1900 years ago and died on the Cross of

## WEDDING OR RECEPTION

### Leon J. Wood

SOME PROPHETIC STUDENTS make a distinction between this occasion, which they call "the marriage of the Lamb," and a later one, which they call "the marriage supper of the Lamb." The reason for this distinction is found especially in three passages which describe a marriage feast: Matthew 22:1–14 and 25:1–13, and Luke 14:16–24. The explanation is that these accounts picture Israel on earth waiting for the return from heaven of Christ, as the Bridegroom, and the church, as His bride, so that the marriage feast might take place. Thus the marriage supper is seen to take place here on earth during the millennium. The marriage itself, which is identified with "the marriage of the Lamb" (Revelation 19:7–9), will have already taken place by the time of Christ's coming. According to this view, it will be only after this coming that the feast in celebration of the marriage will ensue. Only Christ and the church will be involved, then, in the marriage proper, but Israel will additionally act as guests at the later supper. I view this interpretation as possible, but not probable. The matter hinges on the significance of the three "feast" passages. It seems likely that they are better understood, not as predictive of a specific historical event, but merely as revealing truth under the symbolism of a marriage supper, without identifying any particular time or period for that occasion. Arguing against the interpretation, also, is the fact that the event described in Revelation 19:7–9 is already called "the marriage supper of the Lamb" (verse 9).

# THECLA'S HYMN

*Methodius*

> *Chastely I live for Thee,*
> *And holding my lighted lamps,*
> *My Spouse, I go forth to meet Thee.*

1. From on high, there has come, O virgins, the sound of the cry that wakes the dead, bidding us to go to meet the Bridegroom in the east with all speed in white robes and with our lamps. Awake, before the King enters within the gates!

> *Chastely I live for Thee,*
> *And holding my lighted lamps,*
> *My Spouse, I go forth to meet Thee.*

2. Flying from the riches of mortals that brings only wealth of sorrow, from love, from the delights and pleasures of this life, I desire to be sheltered in Thy lifegiving arms and to gaze forever on Thy beauty, Blessed One.

> *Chastely I live for Thee,*
> *And holding my lighted lamps,*
> *My Spouse, I go forth to meet Thee.*

3. For Thee, my King, have I refused a mortal marriage and a home rich in gold, and I have come to Thee in immaculate robes that I may enter with Thee Thy blessed bridal chamber.

> *Chastely I live for Thee,*
> *And holding my lighted lamps,*
> *My Spouse, I go forth to meet Thee.*

4. I have escaped the Dragon's countless bewitching wiles, O Blessed One. Awaiting Thy coming from heaven, I have braved fire and flame and the ravenous assaults of wild beasts.

> *Chastely I live for Thee,*
> *And holding my lighted lamps,*
> *My Spouse, I go forth to meet Thee.*

5. Longing for Thy grace, O Word, I think not of my native city; I think not of the dances of maidens of my own age, the merry life with mother and family. Thou, O Christ, art all these things to me!

> *Chastely I live for Thee,*
> *And holding my lighted lamps,*
> *My Spouse, I go forth to meet Thee.*

6. Provider of life, O Christ, hail, Light that knowest no evening! Receive my cry: the choir of virgins calls upon Thee, perfect Flower, Love, Joy, Prudence, Wisdom, Word!

> *Chastely I live for Thee,*
> *And holding my lighted lamps,*
> *My Spouse, I go forth to meet Thee.*

7. O Queen arrayed in beauty, receive us too with open doors within the bridal bower, O Bride of unsullied body, gloriously triumphant, breathing loveliness! At Christ's side we stand in robes like thine, singing, O youthful maiden of thy blessed nuptials.

> *Chastely I live for Thee,*
> *And holding my lighted lamps,*
> *My Spouse, I go forth to meet Thee.*

8. Now outside the bridal doors are maidens weeping bitterly with deep sobs, and pitiful are their cries. The light of their lamps has gone out, and they have come too late to see the chamber of joy.

> *Chastely I live for Thee,*
> *And holding my lighted lamps,*
> *My Spouse, I go forth to meet Thee.*

9. For, unhappy maidens, they have turned aside from the path of holiness and have neglected to take more oil for life's contingencies. Carrying lamps whose bright flame is dead, they groan inwardly in spirit.

> *Chastely I live for Thee,*
> *And holding my lighted lamps,*
> *My Spouse, I go forth to meet Thee.*

10. Full bowls of sweet nectar stand by. Let us drink! It is a heavenly draught, O virgins, which the Groom has set before all those worthy to be invited to the marriage.

> *Chastely I live for Thee,*
> *And holding my lighted lamps,*
> *My Spouse, I go forth to meet Thee.*

11. Clearly did Abel foreshadow Thy death, O Blessed One, as bleeding he looked to heaven and said: O Word I beseech Thee, receive me cruelly slain by my brother.

> *Chastely I live for Thee,*
> *And holding my lighted lamps,*
> *My Spouse, I go forth to meet Thee.*

12. Thy valiant servant Joseph, O Word, did carry off the greatest prize of chastity, when a woman burning with desire sought to draw him by force to an unlawful bed. But he paid no heed and fled naked, crying aloud:

> *Chastely I live for Thee,*
> *And holding my lighted lamps,*
> *My Spouse, I go forth to meet Thee.*

13. Jephte offered to God in sacrifice his daughter, a maid that knew not man, freshly slain like a lamb before the altar. And she, nobly fulfilling a type of Thy Body, Blessed One, bravely cried out:

> *Chastely I live for Thee,*
> *And holding my lighted lamps,*
> *My Spouse, I go forth to meet Thee.*

14. Bold Judith with a well-planned ruse enticed the general of the enemy hosts with her beauty— nor were her body's members defiled—and then cut off his head. And this was her victory cry:

> *Chastely I live for Thee,*
> *And holding my lighted lamps,*
> *My Spouse, I go forth to meet Thee.*

15. The two judges were inflamed with desire when they saw the texture of Susanna's fair form. Said they: We have come, dear lady, desirous of secret intercourse with you. But she, with timorous cry, said:

> *Chastely I live for Thee,*
> *And holding my lighted lamps,*
> *My Spouse, I go forth to meet Thee.*

16. Far better would it be for me to die than to betray my marriage bed for you, women-mad men, and suffer God's eternal justice in fiery penalties. Save me, O Christ, from these men!

> *Chastely I live for Thee,*
> *And holding my lighted lamps,*
> *My Spouse, I go forth to meet Thee.*

17. Thy forerunner, who bathed multitudes of men in the purifying streams, was unjustly led to slaughter by a wicked man because of his chastity. And as he dampened the dust with his own life's blood, he cried out to Thee, O Blessed One:

*Chastely I live for Thee,*
*And holding my lighted lamps,*
*My Spouse, I go forth to meet Thee.*

18. Even the Virgin who gave Thee life, Grace undefiled, who bore Thee her Child without stain in her virgin womb, was thought to have betrayed her bed. And she, with child, O Blessed One, did say:

*Chastely I live for Thee,*
*And holding my lighted lamps,*
*My Spouse, I go forth to meet Thee.*

19. Eager to see Thy wedding day, Blessed One, all the angels whom Thou their Ruler didst summon, are present with costly gifts, O Word, vested in spotless robes.

*Chastely·I live for Thee,*
*And holding my lighted lamps,*
*My Spouse, I go forth to meet Thee.*

20. Unsullied maid, God's blessed Bride, we thy bridesmaids hymn thy praise, O Church of body snow-white, dark-tressed, chaste, spotless, lovely!

*Chastely I live for Thee,*
*And holding my lighted lamps,*
*My Spouse, I go forth to meet Thee.*

21. Fled is corruption and the tear-flooded pains of disease. Death is made captive, all folly is crushed, heart-melting grief is dead. Of a sudden the lamp of God's joy has shone again on mortals.

*Chastely I live for Thee,*
*And holding my lighted lamps,*
*My Spouse, I go forth to meet Thee.*

22. Paradise is no longer bereft of men. Once again, by God's decree as before, he lives in it who was cast out because of the Serpent's scheming wiles. Now he is incorruptible, blessed, free from fear.

*Chastely I live for Thee,*
*And holding my lighted lamps,*
*My Spouse, I go forth to meet Thee.*

23. Chanting the new strain, our virgin choir escorts thee, our Queen, to heaven, bathed in light. And garlanded with white lily cups, we bear in our hands light-bearing flames.

*Chastely I live for Thee,*
*And holding my lighted lamps,*
*My Spouse, I go forth to meet Thee.*

24. O Blessed One, who dwellest in heaven's pure seat from all eternity, and dost govern all with everlasting sway, behold, we are come! Receive us too, O Father, with Thy Servant, within the Gates of Life.

*Chastely I live for Thee,*
*And holding my lighted lamps,*
*My Spouse, I go forth to meet Thee.*

## NO MORE TEARS FOREVER

*Watchman Nee*

*"God shall wipe away every tear from their eyes."*
　　　　　　　　　—Revelation 7:17

I DELIGHT GREATLY in the New Jerusalem, not because it has a street of pure gold and twelve gates of pearl, but because there will be the presence of the Lord and the absence of any more tears. We may die and rest in Christ, yet we are not just waiting for death but for the coming day when the world shall weep no more.

The New Jerusalem is coming very soon, and this tearful world will pass instantly away. On that day the Lord will give us a resurrection body. I think that that body will be similar to the one we have today, possessing all the different members it has now. But it will be a transformed body. And in this transformed body one thing will be missing—tears in the eyes. The Lord has borne our pain so that we may not suffer again in the future. Thank God for the prospect of no more tears forever.

# ADORATION OF THE LAMB AND HYMN OF THE CHOSEN

*John the Divine (Revelation 14:1–3; 19:1, 3–4)*

AND I LOOKED, and, lo, a Lamb stood on the mount Sion, and with him an hundred forty and four thousand, having his Father's name written in their foreheads.

And I heard a voice from heaven, as the voice of many waters, and as the voice of a great thunder: and I heard the voice of harpers harping with their harps:

And they sung as it were a new song before the throne, and before the four beasts, and the elders: and no man could learn that song but the hundred and forty and four thousand, which were redeemed from the earth. . . .

And after these things I heard a great voice of much people in heaven, saying, Alleluia; Salvation, and glory, and honor, and power, unto the Lord our God. . . .

And again they said, Alleluia. . . .

And the four and twenty elders and the four beasts fell down and worshiped God that sat on the throne, saying, Amen; Alleluia.

# THE ULTIMATE EARTH

*Pierre Teilhard de Chardin*

UNDER THE INCREASING TENSION of the mind on the surface of the globe, we may begin by asking seriously whether life will not perhaps one day succeed in ingeniously forcing the bars of its earthly prison, either by finding the means to invade other inhabited planets or (a still more giddy perspective) by getting into psychical touch with other focal points of consciousness across the abysses of space. The meeting and mutual fecundation of two noospheres is a supposition which may seem at first sight crazy, but which after all is merely extending to psychical phenomena a scope no one would think of denying to material phenomena. Consciousness would thus finally construct itself by a synthesis of planetary units. Why not, in a universe whose astral unity is the galaxy?

Without in any way wishing to discourage such hypotheses—whose realization, though enormously enlarging the dimensions, would leave unchanged both the convergent form and hence the final duration of noogenesis—I consider their probability too remote for them to be worth dwelling on.

The human organism is so extraordinarily complicated and sensitive, and so closely adapted to terrestrial conditions, that it is difficult to see how man could acclimatize himself to another planet, even if he were capable of navigating through interplanetary space. The sidereal durations are so immense that it is difficult to see how, in two different regions of the heavens, two thought systems could coexist and coincide at comparable stages of their development. For these two reasons among others I adopt the supposition that our noosphere is destined to close in upon itself in isolation, and that it is in a psychical rather than a spatial direction that it will find an outlet, without need to leave or overflow the earth. Hence, quite naturally, the notion of change of state recurs.

Noogenesis rises upward in us and through us unceasingly. We have pointed to the principal characteristics of that movement: the closer association of the grains of thought; the synthesis of individuals and of nations or races; the need of an autonomous and supreme personal focus to bind elementary personalities together, without deforming them, in an atmosphere of active sympathy. And, once again: all this results from the combined action of two curvatures—the roundness of the earth and the cosmic convergence of mind—in conformity with the law of complexity and consciousness.

Now when sufficient elements have sufficiently agglomerated, this essentially convergent movement will attain such intensity and such quality that mankind, *taken as a whole*, will be obliged—as happened to the individual forces of instinct—to reflect upon itself at a single point; that is to say, in this case, to abandon its organo-planetary foothold so as to pivot itself on the transcendent center of its increasing concentration. This will be the end and the fulfillment of the spirit of the earth.

The end of the world: the wholesale internal introversion upon itself of the noosphere, which has simultaneously reached the uttermost limit of its complexity and its centrality.

The end of the world: the overthrow of equilibrium, detaching the mind, fulfilled at last, from its material matrix, so that it will henceforth rest with all its weight on God-Omega.

The end of the world: critical point simultaneously of emergence and emersion, of maturation and evasion.

We can entertain two almost contradictory suppositions about the physical and psychical state our planet will be in as it approaches maturation. According to the first hypothesis, which expresses the hopes toward which we ought in any case to turn our efforts as to an ideal, evil on the earth at its final stage will be reduced to a minimum. Disease and hunger will be conquered by science and we will no longer need to fear them in any acute form. And, conquered by the sense of the earth and human sense, hatred and internecine struggles will have disappeared in the ever-warmer radiance of Omega. Some sort of unanimity will reign over the entire mass of the noosphere. The final convergence will take place in *peace*. Such an outcome would of course conform most harmoniously with our theory.

But there is another possibility. Obeying a law from which nothing in the past has ever been exempt, evil may go on growing alongside good, and it too may attain its paroxysm at the end in some specifically new form.

There are no summits without abysses.

Enormous powers will be liberated in mankind by the inner play of its cohesion: though it may be that this energy will still be employed discordantly tomorrow, as today and in the past. Are we to foresee a mechanizing synergy under brute force, or a synergy of sympathy? Are we to foresee man seeking to fulfill himself collectively upon himself, or personally on a greater than himself? Refusal or acceptance of Omega? A conflict may supervene. In that case the noosphere, in the course of and by virtue of the process which draws it together, will, when it has reached its point of unification, split into two zones each attracted to an opposite pole of adoration. Thought has never completely united upon itself here below. Universal love would only vivify and detach finally a fraction of the noosphere so as to consummate it—the part which decided to "cross the threshold," to get outside itself into the other. *Ramification once again, for the last time.*

In this second hypothesis, which is more in conformity with traditional apocalyptic thinking, we may perhaps discern three curves around us rising up at one and the same time into the future: an inevitable reduction in the organic possibilities of the earth, an internal schism of consciousness ever in-creasingly divided on two opposite ideals of evolution, and positive attraction of the center of centers at the heart of those which turn toward it. And the earth would finish at the triple point at which, by a coincidence altogether in keeping with the ways of life, these three curves would meet and attain their maximum at the very same moment.

The death of the materially exhausted planet; the split of the noosphere, divided on the form to be given to its unity; and simultaneously (endowing the event with all its significance and with all its value) the liberation of that percentage of the universe which, across time, space and evil, will have succeeded in laboriously synthesizing itself to the very end.

Not an indefinite progress, which is a hypothesis contradicted by the convergent nature of noogenesis, but an ecstasy transcending the dimensions and the framework of the visible universe.

Ecstasy in concord; or discord; but in either case by excess of interior tension: the only biological outcome proper to or conceivable for the phenomenon of man.

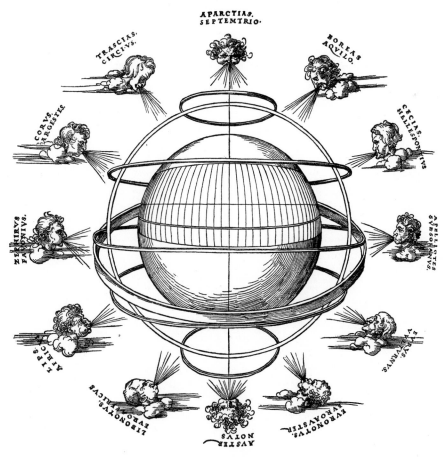

# VI.

# JUDG-MENT

# JUDGMENT OF THE GREAT WHITE THRONE

## W. Herschel Ford

A WAR VETERAN lay dying. A preacher came to see him and asked him the question, "John, are you afraid to die?" The man raised up on his elbow, and said indignantly, "Sir, I have faced death on many bloody battlefields, and I was never afraid. I have faced it often since, and I was not scared. I am no coward. Why do you insult me in my dying hour?" He fell back upon the pillow, exhausted. Then the preacher said, "But, John, are you prepared for what comes after death?" The man sighed and said, "Oh, sir, that is what frightens me. I am afraid of that which comes after death."

The man who is not a Christian well might fear that which comes after death. He may be very brave as he faces the dangers of this world, but it's another matter entirely when he faces the God whom he has spurned in the land where God deals in judgment. A man would be a fool not to have any fears as he faces death without a Savior.

Today men like to pry into the future. They spend thousands on fortune-tellers and quack prophets. But we do not need to go to a fortune-teller to learn about the future life. We have the Bible, the Word of God, which tells us exactly what comes after death. In that book of divine authority, we are told that after death there comes the judgment. "And as it is appointed unto men once to die, but after this the judgment" (Hebrews 9:27).

Many people have a confused picture of the Judgment Day. They picture Christ seated on a throne, with every person who ever lived standing before the throne. Then they see Him judging these people as to salvation, sending some to His right and some to His left, some to heaven and some to hell. This is not a true biblical concept. A man doesn't wait until he stands before the Judgment Seat to be pronounced saved or lost. He is saved or lost right here because of what he has done with Jesus Christ.

The Bible does not tell us of a judgment where saints and sinners will be judged at the same time. The saved man appears before the Judgment Seat of Christ, where his works are judged and his reward determined. But he is saved before he gets there. He is saved because on this earth he received Jesus Christ as his personal Savior. Later the lost man appears before the Great White Throne of Judgment, where Christ judges him according to his evil works, and where the degree of his punishment is determined. Then he is cast into the Lake of Fire. But he is lost before he gets there, because on this earth he rejected the Lord Jesus Christ.

Your salvation comes in this world or not at all. The great question of today is, "What shall I do with Jesus, who is called Christ?" Your answer to that question determines your destiny. Accept Him, and you'll stand before the Judgment Seat and receive your reward. Reject Him, and you'll stand before the Great White Throne and receive your condemnation. In other words, you choose your own judgment, your own destiny. You choose whether your resurrection will be unto eternal life or eternal death.

Let us now think of the judgment of the Great White Throne, the judgment of the unsaved.

    I. The Certainty of This Judgment

    II. The Nature of This Judgment

    III. The Judge of This Judgment

    IV. The People Who Will Be Judged

## I. THE CERTAINTY OF THIS JUDGMENT

Even today judgment is going on everywhere. You cannot violate the laws of nature without suffering. There is no mercy in nature. You violate her laws and you pay the price. Our hospitals are filled with people who have violated these laws and are suffering because of it.

Put your finger in the fire and you'll get burned. Lie and you'll become a liar. Steal and you'll become a thief. Judgment goes on right now. A man goes out for a night of sin and later suffers the tortures of hell. A woman takes one step away from the path of virtue and pays for it the rest of her life. You sow the seeds of sin here and you reap the harvest here.

But there is a greater Judgment Day coming.

Every civilized country has justice of some sort. They have courts and judges that try lawbreakers and punish them. Why? Because our very natures demand justice and judgment. When two men engage in a fight, bystanders demand that each shall receive justice. There is something in man that cries out for justice and for judgment. That thing came from God. He has it in His nature and He puts it in ours.

Here is a man who deals in liquor and becomes rich because of it. His poor victims become poorer, they lose their jobs, their homes, and their souls. Wives weep in sorrow, children are deprived of life's necessities, and homes are broken up. Is there to be no judgment for that liquor man?

Another man leads a girl into ruin and sacrifices her upon the altar of lust. As sure as God lives, there is a judgment for that man.

Another man joins the church, but he is still on the devil's side. He does the devil's work, he tries to ruin the church, and he breaks up its fellowship. I would rather meet God from outside of the church than to meet Him as a church member who played the hypocrite or betrayed Him as Judas did. Do you think that such a man will go free? No, I tell you that God has reserved a judgment for sinners.

In some of the pulpits and schools of the land there are preachers and professors who deny the inspiration of the Bible and the divinity of Christ, and who lead men down the pathway of unbelief. Some years ago I visited in a lovely Georgia home. On the table I saw the picture of a handsome young man. I asked the mother about this boy and she began to weep. She gave me a letter from him, which she asked me to read. In the letter he said, "Mother and Father, I don't believe anymore in those things I learned back home in Sunday school and church. Of course, it's all right for you to believe all these myths and attend church and take an active part, but I am through with such things forever. Here in college I have learned something entirely different." This boy was led astray by false teachers. Will these teachers go free? I say they will not. Men may escape judgment here, but they can't escape God's judgment in the hereafter. He will bring sinners home to judgment.

Aside from reason, the Bible teaches us that there will be a time of judgment. God is a God of love, but He is also a God of justice. When Adam and Eve sinned, He drove them out of the Garden of Eden. God branded Cain after Cain had murdered Abel. He drowned the world in a flood; he burned the cities of the plain; he overthrew many nations —all because of sin. He still punishes sin. He says, "For I am the Lord, I change not . . ." (Malachi 3:6).

Listen to Ecclesiastes 11:9: "Rejoice, O young man, in thy youth; and let thy heart cheer thee in the days of thy youth, and walk in the ways of thine heart, and in the sight of thine eyes; but know thou, that for all of these things God will bring thee into judgment." You are a free moral agent. You can live as you please. But God calls you to remember that there is an accounting day.

Ecclesiastes 12:14 says, "For God shall bring every work into judgment, with every secret thing, whether it be good, or whether it be evil."

A dying infidel said, "I could die in peace, if I

## THE GREAT WHITE THRONE

### John the Divine
### (Revelation 20:11–15)

AND I SAW a great white throne, and him that sat on it, from whose face the earth and the heaven fled away; and there was found no place for them.

And I saw the dead, small and great, stand before God; and the books were opened: and another book was opened, which is the book of life: and the dead were judged out of those things which were written in the books, according to their works.

And the sea gave up the dead which were in it; and death and hell delivered up the dead which were in them: and they were judged every man according to their works.

And death and hell were cast into the lake of fire. This is the second death.

And whosoever was not found written in the book of life was cast into the lake of fire.

## BY GOD'S FINGER

*Gregory of Nazianzus*

YOU HEAR of a book of the living, and a book of those who are not being saved. There we shall all be inscribed or rather have been inscribed already, according to the deserts of each man's life on this earth. Wealth has no advantage there, poverty no disadvantage: nor is justice corrupted, as here, by favor or hatred or any other such influence. We have all been entered in the book by God's finger, and that book will be opened in the day of revelation.

could really believe that the Bible was false." But the Bible is true. It is there to warn you. And as sure as you live and God lives, you will be brought to judgment if you don't repent your sin and come to Jesus. Yes, the Bible plainly teaches that there is a judgment for sinners.

## II. THE NATURE OF THIS JUDGMENT

Acts 17:30–31; Romans 14:12; Revelation 20:11–15

1. *It is an appointed day.* Acts 17:31 says: "Because he hath appointed a day, in the which he will judge the world in righteousness. . . ." God makes appointments and He never fails to keep them. He appointed the day and the night, and they come with clocklike precision. He appointed the sun, the moon, and the stars, and they are never out of place. He appointed the seasons, and they come in regular order. He has appointed a day when He will judge men, and He will not fail to keep that appointment. Some men commit crimes and escape, never to be apprehended, but they cannot escape from God's judgment. He keeps his appointments.

2. *It will be Christ's day.* This is man's day, a day of inventions, improvements, and industry. Man flies through the heavens, sails under the seas, circles in outer space around the globe. This is his day. But Christ's day is coming. You can do as you please now, you can trample Him underfoot, you can spit in His face. But when God's day comes, the Man of Sorrows will be the Man of Wrath. The gentle Jesus will be our judge. The crucified Christ will be the crowned King. And you'll face Him then, if you are not saved.

3. *It will be a day of wrath.* Today is the day of grace and mercy, but there'll be none then. Today you can cry out to God and be saved. In that day your cry will be too late. God offers you tenderness and forgiveness now. At the Great White Throne you'll find only fiery indignation and judgment.

4. *It will be the last day.* Time will have ended, and every opportunity for salvation will be over. God's people, His saints, will be dwelling in everlasting joy and bliss, while the devil's people, the lost sinners, will be standing before the Great White Throne, awaiting judgment and damnation.

## III. THE JUDGE OF THIS JUDGMENT

Acts 17:31 tells us that the judge will be the man whom God raised from the dead, His Son, Jesus Christ. Let me tell you some things about this judge.

1. *He is omnipresent; He is everywhere.* His eyes run to and fro throughout the earth. He sees everything. When you stand before the Great White Throne, He will say, "I was there when you did evil. The darkness could not hide you."

A dying infidel had these words in a sign over his bed: "God is nowhere." A little girl who was just learning to spell spelled out the words, "God is now here." The poor man was so moved by the little girl's words that he broke down and cried out to a willing Savior for salvation. Yes, He is now here. He is everywhere, as you live and as you die.

2. *He is omniscient; He knows everything.* In this world a man is sometimes convicted because of circumstantial evidence. It will not be so at that judgment. He knows the true facts in every case. He knows how men have gone on in their sin, rejecting Him. He knows the punishment they deserve.

3. *He is omnipotent; He has all power.* A criminal may commit a crime and flee to some foreign country, where he escapes the penalty of his crime. But he can't do that when God's judgment falls. With His mighty power, God will bring all sinners

to judgment. Even though God has to burn the world and sift the ashes, He will bring lost men to face the judgment of the Great White Throne. His arm is mighty to save you now, but then He will be the omnipotent judge.

## IV. THE PEOPLE
## WHO WILL BE JUDGED

Who are to be judged? No Christians will be judged; their judgment has passed. The ones to be judged are those whose names "are not written in the Lamb's Book of Life." Not just the bad people, the deep-dyed sinners, but all who have left Christ out of their hearts and lives will be there.

Revelation 21:8—"But the fearful, and unbelieving, and the abominable, and murders and whoremongers, and sorcerers, and idolaters, and all liars, shall have their part in the lake which burneth with fire and brimstone; which is the second death." These are the ones who will be judged at the Great

White Throne. There are many evil people named in this list, but please notice that "the unbelievers," however good they might be, are also included.

Your name may be written on a church roll, but if you haven't been born again, you will stand with this group before the Great White Throne. It is not a question of goodness or works. It is a question of whether or not you have been born again, through your repentance for sin and your faith in the Lord Jesus Christ.

Now God permits every man to make his own choice. You can meet Christ here and be saved, or you can meet Him that day in judgment and be cast into the Lake of Fire. He will receive you now if you come to Him. He says, ". . . him that cometh to me I will in no wise cast out" (John 6:37). But in that day He will cast out all who stand before Him.

The Great White Throne is vacant now. But the mercy throne is occupied by a compassionate and loving Savior. At that throne you find grace, forgiveness, and salvation. But when you stand before the Great White Throne, the day of mercy will be over and the day of condemnation will have begun. Take your choice. But be wise. Choose Jesus now before it is too late.

Over in Scotland two brothers were out on a lake when a storm came up. Their boat overturned, so they swam toward a rock that was jutting up out of the water. The older brother finally reached the rock, but he was completely exhausted. He could not swim another foot, so he just clung to the rock with the little strength he had left. As he looked back, he saw his younger brother battling against the storm. All he could do was call to him. But soon the younger brother drowned as the older brother wept. Soon people from the shore rowed out and rescued the boy from the rock. Over and over he told the story, always ending with the words: "Oh, little brother was nearly saved. Little brother was nearly saved." And every time he recounted his experience, he would finish on that plaintive note, "Little brother was nearly saved."

Oh, friend, will it be that way with you? You come to the services, you hear the Gospel, and you feel God's Holy Spirit knocking at your heart's door. But you go away without making your decision for Christ. You go away lost and condemned. Then on that fateful day, when you stand before the Great White Throne, you'll look back over your life. You'll remember how you rejected Christ, and you'll cry out forever: "I was so near and yet so far. I was nearly saved."

A certain fine couple had only one child, a little boy. When that boy grew up, he began to drink and gamble, bringing his parents to shame and disgrace. Again and again the father helped the boy out of his troubles, only to see him go down again. At last, with his patience exhausted, the father said, "John, if you'll turn away from your life of sin and live a good life, this home and all I have will be yours. But if you continue as in the past, I want you to know that I have paid you out of trouble for the last time." In anger the boy left home.

The boy's mother was heartbroken, and she became ill. The husband called in one doctor after another, but they could not help her. One day one of the doctors said to the father, "She has just a little while to live." Her husband went to her bedside. She looked up and said, "I know I am dying, but I would like to look once more into the face of our son. Grant me my dying wish. It will ease my heart in my last hour." The father soon learned the whereabouts of the boy and wired him to come home.

The boy rushed home and came in to kneel by the bedside of his dying mother. He sobbed, "Oh, Mother, my sin has broken your heart and your health. Can you forgive me? Can God forgive me?" And the mother answered, "Oh, John, I do love you. My love has followed you everywhere. I freely forgive you and I know God will. I am dying, but when I get to heaven I'll have to tell Jesus that heaven will not be complete unless my boy is there. Won't you give your heart to Jesus and meet me in heaven?" And the boy answered, "Yes, Mother, by the grace of God I will."

Then she called her husband to her side and said, "Honey, our boy is home at last. He has given his heart to Jesus, and he'll never cause you any more trouble. Won't you be reconciled to him before I go?" And she reached up one hand and took hold of her husband's hand. She reached up the other hand, took hold of John's hand, and brought their hands together. Then she fell back on her pillow and died.

Oh, friend, won't you be reconciled to God? Christ died on the cross for you. Now He asks you to give Him your hand, that He might place it in the hand of God. There is salvation for you if you'll do this; there is foregiveness for you; there is heaven for you. If you don't come to Christ, there is nothing left for you but eternal death. Come to Him now and you'll never have to face the Great White Throne of Judgment.

# THE SHEEP AND THE GOATS

*Matthew the Evangelist*

*(Matthew 25:31–46)*

WHEN THE SON OF MAN shall come in his glory, and all the holy angels with him, then shall he sit upon the throne of his glory:

And before him shall be gathered all nations: and he shall separate them one from another, as a shepherd divideth his sheep from the goats:

And he shall set the sheep on his right hand, but the goats on the left.

Then shall the King say unto them on his right hand, Come, ye blessed of my Father, inherit the kingdom prepared for you from the foundation of the world:

For I was a hungered, and ye gave me meat: I was thirsty, and ye gave me drink: I was a stranger, and ye took me in:

Naked, and ye clothed me: I was sick, and ye visited me: I was in prison, and ye came unto me.

Then shall the righteous answer him, saying, Lord, when saw we thee a hungered, and fed thee? or thirsty, and gave thee drink?

When saw we thee a stranger, and took thee in? or naked, and clothed thee?

Or when saw we thee sick, or in prison, and came unto thee?

And the King shall answer and say unto them, Verily I say unto you, Inasmuch as ye have done it unto one of the least of these my brethren, ye have done it unto me.

Then shall he say also unto them on the left hand, Depart from me, ye cursed, into everlasting fire, prepared for the devil and his angels:

For I was hungry, and ye gave me no meat: I was thirsty, and ye gave me no drink:

I was a stranger, and ye took me not in: naked, and ye clothed me not: sick, and in prison, and ye visited me not.

Then shall they also answer him, saying, Lord, when saw we thee ahungered, or athirst, or a stranger, or naked, or sick, or in prison, and did not minister unto thee?

Then shall he answer them, saying, Verily I say unto you, Inasmuch as ye did it not to one of the least of these, ye did it not to me.

And these shall go away into everlasting punishment: but the righteous into life eternal.

# THE NIGHT I DREAMED OF JUDGMENT

*Jerome* — strange concept of God.

It was many years ago when, for the sake of the kingdom of heaven, I had cut myself off from my home, my parents, my sister, my kinsmen, and—what was even more difficult—from an accustomed habit of good living. It was going to Jerusalem to be a soldier of Christ. But I could not do without the library which I had collected for myself at Rome by great care and effort. And so, poor wretch that I was, I used to fast and then read Cicero. After frequent night vigils, after shedding tears which the remembrance of past sins brought forth from my inmost heart, I would take in my hands a volume of Plautus. When I came to myself and began to read a prophet again, I rebelled at the uncouth style and—because with my blinded eyes I could not look upon the light—I thought this the fault not of my eyes but of the sun.

While the old serpent was thus having sport with me, in about Mid-Lent a fever attacked my enfeebled body and spread to my very vitals, what I say is almost beyond belief, but without cessation it so wrought havoc upon my wretched limbs that my flesh could scarcely cling to my bones. Meanwhile preparations for my funeral were being made. My entire body was already cold. The vital warmth of life still throbbed feebly only in my poor breast. Suddenly I was caught up in the spirit and dragged before the tribunal of the Judge. Here there was so much light and such a glare from the brightness of those standing around that I cast myself on the ground and dared not look up. Upon being asked my status, I replied that I was a Christian. And He who sat upon the judgment seat said: "Thou liest. Thou are a Ciceronian, not a Christian. 'Where thy treasure is, there is thy heart also.'" I was struck dumb on the spot. Amid the blows—for He had ordered me to be beaten—I was tormented the more by the flame of conscience. I repeated to myself the verse: "And who shall confess thee in hell?" However, I began to cry aloud and to say with lamentation: "Have mercy on me, Lord, have mercy on me." The petition reechoed amid the lashes. Finally, casting themselves before the knees of Him who presided, the bystanders besought Him to have mercy on the young man, granting me opportunity to repent of my error and then to exact the penalty if I ever again read books of pagan literature. Being caught in such an extremity, I would have been willing to make even greater promises. I began to take an oath, swearing by His name, saying: "O Lord, if ever I possess or read secular writings, I have denied thee." After I had uttered the words of this oath, I was discharged and returned to the world above. To the surprise of all, I opened my eyes, which were suffused with such showers of tears that my grief produced belief in the incredulous. That had not been mere sleep or meaningless dreams, by which we are often deceived. As witness I have the tribunal before which I lay, as witness the judgment of which I was afraid. May it never be my fate to undergo such questioning! My shoulders were black and blue, and I felt the blows after I awoke from sleep. After that I read God's word with greater zeal than I had previously read the writings of mortals.

# DIES IRAE

## Thomas of Celano

Day of wrath, the years are keeping,
When the world shall rise from sleeping,
With a clamor of great weeping!

Earth shall fear and tremble greatly
To behold the advent stately
Of the Judge that judgeth straitly.

And the trumpet's fierce impatience
Scatter strange reverberations
Thro' the graves of buried nations.

Death and Nature will stand stricken
When the hollow bones shall quicken
And the air with weeping thicken.

When the Creature, sorrow-smitten,
Rises where the Judge is sitting
And beholds the doom-book written.

For, that so his wrath be slakèd,
All things sleeping shall be wakèd,
All things hidden shall be naked.

When the just are troubled for thee,
Who shall plead for me before thee,
Who shall stand up to implore thee?

Lest my great sin overthrow me,
Let thy mercy, quickened thro' me,
As a fountain overflow me!

For my sake thy soul was movèd;
For my sake thy name reprovèd,
Lose me not whom thou hast lovèd!

Yea, when shame and pain were sorest,
For my love the cross thou borest,
For my love the thorn-plait worest.

By that pain that overbore thee,
By those tears thou weepest for me,
Leave me strength to stand before thee.

For the heart within me yearneth,
And for sin my whole face burneth;
Spare me when thy day returneth.

By the Magdalen forgiven,
By the thief made pure for heaven,
Even to me thy hope was given.

Tho' great shame be heavy on me,
Grant thou, Lord, whose mercy won me,
That hell take not hold upon me.

Thou whom I have loved solely,
Thou whom I have loved wholly,
Leave me place among the holy!

When thy sharp wrath burns like fire,
With the chosen of thy desire,
Call me to the crowned choir!

Prayer, like flame with ashes blending,
From my crushed heart burns ascending;
Have thou care for my last ending.

# THE DAY
# OF WRATH

## Columba of Iona

Day of the king most righteous,
The day is nigh at hand,
The day of wrath and vengeance,
And darkness on the land.

Day of thick clouds and voices,
Of mighty thundering,
A day of narrow anguish
And bitter sorrowing.

The love of women's over,
And ended is desire,
Men's strike with men is quiet,
And the world lusts no more.

# AS THE WIND WHIRLS

## Paulinus of Nola

BLESSED IS THE MAN who isolates his way of life far from the company of irreligious men, no longer dwelling in the path of sinners or sitting in the seat of corruption, but who concentrates his whole heart on God's law, pondering night and day His commands for life's conduct, and ennobling his mind with habits of purity. He will be like a river-tree which feeds on the nourishing moisture of the bank; soon to yield his fruit in fullness at the due time, green with the foliage that never withers, he will endure as living wood with undying leaves.

Such glory as this will not attend the godless. The anger of God will sweep them from His face as the wind whirls off dusty ashes. Accordingly, the hordes of men scattered throughout the world will be divided in such a way that the godless who have denied God the worship which is His due will not rise again for judgment, but will be punished. Blatant guilt needs no investigation to uncover it, because those who do not bear the sign of salvation on their heads will flaunt before them the mark of impending death.

But the great crowd of sinners not hostile to God will rise again not to glory but to be submitted to scrutiny. The man who is to reveal and render an account of his actions, and be approved or condemned according to his differing deeds, cannot sit with the saints.

Those who are ignorant of the law will fall, scattered in the disorder; he who fell while living under the law will be judged by the law. Fire will be the judge, and will rush through every deed. Every act that the flame does not consume but approves will be allotted eternal reward. He who has done deeds which must be burned will suffer injury, but will safely escape the flames; yet wretched because of the marks on his charred body, he will preserve his life without glory. He was conquered by the flesh, but not perverted in mind; therefore, in spite of his denying to the law the allegiance which was its due, by his frequent involvement in many sins, he will never be exiled from the shores of salvation, for he preserves the eternal glory of the faith.

So as long as all of us in this world maintain life's course and our days continue, we must keep our feet firmly on the right path, and not be seduced onto the slippery and broad highway. It is better to struggle on the narrow path and to enter by strenuous exertion. God gladly acknowledges the way of good men, but the path of the godless will be destroyed and leveled.

## MOSES AND LUTHER AT THE LAST JUDGMENT

*Martin Luther*

"I WON'T TOLERATE Moses because he is an enemy of Christ. If he appears with me before the judgment I'll turn him away in the name of the devil and say, 'Here stands Christ.'

"In the last judgment Moses will look at me and say, 'You have known and understood me correctly,' and he will be favorably disposed to me."

## THE RIGHT HAND AND THE LEFT

*Paulinus of Nola*

LET US ALSO be the right hand of Him who is wholly a right hand; in our actions let us have no left hand so that we may deserve to stand on the right hand of the Judge, or, rather, to be His right hand; thus, on the day of retribution, the Lord who repays may count our deeds as the hairs of His head, as He Himself stated in the Gospel. These deeds must be proclaimed at the Judgment, when He will requite the deserving merits of spiritual virtues with divine blessings and with kingly payment.

## THE CONTINUING JUDGMENT

*Augustine of Hippo*

WHEN WE TALK of the Day of Judgment, we add the epithet "Final," or "Last," because God's judgment is happening even now. This judgment began at the start of the human race, when God expelled the first human beings from paradise, and cut them off from the tree of life, because they had committed a great sin. Indeed, it happened when God did not spare the angels who sinned, whose prince first brought about his own ruin, and then through envy brought ruin on mankind: here, beyond doubt, was a judgment. And it is because of God's high and just judgment that the life of men and of demons, on earth and in the sky above us, is most miserable, full of uncertainty and hardship. Even if no one had sinned, it would have been by an act of good and just judgment that God would have kept the whole world of rational creatures attached to himself without faltering. He passes judgment not only generally, on the race of demons and men, so that they are in misery because of the first offenses; but also on the particular acts of individuals, the acts of their own free choice. . . .

# DIALOGUE OF THE BODY WITH THE SOUL, WHICH IS LEADING IT TO JUDGMENT

*Jacopone da Todi*

O flesh now putrified, I'm spirit in agony;
Rise up immediately, we're doomed both to be tried.

The angel is trumpeting in tones dread and severe:
We must before the King without delay appear;
You lived once arguing that we need have no fear:
I erred to trust and hear when you had sin for guide.

Then you're my soul I see, genteel, intelligent!
Since you withdrew from me again to naught I
  went;
Keep me now company that I bear no torment:
I see folk pestilent with faces evil-eyed.

Those are the demons cursed with whom you now
  must dwell;
You should not ask the worst: what you must suffer
  well,
My thoughts are too dispersed to bring myself to
  tell.
Were seas with ink to swell, the sum they could not
  write.

I cannot go ahead for I'm so worn and spent
That I am almost dead, I feel stern death commence;
From me you would have fled: each joint in me you
  rent,
You've wreaked such violence my bones all burst
  inside.

As you and I, humane, were fused with love's deep
  fire,
So are we joined in pain by eternal rancor dire;
The bone shrinks on the vein, sinews with joints
  conspire;
Deranged all humors that prior conditions could
  provide.

Sage Avicenna never, nor Galen, Hippocrates,
The congress could dissever of my infirmities;
They all are joined together and make your rage
  increase:
I feel such catastrophes I wish at birth I'd died.

Rise up, oh cursed and smitten, you can no more
  delay;
Upon your brow is written each sin we did essay:
And that to plain sight hidden which we have done
  each day,
Must be put on display, in view of all spread wide.

Who is this great lord crowned most high king full
  of grace?
I'd sink into the ground, such fear does he upraise;
Where could I flee unfound by his inexorable gaze?
Earth, be my hiding place! His wrath keep from
  my sight.

Lo! This is Christ our Lord, God's only begotten
  Son;
To see his face tear-scored, he loathes the fate I've
  spun:
We could have had reward, his kingdom could have
  won;
Foul, guilty body undone, see what we've gained by
  pride!

# THE GENERAL RECKONING

*from* Everyman

## GOD'S APPRAISAL

(GOD APPEARS AND SPEAKS)

*I perceive here in my majesty,*
*How that all creatures be to me unkind,*
*Living without dread in worldly prosperity.*
*Of spiritual sight the people be so blind,*
*Drowned in sin, they know me not for their God;*
*In worldly riches is all their mind,*
*They fear not my righteousness, the sharp rod;*
*My law that I showed, when I for them died,*
*They clean forget, and shedding of my blood red;*
*I hung between two, it cannot be denied;*
*To get men life I suffered to be dead;*
*I healed their feet, with thorns hurt was my head—*
*I could do no more than I did truly,*
*And now I see the people do clean forsake me.*
*They love the seven deadly sins damnable;*
*And pride, covetize, wrath, and lechery,*
*Now in the world be made commendable;*
*And thus they leave of angels the heavenly*
  *company;*
*Every man liveth so after his own pleasure,*
*And yet of their life they be nothing sure.*
*I see the more that I forbear*
*The worse they be from year to year;*
*All that liveth impaireth fast,*
*Therefore I will with all my haste*
*Have a reckoning of Everyman's person*
*For if I leave the people thus alone*
*In their life and wicked tempests,*
*Verily they will become much worse than beasts;*
*For now one would by envy another eat;*
*Charity they all do clean forget.*
*I hoped well that every man*
*In my glory should make his mansion,*
*And thereto I had them all elect;*
*But now I see, like traitors abject,*
*They thank me not for pleasure that I them meant,*
*Nor yet for their being that I to them have lent;*
*I proffer the people great multitude of mercy,*
*But few there be that ask it heartily;*
*They be so cumbered with worldly riches,*
*That needs on them I must do justice,*
*On Everyman living without fear.*
*Where art thou, Death, thou mightly messenger?*

## EVERYMAN'S PRAYER

*O eternal God, O heavenly figure,*
*O way of righteousness, O goodly vision,*
*Which descended down in a virgin pure*
*Because He would Everyman redeem,*
*Which Adam forfeited by his disobedience.*
*O blessed Godhead, elect and divine,*
*Forgive my grievous offense,*
*Here I cry Thee mercy in this presence.*
*O soul's treasure, O ransomer and redeemer*
*Of all the world, hope and leader,*
*Mirror of joy, and founder of mercy,*
*Which illumineth heaven and earth thereby,*
*Hear my clamorous complaint, thought it late be,*
*Receive my prayers. Unworthy in this heavy life*
*Though I be, a sinner most abominable,*
*Yet let my name be written in Moses' table;*
*O Mary, pray to the Maker of everything,*
*To help me at my ending,*
*And save me from the power of my enemy,*
*For Death assaileth me strongly.*
*And, Lady, that I may by means of thy prayer*
*Of your Son's glory be the partaker,*
*By the pity of his Passion I it crave,*
*I beseech you, help my soul to save.*

"He can't stand the idea of no-fault insurance."

# NOW IS THE TIME TO WORK

*Thomas à Kempis*

AT EVERY TURN of your life, keep the end in view; remember that you will have to stand before a strict Judge, who knows everything, who cannot be won over by gifts or talked around by excuses, who will give you your deserts. What sort of defense will you make before One who knows the worst that can be said against you—poor, sinful fool, so often panic-stricken when you meet with human disapproval! Strange, that you should look forward so little to the Day of Judgment, when there will be no counsel to plead for you, because everyone will be hard put to it to maintain his own cause! Now is the time to work, while there is a harvest to be reaped, now is the time when tears and sighs and lamenting of yours will be taken into account, and listened to, and can make satisfaction for the debt you owe.

Nothing so important, nothing so useful, if you want to clear your soul of that debt, as to be a man who can put up with a great deal. Such a man, if he is wronged, is more distressed over the sin committed than over the wrong done him; he is always ready to say a prayer for his enemies, forgives an injury with all his heart, and is quick to ask forgiveness of others, and you will find him more easily moved to pity than to anger. And all the while he is putting constraint upon himself, doing all he can to make corrupt nature the servant of the spirit.

Much better to get rid of your sins now, prune away your bad habits here, than keep them to be paid for hereafter; it's only our preposterous attachment to creature comforts that blinds us. . . .

Take your sins seriously *now*, be sorry for them *now*, and at the Day of Judgment you will have confidence, the confidence of blessed souls. How fearlessly, then, the just will confront those persecutors of theirs, who kept them down all the time! The man who submitted to human judgments so meekly will now take rank as judge; in perfect calm they will stand there, the poor, the humble, while the proud are daunted by every prospect that meets them.

We shall see, then, what the true wisdom was—learning how to be a fool, and despised, for the love of Christ; troubles endured with patience will be a grateful memory to us, and it will be the turn of the wicked to look foolish. See how all pious souls make merry, and the scoffers go sad; how the body that was mortified shows fairer, now, than if it had been continually pampered; how rags are all the wear, and fine clothes look shabby; how the gilded palace shrinks into insignificance beside the poor man's cottage! The dogged patience you showed here will do you more good than all earth's crowns; you will get more credit for unthinking obedience than for any worldly wisdom.

Philosophy will be less consolation to you than a good clean conscience, and all the treasures on earth won't outweigh the contempt of riches. The devout prayers you offered, not the good meals you ate, will be your comfort then. The silence you kept, not the long chats you had, will be pleasant to think of then. Saintly deeds done, not phrases neatly turned, will avail you then. A well-disciplined life of hard penitential exercise, not a good time here on earth, will be your choice then.

Love God with all your heart, and you've nothing to fear; death or punishment, judgment or hell; love, when it reaches its full growth, is an unfailing passport to God's presence. If we are still hankering after our sinful habits, of course we are afraid of death and judgment. Just as well, all the same, that if love can't succeed in beckoning us away from evil courses, we should be scared away by the fear of hell. Only, if a man doesn't make the fear of God his first consideration, his good resolutions won't last; he will walk into some trap of the Devil's before long.

The following was written by the Rev. JOHN WESLEY, of London, in 1774; and a copy of it was sent to the King of England, which has ever since put a stop to the play, called "The Day of Judgment," which was about that time performing in the London Theatres.

# BY COMMAND OF THE KING OF KINGS,[a]
### *And at the desire of all those who love His appearing.*[b]

SEARCH THE SCRIPTURES.
John v. 39.

a) Rev. xix. 16.—1 Tim. vi. 15.
b) 2 Tim. iv. 3.—Tit. ii. 13.

New Jerusalem.

At the Theatre of the UNIVERSE,[c] on the Eve of Time,[d] will be performed,

c) Rev. 20, 11.—Matth. 24, 26.
d) Rev. 10, 6. 7.—Dan. 12, 18.

# THE GREAT ASSIZE, or
# DAY OF JUDGMENT.[e]

## THE SCENERY,

e) Heb. 9, 27.—Ps. 9, 7. 8.—Rev. 6, 17.
2 Cor. 5, 10.—Zeph. 1, 14 to 17.

WHICH is now actually preparing, will not only surpass every thing that has yet been seen, but will infinitely exceed the utmost stretch of human conception. f) There will be a just representation of all the inhabitants of the world, in their various and proper colours; and their customs and manners will be so exactly and minutely delineated, that the most secret thought will be discovered. g) "For God will bring every work into judgment, with every secret thing, whether it be good, or whether it be evil." Ecc. xii. 14.

This Theatre will be laid out after a new plan, and will consist of PIT and GALLERY, only; and, contrary to all others, the Gallery is fitted up for the reception of people of high (or heavenly) birth; h) and the Pit for those of low (or earthly) rank. i) N. B. The Gallery is very spacious, k) and the Pit without bottom. l)

To prevent inconvenience, there are separate doors for admitting the company; and they are so different, that none can mistake that are not wilfully blind. The door which oppens into the Gallery is very narrow, and the steps up to it are somewhat difficult; for which reason there are seldom many people about it. m) But the door that gives entrance into the Pit, is very wide and commodious, which causes such numbers to flock to it, that it is generally crowded. n) N. B. The straight door leads toward the right hand, and the broad one to the left. o)

It will be in vain for one with a tinselled coat, and borrowed language, to personate one of High Birth, in order to get admittance into the Upper Places, p) for there is One of wonderful and deep penetration, who will search and examine every individual; q) and all who cannot pronounce Shibboleth, r) in the language of Canaan, s) or has not received a White Stone and a new name, t) or cannot prove a clear title to a certain portion of the Land of Promise, u) must be turned in at the left hand door. w)

## THE PRINCIPAL PERFORMERS

Are described in 1 Thes. 4, 19. 2 Thes. 1, 7. 8. 9. Matth. 24, 30. 31.—25, 31. 32. Dan. 7, 9. 10. Judg. 14, 4. Rev. 20, 12 to 15. &c. But as there are some people much better acquainted with the contents of a *Play Bill* than the *Word of God*, it may not be amiss to transcribe a verse or two for their perusal. "The Lord Jesus will be revealed from Heaven with his mighty angels in flaming fire, taking vengeance on them that obey not the gospel, who shall be glorified in his saints. A fiery stream issued and came forth from before him. A thousand thousands ministered unto him, and ten thousand times ten thousand stood before him: The Judgment was set, and the Books were opened, and whosoever was not found written in the Book of Life, was cast into the Lake of Fire."

## Act First of this Grand and Solemn Piece,

Will be opened by an Arch-Angel with the Trump of God. x) "For the trumpet shall sound and the dead shall be raised." 1 Cor. 15, 52.
ACT SECOND—will be a PROCESSION of SAINTS, in white, y) with Golden Harps, accompanied with shouts of joy and songs of praise. z)
ACT THIRD—WILL BE AN ASSEMBLAGE OF THE UNREGENERATE. a)
The Music will consist chiefly of Cries, b) accompanied with Weeping, Wailing, Lamentation and Woe. c)

## To conclude with an Oration by the Son of God.

It is written in the 25th chapter of Matthew, from the 34th verse to the end of the chapter; but for the sake of those who seldom read the Scriptures, I shall here transcribe two verses:— *Then shall the King say unto them on his right hand, 'Come ye blessed of my Father, inherit the Kingdom prepared for you from the foundation of the world.' Then shall he say unto them on his left hand, 'Depart from me, ye cursed, into everlasting fire, prepared for the Devil and his angels."

## AFTER WHICH THE CURTAIN WILL DROP!

Then! O to tell!

| | | |
|---|---|---|
| John 5, 28. 29. | Some raised on high, and others doom'd to hell! | Luke 9, 14. 27. While those who trampled under foot his grace, |
| Rev. 5, 8. 9. | These praise the Lamb, and sing redeeming love, | Matth. 25, 30. Are banish'd now forever from his face. |
| Luke 16, 22. 23. | Lodg'd in his bosom, all his goodness prove: | Luke 16, 29. Divided thus, a gulph is fixed between, |
| | | Matth. 25, 46. And [everlasting] closes up the scene. |

*Thus will I do unto thee, O Israel; and because I will do thus unto thee, prepare to meet thy God. Amos 4, 12.*

Tickets for the PIT at the easy purchase of following the pomps and vanities of the fashionable world, and the desires and amusements of the flesh: d) to be had at every flesh-pleasing assembly. "If ye live after the flesh, ye shall die." Rom. 8, 13.

Tickets for the GALLERY, at no less rate than being converted, e) forsaking all, f) denying self, taking up the cross, g) and following Christ in the regeneration: h) To be had nowhere but in the *Word of God*, and where that word appoints. "He that hath ears to hear, let him hear, and be not deceived; God is not mocked; for whatsoever a man soweth, that shall he also reap." Matth. 11, 15. Gal. 6, 7.

N. B. No money will be taken at the door; i) nor will any tickets give admittance into the Gallery, but those sealed by the Holy Ghost, k) with Immanuel's signet: l) Watch therefore; be ye also ready, for in such an hour, as ye think not, the Son of Man cometh. Math. 24, 42. 44.

f) 1 Cor. 2, 9.—Isa. 64, 4.—Ps. 31, 19.
g) Matth. 12, 36.—1 Cor. 4, 5.—Rom. 2, 15. 16.
h) John 3, 3. 5.—1 Pet. 1, 23.—Rom. 8, 14.
i) James 3, 14. 15.—Rom. 8, 6. 7. 8.—Gal. 5, 19 to 21.
k) Luke 14, 22.—John 14, 2.
l) Rev. 9, 12.—19, 20.

m) Matth. 7, 14.
n) ——— 7, 13.
o) ——— 25, 33.
p) ——— 7, 21 to 28.
q) Ps. 44, 20. 21.—Jer. 17, 10.—Zeph. 1, 12.—2 Tim. 2, 19.—John 10, 14.
r) Judges 12, 6.
s) Isa. 19, 11.—Zeph. 3, 9.
t) Rev. 2, 17. u) Heb. 11, 1. 8. 9.—Gal. 3, 9. 29.—2 Cor. 18, 5.
w) Ps. 9, 17.—Heb. 3, 17 to 19.

x) 1 Thes. 4, 16.—Matth. 24, 31.
y) Rev. 7, 14.—19, 14.
z) ——— 14, 2. 3.—15, 2 to 4.
a) 1 Cor. 6, 9. 10.—Matth. 13, 41.
b) Luke 23, 3.—Rev. 6, 16.
c) Luke 13, 28.—Matth. 18, 49. 50.—Rev. 1, 7.—Ezek. . . . . 10.

[d] James 4, 2.—1, 15. 16. 17.—Col. 3, 5. 6. 1 Tim. 5, 6.—Ephes. 5, 3 to 7.
e) Matth. 18, 8.—Acts 3, 19.
f) Luke 14, 33.—18, 29. 36.
g) ——— 9, 23 to 26.—14, 27.
h) Matth. 19, 28. 29.—Galater 5, 24. 25. Eph. 5, 1. 2.
i) Acts 8, 20 to 23.—Zeph. 1, 18.
k) 2 Cor. 1, 22.—4, 30.—Ephs. 1, 13.
l) Rev. 7, 2.—14, 1.—Ezek. 9, 4.

Printed and for Sale by G. S. Peters, Harrisburg, Pa.

# DAY IN COURT

## C. S. Lewis

IF THERE IS any thought at which a Christian trembles, it is the thought of God's "judgment." The "Day" of Judgment is "that day of wrath, that dreadful day." We pray to God to deliver us "in the hour of death and at the day of judgment." Christian art and literature for centuries have depicted its terrors. This note in Christianity certainly goes back to the teaching of Our Lord Himself; especially to the terrible parable of the sheep and the goats. This can leave no conscience untouched, for in it the "goats" are condemned entirely for their sins of omission; as if to make us fairly sure that the heaviest charge against each of us turns not upon things he has done but on those he never did—perhaps never dreamed of doing.

It was therefore with great surprise that I first noticed how the Psalmists talk about the judgments of God. They talk like this: "O let the nations rejoice and be glad, for thou shalt judge the folk righteously" (Psalm 67:4), "Let the field be joyful . . . all the trees of the wood shall rejoice before the Lord, for he cometh, for he cometh to judge the earth" (Psalm 96:12–13). Judgment is apparently an occasion of universal rejoicing. People ask for it: "Judge me, O Lord my God, according to thy righteousness" (Psalm 35:24).

The reason for this soon becomes very plain. The ancient Jews, like ourselves, think of God's judgment in terms of an earthly court of justice. The difference is that the Christian pictures the case to be tried as a criminal case with himself as the plaintiff. The one hopes for acquittal, or rather for pardon; the other hopes for a resounding triumph with heavy damages. Hence he prays "judge my quarrel" or "avenge my cause" (Psalm 35:23). And

though, as I said a minute ago, Our Lord in the parable of the sheep and the goats painted the characteristically Christian picture in another place, He is very characteristically Jewish. Notice what He means by "an unjust judge." By those words most of us would mean someone like Judge Jeffreys or the creatures who sat on the benches of German tribunals during the Nazi regime: someone who bullies witnesses and jurymen in order to convict, and then savagely, to punish innocent men. Once again, we are thinking of a criminal trial. We hope we shall never appear in the dock before such a judge. But the unjust judge in the parable is quite a different character. There is no danger of appearing in his court against your will: the difficulty is the opposite —to get into it. It is clearly a civil action. The poor woman (Luke 18:1–5) has had her little strip of land—room for a pigsty or a hen run—taken away from her by a richer and more powerful neighbor (nowadays it would be town planners or some other "body"). And she knows she has a perfectly watertight case. If once she could get it into court and have it tried by the laws of the land, she would be bound to get that strip back. But no one will listen to her, she can't get it tried. No wonder she is anxious for "judgment."

Behind this lies an age-old and almost worldwide experience which we have been spared. In most places and times it has been very difficult for the "small man" to get his case heard. The judge (and, doubtless, one or two of his underlings) has to be bribed. If you can't afford to "oil his palm," your case will never reach court. Our judges do not receive bribes. (We probably take this blessing too much for granted; it will not remain with us automatically). We need not therefore be surprised if the Psalms, and the Prophets, are full of longing for judgment, and regard the announcement that "judgment" is coming as good news. Hundreds of thousands of people who have been stripped of all they possess and who have the right entirely on their side will at last be heard. Of course, they are not afraid of judgment. They know their case is unanswerable—if only it could be heard. When God comes to judge, at last it will.

Seymour Chwast

# THE GRACIOUS JUDGE

## *Andrew Murray*

GOD IS A GOD OF MERCY and a God of judgment. Mercy and judgment are ever together in His dealings. In the Flood, in the deliverance of Israel out of Egypt, in the overthrow of the Canaanites, we ever see mercy in the midst of judgment. In these, the inner circle of His own people, we see it too. The judgment punishes the sin, while mercy saves the sinner. Or, rather, mercy saves the sinner, not in spite of, but by means of, the very judgment that came upon his sin. In waiting on God, we must beware of forgetting this—as we wait we must expect Him as a God of judgment.

"In the way of thy judgments, O Lord, have we waited for thee." That will prove true in our inner experience. If we are honest in our longing for holiness, in our prayer to be wholly the Lord's, His holy presence will stir up and discover hidden sin, and bring us very low in the bitter conviction of the evil of our nature, its opposition to God's law, its impotence to fulfill that law. The words will come true: "Who may abide the day of his coming, for he is like a refiner's fire." "O that thou wouldest come down, as when the melting fire burneth!" In great mercy God executes, within the soul, His judgments upon sin, as He makes it feel its wickedness and guilt. Many a one tries to flee from these judgments. The soul that longs for God, and for deliverance from sin, bows under them in humility and in hope. In silence of soul it says: "Arise, O Lord! and let thine enemies be scattered. In the way of thy judgments we have waited for thee."

Let no one, who seeks to learn the blessed art of waiting on God, wonder if at first the attempt to wait on Him only discovers more of his sin and darkness. Let no one despair because unconquered sins, or evil thoughts, or great darkness appear to hide God's face. Was not, in His own beloved Son, the gift and bearer of His mercy on Calvary, the mercy as hidden and lost in the judgment? Oh, submit and sink down deep under the judgment of your every sin. Judgment prepares the way, and breaks out in wonderful mercy. It is written: "Thou shalt be redeemed with judgment." Wait on God, in the faith that His tender mercy is working out His redemption in the midst of judgment. Wait for Him, He will be gracious to you.

There is another application still, one of unspeakable solemnity. We are expecting God, in the way of His judgments, to visit this earth: we are waiting for Him. What a thought! We know of these coming judgments; we know that there are tens of thousands of professing Christians who live on in carelessness, and who, if no change come, must perish under God's hand. Oh, shall we not do our utmost to warn them, to plead with and for them, if God may have mercy on them! If we feel our want of boldness, want of zeal, want of power, shall we not begin to wait on God more definitely and persistently as a God of judgment, asking Him so to reveal Himself in the judgments that are coming on our very friends, that we may be inspired with a new fear of Him and them, and constrained to speak and pray as never yet. Verily, waiting on God is not meant to be a spiritual self-indulgence. Its object is to let God and His holiness, Christ and the love that died on Calvary, the Spirit and fire that burns in Heaven and came to earth, get possession of us, to warn and rouse men with the message that we are waiting for God in the way of His judgments. O Christian, prove that you really believe in the God of judgment!

*My soul, wait thou only upon God!*

## THE APPREHEN-SIVE DEFENDANT

### *Rufinus*

I THINK IT necessary to remind you of the intention behind the doctrine [of judgment], namely, that we should be daily apprehensive of the coming of the Judge. We are to frame our behavior on the assumption that we shall have to give an account to a Judge who is at hand. This is what the prophet meant by his saying about the man who is blessed: *Forasmuch as he orders his words with judgment.*

# THE WRATHFUL JUDGE *Bonaventure*

WHEN THE SIGN of the omnipotent Son of God appears in the clouds and the powers "of heaven are shaken" (Matthew 24:29) and fire engulfs the earth in the conflagration of the world and all the just are placed on the right and the wicked on the left, then the Judge of the universe will appear so wrathful to the reprobate that "they will say to the mountains and to the rocks: 'Fall upon us and hide us from the face of him who sits upon the throne and from the wrath of the Lamb'" (Revelations 6:16). "He shall don justice for a breastplate and shall wear sure judgment for a helmet. He shall take invincible equity as a shield and whet his dire anger for a spear, and the universe shall war with him against the foolhardy" (Wisdom of Solomon 5:18–20); so that those who fought insolently against the Creator of all will then, by God's just judgment, be conquered by all creatures.

*"On high
the wrathful Judge
will then appear;
below,
hell will open up
as a horrible chaos.
On the right
will be the accusing sins,
on the left
countless demons.
Thus surrounded,
where will the sinner flee?
Certainly, to hide will be impossible
and to be seen, intolerable.
For 'if the just man scarcely will
be saved,
where will the impious and sinner
appear?'"
"Do not, therefore, enter into judgment
with your servant,
O Lord!"*

R. Pryor

# AN ENDTIME MUSICAL

## *William Griffin*

A CHORUS LINE may be the simplest, profoundest, dancingest, most riveting, theatrical, imaginative musical ever to appear on the Broadway stage. It is also, I would like to think, a work of great spiritual beauty.

As lights come up on the stage, bare of scenery except for floor-to-ceiling mirrors, dozens of dancers are pounding the boards to the familiar rhythms of a rehearsal piano. They are being put through their paces by an unbending choreographer who barks at them meticulously, mercilessly: *Step! Kick! Leap! Touch! Pivot! Walk! Turn!* They are a mixed group: children of the rich, children of the poor; Occidental, Oriental; some bosomy, some bony; some muscular, some angular; but all athletic; and they move about the stage with professional, if unspectacular, ease. No stars here; no Nureyevs or Fonteyns, no Villellas or Tallchiefs. Just the common, ordinary, run-of-the-show dancers who provide background and bounce to Broadway musicals. Just twenty-seven dancers auditioning for eight jobs in a chorus line, any chorus line, in any musical show, anywhere in the universe.

The twenty-seven are quickly cut to seventeen. Not only must the survivors be able to perform tap, ballet, and jazz, but they must also—at the insistence of the choreographer—justify their existence, tell their life story, how they began dancing, how they got through adolescence, what their sexual orientation is, whether they have danced in a Broadway show before, and what they will do when they are able to dance no longer. Although they are more physically than verbally articulate, they do manage to blurt out quite poignantly, and sometimes quite

beautifully, their unhappy childhood, their raunchy adolescence, and their uneasy introduction to the harshnesses of the professional dance world. Dancing, it seems, was a refuge from reality, a release for their fantasy; it was also something they did extremely well. However loveless their lives had been, love now motivates their movements, and they dance only for the moment.

The seventeen are quickly cut to eight, four boys and four girls. Those who didn't make it simply fade out of the spotlights; those who did make it simply weep and gasp in relief. Ahead lies job security of a sort: a minimum-wage union contract, six weeks of rugged rehearsal, more weeks touring the show, then opening night on Broadway.

Painted across the width of the stage floor is a wide white line. On one side stands the literal meaning of *A Chorus Line*; on the other stand several possible figurative meanings of the work. On one side stands the choreographer, who can also be construed as a job interviewer, union steward, judge, football coach, drill sergeant. On the other side stand the dancers, who can also be seen as job applicants, stevedores, contestants, rookies, raw recruits. And by virtue of my tropological trampoline, that mode of conveyance by which a nimble-minded critic gets from one level of meaning to another, I suppose I could even say that God the dance master stands on one side of the white line and on the other are a myriad of souls auditioning for salvation, having not only to face the music but also to sing and dance to it, mankind hoofing its way on horn-hard soles, hoping to earn the definitely limited places in the kingdom of heaven.

A little far-fetched, you might say, and of course these figurative interpretations, especially the last, are by no means a perfect fit for what happens on the stage. Experiencing *A Chorus Line* in the theater may not make your soul want to trip the light fantatisc, but it will set your blood dancing. It will make you want to grab your sweater or sweatshirt, slip into your leotards or Levi's, lace up your Keds or Pumas or Adidases or whatever. It will make you want to stop slouching and start limbering up, to sweat the alcohol and cholesterol out of your veins and arteries, to articulate, in a bodily way, more pronounced and pulsating rhythms than your own. It's that kind of show.

# BOOK OF ACTIONS,
# BOOK OF LIFE

*Jacques Ellul*

Now THE DOUBLE PROBLEM appears: the Book of Life, the judgment according to works. I believe, on this second point, that we have already little by little perceived that it is not at all a matter of morality, nor of works in the narrowly Christian sense. The work of man is the total product of his life itself. The biblical teaching appears to me very clear. We have seen, on the other hand, that all that which had to be condemned has been condemned in the destruction of the nations. That in the life of man there is in reality the work of power, of death, of aggression, etc., which is abolished. But man himself? We are told that each is *judged* according to his works, and we have already encountered, in the overturning of the bowls, the judgment driving man into a corner. It is not said that men are *condemned* because of their works. Their works can be condemned: we have also seen that dissociation in the opposition between the overturning of the bowls which concerns men, and the condemnation of man's works of power with the Woman and Babylon. We see here not condemnations because the works are bad but a wholly different distinction: the inscription or noninscription in the Book of Life. There are the books of the actions of man, of the realizations brought about precisely during the thousand years when Satan was bound, of those works which had to be the expression of the liberation of man and which are the responsibility of man.

And then there is *the* Book of Life. In this passage there is an intermingling of two themes: on the one hand, that of the resurrection with the end of death; on the other, the theme of the Book of Life. Only those who are not written in the Book of Life (and not those who have produced bad works) are thrown into the second death. There is no correlation between the judgment of works and the gift of eternal life or rejection into death. The sole criterion is: one who was not found written in the Book of Life. "Was not"; then it was written before the judgment of works! And then the crucial question is posed, but without answer: Is it possible that some men have not been written in the Book of

Life? Is it possible that love rejects? Is it possible that the Living One destroys anything other than destruction? That the one who renews all things perpetuates the ancient status of death? That the one who has come to save all men has not completed his task and has saved only some? Is it possible that the Eternal abandon the temporal? That the one who is All leave outside himself an indistinct group of "Outside of Life"? That the Father expel his sons ("a man had two sons")? That the Omnipotent—for he is also the Omnipotent—finally be limited in his power by the rebellious work of men, which, we have seen, is annihilated? That the justice of God be expressed not in his wrath, which is very normal and well expressed in judgment and plagues, but in an eternal wrath? A wrath continuing forever? Have we not seen the impossibility of considering that the New Creation, that admirable symphony of love, could exist *beside* the world of wrath? Is God still double-faced: a visage of love turned toward his celestial Jerusalem and a visage of wrath turned toward this "hell"? Are then the peace of joy of God complete, since he continues as a God of wrath and of fulmination? Could paradise be what Romain Gary has so marvelously described in *Tulipe*, when he said that the trouble is not the concentration camp but "the very peaceable, very happy little village *beside* the camp"—the little village alongside, where people were undisturbed while millions died atrociously in the camp?

The evangelical image of the justice of God is not that. It is not that of the magistrate who dispatches condemnations. The evangelical image of the justice of God is the parables of the worker at the eleventh hour, and the lost sheep, and the pearl of great price (he has given all that he has, this God, in order to obtain what was in his eyes the pearl of great price —man; then is he going to break this pearl in pieces in order to throw some away?), and the prodigal son and the unfaithful steward—such is the justice of God. Neither retributive nor distributive. It is the justice of Love itself, who cannot see the one he judges except through his love, and who is always able to find in that fallen miserable being—rebel, blasphemer, slave, powerful, without shame, hating, devourer—the last tiny particle, invisible to any other than his love, and which he is going to gather up and save. Not all that this man has done in his life, not all the evil that he has been, but himself, this ultimate breath that God has loved. It is not theologically possible that there be damned men. That would mean, in a word, that there is an external limit to the love of God. Only the nothingness is annihilated. And in the second death there are not men, there are not lives; there are the evil works of man, there are Satan and the Devil, there are the incarnations (invented by man!) of these powers, there is death. Nothing more.

# AT EVENING
# WE SHALL
# BE JUDGED
# BY LOVE

*Robert W. Gleason*

CHRIST WILL COME to judge this world, this scene of His sufferings and humiliations, and He will come as Victor and Illuminator. Then will He be definitely revealed as King of a universe now entirely submissive to His regal power. Then will He unveil the mysteries of His providence over the world. The effects of all human actions upon the destiny of this cosmos will be made clear, and justice will triumph with a triumph which is absolute. During the course of temporal existence it was impossible to pass a final judgment upon the ensemble of created reality or upon the individual acts which inserted themselves into the context of history. Now Christ will be manifested as the living center of humanity, whose whole significance flows from Him. He will exercise His judicial power to glorify His Church and to proclaim the existence of sovereign goodness operative in the redemption of the world. The record of every individual with all its actions and motives will be reviewed and receive its reward or punishment. All existence, all that was done in time, will be submitted to this clarifying light of judgment.

This judgment, moreover, will disclose the vast plan for the redemption of humanity and the roles played by individuals and groups as this plan worked itself out. The confusions and obscurity of history will be dissolved as all things are seen in relation to that divine Word in whom they were made.

Beyond all else, it is the triumphant proof of God's redemptive love that will then emerge. For the judgment is ordained to manifest not the punitive powers of God but His all-conquering goodness. It will be discovered then by everyone how truly Jesus is to be defined in terms of love and how fitting it is for men to be appraised in terms of their relationship to Jesus. The position which a man took up on earth toward the Savior and His atonement will be decisive here. Sin will be unmasked and shown as the suicidal madness it is. The sinner who refused the advances of Christ will see absurdity streaming through the whole range of his being. The self-hatred which was the wellspring of the rejection which sin implies will be disclosed.

Any effort to interpret God's will expressed in the moral law as a frustrating burden upon man is annihilated now in the blinding vision of salvific love. All the demands of God upon man will be set forth in their true nature, as an espousal of the interests of man. The commandments of God will put off their exterior aspects of imposed authority and reveal their inner nature as the laws according to which man's being expands. They will be grasped even by the sinner as exteriorizations of an inner attitude of love on God's part. The dynamism of Christian life will yield up its secret to examination and will be revealed as love. "At evening we shall be judged by Love," and Love will judge our deeds and character, omissions and motives. In the light of eternity the Christian vocation will be understood as what it is: a vocation to love which affects the growth of man to maturity. Law and love will be seen in their original unity. The revelation of God concerning Himself will be seized in its full implications, and the liberty of the children of God will be made manifest.

The Christian, moreover, has lived in the close unity of the body of the Church, supported by the efforts of others, and himself giving impetus to the life of the whole. All the activities of the individual Christian have had their effects upon the whole body, and this interreaction of individual upon individual and upon the Church will be revealed to the society of the faithful in all its social import. A collective illumination will aid the faithful to judge the universal moral order, and there will be no more room for the questioning of history; it will have yielded up its innermost secrets, and all the intertwining series of causes and effects will be laid bare. The labors of the saints will be seen in their full depth and extent, which exceed the dimensions of their particular historical period. The collaboration of man with the labor of the eternal Father and Christ will be unmistakable. It will be the triumph of a society: the Church.

As the Christian has begun his life as a member of a society and has fostered that life within a society, so his final judgment will be social. The consummation of all things within the unity of the Mystical Body of Christ being now completed, the Christian will pass to the social life of the new Jerusalem.

# VII.
# HELL

"I only said you could take it with you.
I didn't say you could keep it!"

# IS HELL STILL A BURNING QUESTION?

## James Breig

BE IT EVER so horrible, there's no place like hell. That charming place of everlasting fire, pitchfork-bearing demons, and constant gnashing of teeth is going out of style for many contemporary believers, partly because they have focused their attention on heaven, partly because they cannot reconcile a merciful God with a damning divinity, partly because hell seems like such a childish belief, and partly because they don't really understand what hell is supposed to be. Threat? Punishment? Myth? Reality? Just what is hell?

According to Woody Allen, it is the abode of all the people who annoy him. In his recent film, *Annie Hall*, you will not see this sequence (filmed, edited, and then discarded): Allen descends in an elevator through the levels of hell. At each floor, some nemesis of his life steps on—CIA agents and fast-food waiters among them. At the final level a great blast of flame engulfs the elevator as Richard Nixon boards. That image of hell is what many Christians hold.

Hell is sort of a whimsical place, more of a joke than an eschatological reality. It is a fictional domain, created from one part Dante and one part Milton with a dash of religious art thrown in. The picture conjured up is most often the one presented in a campy movie of the '30s called *Dante's Inferno* in which Spencer Tracy (playing, ironically, a carnival con man named Jimmy Carter) presides over a sideshow attraction purporting to show the agonies of the damned. In mid-movie, illustrations of Dante's allegory come to life to show us what real gnashing of teeth is all about.

How can you take it seriously? Hell has become so trivialized that it has even lost its force as a curse. "Go to hell" is a suggestion friends share. "The hell it is" is an exclamation of surprise and incredulity. "Dammit" is something we utter when we stub our toes, not an eternal sentence.

And that's another thing. If the Church really wants us to believe in hell, then why don't we ever pick up the paper and read something like this?

> VATICAN CITY—*In colorful ceremonies today, full of traditional pageantry, Pope Paul VI solemnly declared that Adolf Hitler has been damned to hell.*
>
> *Thousands of pilgrims from Germany attended the outdoor rite as the pontiff announced the church's belief that Hitler deserved everlasting torment. His condemnation followed years of Vatican study and research, including the counterarguments presented by the angel's advocate of the church.*

After all, if we can canonize people, why can't we cast them down into the pit? Is it because the church always holds out some hope for forgiveness and mercy?

Many individual Catholics hold out that hope. Father Andrew Greeley has done a study showing that while seventy percent of Catholics believe in life after death, only one-third of them believe in hell.

What we may have here is a case of closing our eyes and hoping it will go away. Cardinal Newman recognized that symptom a century ago, writing, "I have held with a full, inward assent and belief the doctrine of eternal punishment, though I have tried by various ways to make the truth less terrible to the imagination."

What is the truth of hell? Does it exist? What is it like? Could someone really so order his life that he would choose to go there?

The origins of hell reach back into history. Early religions believed that the soul went somewhere, even if it only hung around the grave for all time.

Old Testament Jews called this location Sheol, and whether you were good or bad didn't make any difference. Everyone ended up in the same place.

After that the notion developed that how people lived should determine where they spent eternity. So good people stayed in Sheol—a sort of dark, cold region where nothing much went on—while the evil ones (primarily those who had sinned against the faith) where sent to Gehenna—the burning dump.

Picture an ancient Jewish mother strolling along Jerusalem's main drag with her cranky child in hand. Finally fed up with his antics along the food market's aisles, she points to the dump—a mound of rotting garbage, bones, rats, and worms—and warns him: "Keep it up and that's where you'll end up." And thus, according to some scholars, hell was born.

"I've seen it," says Dr. Martin Marty. "The fires we now associate with hell are symbols of

Gehenna" where fires burned constantly to keep the pile of rubbish manageable.

Add to this notion that Gehenna's location had once been the site of pagan child sacrifices and one understands how hell got such a bad name. It was the name Jesus used when he spoke several times in the Gospels about hell.

Christianity accepted the notion of hell as a place of fire and physical torment and thus spawned "fire-and-brimstone" sermons.

Such sermons are often referred to by people who have no idea what brimstone is much less what those sermons were like. (Fire-and-brimstone sermons are, in the scheme of homiletics, perhaps not as scary as hellfire-and-damnation preachings.) Let us journey back to the thirteenth century to hear one Berthold of Regensburg describe hell:

"The best man in hell has such comfort as if the whole world were on fire, even to the firmament on high, and he were in the midst of that fire in his shirt or stark naked."

Think that's bad? That was the guy on top. "But another man may have it tenfold worse or thirtyfold or sixtyfold"—wait, he's just getting started—"or an hundredfold or a thousandfold or sixty-thousand-fold worse, for the more his sins, the deeper his place in hell and the hotter his fire." Whew! Can't you just hear Berthold building up those "folds" until your pew started to get hot?

St. Cyprian announced to his readers that "ever-

burning Gehenna will burn up the condemned with living flames; nor will there be . . . respite. . . . Weeping will be useless and prayer ineffectual."

Pope Gregory I announced that it was his opinion that the fire of hell was one temperature, but it tormented each occupant in different ways depending on his or her sins.

Francis de Sales pictured hell as "a city involved in darkness, burning with brimstone and stinking pitch and full of inhabitants who cannot make their escape". . . .

Thomas Merton thought that "hell is where no one has anything in common with anybody else except the fact that they all hate one another and cannot get away from one another." Hell as a cocktail party.

Along about the seventeenth century, great thinkers, theologians, and educators began debating what hell was paved with. They came up with everything but yellow bricks.

A gaggle of them chose "good intentions," a saw we still use today.

Richard Baxter, a theologian with an active imagination, decided that "hell is paved with infants' skulls."

John Chrysostom had a happier thought: "Hell is paved with priests' skulls."

An English physician chose the "skulls of scholars" while a German educator was naturally dissatisfied with that and with craniums. "Hell," he proclaimed, "is paved with monks' cowls, priests' drapery, and spike helmets." Try to walk that road in your earth shoes.

There was a countermovement to all this pavement work. Francis de Sales wrote a letter to a friend and said simply, "Do not be troubled by the saying 'Hell is full of good intentions and wills.'" Poet Robert Southey put things into perspective by stating flatly that "it has been more wittily than charitably said that hell is paved with good intentions; they have their place in heaven also."

As to the location of hell, people have long held it to be in the center of the earth, an opinion geothermal proponents heartily support. No less an authority than Thomas Aquinas opined that "concerning the inquiry whether hell is at or near the center of the earth, my opinion is that nothing should be rashly asserted." This is so, he went on, because Augustine "reckoned that nobody knows where hell is." And besides, "I do not believe that man can know the position of hell."

Not everyone in the early church, however, was wrapped up in painting a picture of hell. There was a movement afoot that questioned not only the eternity of hell but also that its punishment consisted of physical fire. Origen, in the third century, was one who mulled over these problems.

Speculation and debate continue today, but the church's position remains firm if rooted in rather loose soil. Hell exists, says the church, because Christ will come to judge the living and the dead. The existence of hell is assumed, in other words, because of the doctrine of the last judgment.

Which doesn't clear up much. Is hell full of worms and fire like Gehenna? Or is it something else?

Many average Catholics will tell you that hell is here on earth; life is our punishment, they declare. It is a feeling voiced by philosopher Thomas Browne a few hundred years ago: "I feel sometimes a hell dwells within myself." The torment of living, of existing, of working out our problems and pains, of experiencing loss and failure and humiliation—all this, these people assert, is hell and nothing could be worse.

It is a feeling that Augustine understood and rejected: "The perpetual death of the damned will go on without end and will be their common lot, regardless of what people prompted by human sentiments may conjure up about different kinds of punishment and a mitigation or interruption of their torment."

Augustine was rejecting not only the belief that hell is now, but the feeling that the hell after life is only a brief punishment—God's penalty box—or a sort of divine closet to which we are banished for a while, the time limit determined by how long the punisher can stand the thought of us cowering in the gloom among the winter coats, surrounded by brooms. In this theory, God will one day drop down to hell to surprise everyone with instant parole.

The idea that hell is here is an appealing one since it would mean we are simultaneously committing our crimes and serving our sentence. But, in the final analysis, it is an untenable position. *The New Catholic Encyclopedia* puts it strongly: "It is impossible to soften the severity of Jesus's warning against unrepented sin and the sentimentalism that seeks to do so in distortion of his teaching and that of the New Testament as a whole."

Those who find the accusation that they are going against Christ and the Bible to be somewhat exaggerated could, instead, ponder this argument: How can this life be hell when that would mean hell contains not only Michelangelo's sculpture and Mozart's music and all else of beauty but the Eucharist as well?

Archbishop Fulton J. Sheen put it simply: "Some say we have our hell on this earth. We do. We can start here but it does not finish here."

A more pressing problem than the location of hell is the lack of acceptance of church teaching. Catholics are not so much denying hell as just ignoring it. That is due, in part, to the leftover and no longer effective imagery of Gehenna.

"Today," says Martin Marty, "fire and brimstone convey in no way what hell is. As time has passed, hell has lost its power to terrify."

Are we in need, then, of new imagery, of metaphors that will present hell in modern terms and make it more real to people? Will people two thousand years from now have to explain why, in our day, it was thought that hell was an eternal subway ride or everlasting underarm odor?

Or is there something more basic behind the refusal to accept the existence of hell? Rather than an unfamiliarity with symbols, might it not be an unwillingness to accept the possibility, first, that God would ever condemn a person to eternal suffering; and second, that a human, given the choice of heaven or hell, would ever choose the nether region?

Consider the quotation from Martin Marty: "Only one in eight who believe in hell believes it is a threat to him." In other words, there is a blindness in people that refuses to see not the imagery of hell but the application of that imagery to themselves.

An interesting theory developed from the babies-in-limbo debate. A common answer to those who wondered about unbaptized infants was to say that at the moment of death the child was given maturity and the choice of God or the Devil. Everyone breathed a sigh. Of course, the kid would select God. Then people began to wonder. Might not this same thing happen to each of us? Might not the final judgment be a case of everyone being given one last choice: pearly gates or fiery caverns? It is a consoling thought: no matter what I do, I'll have one last swing of the bat.

Under such circumstances, who would choose hell? Perhaps this is why the church has no condemnation ceremonies because, in fact, there is a hell but it is unoccupied except for Lucifer and company. Is it possible?

Dr. Marty: "No. People would choose hell."

Then how does he reconcile God's mercy and his justice? "I don't," says Dr. Marty, "but He does. I picture his love as encompassing but resistible."

Resistible because God gave humans free will, a will He does not usurp even at the last moment when the choice may not be between clouds of gold and walls of worms but the same choice one has been making for a lifetime: other or self, reaching out or holding back, love or hate.

*Drawing by Dedini;* © *1978*
THE NEW YORKER MAGAZINE, INC.

*"What gravels me is it's legal in Denmark."*

Looked at this way, hell acquires new dimensions. It is not Gehenna and it is not a subway. It is, to use Dr. Marty's words, "an absence from love, from God."

Hell thus becomes the reverse of what we are being called to by God. As the *Catholic Encyclopedia states,* "The possibility of hell is made intelligible by the conception of unbelief."

What is hell like then? In the end we cannot say, no images will suffice. If eye has not seen nor ear heard what heaven is like, the same holds true for hell. It must consist of abstractions like dissatisfaction, deprivation, loss, absence. What we know of these from this life can give us a clue to what they would be like for an eternity.

While pondering hell's dimensions is a fascinating exercise, it is ultimately useless and distracts from what we should be considering. The stress of the Second Vatican Council laid it out for us. Its focus was not on failure and sin and damnation, but on triumph and virtue and salvation. Look in the index to *The Documents of Vatican II*. Hell is not listed. Under "love" there are forty-five entries. That is where the church is asking us to go—away from hellfire and toward a new understanding of what God is asking of us.

If there is a reason for ignoring hell, therefore, it is not because of its ancient imagery or our pride or inability to comprehend God's justice, but because our eyes should turn to what we are to do rather than what we are to avoid. "One is to love God for his own sake, not out of fear of hell or hope in heaven," concludes Dr. Marty. "The accent should be on the character of God, not the temperature or geography of personal fate. Then all will be well."

Place the emphasis on finding out who God is and what He wants of us; Gehenna will take care of itself. A people who care about God will not have to worry about hell.

# The Roads to Heaven and Hell.

## Die Wege zum Himmel und zur Hölle.

. . . Come unto me all ye that labour and are heavy laden, and I will give you rest.   Mat. 11, 28. . .

Kommt alle her zu mir, die ihr mühselig und beladen seid,  ich will euch erquicken.   Matth. 11, 28.

# GEHENNA

## John L. McKenzie

GREEK *geenna* represents Aramaic *ge-hinnam*, which in turn represents Hebrew *ge-hinnōm*, an abbreviation of the full title, "valley of the son of Hinnom."

The name probably is that of the original Jebusite owner of the property.

In the Old Testament this is a geographical term which divides ancient Jerusalem (Zion) from the hills to the south and west. It is the modern Wadi er Rababi, which joins the Wadi en Nar (the Kidron) at the southern extremity of the hill of Zion.

The valley was a point on the boundary between Judah and Benjamin (Joshua 15:8; 18:16). This usage is reflected in Nehemiah 11:30. The valley had an unholy reputation in later Old Testament books because it was the site of Tophet, a cultic shrine where human sacrifice was offered (2 Kings 23:10; 2 Chronicles 28:3, 33:6; Jeremiah 7:31, 19:2ff, 32:35). It is called simply "the valley" (Jeremiah 2:23). Because of this cult Jeremiah cursed the place and predicted that it would be a place of death and corruption (7:32, 19:6ff). The valley is referred to, not by name in Isaiah 66:24, as a place where the dead bodies of the rebels against Yahweh shall lie. Their worm shall not die nor shall their fire be quenched—an allusion to the passages of Jeremiah cited above. . . .

Gehenna in the New Testament is mentioned seven times in Matthew, three times in Mark, once in Luke, once in James.

It is a place of fire (Matthew 5:22, 18:9; James 3:6).

The fire is unquenchable (Mark 9:43).

It is a pit into which people are cast (Matthew 5:29–30, 18:9; Mark 9:45, 47; Luke 12:5).

It is a place where the wicked are destroyed body and soul, which perhaps echoes the idea of annihilation (Matthew 10:28).

The Pharisees are sons of Gehenna—in Semitic idiom destined to Gehenna (Matthew 23:15), and they will incur the judgment of Gehenna (Matthew 23:33).

*"You're damn right it's polluted!"*

## SHEOL AND HADES

### John L. McKenzie

SHEOL IS THE UNDERWORLD as the abode of the dead. Ancient Near Eastern thought conceived the world as structured in three levels: the heavens, the earth, and the underworld. The underworld consists of the subterranean ocean, beneath which is Sheol, the abode of the dead. The picture is not entirely consistent, for Sheol is often mentioned parallel with the "pit," the grave; when the earth is opened for burial of the dead, the grave is an entrance to Sheol. . . .

In the New Testament Sheol (Greek *hadēs*) appears in several forms, although the word is not common. Psalm 16:10 is quoted and applied to Jesus in Acts of the Apostles 2:27 in connection with the resurrection, deliverance from death. 1 Colossians 15:55 quotes Hosea 13:14, but it is to be noted that Sheol/Hades is replaced by death. Capernaum will be brought down to Hades (Matthew 11:23; Luke 10:15), which here means destruction. The power of the risen Christ is shown by His possession of the keys of death and Hades (Revelation 1:18).

Hades as a destructive power follows death, the fourth horseman of the Apocalypse (6:8). Apocalypse 20:13–14 exhibits a conception of Sheol which is found in Judaism also: in the final catastrophe death and Sheol, which are temporary places of storage for the deceased, give up the dead for final judgment, and then are themselves destroyed. Hades becomes a place of torment, scarcely to be distinguished from Gehenna, in Luke 16:23. Hades is also a destructive power in Matthew 16:18, where Jesus promises that the gates of Hades shall not overcome His church. The gates are here the power of the palace fortress; Hades is the agent of destruction, not expressly identified with cosmic or human agents, and the passage means that the church is indestructible.

# A PITFUL OF FIRE FOREVER

*Mark the Evangelist (Mark 9:43–48)*

IF THY HAND offend thee, cut it off: it is better for thee to enter into life maimed, than having two hands to go into hell, into the fire that never shall be quenched:

Where their worm dieth not, and the fire is not quenched.

And if thy foot offend thee, cut it off: it is better for thee to enter halt into life, than having two feet to be cast into hell, into the fire that never shall be quenched:

Where their worm dieth not, and the fire is not quenched.

And if thine eye offend thee, pluck it out: it is better for thee to enter into the kingdom of God with one eye, than having two eyes to be cast into hell fire:

Where their worm dieth not, and the fire is not quenched.

## THE WORM
## AND THE FIRE

### Augustine of Hippo

THERE ARE SOME who think that both the "fire" and the "worm" . . . are meant as pains of the soul rather than of the body. Their argument is that, since those who repent too late and, therefore, in vain (because cut off from the kingdom of God) burn with anguish of soul, the "fire" can be taken very well to symbolize this burning anguish. They quote the words of the apostle: "Who is made to stumble, and I am not inflamed?" (2 Corinthians 11:29). They hold that the "worm" also must be taken to mean the soul, as can be seen, they think, in the text: "As a moth doth by a garment, and a worm by the wood, so the sadness of a man consumeth the heart" (Proverbs 25: 30).

However, those who have no doubt that in hell there will be sufferings for both soul and body hold that the body will be burned in fire while the soul will be gnawed, as it were, by the "worm" of grief. This is certainly a probable enough view, since it is absurd to think that either pain of body or anguish of soul will be lacking there. For myself, however, it seems preferable to say that both "fire" and the "worm" apply to the body, and that the reason for making no mention in Scripture of the anguish of the soul is that it is implied, though not made explicit. When the body is in such pain, the soul must be tortured by fruitless repentance.

## UNDYING AND
## UNQUENCHABLE

### Basil of Caesarea

THE "UNDYING" WORM may inflict gentler or fiercer torture, the "unquenchable" fire may burn freely or violently, according to desert. Hell surely has different kinds of chastisement: one man is consigned to outer darkness, where for some there is only weeping, while for others there is the gnashing of teeth. And outer darkness inevitably suggests an inner darkness.

## A VERITABLE
## VESUVIUS

### Minucius Felix

THE FIRE there below, endowed with ingenuity, consumes and renews, wears away and sustains the limbs. As the fiery flashes of lightning strike the bodies without consuming them, as the fires of Etna and Vesuvius and volcanoes all the world over burn without being exhausted, so the avenging fire is fed not by destroying those who are exposed to the flames, but is sustained by the never-ending mangling of their bodies.

"Frankly, I don't take much stock in this business of the gods being angry. The way I got it doped out is that at great depths the heat caused by the enormous pressure of the earth's crust melts the stone and turns some of it into gases. See? Then you got down there a vapor tension strong enough to blow the whole works to the surface, providing, of course, a channel of weakness opens up for it."

# AS MANY GO
# TO HELL
# AS HEAVEN

*Arline Brecher*

"I'M THOROUGHLY convinced that there is life after death—and that there are at least as many going to hell as to heaven!" declared Dr. Maurice Rawlings, a top cardiologist who has talked to patients who had "died" and been resuscitated.

Dr. Rawlings—a fellow of the American College of Cardiology, and a clinical associate professor of medicine at the University of Tennessee at Chattanooga—told *The Enquirer* that until he began collecting accounts three years ago he could find no support for the biblical accounts of heaven or hell.

But the incredible experiences and too vivid accounts of about a hundred patients whose hearts had stopped dramatically changed all that and led Dr. Rawlings to write the soon-to-be-published book, *Beyond Death's Door*.

"About fifty percent of the revived persons told of having gone to a place of great darkness, filled with grotesque moaning and writhing bodies, crying out to be rescued from this place with an overwhelming feeling of eerie and nightmarish terror," he said.

"Patients also described things that had gone on in the emergency room during the time they were dead—able to give precise information as to what had been said and done while they were gone!"

Typical of the chilling reports of the afterlife was the grim recollection of a man who was "clinically dead of a heart attack for four or five minutes."

"I was at his side when he revived," Dr. Rawlings recalled, "and he immediately began telling me of his visit to hell. He said he felt as if his body was falling down a shaft until he emerged into an enormous cave. He saw a lake of fire and brimstone. All around him, he said, were the bony bodies of people moaning helplessly."

It wasn't until the patient was able to momentarily draw the attention of a robed, Christlike figure that he was able to escape. "He told me, 'The next thing I knew, I was back in my body,'" Dr. Rawlings said.

Another man reportedly had three life-after-death experiences. "The first time he 'died' he found himself in hell," Dr. Rawlings remembered. Summoned out of the hospital emergency room by a "giant and several implike figures," the patient said he "descended through a tunnel-like passageway which eventually emptied into a cavern, piled high with glowing-hot rocks." He told Dr. Rawlings that he experienced "unbearable heat and felt oozing, slimy, writhing creatures slithering all over his feet."

He was able to escape only after a loud voice boomed, "Come out!" He instantly "found himself back in his hospital bed, being shocked back to life."

One patient was so shaken by his experience that he quit his job to join the ministry.

Such incredible experiences are more frequent than is generally believed, according to Dr. Rawlings, who maintains that they are often not reported because people are too embarrassed to admit them.

Dr. Rawlings added that their doctors are embarrassed "to make inquiries into such spiritual matters." Instead, we hear mostly of heavenly life-after-death experiences.

"But nobody can afford to ignore the reports of these patients," he cautioned.

"I'm convinced that there is a hell and that we must conduct ourselves in such a way as to avoid being sent there at all costs."

# MARRIAGE OF THE KING'S SON— A PARABLE

*Matthew the Evangelist*

*(Matthew 22:2–14)*

THE KINGDOM OF HEAVEN is like unto a certain king, which made a marriage for his son,

And sent forth his servants to call them that were bidden to the wedding: and they would not come.

Again, he sent forth other servants, saying, Tell them which are bidden, Behold, I have prepared my dinner: my oxen and my fatlings are killed, and all things are ready: come into the marriage.

But they made light of it, and went their ways, one to his farm, another to his merchandise:

And the remnant took his servants, and entreated them spitefully, and slew them.

But when the king heard thereof, he was wroth: and he sent forth his armies, and destroyed those murderers, and burned up their city.

Then saith he to his servants, The wedding is ready, but they which were bidden were not worthy.

Go ye therefore into the highways, and as many as ye shall find, bid to the marriage.

So those servants went out into the highways, and gathered together all as many as they found, both bad and good: and the wedding was furnished with guests.

And when the king came in to see the guests, he saw a man which had not on a wedding garment:

And he saith unto him, Friend, how camest thou in hither not having a wedding garment? And he was speechless.

Then said the king to the servants, Bind him hand and foot, and take him away, and cast him into outer darkness; there shall be weeping and gnashing of teeth. For many are called, but few are chosen.

---

# DRESSING FOR THE PARTY

*Helmut Thielicke*

WE CAN ACCEPT the call to come into the Father's house just as we are. We need not be ashamed of the highways and hedges from which we have come. It is our very pitableness that proves the Father's pity. We can come just as we are.

But this by no means implies that we can *enter* the Father's house as we are. And this is precisely what the parable means by this metaphor of the wedding garment. We seat ourselves at the banquet table without a wedding garment when we allow our sins to be forgiven but still want to hang on to them. We do this, in other words, when we say to ourselves, consciously or unconsciously, "This is great stuff; a man can remain in his sins without worrying since this God of love can never be really angry; he shuts both eyes; he will let it pass." . . .

And right here is where God's warning comes in: the person who comes without the wedding garment, the person who permits the fact that he can come as he is to make him shameless instead of humble, who, instead of being concerned with sanctification and discipline, allows himself to play a frivolous game with the grace of God, that person is just as badly off as the people who refuse *altogether*, who, indeed, kill the messengers of the king.

Even Christians, not only pagans, can be cast into outer darkness. Even the grace of God can become our doom. This is why there is such great sense in the custom of making confession and setting various things to rights before going to Holy Communion. This is comparable to our putting on the wedding garment.

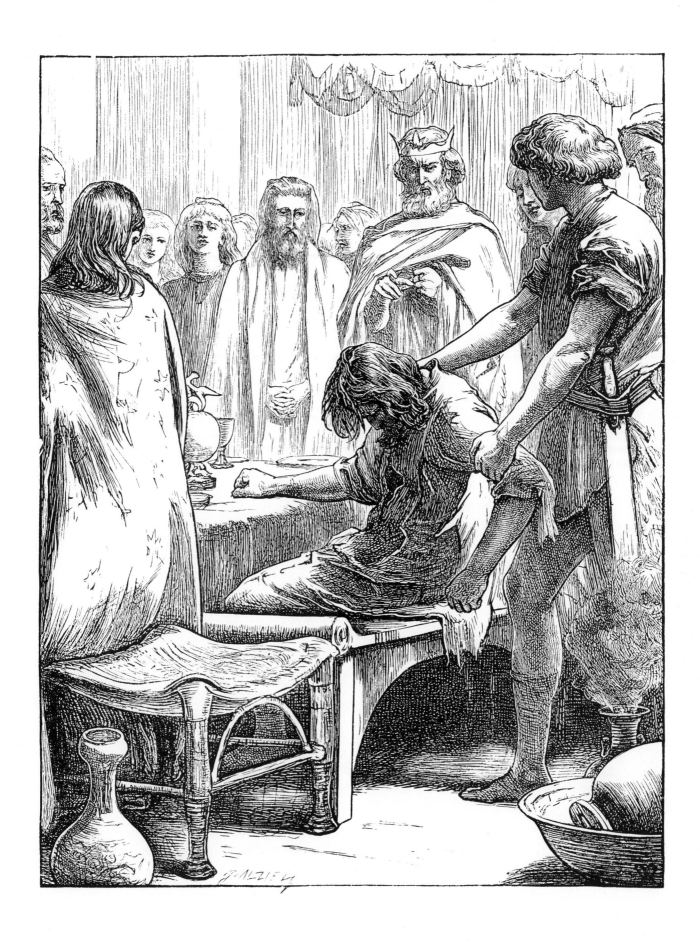

# THE TEN VIRGINS— A PARABLE

*Matthew the Evangelist*

*(Matthew 25:1–13)*

THEN SHALL THE KINGDOM of heaven be likened unto ten virgins, which took their lamps, and went forth to meet the bridegroom.

And five of them were wise, and five were foolish.

They that were foolish took their lamps, and took no oil with them:

But the wise took oil in their vessels with their lamps.

While the bridegroom tarried, they all slumbered and slept.

And at midnight there was a cry made, Behold, the bridegroom cometh; go ye out to meet him.

Then all those virgins arose, and trimmed their lamps.

And the foolish said unto the wise, Give us of your oil; for our lamps are gone out.

But the wise answered, saying, Not so; lest there be not enough for us and you: but go ye rather to them that sell, and buy for yourselves.

And while they went to buy, the bridegroom came; and they that were ready went in with him to the marriage: and the door was shut.

Afterward came also the other virgins, saying, Lord, Lord, open to us.

But he answered and said, Verily I say unto you, I know you not.

Watch therefore, for ye know neither the day nor the hour wherein the Son of man cometh.

---

## "SLEEPERS, AWAKE!"

*Helmut Thielicke*

NATURALLY, this sleeping must not be taken literally. It is possible for us to fall asleep while waiting in such a way that we turn to other things altogether and throw ourselves into frantic action. A man can put his expectancy, his hope, his faith, his conscience to sleep by plunging into all kinds of activity, by working "like blazes," by rushing about his business like a madman, and taking every free minute to listen to the radio or to look at the pictures in the magazines—as the people before the Flood did in their way. For they too fell asleep and gave no thought to the coming judgment of God. But their sleep was such that they were highly active; "they were eating and drinking, marrying and giving in marriage." . . .

The same is true of us who dance around the golden calf of our standard of living and forget why we are here and who is waiting for us. And I am sure that when the Lord Christ returns and his cry, "Sleepers, awake!" reverberates like a peal of thunder over the earth, only the fewest of men will rise from their beds; the majority at their benches and their desks, in the trains and in their cars, in the movies or the taverns, and certainly not least in the churches, will rise up in terror. . . . They will remember that once in their lives that light had gleamed, that once they took some hesitant steps toward it. But now they snatch at emptiness and darkness. The oil has long since been consumed, and what once was a flickering gleam has guttered into doom.

# A MEDITATION ON HELL

*Ignatius Loyola*

AFTER THE PREPARATORY PRAYER and two preliminaries, it consists of five headings and a colloquy.

The preparatory prayer will be the usual one.

*First preliminary.* The picture. In this case it is a vivid portrayal in the imagination of the length, breadth, and depth of hell.

*Second preliminary.* Asking for what I want. Here it will be to obtain a deep-felt consciousness of the sufferings of those who are damned so that, should my faults cause me to forget my love for the eternal Lord, at least the fear of these sufferings will help to keep me out of sin.

*First heading.* To see in the imagination those enormous fires, and the souls, as it were, with bodies of fire.

*Second heading.* To hear in the imagination the shrieks and groans and the blasphemous shouts against Christ our Lord and all the saints.

*Third heading.* To smell in imagination the fumes of sulfur and the stench of filth and corruption.

*Fourth heading.* To taste in imagination all the bitterness of tears and melancholy and a gnawing conscience.

*Fifth heading.* To feel in imagination the heat of the flames that play on and burn the souls.

*Colloquy.* Talk to Christ our Lord. Remember that some souls are in hell because they did not believe He would come; others because, though they believed, they did not obey His commandments. They fall into three classes: (1) before His coming; (2) during His lifetime; (3) after His life on earth. Remembering this, I will thank Him that He has not allowed me to die and so to fall into one of these classes. I will also thank Him for having shown me such tender mercy all my life long until now; and will close with an *Our Father.*

# MEANING OF THE MEDITATION ON HELL

## Karl Rahner

IF THIS MEDITATION is to be a truly existential experience, then it cannot stop at the application of the senses. Because I have every chance in the world not to end up in hell, I must place myself with all the seriousness of the hell meditation under the cross of my Lord. There, where I can see the love of God portrayed as nowhere else, and where I am challenged to return that love, with piercing fright I should feel the fickleness of my love. When I offer my love to God in temptation and want, I should say: "I will see to it that I will love You even when I don't want to love You anymore. I will remain true to You then out of fear of myself."

I know that I can abandon my love, that I can let it fall away from me in the heat of temptation. I also know the basic reason for this state of temptation of my love: it does not proceed from me alone—it is a gift from without. Even as a love that moves me, it is always something given, even in its most personal aspect. When I am able to love God to such an extent that my love is really capable of creating an eternity of bliss, I am still moved by God, and I am still under his influence. A true knowledge of man's love of God always implies, therefore, an awareness that it is a gift of grace and that it is always subject to temptation. Where this love becomes a reality, it must also be very humble. Only by encountering opposition and strangeness do we come to realize who we are and what we should be; and we also attain that "chaste fear" of ourselves that is supposed to be the fruit of this meditation.

The continually present background of this meditation and its final end must be the One who is our measure: the crucified Christ. He is the one Who stirs up our love. He is the one Who sends us His love day after day. His cross and His terrible death, that is also our judgment, speak to us in urgent tones that we can be unfaithful to our love and that we can sink into the bottomless emptiness of our own self-love.

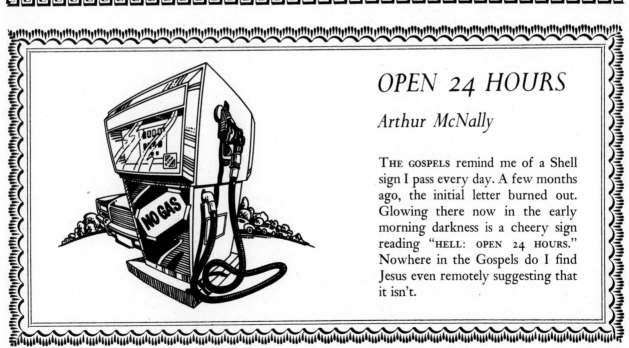

# OPEN 24 HOURS

## Arthur McNally

THE GOSPELS remind me of a Shell sign I pass every day. A few months ago, the initial letter burned out. Glowing there now in the early morning darkness is a cheery sign reading "HELL: OPEN 24 HOURS." Nowhere in the Gospels do I find Jesus even remotely suggesting that it isn't.

# THE SEVEN DEADLY SINS

THESE SEVEN WOODCUTS appeared in *Le grant kalendrier et compost des Bergiers*, printed by Nicolas Le Rouge, Troyes, 1496. *Right*, the angry are dismembered while still alive. *Below left*, the envious are immersed in freezing water. *Below right*, the gluttonous are force-fed with toads, rats, and snakes. *Next page. Top left*, the greedy are put into caldrons of boiling oil. *Top right*, the slothful are thrown into snake pits. *Bottom left*, the prideful are broken on the wheel. *Bottom right*, the lustful are smothered in fire and brimstone.

# A SAINT'S VISION

*Teresa of Avila*

I WAS AT PRAYER one day when suddenly, without knowing how, I found myself, as I thought, plunged right into hell. I realized that it was the Lord's will that I should see the place which the devils had prepared for me there and which I had merited for my sins. This happened in the briefest space of time, but, even if I were to live for many years, I believe it would be impossible for me to forget it.

The entrance, I thought, resembled a very long, narrow passage, like a furnace, very low, dark, and closely confined; the ground seemed to be full of water which looked like filthy, evil-smelling mud, and in it were many wicked-looking reptiles. At the end there was a hollow place scooped out of a wall, like a cupboard, and it was here that I found myself in close confinement. But the sight of all this was pleasant in comparison with what I felt there. What I have said is in no way an exaggeration. . . .

# A NUN'S GLIMPSE

*Sister Lucia*

[Our Lady] opened her hands once more, as she had done during the two previous months. The rays of light seemed to penetrate the earth, and we saw as it were a sea of fire. Plunged in this fire were demons and souls in human form, like transparent burning embers, all blackened or burnished bronze, floating about in the conflagration, now raised into the air by the flames that issued from within themselves together with great clouds of smoke, now falling back on every side like sparks in huge fires, without weight or equilibrium, amid shrieks and groans of pain and despair, which horrified us and made us tremble with fear. (It must have been this sight which caused me to cry out, as people say they heard me.) The demons could be distinguished by their terrifying and repellent likeness to frightful and unknown animals, black and transparent like burning coals. Terrified and as if to plead for succor, we looked up at Our Lady, who said to us, so kindly and so sadly:

"You have seen hell where the souls of poor sinners go."

I felt a fire within my soul the nature of which I am utterly incapable of describing. My bodily sufferings were so intolerable that, though in my life I have endured the severest sufferings of this kind . . . none of them is of the smallest account by comparison with what I felt then, to say nothing of the knowledge that they would be endless and never-ceasing. . . . To say that it is as if, the soul were continually being torn from the body is very little, for that would mean that one's life was being taken by another; whereas in this case it is the soul itself that is tearing itself to pieces. The fact is that I cannot find words to describe that interior fire and that despair, which is greater than the most grievous tortures and pains. I could not see who was the cause of them, but I felt, I think, as if I were being both burned and dismembered; and I repeat that that interior fire and despair are the worst things of all.

In that pestilential spot, where I was quite powerless to hope for comfort, it was impossible to sit or lie, for there was no room to do so. I had been put in this place which looked like a hole in the wall, and those very walls, so terrible to the sight, bore down upon me and completely stifled me. There was no light and everything was in the blackest darkness. I do not understand how this can be, but, although there was no light, it was possible to see everything the sight of which can cause affliction. . . .

I was terrified by all this, and, though it happened nearly six years ago, I still am as I write: even as I sit here, fear seems to be depriving my body of its natural warmth.

---

# A LUMBERMAN'S EXPERIENCE

*Thomas Welch*

I WENT OUT on the trestle to straighten out some timbers which were crossed and not moving on a conveyor. Suddenly I fell off the trestle and tumbled down between the timbers and into the pond, which was ten feet deep. An engineer sitting in the cab of his locomotive unloading logs into the pond saw me fall. I landed on my head on the first beam thirty feet down, and then tumbled from one beam to another until I fell into the water and disappeared from his view. . . .

The next thing I knew I was standing near a shoreline of a great ocean of fire. It happened to be what the Bible says it is in Revelation 21:8: ". . . the lake which burneth with fire and brimstone." This is the most awesome sight one could ever see this side of the final judgment.

I remember more clearly than any other thing that has ever happened to me in my lifetime every detail of every moment, what I saw and what happened during that hour I was gone from this world. I was standing some distance from this burning, turbulent, rolling mass of blue fire. As far as my eyes could see it was just the same. A lake of fire and brimstone. There was nobody in it. I was not in it.

# WHO'S WHERE IN DANTE'S INFERNO

## William Griffin

WITH POETIC INGENUITY not unlike Frank Lloyd Wright's, Dante has designed a subterranean hell that descends in circles like the Guggenheim Museum in New York. At each level Dante has grouped sinners of a certain sort.

- At the entrance to hell are the opportunists.
- In circle one are the virtuous pagans.
- In circle two are the carnal.
- In circle three are the gluttons.
- In circle four are the hoarders and the wasters.
- In circle five are the wrathful and the sullen.
- In circle six are the fallen angels and the heretics.
- In circle seven are those who have acted violently against themselves or their neighbors and against God, Nature, and Art.
- In circle eight are the fraudulent and malicious, the panderers and seducers, the flatterers, the simoniacs, the fortune-tellers and diviners, the grafters, the hypocrites, the thieves, the evil counselors, the sowers of discord, and the falsifiers (people like alchemists, evil impersonators, counterfeiters, and false witnesses).
- In circle nine are those who have committed compound fraud and those who have been treacherous to kin, country, guests, hosts, or their masters.

# THE GATE
# OF HELL

## Dante Alighieri
## *from* The Inferno

I am the way into the city of woe.
I am the way to a forsaken people.
I am the way to eternal sorrow.

Sacred justice moved my architect.
I was raise here by divine
  omipotence,
Primordial love and ultimate
  intelligence.

Only those elements time cannot
  wear
Were made before me, and beyond
  time I stand.
Abandon all hope ye who enter
  here.

# THE DISMAL SITUATION

*John Milton*
*(from* Paradise Lost)

*A dungeon horrible, on all sides round*
*As one great furnace flamed, yet from those flames*
*No light, but rather darkness visible*
*Served only to discover sights of woe,*
*Regions of sorrow, doleful shades, where peace*
*And rest can never dwell, hope never comes*
*That comes to all; but torture without end*
*Still urges, and a fiery deluge, fed*
*With ever-burning sulfur unconsumed:*
*Such place eternal justice had prepared*
*For those rebellious, here their prison ordained*
*In utter darkness, and their portion set*
*As far removed from God and light of heaven*
*As from the center thrice to the utmost pole.*
*O how unlike the place from whence they fell!*

# THE DEVIL ON DANTE AND MILTON

*George Bernard Shaw*

HELL IS A PLACE far above the common people's comprehension: they derive their notion of it from two of the greatest fools that ever lived, an Italian and an English-man. The Italian described it as a place of mud, frost, filth, fire, and venomous serpents: all torture. This ass, when he was not lying about me, was maundering about some woman whom he saw once in the street. The Englishman described me as being expelled from heaven by cannons and gunpowder; and to this day every Briton believes that the whole of his silly story is in the Bible. What else he says I do not know; for it is all in a long poem which neither I nor anyone else ever succeeded in wading through.

# DON JUAN ON HELL

*from* Don Juan in Hell
*George Bernard Shaw*

- In hell the Devil is the leader of the best society.
- Hell . . . is a place for the wicked. The wicked are quite comfortable in it: it was made for them.
- Hell is the home of honor, duty, justice, and the rest of the seven deadly virtues. All the wickedness on earth is done in their name: where else but in hell should they have their reward? Have I not told you that the truly damned are those who are happy in hell?
- Nothing is real here. That is the horror of damnation.
- In hell old age is not tolerated. It is too real. Here we worship Love and Beauty. Our souls being entirely damned, we cultivate our hearts.

# WHY FEAR OF HELL IS HEALTHY

*Frederick William Faber*

I DO NOT THINK that if we kept in view the perfections of God, we should venture to believe, unless the church taught us, that there was in creation such a place as hell. When it has been revealed to us, we can perceive, not only its reasonableness but also how admirably in keeping with the various attributes of God, and, not least of all, with the exquisiteness of His mercy. There is an awful beauty about that kingdom of eternal chastisement; there is a shadow cast upon its fires, which we admire even while we tremble, the shadow of the gigantic proportions of a justice which is omnipotent; there is an austere grandeur about the equity of God's vindictive wrath, which makes us nestle closer to Him in love, even while we shudder at the vision. But to us who live and strive, who have grace given us and yet have the power of resisting it, who have room for penance but are liable to relapse, who are right now but can at any time go wrong—who can doubt that hell is a pure mercy, a thrilling admonition, a solemn passage in God's pathetic eloquence, pleading with us to save our souls and to go to Him in heaven?

There is no class of Christians to whom hell is not an assistance. The conversion of a sinner is never complete without the fear of hell. Otherwise the work cannot be depended on. It has a flaw in its origin, a seed of decay in its very root. It is unstable and insecure. It is shortlived and unpersevering, like the seed in our Savior's parable which fell upon a rock, sprang up for a season, and then withered away. Hell teaches us God when we are too gross to learn Him otherwise. It lights up the depths of sin's malignity, that we may look down and tremble, and grow wise. Its fires turn to water, and quench the fiery darts of the tempter. They rage around us, so that we dare not rise up from prayer. They follow us, like the many-tongued pursuing flames of a burning prairie, and drive us swiftly on, and out of breath, along the path of God's commandments. O hell! Thou desolate creation of eternal justice! Whoever thought of finding a friend in thee!

**"I'm terribly mixed up."**

# WHY
# FEAR OF
# HELL
# IS
# NEUROTIC

*Ignace Lepp*

IT WAS LONG BELIEVED that punishment was a particularly efficacious means of education. If a child misbehaved, its mother or nurse threatened to "tell everything to father." The bogey man, Santa Claus, and a host of other mythological figures were called upon to make children toe the line. Religion itself was thought to contribute to the education of children and the maintenance of the social order because its teachings contained terrible threats of punishment for the "wicked." I have heard altogether reasonable men say, "If the Bible didn't teach the existence of hell, we would have to invent it to preserve social order and peace." We have only to look at paintings and sculptures of our cathedrals to realize the primordial role threats of hellfire played in the education of our ancestors.

Nor is it necessary to go back to the Middle Ages. In the very recent past, Lenten preachers and parochial missionaries hoped to convert the lukewarm and sinful with detailed descriptions of the torments of hell. Fire, caldrons of boiling oil, and Satan and his demon helpers were taken as fundamental religious truths. Most ministers of religion today follow the general direction of modern pedagogy and no longer believe in the moral efficacy of fear. Thus they no longer preach on hell. Yet the concept continues to haunt many imaginations. Certain Protestant sects such as the Adventists and Jehovah's Witnesses still hold the fear of hell to be the best means of converting sinners. The same is true of certain segments of Catholicism. I once heard a preacher in a respected retreat house claim that he knew that all the "wicked" (among them those who did not share his conservative political ideas) would be victims of eternal hellfire. On another

occasion I actually saw the presumably enlightened author of one of these spiritual exercises enter into a sort of ecstasy and, with hands raised to heaven, shout, "I see him. . . . I see him. . . . How horrible. . . . He is burning in Hell. . . . The devil sneers and attacks. . . ." I later learned that the subject of this horrifying vision was a recently deceased archbishop of Paris who was guilty, in the eyes of the integralists, of favoring social reform in Léon Blum's government of 1936. It is astonishing that illuminism of this sort is still effective in a skeptical age. I know any number of educated men whose lives have been changed by meditation on the horrors of hell. But in other cases serious neurotic anxieties result.

Sects of illuminati (as well as certain backward regions where religious life is always dominated by Jansenist theology) apart, the fear of hell still plays a fairly important role in the psychic lives of well-educated men and women who live in dechristianized areas. This is particularly true of neurotics, whether believers or not.

Maurice is a militant atheist and bitterly anticlerical. Suffering from anxiety and other psychic troubles, he underwent psychotherapy. He was haunted by fear of death and troubled by "ridiculous" nightmares dominated by the imagery of hell. The humor of the situation struck him: "If I don't believe in God, would I be stupid enough to believe old wives' tales about Satan and hell?" Yet he does believe and is terribly afraid. Consciously he is an atheist, but ancient archetypes are at work in his unconscious. In Maurice's case, his fear of hell ceased only when he adopted a positive religion of love.

We should resist the temptation to draw an apologetic argument from this particular case. Other neurotics get rid of their fear of hell and still remain atheists, and religious neurotics often lose their faith in God along with their fear of hell. Belief, like unbelief, can be neurotic in origin and disappear after the neurosis has been cured. Again, both can be expressions of a healthy psyche and remain intact when neurotic fears have been liquidated.

As a rule, well-educated and dedicated Christians are least afraid of hell. They do not take all the pious (?) imagery about hell literally. If out of fidelity to the traditional teachings of their Church, they do not explicitly deny the reality of hell, they at least entertain a purified, highly spiritual idea of it. But it is significant that even these Christians are plagued by thoughts of hell when the moment of death approaches. They understand hell as the frightening possibility of being separated from God, in whom they believe, and this perspective is as fearsome to them as the cruder conceptions of hell to others.

# A COMFORTABLE DOCTRINE

*Frederick William Faber*

HELL TEACHES the same comfortable doctrine as heaven, although in a rougher strain. Finite evil is almost infinitely punished, limited sin almost illimitably tormented. One mortal sin is chastised eternally. There may be many in hell who have committed a lesser amount of sin than many who are in heaven, only they would not lay hold of the Cross of Christ and do penance and have easy absolution. There is no life of self-denying virtue, however long and however laborious, but if it ends in impenitence and mortal sin, must be continued among the unending pains of hell. One mortal sin, and straightway a death without contrition, and everlasting despair alone remains.

Now will evil be more punished than good is rewarded? Will they even be on equal terms? Theology teaches that the chastisements of hell are for the sake of Christ far less than the wretched sufferers deserve. There is mercy even there, whence hope has long since fled, compassion even there where its tenderness seems so wholly out of place, and its forbearance thankless and unavailing. Hell is less than sin deserves. Then is there no corner of creation where the divine justice enjoys all its rights? At least it is not in hell; for hell is less than sin deserves. O beautiful ubiquity of mercy!

The Gospel nowhere tells us that sinners shall be punished up to the plentitude of their demerits; but it does tell us about the reward of virtue, that it shall be "good measure, and pressed down, and shaken together, and running over." You see, it is in heaven only that justice shall enjoy its royalties! Shall not then God's rewarding of good be in all respects far beyond in fullness and completeness, His punishment of evil?—Shall not a little good, a very little good, be much rewarded? And is not the number who are rewarded a chief feature in the magnificence of the reward? Surely not only will heaven be unspeakably beyond our deservings, but many will go there, whom only the generosity of divine love and the determination of persisting grace could have made deserving.

These are things which we cannot know. . . .

"Seems like *everyone's* coming out of the closet!"

# THE INTOLERABLE DOCTRINE

*C. S. Lewis*

I AM NOT GOING to try to prove the doctrine tolerable. Let us make no mistake; it is *not* tolerable. But I think the doctrine can be shown to be moral by a critique of the objections ordinarily made, or felt, against it.

First, there is an objection, in many minds, the idea of retributive punishment as such. . . . Let us try to be honest with ourselves. Picture to yourself a man who has risen to wealth or power by a continued course of treachery and cruelty, by exploiting for purely selfish ends the noble motions of his victims, laughing the while at their simplicity; who, having thus attained success, uses it for the gratification of lust and hatred and finally parts with the last rag of honor among thieves by betraying his own accomplices and jeering at their last moments of bewildered disillusionment. Suppose further that he does all this, not (as we like to imagine) tormented by remorse or even misgiving, but eating like a schoolboy and sleeping like a healthy infant—a jolly ruddy-cheeked man, without a care in the world, unshakably confident to the very end that he alone has found the answer to the riddle of life, that God and man are fools whom he has got the better of, that his way of life is utterly successful, satisfactory, unassailable. We must be careful at this point. The least indulgence of the passion for revenge is very deadly sin. Christian charity counsels us to make every effort for the conversion, at the peril of our own lives, perhaps of our own souls, to his punishment; to prefer it infinitely. But that is not the question. Supposing he *will* not be converted, what destiny in the eternal world can you regard as proper for him? Can you really desire that such a man, *remaining what he is* (and he must be able to do that if he has free will), should be confirmed forever in his present happiness—should continue, for all eternity, to be perfectly convinced that the laugh is on his side? And if you cannot regard this as tolerable, is it only your wickedness—only spite—that prevents you from doing so? Or do you find that conflict between justice and mercy, which has sometimes seemed to you such an outmoded piece of theology, now actually at work in your own mind, and feeling very much as if it came to you from above, not from below? You are moved, not by a desire for the wretched creature's pain as such, but by a truly ethical demand that, soon or late, the right should be asserted, the flag planted in this horribly rebellious soul, even if no fuller and better conquest is to follow. In a sense, it is better for the creature itself, even if it never becomes good, that it should know itself a failure, a mistake. Even mercy can hardly wish to such a man his eternal, contented continuance in such ghastly illusion. Thomas Aquinas said of suffering, as Aristotle had said of shame, that it was a thing not good in itself, but a thing which might have a certain goodness in particular circumstances. That is to say, if evil is present, pain at recognition of the evil, being a kind of knowledge, is relatively good; for the alternative is that the soul should be ignorant of the evil, or ignorant that the evil is contrary to its nature, "either of which," says the philosopher, "is *manifestly* bad." And I think, though we tremble, we agree. . . .

Another objection turns on the apparent disproportion between eternal damnation and transitory sin. And if we think of eternity as a mere prolongation of time, it is disproportionate. But many would reject this idea of eternity. If we think of time as a line—which is a good image, because the parts of time are successive and no two of them can coexist; that is, there is no *width* in time, only length—we probably ought to think of eternity as a plane or even a solid. Thus the whole reality of a human being would be represented by a solid figure. That solid would be mainly the work of God, acting through grace and nature, but human free will would have contributed the base line which we call earthly life: and if you draw your base line askew, the whole solid will be in the wrong place. The fact that life is short, or, in the symbol, that we contribute only one little line to the whole complex figure, might be regarded as a divine mercy. For even if the drawing of that little line, left to our free will, is sometimes so badly done as to spoil the whole, how much worse a mess might we have made of the figure if more had been entrusted to us? . . .

A third objection turns on the frightful intensity of the pains of hell as suggested by medieval art and, indeed, by certain passages in Scripture. Von Hugel here warns us not to confuse the doctrine itself with the *imagery* by which it may be conveyed. Our

Lord speaks of hell under three symbols: first, that of punishment ("everlasting punishment," Matthew 25:46); second, that of destruction ("fear Him who is able to destroy both body and soul in hell," Matthew 10:28); and thirdly, that of privation, exclusion, or banishment into "the darkness outside," as in the parables of the man without a wedding garment or of the wise and foolish virgins. The prevalent idea of fire is significant because it combines the ideas of torment and destruction. Now it is quite certain that all these expressions are intended to suggest something unspeakably horrible, and any interpretation which does not face that fact is, I am afraid, out of court from the beginning. But it is not necessary to concentrate on the images of torture to the exclusion of those suggesting destruction and privation. What can that be whereof all three images are equally proper symbols? Destruction, we should naturally assume, means the making, or cessation, of the destroyed. And people often talk as if the "annihilation" of a soul were intrinsically possible. In all our experience, however, the destruction of one thing means the emergence of something else. Burn a log, and you have gases, heat, and ash. To *have been* a log means now being those three things. If a soul can be destroyed, must there not be a state of *having been* a human soul? And is not that, perhaps, the state which is equally well described as torment, destruction, and privation? . . .

A fourth objection is that no charitable man could himself be blessed in heaven while he knew that even one human soul was still in hell; and if so, are we more merciful than God? At the back of this objection lies a mental picture of heaven and hell coexisting in unilinear time as the histories of England and America coexist: so that at each moment the blessed could say "The miseries of hell are *now* going on." But I notice that our Lord, while stressing the terror of hell with unsparing severity, usually emphasizes the idea not of duration but of *finality.* Consignment to the destroying fire is usually treated as the end of the story—not as the beginning of a new story. That the lost soul is eternally fixed in its diabolical attitude we cannot doubt: but whether this eternal fixity implies endless duration— or duration at all—we cannot say. . . .

Finally, it is objected that the ultimate loss of a single soul means the defeat of omipotence. And so it does in creating beings with free will, omnipotence from the outset submits to the possibility of such defeat. What you call defeat, I call miracle: for to make things which are not itself, and thus to become, in a sense, capable of being resisted by its own handiwork, is the most astonishing and unimaginable of all the feats we attribute to the Deity.

I willingly believe that the damned are, in one sense, successful rebels to the end; that the doors of hell are locked on the *inside.* I do not mean that the ghosts may not *wish* to come out of hell, in the vague fashion wherein an envious man "wishes" to be happy: but they certainly do not will even the first preliminary stages of that self-abandonment through which alone the soul can reach any good. They enjoy forever the horrible freedom they have demanded, and are therefore self-enslaved just as the blessed, forever submitting to obedience, become through all eternity more and more free.

## HELL

### W. H. Auden

Hell is neither here nor there
Hell is not anywhere
Hell is hard to bear.

It is so hard to dream posterity
Or haunt a ruined century
And so much easier to be.

Only the challenge to our will,
Our pride in learning any skill,
Sustains our effort to be ill.

To talk the dictionary through
Without a chance word coming
    true
Is more than Darwin's apes could
    do.

Yet pride alone could not insist
Did we not hope, if we persist,
That one day Hell might actually
    exist.

In time, pretending to be blind
And universally unkind
Might really send us out of our
    mind.

If we were really wretched and
    asleep
It would be then de trop to weep,
It would be natural to lie,
There'd be no living left to die.

# A DIABOLICAL DEFINITION

## Ambrose Bierce

ONE OF THE Creator's lamentable mistakes, repented in sackcloth and ashes. Being instated as an archangel, Satan made himself multifariously objectionable and was finally expelled from Heaven. Halfway in his descent he paused, bent his head in thought a moment, and at last went back. "There is one favor that I should like to ask," said he.

"Name it."

"Man, I understand, is about to be created. He will need laws."

"What, wretch! you his appointed adversary, charged from the dawn of eternity with hatred of his soul—you ask for the right to make his laws?"

"Pardon; what I have to ask is that he be permitted to make them himself."

It was so ordered.

# APOCATASTASIS

## Van A. Harvey

APOCATASTASIS is a Greek word referring to the final and complete salvation of all beings. It suggests universal redemption or universalism. It is to be found in the works of those theologians, like Clement and Origen of Alexandria, who emphasized the perfection of the divine love and who could not believe that the wrath of God is the final expression of that love. Origen's teachings were later condemned.

# VIII.

# HEAVEN

# WILL PEOPLE THROW PARTIES IN HEAVEN?

*Yvonne Goulet*

WHAT WILL LIFE after death be like? That is a subject increasingly discussed these days, especially in light of investigations into near-death experiences by people such as Elisabeth Kübler-Ross and Raymond Moody.

According to Kübler-Ross, clergy have been particularly critical of such research. One priest, she notes, referred to such investigations as "selling cheap grace." Others feel that the question of life after death should remain an issue of "blind faith."

Regardless of the controversy, it is clear that near-death experiences are not common among the living. Hope in everlasting life, however, is at the heart of Christian belief. "If Christ be not risen from the dead," St. Paul said, "our faith is in vain."

Between the two extremes of blind faith and scientific proof, however, is simply curiosity and creative reflection about what life after death might be like. What is it precisely we hope for when we long to live eternally? Seven Christian thinkers and writers from a variety of backgrounds agreed to share their reflections on the subject.

Enthusiasm varied. Naomi Burton, a retired literary editor, said she is "not sure people need to be concerned in this area." Morton Kelsey, author and professor of theology at the University of Notre Dame, however, was very much concerned about the subject. Not only has he written a book on life after death, but the subject has been one of his major interests for thirty years. He believes discussion of the subject is absolutely essential because of the failure of theologians to address this question.

All seven people questioned believe in heaven, but not all are certain about the existence of hell. Most agree eternal life will involve not just *being* but also *doing*. Martin Marty, a professor and theologian at the University of Chicago Divinity School, even

finds it "unbearable to endure a long rainy Sunday afternoon with nothing to do."

When asked what we will *do* in heaven, Harold Lindsell, editor of *Christianity Today*, replied, "We will work forever and enjoy it." He finds it impossible, however, to describe heaven or hell. "There is nothing that comes close to the idea of heaven and hell" for him although he believes hell does exist.

Marty believes that "heaven and hell are too specifically locational terms for me to imagine them as anything more than adapted, symbolic expressions of the fact that 'love is stronger than death' and 'nothing shall separate us from the love of God.' Hell I leave to God, who has the problem of squaring his sure justice with his encompassing love.

"I have no basis of analogy, but from what I've seen on earth, not to be in situations that make for creative response would be hell, to be in such situations would be toward heaven."

Kelsey believes in both heaven and hell and describes heaven as "growing." The earthly experiences that would be closest to those of heaven and hell for him are "the mystical experience and the anxiety neurosis."

Msgr. Charles M. Murphy, dean of the North American College in Rome, qualified his comments about heaven and hell by saying that "neither Christianity nor Judaism has any mythology developed around these themes. In fact, this total blank about life after death provided the best possible preparation for the Christian teaching of the Resurrection because there was no possibility of its becoming intermingled with mythological elements." As for what heaven might be like, Murphy cited Paul Tillich, who says that the condition will be either unlimited vision or love. Thomas Aquinas stressed vision, but there is another Catholic tradition that stresses love. "If we go with love as the essence of eternity, then it is possible to understand what St. John means when he says that in the love we experience from each other, we have already seen God and been brought into eternal life."

Murphy commented that "the only portions of the creation of God to have no future (in the afterlife) are those which are in opposition to God and contradict the life of God. This would include sickness, death, war, injustice, and all the many other manifestations of human sinfulness." He is unsure about hell: "I think the Christian tradition is remarkably optimistic about the possibilities of salvation for everyone, given the unbounded desire of God that all should be saved."

Sister Margaret Dorgan, a contemplative who lives on a farm in Maine, spoke of "lots of *doing* in heaven, flowing out of our *being*. I think of every-

thing I've loved on earth as being present in a more wonderful way in the existence I'll have in heaven—music, dance, my delightful dog Plotinus, the joy of swimming, running. And the marvelous exhilaration of pursuing ideas right into the mystery of God." Prayer is the earthly experience that brings her closest to heaven. "The presence of God absorbing my whole being takes many forms." For her, hell would be the absence of love—"rejection, hate, or bitterness"—but more for the one rejecting than the one being rejected.

Burton handles doubts about the existence of heaven "by thinking of the rafts of more brilliant men and women who have believed." She described heaven as " a life of praise of God. I think we'll be at peace, 'be lost forever in thy glory's sight.' If heaven is heaven it will be what the best in us most longs for."

She says an earthly experience that would be most analogous to the experience of heaven would be "probably a mixture of natural beauty and time spent surrounded with family and friends when everything goes right." An earthly experience like hell would be "quarreling and being unable, physically unable, through distance, broken phone lines, to make up or to say you're sorry; alienation from others through one's own fault; doing crummy things that can't be undone."

Stanley A. Moody, who owns a chain of religious bookstores, believes heaven will be "the ultimate fulfillment of our creative selves." The earthly experience most like heaven, he says, is the love in the human family which mirrors God's love. An earthly experience of hell would be a "conscious decision to live in control of one's own destiny. . . . I think hell visits the executive boardrooms and religious headquarters every day. It exists where men and women take control of their own lives and the lives of others and regulate with dispassion." As for the ultimate destiny of nonbelievers, "I would accept the thought of final annihilation," he says.

For Murphy, the meaning of the resurrection of the body is that "the total human person participates in the Resurrection of Christ. There is one who is eternal and that is God, and the only survival possible for a creature after death is by some mystical participation in the life on God's terms alone."

According to Marty, "Paul calls them resurrected 'spiritual bodies,' which shows that he was coining, and didn't know, and so I certainly do not either."

Kelsey believes that in life the human person "participates in two totally different dimensions of reality. One is space-time reality and the other is non-space-time or spiritual reality. The human being participates in both while alive and continues living on in the other one after the dissolution of the body." The spiritual reality of the person "is as real as the physical, and [the afterlife] is the enhancement of one's spiritual being, individuality, personality. This is described very well by Raymond Moody. We have a body, but it's not a crass physical body; it's a spiritual body. We have our own being,

*Drawing by Ed Fisher;* © *1979*
THE NEW YORKER MAGAZINE, INC.

individuality, personality, and body, our uniqueness, our separateness."

Dorgan made a similar point: "I think of [the afterlife] as my humanity raised to its fullness, the me transformed in God, radiant with his life but strongly individual. I'm repelled by any spirituality that wipes out the personal either in this life or hereafter." The spiritual bodies, she says, would be "perfect in beauty and sense activity." Everyone's age would be the age of the "fullness of our powers, before decline sets in and when potential has been reached."

Burton thinks that "perhaps we'd appear to have bodies yet be able to move through things. Maybe like the resurrected Jesus." She does not envision that we'll be "any age really. Age won't matter; I doubt we'll take a lot of baggage with us."

Moody believes our bodies "will be in their creative prime. There will be no age consciousness. We will, however, be recognizable to each other."

Many think communication with others on earth and in heaven will be an important part of the afterlife. For Kelsey it is "what the communion of saints is all about."

Lindsell does not think we will be omniscient in the afterlife, or that we will be able to communicate with those on earth, but he does believe we will be able to communicate with others in heaven. He also doubts that we will retain relationships with friends and family after death.

Marty also doubts we will be omniscient or that we will communicate with others on earth. "I cannot conceive of eternal existence without 'I-Thou.'" As for relationships with family and friends in heaven, "Jesus said that intimate bonding will be transcended."

For Kelsey, however, "the communion of saints means you are more in touch with the deceased after death than you are with non-Christians in the space-time world. The whole idea of Jesus Christ that the kingdom of heaven is at hand means that the whole dimension of the nonphysical, spiritual reality into which the deceased pass at death is available to us here and now."

The reason so many contemporary theologians fail to believe this, he said, is that they have capitulated to rationalism and the notion that there is nothing that cannot be perceived by the senses.

## HEAVEN IN SCRIPTURE

### L. L. Morris

HEAVEN is the abode of God, and of those closely associated with Him. The Israelite is to pray, "Look down from thy holy habitation, from heaven" (Deuteronomy 26:15). God is "the God of heaven" (Jonathan 1:9), or "the Lord God of heaven" (Ezra 1:2), or the "Father which is in heaven" (Matthew 5:45, 7:21, etc.). God is not alone there, for we read of "the host of heaven" which worships Him (Nehemiah 9:6), and of "the angels which are in heaven" (Mark 13:32). Believers also may look forward to "an inheritance . . . reserved in heaven" for them (1 Peter 1:4).

Heaven is thus the present abode of God and His angels, and the ultimate destination of His saints on earth. . . .

Heaven comes to be used as a reverent periphrasis for God. Thus when the prodigal says, "I have sinned against heaven" (Luke 15:18, 21), he means, "I have sinned against God." So with John 3:27, "it be given him from heaven." The most important example of this is Matthew's use of the expression "the kingdom of heaven," which seems to be identical with "the kingdom of God."

Finally, we must notice an eschatological use of the term. In both Old and New Testaments it is recognized that the present physical universe is not eternal, but will vanish away and be replaced by "a new heaven and a new earth" (Isaiah 65:17, 66:22; 2 Peter 3:10–13; Revelation 21:1). We should understand such passages as indicating that the final condition of things will be such as fully expresses the will of God.

Dorgan does not believe we will be omniscient in the afterlife. "That would be to equal God. But our knowledge will be expanded tremendously." She says those who have died "will be aware of those on earth and powerful enough to help them—not explicit communication but communication all the same." Relationships with friends and family will continue, "but much better. No misunderstandings, no bitterness, no fights, no jealousies."

Burton does not think we will be omniscient "since surely only God is that," but that "yes, dead people can communicate with us. We don't hear them most of the time. I feel that this takes place only rarely, when there's a need for the one on earth." Of the possibility of communicating with others in heaven, she says, "So many people—my mother for one—are convinced that at the time of death they will see children who died earlier or others who have died. God isn't a cheat."

She hopes in the afterlife "to see my mother, perhaps by then to be what she'd hoped for me, not a silly little nine-year-old. Again, it won't matter."

Moody said that "since heaven is portrayed in scripture as perfect love, communication will be an absolute necessity. We will be expressing that love to each other and to our Creator and his Son." He does not believe in communication between the deceased and those on earth "because I feel that God will be setting up his kingdom here on earth. Life as we know it now will be no more."

Moody does not think relationships with family and friends will continue. "Those relationships will be entirely different. There will be forgiveness so that we will not be haunted by those who have slighted or divorced or whatever." Family relationships will change, he said, "because in the presence of perfect love, how could one feel more love for one person than another?"

All seven were asked to describe their concept of the experience of God after death.

Lindsell's answer was simply, "Beyond description."

Marty simply replied, "I-Thou."

Murphy believes that "in the love we experience from each other we have already seen God."

Kelsey sees God as "the divine lover with whom we'll have an ideal relationship of becoming. We will experience transformation in the presence of divine love-light." He said relationships will be horizontal as well as with God. "Heaven is not the flight of the alone to the alone. Jesus speaks of the kingdom of heaven and other subjects as well as the King."

For Dorgan, God will be "Ah. Ah. Ah. All love.

Ineffable. Beyond thought. Glorious. I can hardly wait." "Since no one has ever seen God, how can we know?" Burton asks. "The mystics give us clues but only clues. I suppose I'd say perfect unselfish love, enjoyment, laughter. All the time. No letdowns."

Moody thinks that "all those unanswered questions will be instantly and automatically known. We will become spirits in the same sense that God is a spirit. . . . We will become creators in the presence of the ultimate Creator. God's spirit will be the wellhead of love."

What is the consensus, then, of these thoughtful Christians about the afterlife? There is a heaven and a hell, but hell may not be everlasting. The essence of heaven will be creative love. We will have bodies, but they will be unlike our earthly bodies. We will not simply *be* in heaven; we will be involved in creative, joyous activity. We will be able to communicate with others in heaven and possibly with those on earth, to some extent. We will be able to recognize family and friends, but our relationships will be transformed in the love that we feel for everyone.

Is such speculation valuable or even healthy? Is there a place for it in the Christian life? What connection is there between such speculation and the research being done on experiences of life after death?

Kelsey believes such questioning is absolutely essential in the light of the rationalism that pervades much modern Christian theology. Before rationalism gained popularity in the seventeenth and eighteenth centuries, Christians were always aware of the reality of the spiritual world. To early Christians, "the spiritual reality was as real as the physical. Dying meant the enhancement of one's spiritual being, individuality, personality." St. Ambrose wrote at length about his exchanges with his brother who had died.

Kelsey sees the renewed interest in scientific investigation of life after death as healthy. He doesn't think the scientific and the faith approaches can be separated. He believes the church largely has capitulated to the rationalistic world view "and forgotten there is another dimension to reality. It's only as you bring out what is in the other dimension that life after death seems a natural thing."

For many persons, everlasting life sounds like a colossal bore. But everlasting joy, creativity, love, light, and laughter sound more attractive. Perhaps if there were more speculation on the afterlife, more people would conclude it is worth striving for.

# THE CELESTIAL CITY

*Paul Bunyan*

CHRISTIAN AND HOPEFUL went easily up the hill on which the City stood, because the angels helped them. They went up through the air, for the City was higher than the clouds. As they went they saw countless angels and talked with them. The angels said, "You will never again see sorrow, sickness, or death, and you will receive rewards for all you have done and suffered for the King on your way here. You will serve Him continually with joy, and never be tired or weary. Besides this, you will enjoy your friends who have gone on before you, and you will welcome with joy everyone who follows you into the City."

As the four men were coming near the gate, a great number of angels came out to meet them. The two angels said to the throng, "Here are two men who loved the Lord Jesus when they were in the world, and who left all for Him."

Then the heavenly host shouted, and several of the King's trumpeters came out, clothed in shining white garments, and welcomed Christian and Hopeful. They surrounded them as if to guard them through the upper regions. As they went, they continued to blow their trumpets, making sweet music to show how glad they were to have Christian and Hopeful in their company. The pilgrims could see the City and hear the bells ringing to welcome them. No tongue could tell how happy they were to be in such company forever.

When they came to the gate, they saw written over it, "Blessed are they who have lived to please the King. They may enter through the gate into the City."

Then Christian and Hopeful handed in their certificates or rolls. These were carried to the King, who, when He read them, commanded the gate to be opened. As Christian and Hopeful went through it, they were transfigured and had garments put on them that shone like gold. Harps were given to them on which to praise the King, and crowns were given them to show them honor. All the bells in the City rang for joy, and the pilgrims sang, "Blessing, honor, and glory to Him who sitteth on the throne and to the Lamb forever."

The City shone like the sun; the streets were paved with gold, and on them many walked with crowns on their heads, palm branches in their hands, and golden harps with which to praise the King. The heavenly beings sang, "Holy, holy is the Lord!" Then the gate was closed.

Shortly after, Ignorance came to the river. A man called Vain-hope was there with a boat and took him over. Ignorance had far less difficulty crossing the river than had Christian and Hopeful. He went up the hill and knocked, but no one welcomed him. Those at the gate asked him for his certificate or roll, but he had none. When they told the King that Ignorance had arrived, the King commanded the two angels to bind him hand and foot and take him away. The angels carried him to the door at the side of the hill, opened it, and cast him inside. That way was the way of hell, even at the gates of heaven, as well as from the City of Destruction.

So I awoke, and behold, it was a dream.

"IT IS EASIER FOR A CAMEL TO GO

FOR A RICH MAN TO ENTER INTO

*THROUGH THE EYE OF A NEEDLE THAN*

*THE KINGDOM OF GOD."*   *Mark 10:25*

# THE CITY OF GOD

## *Augustine of Hippo*

BUT THAT WHICH is the house of God is also a city. For the house of God is the people of God; for the house of God is the temple of God. And what doth the apostle say? The temple of God is holy, which are ye. But all the faithful who are the house of God are not only those who now exist, but those also who have been before us and have already slept, and those who are to come after us, unto the world's end. Innumerable hosts of the faithful gathered into one body, but counted by the Lord of whom the apostle said, "The Lord knoweth them that are His; those grains which as yet groan among the chaff, which will constitute one mass, when the floor shall in the end have been winnowed; the whole number of faithful saints, destined to be changed from the human state that they may become equal with the angels of God; themselves, joined unto the angels, who are no longer pilgrims, all make together one house of God, and one city."

# THE IOWA POLL: HEAVEN OR HELL

## *Arnold Garson*

PERHAPS THERE'S NOT as much goodwill floating around right now as you'd like to think.

That'd be a helluva note on Christmas Day. But the *Register*'s Iowa Poll offers some scientific evidence to that effect.

The chances are one in three that your neighbor thinks you're going to hell—literally—the poll shows.

At the same time, however, the chances are very good that you think your neighbor is wrong.

The situation is this: The poll shows that thirty-one percent of the adults in Iowa think they know someone who's going to hell. But on the other hand, only five percent think they're going to hell themselves.

Translation: Somewhere between 100,000 (five percent) and 620,000 (thirty-one percent) of the state's 2,000,000 adults may be headed for Hades.

Unfortunately, the precise figure cannot be pinpointed since there are two divergent points of view —yours and your neighbor's. Perhaps you should just be satisfied to know that some things are beyond the scope of public-opinion surveys, and the Iowa Poll could not devise a test to determine whether you or your neighbor is right.

The poll does show, however, that while 100,000 Iowans believe they're going to hell, another 1,300,000 believe they're going to heaven. The remaining 600,000 are holding their options open by saying they have no opinion.

(In case you're prepared to argue that all of this is meaningless since most people don't believe in such things as heaven and hell, the Iowa Poll points out that is not the case. It was determined in April that an overwhelming majority of Iowans do believe in heaven and hell.)

Statewide, the poll shows that the chances of going to hell as opposed to heaven are one in thirteen, based on how Iowans perceive their own futures.

But the poll also shows that if you happen to be under the age of thirty-five, a political independent, someone who disapproves of the job Governor Robert Ray is doing, or a member of a labor union, the chances are much better than average that you think you're going to hell.

On the other hand, if you're a farmer, a Republican, over the age of sixty-five, someone who voted for Gerald Ford last year, or a member of the upper-income crowd, the chances of you thinking you're going to hell are much less than average.

Here is a closer look at the exact chances of going to heaven as opposed to hell for a variety of groups —still based on how Iowans view themselves.

• Men, 9–1; women, 14–1 (for every nine men who think they're going to heaven, one thinks he's going to hell; for every fourteen women who think they're going to heaven, one thinks she's going to hell).

• Residents of metropolitan areas, 9–1; residents of cities outside the state's seven metropolitan areas, 11–1; farmers, 30–1.

• Persons whose family income is less than $5,000 a year, 16–1; persons whose family income is between $5,000 and $25,000, 11–1; persons whose family income is over $25,000 a year, 34–1.

• Persons under the age of thirty-five, 8–1; persons between thirty-five and sixty-four, 11–1; persons age sixty-five and over, 63–1 (the best odds of any group measured).

• University of Iowa football fans, 10–1; Iowa State football fans, 13–1.

• Republicans, 35–1; Democrats, 9–1, independents, 8–1.

• Iowans who approve of the job President Carter is doing, 13–1; Iowans who disapprove of Carter, 16–1.

• Iowans who voted for Carter, 10–1; Iowans who voted for Ford, 24–1; Iowans who didn't vote, 13–1.

Iowans who approve of Governor Ray, 13–1; Iowans who disapprove of Ray, 8–1.

• Members of labor unions, 4–1 (the worst odds of any group measured); nonunion members, 13–1.

Converting a few of these items to percentages, the number of Iowans perceiving themselves as going to hell ranges from one percent among persons over age sixty-five to fourteen percent among members of labor unions. The number of Iowans perceiving themselves as going to heaven ranges from fifty-seven percent among men to seventy-two percent among women.

It should be noted that the figures are subject to change based on the future behavior of the state's residents.

A young Fairfield farmer, for example, said he thinks he's going to heaven, but added: "It'll be a fight all the way."

All of which prompts still another question: Is there room enough for all the Iowans who may be going there? That, too, however, appears beyond the scope of a public-opinion poll.

The poll upon which this story is based was conducted August 24–27. The following questions were asked:

*A recent poll showed that most Iowans believe in heaven or hell. In line with this, can you think of anyone you know who might end up in hell?*

*On a personal basis, how do you think you might end up—in heaven or hell?*

## THE IOWA POLL HEAVEN AND HELL

| | ALL IOWANS | MEN | WOMEN |
|---|---|---|---|
| GOING TO END UP IN HEAVEN | 65% | 57% | 72% |
| GOING TO END UP IN HELL | 5 | 6 | 5 |
| NOT SURE OR NO OPINION | 30 | 37 | 23 |
| KNOW SOMEONE ELSE WHO'S GOING TO HELL | 31 | 33 | 29 |

# HOW JESUS IS HEAVEN

## *Walter Hilton*

WHAT IS HEAVEN to a reasoning soul? Surely, nothing other than Jesus, our God. For if heaven is that which is above all things, then God alone is heaven to a man's soul, for he alone is superior to the nature of the soul. Therefore if grace enables a soul to perceive the divine nature of Jesus, it sees heaven itself, for it sees God.

Many people misunderstand certain sayings about God because they do not interpret them in a spiritual sense. Holy Scripture says that a soul that seeks God must lift up its eyes and seek God above itself. Some who wish to follow this injunction understand the words "above itself" as meaning a higher or nobler level in a worldly sense, in the same way that one element or planet is regarded as superior to another. But this does not apply to spiritual matters, for the soul is superior to all material things, not because of its position in the world but because of the dignity of its nature. Similarly, God is superior to all created things, both spiritual and material, not because of his lofty place in the universe, but because of the spiritual dignity of his Being, blessed and unchanging. Therefore, anyone who desires to seek God wisely and to find him must not allow his thoughts to soar above the sun and circle the firmament, picturing the majesty of God as the light of a hundred suns. Instead, let him forget the sun and all the firmament, regarding them as inferior to himself, and think both of God and himself on a spiritual plane. If the soul can do this, it then looks beyond itself and sees heaven.

The word "within" must be understood in the same way. It is commonly said that a soul shall see God in all things and within itself. It is true that God is in all created things, but not in the way that a kernel is hidden within the shell of a nut, or as a small object is contained within a greater. He is within all things, maintaining and preserving them in being, but he is present in a spiritual way, exercising the power of his own blessed nature and invisible purity. For just as an object that is very precious and pure is laid in a secure place, so by the same analogy the nature of God, which is supremely precious, pure, and spiritual, utterly unlike any physical nature, is hidden within all things. Anyone who desires to seek God within must therefore forget all material things, for these are exterior; he must cease to consider his own body or even his own soul, and consider the uncreated nature of God who made him, endowed him with life, upholds him, and gives him reason, memory, and love. All these gifts come to him through the power and sovereign grace of God. This must be the soul's course of action when it is touched by grace; otherwise it will be of little use to seek God within itself or in his creation.

In Holy Scripture God is described as light. St. John says: *Deus lux est* (1 John 1:5). God is light. This light is not to be understood as physical light, but in this way. God is light; that is, God is truth itself, since truth is spiritual light. Therefore the soul that by grace possesses the fullest knowledge of truth has the clearest vision of God. But it may be compared with physical light in this sense: for as the sun reveals itself and all material things to the eye by its own light, so God, who is also truth, reveals himself first to the understanding of the soul, and by this means bestows all the spiritual knowledge that the soul requires. For the prophet says: *Domine, in lumine tuo videbimus lumen* (Psalm 36:9). Lord, in your light we shall see all light. That is: we shall see that you are truth by the light of yourself.

In the same way, God is described as fire: *Deus noster ignis consumens est.* Our God is a consuming fire. This does not mean that God is the element of fire which heats and consumes physical objects, but that God is love and charity. For just as fire consumes all material objects that can be destroyed by it, so the love of God burns and consumes all sin out of the soul and makes it clean, as fire purifies all kinds of metal. These descriptions and all other material comparisons applied to God in holy scripture must be understood in a spiritual sense, for otherwise they are meaningless. But the reason why such words are employed to describe God is that we are so worldly in our outlook that we cannot speak of God without at first using such expressions. However, when the eyes of the soul are opened by grace, and we are enabled to catch a glimpse of God, then our souls can quite easily interpret these material descriptions in a spiritual sense.

This opening of the eyes of the soul to the knowledge of the Godhead I call reform in faith and feeling. For the soul then has some experience of what it once knew by faith alone. This is the beginning of contemplation, of which St. Paul said: *Non contemplantibus nobis quae videntur, sed quae non videntur; quae enim videntur, temporalia sunt, quae autem non videntur, aeterna sunt* (2 Corinthians 4: 18). We do not contemplate the things that are seen, but those that are not seen; for the things that are seen are temporal, but those that are not seen are eternal. It is these things that the soul should aspire to gain, partially indeed in this present life, but fully in the bliss of heaven. For the full bliss and eternal life of the rational soul consist in this vision and knowledge of God. *Haec est autem vita aeterna; ut cognoscant te unum Deum, et quem misisti, Jesum Christum* (John 17:3). Father, this is eternal life, that your chosen souls should know you, and Jesus Christ your son whom you have sent, to be the one true God.

## WHAT IS GOD DOING IN HEAVEN?

*Meister Eckhart*

I HAVE BEEN ASKED what God is doing in heaven. I answer, He has been giving His Son birth eternally, is giving birth now and will go on giving birth forever, the Father being in childbed in every virtuous soul. Blessed, thrice blessed is the man within whose soul the heavenly Father is thus brought to bed. All she surrenders to Him here she shall enjoy from Him in life eternal. God made the soul on purpose for her to bear His onebegotten Son. His ghostly birth in Mary was to God better pleasing than His nativity of her in flesh. When this birth happens nowadays in the good loving soul it gives God greater pleasure than His creation of the heavens and earth.

## HOW GOD IS HEAVEN

*Augustine of Hippo*

THE REWARD of virtue will be God himself, who gave the virtue, and promised to give himself; and there could be no better or greater gift. For when he said by the prophet, "I shall be their God, and they will be my people," he surely meant just this: "I shall be their satisfaction; I shall be everything that men can honestly desire: life, health, food, abundance, glory, honor, peace, and all good things." This is the right interpretation of the apostle's words, "That God may be all in all." He will be the end of our desires, and we shall see him without end, love him without revulsion, praise him without weariness. This gift, this emotion, this activity will be shared by all, just as life eternal will be the common condition of all.

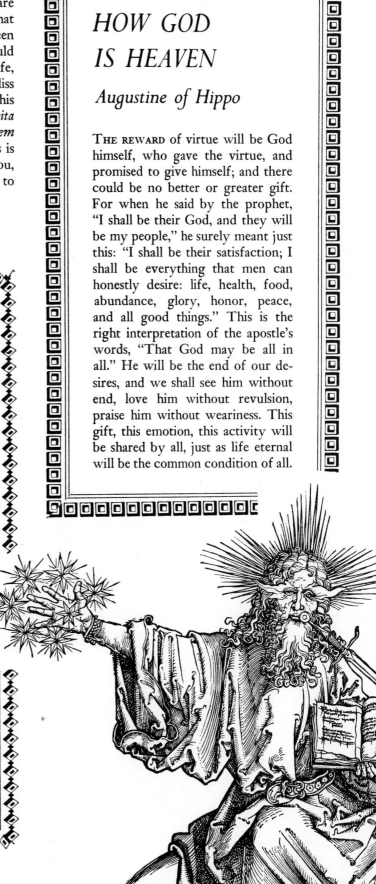

# THE EXCELLENCIES OF THE SAINTS' REST

*Richard Baxter*

LET US DRAW a little nearer, and see what further excellencies this rest affordeth. The Lord hide us in the clefts of the rock, and cover us with the hands of indulgent grace, while we approach to take this view! This rest is excellent for being—a purchased possession;—a free gift;—peculiar to saints;—an association with saints and angels;—yet deriving its joys immediately from God;—and because it will be a seasonable,—suitable,—perfect,—and eternal rest.

It is a most singular honor of the saints' Rest, to be called "the purchased possession" (Ephesians 1:14). That is, the fruit of the blood of the Son of God; yea, the chief fruit, the end and perfection of all the fruits and efficacy of that blood. Greater love than this there is not, to lay down the life of the lover. And to have this our Redeemer ever before our eyes, and the liveliest sense and freshest remembrance of that dying, bleeding love still upon our souls: how will it fill our souls with perpetual joy, to think that in the streams of this blood we have swum through the violence of the world, the snares of Satan, the seducements of flesh, the curse of the law, the wrath of an offended God, the accusations of a guilty conscience, and the vexing doubts and fears of an unbelieving heart, and are arrived safe at the presence of God! . . .

Another pearl in the saints' diadem is, that it's a free gift. These two, "purchased" and "free," are the chains of gold which make up the wreaths for the tops of the pillars in the temple of God (1 Kings 7:17). It was dear to Christ, but free to us. When Christ was to buy, silver and gold were nothing worth; prayers and tears could not suffice, nor anything below his blood. But our buying is receiving; we have it freely, "without money, and without price" (Isaiah 4:1). A thankful acceptance of a free acquittance, is no paying of the debt. Here is all free; if the Father freely give the Son, and the Son freely pay the debt; and if God freely accepts that way of payment, when he might have required it

of the principal; and if both Father and Son freely offer us the purchased life on our cordial acceptance, and if they freely send the Spirit to enable us to accept; what is here then that is not free? Oh the everlasting admiration that must needs surprise the saints to think of this freeness! . . .

If it were only for nothing, and without our merit, the wonder were great; but it is moreover against our merit, and against our long endeavoring our own ruin. What an astonishing thought it will be, to think of the unmeasurable difference between our deservings and receivings! Between the state we should have been in, and the state we are in! To look down upon hell, and see the vast difference that grace hath made betwixt us and them! To see the inheritance there, which we were born to, so different from that which we are adopted to! What pangs of love will it cause within us, to think, "Yonder was the place that sin would have brought me to, but this is it that Christ hath brought me to! Yonder 'death' was 'the wages of' my 'sin,' but this 'eternal life is the gift of God, through Jesus Christ my Lord' (Romans 6:23)! 'Who made me to differ' (1 Corinthians 4:7)? Had I now now been in those flames, if I had had my own way, and been let alone to my own will? Should I not have 'lingered in Sodom,' till the flames had seized on me, if God had not in mercy 'brought me out'? (Genesis 19:16)." Doubtless this will be our everlasting admiration, that so rich a crown should sit the head of so vile a sinner! . . .

This rest is peculiar to saints, belongs to no other of all the sons of men. If all Egypt had been light, the Israelites would not have had the less; but to enjoy that light alone, while their neighbors lived in thick darkness, must make them more sensible of their privilege. Distinguishing mercy affects more than any mercy. If Pharaoh had passed as safely as Israel, the Red Sea would have been less remembered. If the rest of the world had not been drowned, the rest of Sodom and Gomorrah not burned, the saving of Noah had been no wonder, nor Lot's deliverance so much talked of. When one is enlighted, and another left in darkness; one reformed, and another by his lust enslaved; it makes the saints cry out, "Lord, how is it that thou wilt manifest thyself unto us, and not unto the world!" (John 14:22) When the prophet is sent to one "widow" only of all that were in Israel, and to cleanse one Naaman of all the lepers (Luke 4:25, 27), the mercy is more observable. That will surely be a day of passionate sense on both sides, when "there shall be two in one bed," and "two in the field, the one taken, and the other left" (Luke 17:34, 36). The saints shall look down upon the burning lake, and in

the sense of their own happiness, and in the approbation of God's just proceedings, they shall rejoice and sing, "Thou art righteous, O Lord, which wast, art, and shalt be, because thou hast judged thus" (Revelation 16:5).

But though this rest be proper to the saints, yet it is common to all the saints; for it is an association of blessed spirits, both saints and angels; a corporation of perfected saints, whereof Christ is the head; the communion of saints completed. As we have been together in the labor, duty, danger, and distress, so shall we be in the great recompense and deliverance. As we have been scorned and despised, so shall we be owned and honored together. We, who have gone through the day of sadness, shall enjoy together that day of gladness. Those who have been with us in persecution and prison shall be with us also in that palace of consolation. How oft have our groans made, as it were, one sound? our tears one stream? and our desires one prayer? But now all our praises shall make up one melody; all our churches, one church; and all ourselves, one body; for we shall be

"all one" in Christ, even "as he and the Father are one" (John 17:21). . . .

As another property of our rest, we shall derive its joys immediately from God. Now we have nothing at all immediately, but at the second, or third, hand, or how many, who knows? From the earth, from man, from sun and moon, from the ministration of angels, and from the Spirit, and Christ. Though, in the hand of angels, the stream favors not of the imperfection of creatures; and as it comes from man, it favors of both. How "quick and piercing is the word" (Hebrews 4:12) in itself? . . .

A further excellence of this rest is that it will be seasonable. He that expects "the fruit of his vineyard at the season" (Mark 12:2), and makes his people "like a tree planted by the rivers of water, that bringeth forth his fruit in his season" (Psalm 1:3), will also give them the crown in season. He that will have "a word of joy spoken in season to him that is weary" (Isaiah 1:4), will surely cause the time of joy to appear in the fittest season. They who "are not weary in well doing, shall if they faint not, reap in due season" (Galatians 6:9). If God "giveth rain," even to his enemies, "both the former and the latter in his season," and "reserveth the appointed weeks of harvest, and covenants that there shall be day and night in their season" (Jeremiah 5:24; 33:20), then surely the glorious harvest of the saints shall not miss its season. . . .

As this rest will be seasonable, so it will be suitable. The new nature of the saints doth suit their spirits to this rest. Indeed their holiness is nothing else but a spark taken from this element, and by the spirit of Christ kindled in their hearts, the flame whereof, mindful of its own divine original, ever tends to the place from whence it comes. Temporal crowns and kingdoms could not make a rest for saints. As they "were not redeemed with" (1 Peter 1:18) so low a price, neither are they endowed with so low a nature. As God will have from them a spiritual worship, suited to his own spiritual Being, he will provide them a spiritual rest, suitable to their spiritual nature. The knowledge of God and his Christ, a delightful complacency in that mutual love, and everlasting rejoicing in the enjoyment of our God, with a perpetual singing of his high praises; this is a heaven for a saint. . . .

Still more, this rest will be absolutely perfect. We shall then have joy without sorrow, and rest without weariness. There is no mixture of corruption with our graces, nor of suffering with our comfort. There are none of those waves in that harbor, which now so toss us up and down. Today we are well, tomorrow sick; today in esteem, tomorrow in disgrace; today we have friends, tomorrow none; nay, we have wine and vinegar in the same cup. If revelations raise us "to the third heaven, the messenger of Satan" must presently "buffet" us, and "the thorn in the flesh" fetch us down (2 Corinthians 12:2, 7). But there is none of this inconstancy in heaven. If "perfect love casteth out fear" (1 John 4:18), then perfect joy must needs cast out sorrow, and perfect happiness exclude all the relics of misery. We shall there rest from all the evil of sin and of suffering.

"It's just as I'd always hoped it would be."

Gahan Wilson

# THE BEATIFIC VISION

*P. J. Boudreaux*

"BEATIFIC VISION" is composed of three Latin words —*beatus*, happy; *facio*, I make; and *visio*, a sight— all of which taken together make up and mean a happy-making sight. Therefore, in its very etymology, Beatific Vision means a sight which contains in itself the power of banishing all pain, all sorrow from the beholder, and of infusing, in their stead, joy and happiness. We shall now analyze it, and see wherein it consists; for it is only by doing so that we can arrive at the clear idea of it, which we are seeking.

Theologians tell us that the Beatific Vision, considered as a perfect and permanent state, consists of three acts—which are so many elements essential to its integrity and perfection. These are, first, the sight or vision of God; second, the love of God; and third, the enjoyment of God. These three acts, though really distinct from each other, are not separable; for, if even one of them be excluded, the Beatific Vision no longer exists in its integrity. We shall now say a few words on each of these constituents of heavenly bliss.

1. First, the sight or vision of God means that the intellect—which is the noblest faculty of the soul—is suddenly elevated by the light of glory, and enabled to see God as He is, by a clear and unclouded perception of his Divine Essence. It is, therefore, a vision in which the soul sees God, face to face; not indeed with the eyes of the body, but with the intellect. For God is a Spirit, and cannot be seen with material eyes. And if our bodily eyes were necessary for that vision, we could not see God until the day of judgment; for it is only then that our eyes will be restored to us. Hence, it is the soul that sees God; but then, she sees Him more clearly and perfectly than she can now see anything with her material eyes.

This vision of God is an intellectual act by which the soul is filled to overflowing with an intuitive knowledge of God; a knowledge so perfect and complete that all the knowledge of Him attainable, in this world, by prayer and study, is like the feeble glimmer of the lamp compared to the dazzling splendor of the noonday sun.

This perfect vision, or knowledge of God, is not only the first essential element of the Beatific Vision, but it is, moreover, the very root or fountainhead of the other acts which are necessary for its completeness. Thus we say of the sun that he is the source of the light, heat, life, and beauty of this material world; for, if he were blotted out from the heavens, this now beautiful world would, in one instant, be left the dark and silent grave of every living creature. This is only a faint image of the darkness and sadness which would seize upon the blessed, could we suppose that God would at any time withdraw from them the clear and unclouded vision of Himself. Therefore, we say, that the vision of the Divine Essence is the root or source of the Beatific Vision.

Yet, although this is true, it does not follow that the vision of the Divine Essence constitutes the whole Beatific Vision; for the human mind cannot rest satisfied with knowledge alone, how perfect soever it may be. It must also love and enjoy the object of its knowledge. Therefore, the vision of God produces the two other acts which we shall now briefly consider.

2. The second element of the Beatific Vision is an act of perfect and inexpressible love. It is the sight or knowledge of God as He is, that produces this love; because it is impossible for the soul to see God in his divine beauty, goodness, and unspeakable love for her, without loving Him with all the power of her being. It were easier to go near an immense fire and not feel the heat, than to see God in His very essence, and yet not be set on fire with divine love. It is, therefore, a necessary act; that, one which the blessed could not possibly withhold, as we now can do in this world. For, with our imperfect vision of God, as He is reflected from the mirror of creation, we can, and unfortunately do, withhold our love from him—even when the light of faith is superadded to the knowledge we may have of him from the teachings of nature. Not so in heaven. There, the blessed see God as He is; and therefore, they love him spontaneously, intensely, and supremely.

3. The third element of the Beatific Vision is an act of excessive joy, which proceeds spontaneously from both the vision and the love of God. It is an act by which the soul rejoices in the possession of God, who is the Supreme Good. He is her own God, her own possession, and in the enjoyment of Him her cravings for happiness are completely

gratified. Evidently, then, the Beatific Vision necessarily includes the possession of God; for without it, this last act could have no existence, and the happiness of the blessed would not be complete, could we suppose it to have existence at all. A moment's reflection will make this as evident as the light of day.

A beggar, for instance, gazes upon a magnificent palace, filled with untold wealth, and all that can gratify sense. Does the mere sight of it make him happy? It certainly does not, because it is not and never can be his. He may admire its grand architecture and exquisite workmanship, and thus receive some trifling pleasure; but, as he can never call that palace nor its wealth his own, the mere gazing upon it, and even loving its beauty, can never render him happy. For this, the possession of it is essential.

Again, the starving beggar gazes upon the rich man's table loaded with every imaginable luxury. Does that mere sight relieve the pangs of hunger? It certainly does not. It rather adds to his wretchedness, by intensifying his hunger, without satisfying its cravings. Even so would it be in heaven, could we suppose a soul admitted there, and allowed to gaze upon the beauty of God, while she cannot possess or enjoy Him. Such a sight would be no Beatific Vision for her. The possession of God is, therefore, absolutely necessary in order that the soul may enjoy Him, and rest in Him as her last end. Hence, the act of seeing God is also the act by which the blessed possess God, and enter into the joy of their Lord.

But this is not yet all. We have been considering the acts by which the soul appropriates God to herself; meanwhile, we must not forget that the active concurrence of God is as essential in the Beatific Vision as the action of the creature. The Beatific Vision means, therefore, that God not only enables the soul to see Him in all his surpassing beauty, but also that he takes her to his bosom as a beloved child, and bestows upon her the happiness which mortal eye cannot see. It means, furthermore, that God unites the soul to Himself in so wonderful and intimate a manner, that, without losing her created nature or personal identity, she is transformed into God, according to the forcible expression of St. Peter, when he asserts that we are "made partakers of the divine nature." This is the highest glory to which a rational nature can be elevated. . . .

# THE FACE OF GOD

*Nicholas of Cusa*

O LORD, how marvelous is Thy face, which a young man, if he strove to imagine it, would conceive as a youth's; a full-grown man, as manly; an aged man, as an aged man's! Who could imagine this sole pattern, most true and most adequate, of all faces—of all even as of each—this pattern so very perfectly of each as if it were of none other? He would have need to go beyond all forms of faces that may be formed, and all figures. And how could he imagine a face when he must go beyond all faces, and all likenesses and figures of all faces, and all concepts which can be formed of a face, and all color, adornment, and beauty of fall faces? Wherefore he that goeth forward to behold Thy face, so long as he formeth any concept thereof, is far from Thy face. For all concept of a face falleth short, Lord, of Thy face, and all beauty which can be conceived is less than the beauty of Thy face; every face hath beauty, yet none is beauty's self, but Thy face, Lord, hath beauty and this having is being. 'Tis therefore Absolute Beauty itself, which is the form that giveth being to every beautiful form. O face exceed-ing comely, whose beauty all things to whom it is granted to behold it, suffice not to admire!

In all faces is seen the Face of faces, veiled, and in a riddle; howbeit, unveiled it is not seen, until above all faces a man enter into a certain secret and mystic silence where there is no knowledge or concept of a face. This mist, cloud, darkness, or ignorance into which he that seeketh Thy face entereth when he goeth beyond all knowledge or concept is the state below which Thy face cannot be found except veiled; but that very darkness revealeth Thy face to be there, beyond all veils. 'Tis as when our eye seeketh to look on the light of the sun which is its face; first it beholdeth it veiled in the stars, and in colors and in all things that share its light. But then it striveth to behold the light un-veiled, or goeth beyond all visible light, because all this is less than that which it seeketh. A man seeking to see a light beyond his seeing knoweth that, so long as he seeth aught, it is not that which he seeketh. Wherefore it behooveth him to go beyond all visible light. For him, then, who must go beyond all light, the place he entereth must needs lack visible light, and is thus, so to speak, darkness to the eye. And while he is in that darkness which is a mist, if he there knows himself to be in a mist, he knoweth that he hath drawn nigh the face of the sun; for that mist in his eye proceedeth from the exceeding bright shining of the sun. Wherefore, the denser he knoweth the mist to be, by so much the more truly doth he attain in the mist unto the light invisible. I perceive that 'tis thus and not otherwise, Lord, that the light inaccessible, the beauty and radiance of Thy face, may, unveiled, be approached.

---

# THE LONG-AWAITED BRIGHTNESS *Bonaventure*

Now THAT the combat of the passion was over, and the bloody dragon and raging lion thought that he had secured a victory by killing the Lamb, the power of the divinity began to shine forth in his soul as it de-scended into hell. By this power our strong "Lion of the tribe of Judah" (Revelation 5:5), rising against the "strong man who was fully armed" (Luke 11:21), tore the prey away from him, broke down the gates of hell and bound the serpent. "Disarming the Principalities and Powers, he led them away boldly, displaying them openly in triumph in himself" (Colossians 2:15). Then the "Leviathan was led about with a hook" (Job 40:25), his jaw pierced by Christ so that he who had no right over the Head which he had attacked, also lost what he had seemed to have over the body. Then the true Samson, as he dies, laid prostrate an army of the enemy (cf. Judges 16:30). Then the Lamb without stain "by the blood of his Testament led forth the prisoners from the pit in which there was no water" (Zachariah 9:11). Then the long-awaited brightness of a new light shone upon those "that dwelt in the region of the shadow of death" (Isaiah 9:2).

# ANIMALS HAVE SOULS JUST LIKE OTHER PEOPLE

## *Arnobius of Sicca*

ARE YOU WILLING, gentlepersons, to lay aside that deep-seated arrogance and conceit, you . . . who claim God as your Father and maintain that you have the same immortality as He? Are you willing to inquire, to search out, to investigate what you yourselves are, whose you are, of what father you are thought to be, what you are doing in the world, how you were born, in which manner your leap into life? Are you willing, having laid aside partiality, to reach the conclusion in your silent thought that we are animate beings either in all respects like the rest or separated from them by no great difference? After all, what is there to show that we differ from them? Or what extraordinary quality is there in us so that we should refuse to be enrolled in the number of animals?

Their bodies are founded upon bones and are bound together by a network of sinews: and in like manner our bodies are founded upon bones and are bound together by sinews. They breathe in the air through nostrils and give it out again in exhalations: and we in the same way draw in our breath and breathe it out again in a continuous to-and-fro. They are separated in female and male kinds: and we too have been fashioned by our Creator into as many sexes. They produce their young from wombs and beget them through bodily union: we, too, are born from bodily embraces and are brought forth and sent out from the wombs of mothers. By food they are sustained and by drink, and the impure excess they cast out from the lower parts: we, too, are sustained by food and by drink, and what nature is ready to reject, we pour out by the same channels.

All of them take care to repel death-bringing hunger and of necessity to watch for food. What else do we do in life's great preoccupations except to seek for those things by which the danger of hunger is avoided and unhappy anxiety is laid aside? They feel diseases and starvation and in the end are weakened by old age. Are we by any chance immune to these evils and not broken in the same manner by the inconvenience of diseases and destroyed by the decline of old age?

But if this also is true, as is said in the more hidden mysteries, that the souls of the wicked go into cattle and other beasts after they have been removed from human bodies, it is more clearly demonstrated that we are near them and not removed from them by any appreciable difference; for there is a factor in both us and them by reason of which animate beings are said to exist and to have the power of living motion.

"But *we* possess reason and surpass in understanding every species of dumb animals."

I would believe this to be most truly spoken, if all men lived rationally and wisely, held to the course of duty, refrained from the forbidden, had nothing to do with base activities, and no one through his depraved intellect and blindness of ignorance asked for what is alien and even hostile to himself. I should however, like to know what this reason is by which we are to be preferred to all species of animals. Because we have made dwellings for ourselves in which we can avoid the cold of winter and heat of summer? Do you mean to say that other animate beings have no foresight of this kind? Do we not see some building dwellings of nests for themselves in rocks and hanging crags; still others burrowing into the soil of the earth and preparing in dug-out pits places of protection and lairs for themselves? And if Mother Nature had been willing to give them hands to help them, there would be no doubt that they themselves would also have built towering fortifications and would have struck out new works of art. Yet even in those things which they make with their beaks and claws, we see that there are many images of reason and wisdom which we human beings are unable to copy with any amount of thought, although we have hands that work for us and are masters of every sort of perfection.

"They have not learned to fashion clothing, chairs, ships, and plows, nor the other equipment which daily life demands."

These are not the blessings of knowledge but the inventions of paupers—necessity. Nor did the arts drop down with the souls from the innermost heart of heaven, but they have all been carefully sought for and come to birth here on earth and through painstaking thought have been devised gradually in the progress of time. And if in this regard the souls possessed the knowledge which a race that is divine and immortal ought by all rights fittingly to have, all men would have known all things from the beginning and there would have been no age unacquainted with any art or not possessed of the advantage of experience with things. But now a life that is destitute and lacking many things, observing that certain things happen to its advantage by chance, while it imitates, experiments, and tries, while it makes errors, revises, makes changes, by a constant process of rejection has assembled little smatterings in the arts and has brought them to one issue, the joint improvements of many ages.

Now if men either knew themselves through and through or had received an understanding of God to the extent of even the slightest conjecture, never would they claim for themselves a divine and immortal nature, nor would they think themselves something great because they have made for themselves gridirons, basins, and bowls; because they have made undershirts, linen jackets, mantles, cloaks, ceremonial robes, knives, breastplates, and swords; because they have made rakes, hatchets, the plowshare. Never, I say, would they believe, exalted by their arrogance and conceit, that they are deities of the first class and equals of the Highest in His sublimity, just because they had begotten grammar, music, oratory, and geometrical forms. We do not see what is so surprising in these arts that from their discovery it should be believed that the souls are superior to the sun and all the stars, surpassing in glory and substance this whole world of which these things are only parts.

*"Wonderful seeing you!"*

*Drawing by Koren;* © *1975*
THE NEW YORKER MAGAZINE, INC.

## SPIRITUAL FRIENDSHIP

### Aelred of Rievaulx

How THEY RUN after one another, play with one another, so express and betray their love by sound and movement, so eagerly and happily do they enjoy their mutual company that they seem to prize nothing else so much as they do whatever pertains to friendship!

## IF ANIMALS HAVE NO SOULS

### Cleveland Amory

IF IT'S TRUE that animals have no souls and that we're all going to some wonderful Elysian Fields and they're not, then that is all the more reason to give them a better shake in the one life they do have.

# THE VICAR'S REMORSE

*Having blessed the foxhounds in accordance with tradition, he feels the prick of conscience*

# GOD OF THE SPARROW

*George MacDonald*

To BELIEVE THAT GOD made many of the lower creatures merely for prey, or to be the slaves of a slave, and writhe under the tyrannies of a cruel master who will not serve his own master; that He created and is creating an endless succession of them to reap little or no good of life but its cessation —a doctrine held by some, and practically accepted by multitudes—is to believe in a God who, so far as one portion at least of His creation is concerned, is a demon. But a creative demon is an absurdity; and were such a creator possible, he would not be God, but must one day be found and destroyed by the real God.

Not the less the fact remains that miserable suffering abounds among them, and that, even supposing God did not foresee how creation would turn out for them, the thing lies at His door. He has besides made them so far dumb that they cannot move the hearts of the oppressors into whose hands He has given them, telling how hard they find the world, how sore their life in it. The apostle takes up their case, and gives us material for an answer to such as blame God for their sad condition. . . .

What many men call their beliefs are but the prejudices they happen to have picked up. . . . There are not a few who would be indignant at having their belief in God questioned, who yet seem greatly to fear imagining Him better than He is. "You see the plain facts of the case!" they say. "There is no questioning them. What can be done for the poor things—except, indeed, you take the absurd notion into your head, that they too have a life beyond the grave?"

Why should such a notion seem to you absurd? I answer. The teachers of the nation have unwittingly, it seems to me through unbelief, wronged the animals deeply by their silence anent the thoughtless popular presumption that they have no hereafter, thus leaving them deprived of a great advantage to their position among men. But I sup-pose they too have taken it for granted that the Preserver of man and beast never had a thought of keeping one beast alive beyond a certain time; in which case heartless men might well argue He did not care how they wronged them, for He meant them no redress. Their immortality is no new faith with me, but as old as my childhood.

Do you believe in immortality for yourself? I would ask any reader who is not in sympathy with my hope for the animals. If not, I have no argument with you. But if you do, why not believe in it for them? . . . Are you the lowest kind of creature that could be permitted to live? Had God been of like heart with you, would He have given life and immortality to creatures so much less than Himself as we?

Are these not worth making immortal? How, then, were they worth calling out of the depth of no-being? It is a greater deed to make be that which was not than to seal it with an infinite immortality: did God do that which was not worth doing? What He thought worth making, you think not worth continuing made! You would have Him go on forever creating new things with one hand, and annihilating those He had made with the other—for I presume you would not prefer the earth to be without animals. If it were harder for God to make the former go on living than to send forth new, then His creatures were no better than the toys which a child makes, and destroys as he makes them.

For what good, for what divine purpose is the Maker of the sparrow present at its death, if He does not care what becomes of it? What is He there for, I repeat, if He have no care that it go well with His bird in its dying, that it be neither comfortless nor lost in the abyss? If His presence be no good to the sparrow, are you very sure what good it will be to you when your hour comes? Believe it is not by a little only that the heart of the universe is tenderer, more loving, more just and fair, than yours or mine.

If you did not believe you were yourself to out-live death, I could not blame you for thinking all was over with the sparrow; but to believe in im-mortality for yourself, and not care to believe in it for the sparrow, would be simply hard-hearted and selfish. If it would make you happy to think there was life beyond death for the sparrow as well as for yourself, I would gladly help you at least to hope that there may be.

I know of no reason why I should not look for the animals to rise again, in the same sense in which I hope myself to rise again—which is, to reappear, clothed with another and better form of life than before. If the Father will raise His children, why should He not also raise those whom He has taught His little ones to love? Love is the bond of the universe, the heart of God, the life of His children: if animals can be loved, they are lovable; if they can love, they are yet more plainly lovable: love is eternal; how then should its object perish? Must the love live on forever without its object? or, worse still, must the love die with its object, and be eternal no more than it? What a misinvented correlation in which the one side was eternal, the other, where not yet annihilated, constantly perishing!

Is not our love to the animals a precious variety of love? And if God gave the creatures to us, that a new phase of love might be born in us toward another kind of life from the same fountain, why should the new life be more perishing than the new love?

Can you imagine that, if, hereafter, one of God's little ones were to ask Him to give again one of the earth's old loves—kitten, or pony, or squirrel, or dog —which He had taken from him, the Father would say no? If the thing was so good that God made it for and gave it to the child at first who never asked for it, why should He not give it again to the child who prays for it because the Father had made him love it? What a child may ask for, the Father will keep ready.

# WILL I HAVE MY CAT IN HEAVEN?

### F. J. Sheed

"WILL I HAVE my cat—or my whatever it is I can't imagine living without—in heaven?"—that through the ages was the child's question. And "If you want it, you will have it"— that through the ages was the grownup's answer. The grownup knew that the child would grow up out of his present blisses: the child did not know it: both were satisfied. I fancy even grownups have their own slightly less infantile, but infantile still, variant of that question and answer. If they get around to 1 Corinthians they may be startled by Paul's answer to one who asked what life in heaven would be like—"Don't be silly."

# WHERE WILL YOU PUT ALL THE MOSQUITOES?

### C. S. Lewis

I HAVE BEEN WARNED not even to raise the question of animal immortality, lest I find myself "in company with all the old maids." I have no objection to the company. I do not think either virginity or old age contemptible, and some of the shrewdest minds I have met inhabited the bodies of old maids. Nor am I greatly moved by jocular inquiries such as "Where will you put all the mosquitoes?"—a question to be answered on its own level by pointing out that, if the worst came to the worst, a heaven for mosquitoes and a hell for men could be very conveniently combined.

# THE HEAVEN OF ANIMALS

## James Dickey

Here they are. The soft eyes open.
If they have lived in wood
It is a wood.
If they have lived on plains
It is grass rolling
Under their feet forever.

Having no souls, they have come,
Anyway, beyond their knowing.
Their instincts wholly bloom
And they rise.
The soft eyes open.

To match them, the landscape flowers,
Outdoing, desperately
Outdoing what is required:
The richest wood,
The deepest field.

For some of these,
It could not be the place
It is, without blood.
These hunt, as they have done,
But with claws and teeth grown perfect.

More deadly than they can believe.
They stalk more silently,
And crouch on the limbs of trees,
And their descent
Upon the bright backs of their prey

May take years
In a sovereign floating of joy.
And those that art hunted
Know this as their life,
Their reward: to walk

Under such trees in full knowledge
Of what is in glory above them,
And to feel no fear,
But acceptance, compliance.
Fulfilling themselves without pain

At the cycle's center,
They tremble, they walk
Under the tree,
They fall, they are torn,
They rise, they walk again.

Drawing by Koren; © 1974
THE NEW YORKER MAGAZINE, INC.

"May I join your rumination group?"

# THE SOCIAL JOYS OF HEAVEN

## P. J. Boudreaux

LET US NOW RAISE our eyes to our heavenly home, and there contemplate a life of the purest, and most perfect social pleasures. There, neither selfishness, nor uncharitableness, nor any unruly passion can exist, and, consequently, our social joys will never be mingled with the gall of bitterness. Putting aside, for a moment all the shortcomings and imperfections that mar our social joys in this world, let us look at their bright side only, and see what it is that makes our social intercourse with others a pleasure. This will be as a mirror wherein we shall behold some faint reflections of social joys as they exist in heaven. What are the personal attributes or qualities in others that make our social intercourse with them a pleasure? They may be reduced to six, which really include all others that could be mentioned. These are virtue, learning, beauty, refinement, mutual love, and the ties of kindred. We shall say a few words on each of these.

(1) Virtue is the attribute which gives us our highest similitude to God, and it is this also which imparts to us some of the purest social pleasures we enjoy on earth. Purity of life, or at least the absence of gross vices, is a condition without which we can enjoy no one's society, unless we ourselves are depraved. Neither beauty, nor learning, nor any other endowment can replace virtue, while it alone can, to a great extent, supply all other deficiencies. Hence it is that when depraved persons are in the society of the good, they feel compelled to be guarded in their words and actions. They must put on an exterior appearance, at least, of virtue, well knowing that otherwise their presence would be extremely offensive, and calculated to mar the pleasures of others.

When we meet with one who is evidently a man of God, one whose every word is instinct with the spirit of God, whose whole exterior betokens the intimate union of his soul with God, in whose very countenance the beauty of angelical purity shines forth, we deem it a happiness to spend a few moments in his society. The pleasures enjoyed in his company are not only exquisite—they are also sanctifying. If that is so in this world, where all holiness is imperfect, what shall we say of the pleasures of heavenly society? Holiness is an essential attribute of every inhabitant of heaven. They are all pure; for none else can see God. They are all made partakers of the Divine Nature in a far higher degree than is attainable in this world, and consequently they are all clothed with the spotless purity of God himself. Not only are they all pure, but they are, moreover, totally free from those natural defects of character, which, in this world, make many holy persons unamiable, and even repulsive. As nature is not destroyed, but perfected by glory, our natural character will not be destroyed by our union with God. But whatever is faulty in it, or offensive to others, will disappear, leaving it amiable and perfect in its own kind. Hence, our social intercourse with the saints will ever be the source of the purest pleasures.

(2) Learning, in those with whom we associate, is another source of pleasure. We can sit for hours listening to the interesting conversation of a learned man, even if he lacks virtue, and only wears its exterior appearance. In such a man's society we drink in, as it were, torrents of pleasures, which are among the most rational we can enjoy in this world. If these pleasures are so exquisite here below, where, after all, the wisest know so little, what shall we say of those same pleasures in heaven? There all are learned, all are filled with knowledge, though all do not possess it in the same degree. Nevertheless, each one's knowledge will be a source of pleasure to others.

(3) Personal beauty is also a source of pleasure in this world. Everyone knows that perfect personal beauty sweetly but powerfully draws men to itself, and that one endowed therewith gives far greater pleasure than another who does not possess this attribute. It is in heaven, and there only, that everyone will possess the attribute of beauty in its fullest perfection. For the soul is clothed with the beauty of God Himself, which He communicates to her in the Beatific Vision; while the whole body is beautified and glorified after the likeness of Christ's glorious body. Every saint is therefore clothed with a loveliness far superior to anything we ever can see on earth. If, then, it is so great a pleasure to associate with persons who possess the natural and perishable beauty of this world, what shall we say of the pleasures which must flow from our intercourse with persons who are clothed with the beauty of God himself!

(4) Refinement is another attribute which makes our social intercourse with others pleasurable. A great personal beauty that might at first attract others to itself would soon repel and even disgust them, should they perceive in its possessor unpolished manners, coarseness, and stupidity. A cultivated intellect, refined feelings, and elegant manners are necessary to adorn personal beauty, and make it a source of pleasure to those who are attracted thereby. It is very certain that in heaven, where our whole nature is to be elevated and perfected, this refinement of mind and heart, as well as the elegance of personal bearing which flows from both, will exist in its highest perfection, and ever be the source of exquisite pleasures in our social intercourse with the blessed.

(5) Another source of social joys is mutual love. The four personal attributes we have been considering make up an amiable character; that is, one which we love spontaneously, and whose love we are certain to have in return for ours. It is this love which crowns and perfects a character of this kind, and produces a very large share of the pure pleasures we enjoy in the society of such persons. But, however pure human love may be, even when elevated by grace to the virtue of charity, it never can produce unalloyed social pleasures; because it never reaches its full perfection in this world.

It is in heaven only that charity is perfect. There we shall love everyone with a most tender charity, and see ourselves loved as tenderly and as purely in return. Our charity will be mutual, and, therefore, our intercourse with the blessed will produce joys and pleasures second only to the unspeakable happiness of the Beatific Vision. Meditate well, Christian soul, on these exquisite delights. Think what an unspeakable pleasure that mutual and perfect charity must be to the inhabitants of heaven. That feature alone would almost change for any one of us this cold world into a heaven. . . .

(6) Besides the things already enumerated, there is one more which is to be the source of still greater joy. And what may that be? It is the meeting, in heaven, of them whom we loved so well here, because they were bound to us by the sacred ties of kindred, or true friendship.

## THE SERIOUS BUSINESS OF HEAVEN

### C. S. Lewis

I DO *not* THINK that the life of heaven bears any analogy to play or dance in respect of frivolity. I do think that while we are in this "valley of tears," cursed with labor, hemmed around with necessities, tripped up with frustrations, doomed to perpetual plannings, puzzlings, and anxieties, certain qualities that must belong to the celestial condition have no chance to get through, can project no image of themselves, except in activities which, for us here and now, are frivolous. For surely we must suppose the life of the blessed to be an end in itself, indeed The End: to be utterly spontaneous; to be the complete reconciliation of boundless freedom with order—with the most delicately adjusted, supple, intricate, and beautiful order? How can you find any image of this in the "serious" activities either of our natural or of our (present) spiritual life? Either in our precariousness and heartbroken affections or in the Way which is always, in some degree, a *via crucis*? No. . . . It is only in our "hours off," only in our moments of permitted festivity, that we find an analogy. Dance and game *are* frivolous, unimportant, down here; for "down here" is not their natural place. Here, they are a moment's rest from the life we were placed here to live. But in this world everything is upside down. That which, if it could be prolonged here, would be a truancy, is likest that which in a better country is the End of Ends. Joy is the serious business of heaven.

# HALO, NIMBUS, AUREOLE

## Gertrude Grace Sill

HALOS ARE the visual expression of a supernatural light, a mystical force. Familiar in Oriental as well as Western art, halos form a symbolic crown. In ancient art halos identified deities. In their circular shapes, their lightness and brightness, they resemble the sun. (The word *halo* most likely evolves from the Greek *helias*, meaning sun. *Nimbus* is Latin for cloud.) The halo is the attribute of sanctity in Christian art, and identifies important personages. In Eastern art the halo was exclusively an attribute of power. In some early medieval miniatures Satan and the seven-headed beast of the Apocalypse wear halos as symbols of power, not holiness.

The *aureole* or *glory* is an orbit of light that surrounds the entire body of God the Father, God the Son, the Holy Ghost, the Virgin, or a person representing the Trinity. It is the symbol of divinity, or supreme power. The rays of the aureole frequently end in multicolored flames. Aureoles may be gold, white, blue, or rainbow-hued. *Aureus* in Latin means gold.

The *cruciform halo*, used behind the head of Christ or God and Christ in one, suggests redemption through the Crucifixion. The Sacred Monogram may also be included in the cruciform halo . . .

*Hexagonal* or *lozenge-shaped halos* are used to distinguish the Virtues or allegorical figures, Old Testament and pre-Christian figures of noble life.

The *mandorla* is an oval frame enclosing an important figure. (*Mandorla*, Italian for "almond," refers to the seed or womb, a similar shape, as well as the oval frame itself.) In Latin the mandorla is called the *vesica piscis*, or fish bladder, another oval shape. The mandorla often includes Christ in Majesty with the four animal symbols of the Evangelists.

The *square halo* identifies a living person. It is used to distinguish donors and other important living people from saints. The square is an earthly symbol, inferior to the perfection of the circle as the earth is inferior to heaven.

The *triangular halo* refers to the Trinity and is used to identify God the Father.

*Three rays of light* emanating from the head are reserved for any of the three members of the Trinity.

# HEAV'M IN GOSPEL SONG

*John Lovell, Jr.*

IF YOU ARE ONE of the sanctified, says the spiritual poet, to heav'm by one way or another you are headed. The nature of being saved has a built-in magnetism which propels you to heav'm. Everything else is incidental.

Sometimes, the song stresses the fact of going, including the being on the way. Sometimes, it shows the irresistibility of the driving impulse. Again, it may concentrate on the desire, but that is no different from the going itself. If you are determined to go and have been permitted into the magnetic stream, forget everything else, you are going! Saying you want to, longing and yearning for the day are mere fillips. Again and again, the song describes the method—ship, chariot, or someone coming to get you who can take you right in.

If heav'm is free land, one can understand the emphasis on the irresistibility through the slave's need to be saved. If he was going to attempt this variety of salvation, he would certainly want to feel that his chances of failure were minimal. There is plenty of evidence that he yearned for the day of freedom, no matter what the method. He would want to feel that he was "on the way" and "bound to go" and that nothing could stop him. His enthusiasm would be without bounds, as it was in these songs.

If heav'm is the land of reward for the sanctified beyond the grave, then the irresistibility is appropriate, but in a different sense. Frankly, the slave's preoccupation with the things of the earth is so great that it does not seem likely that he would have so deep a concern for a land beyond the grave so early in his career. If, in spite of appearances, he had such a concern, he had given up hope of earthly betterment and was putting all his hopes and plans into his postearthly career. If this is indeed the case, he would want nothing to interfere with that sole remaining hope, however far away its time of materialization.

It is easy to see that the songs are more insistent if the immediate hope and enthusiasm are greater. It is also quite clear that the slave was like most of the rest of us; we have our heav'ms within reach and those far away. Very few of us surrender all the immediate ones and resign ourselves totally to those far away. If we do, we rarely write songs of vigorous enthusiasm about the process.

In certain essential respects, you could have either polar interpretation and still have the same songs. The poet is having a wonderful time talking about rewards and goals. Incidentally, he is talking about the good life (that people of soul and energy and spirit have discussed in literature from time immemorial) and why it is a fine thing to lead. To have strong goals is a sign of character; to work unremittingly for them is an even better sign. To expect the rewards of good living is natural and inspirational; it makes you keep up your standards and steels you against discouragement and defeat. In the case of the spiritual poet, it developed his fine, aesthetic sense, as we shall see in the next section of this chapter.

So, heav'm is a place to which the sanctified are on the way. "Thank God, I'm on my way to heav'n," they sing in one song. "Let us cheer the weary traveler, Along the heavenly way," they sing in another. "Gwineter sing all along de way," they sing in still another. While singing, they raise high a golden banner upon which is written: "Repentance and Salvation."

They are going, going, going, and nothing can stop them.

> *For I'm goin' to heav'n above,*
> *Goin' to the God I love.*

So mother, do not weep; just get ready to go, too, when your turn comes.

I am "goin' meet King Jesus in the air," says still another. "Goin' to take my wings an' cleave the air" is a common declaration, although never is it told when and where "my wings" are to be issued, tested, and certified. "Oh, yes, I'm gwine up to see de heavenly land," and presumably to visit there a while. "Gwine reach heab'n by an' by" is another statement delivered with certainty. "Anyhow, anyhow, anyhow, my Lord! Anyhow, yes, anyhow; I'm gwine up to heab'n anyhow."

All these declarations presuppose the proper credentials, knowledge of the route, and no hitches caused either by the individual's relaxation of his good life or by some authority's disagreeable manner or error. Some of the declarations, however, are stronger still; some people are bound to go. "But still my soul is heavenly bound," says one. "My soul is boun' for that bright land," says another. "I will go, I shall go," says one. Nothing can stop me, indicates another, because "de Angels in de heab'n gwineter write my name . . . in de Book of life . . . wid a

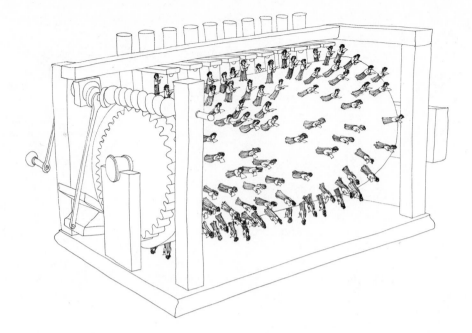

golden pen . . . in de drippin' blood." "You shall have a new hiding place that day," is the firm assurance granted by still another.

Sometimes, although the arrival is sure, the method is of some concern. "Got my letter, goin' to ride the train" is all the message that is necessary in the heart of one poet. For another poet, to be on a ship that is definitely going is the right way, "My ship is on the ocean, We'll anchor bye and bye." For another whose ship is on the ocean, there is no thought of the sureness of the voyage and the landing; he has time to think of whom he wishes to see after arriving; he chooses "good ol' Daniel" and "weepin' Mary." For a more particular passenger, "gwineter ride up in de chariot, Soon-a in de mornin' '" is adequate.

One singer ignores the method but says he sees the angels beckoning and adds:

*I tell you what I mean to do; . . .*
*I mean to go to heav'n, too.*

Another wants to be escorted:

*My way-my way's cloudy, my way,*
*Go sen'-a dem angels down.*

Another will be satisfied with no less than Jesus himself:

*How can I die when I'm in de Lord?*
*Massa Jesus is comin' bye and bye.*

Another suggests that you "hang on behin' the old chariot that's headed for heav'n." This one adds that:

# THE SWEET FOREVER

*George Eldon Ladd*

*There's a land beyond the river*
*That they call the sweet forever,*
*And we only reach that shore by*
*faith's decree;*
*One by one we reach the portals,*
*There to dwell with the immortals,*
*When they ring those golden bells*
*for you and me.*

This old evangelistic song expresses the idea many Christians have of life after death. When we die, "we go to heaven." The popular idea is that heaven is a state of blessedness —"the sweet forever"—through whose portals the man of faith passes when he dies and crosses the river of death. There, in a state of disembodied blessedness, he will "dwell with the immortals." . . .

"It's from the Consumer Protection Agency, demanding that we
submit proof that the gates *are* made of pearl."

*Ef yo' mother want to go,*
*She shall wear a starry crown.*
*An' she must hang on behin'.*

One other is telling sinners, liars, gamblers, and backsliders that they cannot cross "de ribbuh ob Jordan" and implies that he himself can. Still one other gives assurance that "dere's one mo' river to cross," but this one ("Jordan, Lord") is very wide indeed.

Many make the declaration that they want to go without saying precisely that they are going. Such a declaration is tantamount to already being in the magnetic stream.

*Say, don't you want to go to heav'n,*
*How I long to see dat day.*

The writer of a very famous song put it this way: "I want to go to Heaven when I die." A colleague wants to go after he dies "to hear old Jordan roll." Another writer repeats the wish, includes a desire to see mother, father, sister, and Jesus, and ends with:

*Good Lord, when I die,*
*Good Lord, when I die.*

Perhaps, there is no doubt that these two refer to the afterlife for sure.

The sister in "The Old Ark's A-Movering" wants "to go to heav'n 'fore the heaven doors close," a reasonable wish. Another maker of good wishes intones:

*I know I have another building,*
*I know it's not made with hands, O brethren,*
*I want to go to Heaven, and I want to go right,*
*Not made with hands;*
*O, I want to go to Heaven all robed in white,*
*Not made with hands, O brethren.*

This one also has:

*A holy band of angels coming after me,*
*Not made with hands, O yes.*

"This holy band" might just be Quakers in the Underground Railroad. Still another, besides being dressed in white, wanted "to be in Heaven when the roll is called." Already he can hear:

*Heav'n bells a-ringing,*
*The saints all a-singing.*

In one version of still another very famous song, "Lis'en to de Lam's," are these lines:

*Come on sister wid yo' ups an' downs,*
*Wan'-ta go to heaben, when I die.*
*De angel's waitin' for to give you a crown,*
*Wan'-ta go heaben when I die.*

Another declarer wants:

*to go to heab'n, when I die . . .*
*To see God's bleedin' lamb.*

Another sweet singer makes clear his preference after what seems to have been a long period of meditation and soul-searching:

*Yes, I want God's heav'n to be mine;*
*To be mine, to be mine;*
*Yes, I want God's heab'n to be mine,*
*Save me, Lord, save me.*

Once in Heav'm, he is there for good:

*When I get to heav'n, gonna sing and shout,*
*Nobody there for to turn me out.*

# IN THE STOREHOUSE OF YOUR MEMORY

*Fulton J. Sheen*

GO BACK IN THE STOREHOUSE of your memory, and you will find ample proof that it is always in those moments when you are least conscious of the passing of time that you most thoroughly enjoy the pleasures of time. How often it happens, for example, when listening to an absorbing conversation or the thrilling experiences of a much-traveled man, that the hours pass by so quickly we are hardly conscious of them, and we say, "The time passes like everything." What is true of a delightful conversation is also true of aesthetic pleasures. I dare say that very few would ever notice the passing of time listening to an orchestra translate the beauty of one of Beethoven's works. In just the proportion that it pleases and thrills, it makes us unconscious of how long we were absorbed by its melodies. The contrary fact illustrates the same truth. The more we notice time, the less we are being interested. If our friends keep looking at their watches while we tell a story, we can be very sure that they are being bored by our story. A man who keeps his eye on the clock is not the man who is interested in his work. The more we notice the passing of time, the less is our pleasure, and the less we notice the passing of time, the greater is our pleasure.

These psychological facts of experience testify that not only is time the obstacle of enjoyment, but escape from it is the essential of happiness. Suppose we could enlarge upon our experience in such a way as to imagine ourselves completely outside of time and succession, in a world where there would never be a "before" nor an "after," but only a "now." Suppose we could go out to another existence where the great pleasures of history would not be denied us because of their historical incompatibility, but all unified in a beautiful hierarchial order, like a pyramid in that all would minister to the very unity of our personality. Suppose I say that I could reach a point of timelessness at which all the enjoyments and beauties and happinesses of time could be reduced to those three fundamental unities which constitute the perfection of our being, namely, life, and truth, and love, for into these three all pleasures can be resolved.

Suppose first of all that I could reduce to a single focal point all the pleasures of life, so that in the now which never looked before nor after, I could enjoy the life that seems to be in the sea when its restless bosom is dimpled with calm, as well as the urge of life that seems to be in all the hill-encircling brooks that loiter to the sea; the life which provokes the dumb, dead sod to tell its thoughts in violets; the life which pulsates through a springtime blossom as the swinging cradle for the fruit; the life of the flowers as they open the chalice of their perfume to the sun; the life of the birds as the great heralds of song and messengers of joy; the life of all the children that run shouting to their mothers' arms; the life of all the parents that beget a life like unto their own; and the life of the mind that on the wings of an invisible thought strikes out to the hid battlements of eternity to the life whence all living comes. . . .

Suppose that in addition to concentrating all the life of the universe in a single point, I could also concentrate in another focal point all the truths of the world, so that I could know the truth the astronomer seeks as he looks up through his telescope, and the truth the biologist seeks as he looks down through his microscope; the truth about the heavens, and who shut up the sea with doors when it did burst forth as issuing from a womb; the truth about the hiding place of darkness and the treasure house of hail, and the cave of the winds; the truth about the common things: why fire, like a spirit, mounts to the heavens heavenly, and why gold, like clay, falls to the earth earthly; the truth the philosopher seeks as he tears apart with his mind the very wheels of the universe; the truth the theologian seeks as he uses Revelation to unravel the secrets of God which far surpass those that John heard as he leaned his head upon the breast of his Master. . . .

Suppose that over and above all these pleasures of life and truth, there could be unified in another focal point all the delights and beauties of love that have contributed to the happiness of the universe: the love of the patriot for his country; the love of the soldier for his cause; the love of the scientist for his discovery; the love of the flowers as they smile upon the sun; the love of the earth at whose breast all creation drinks the milk of life; the love of mothers, who swing open the great portals of life that a child may see the light of day; the love of friend for friend to whom he could reveal his heart through words; the love of spouse for spouse; the love of husband for wife; and even the love of angel for angel, and the angel for God with a fire and heat sufficient to enkindle the hearts of ten thousand times ten thousand worlds. . . .

Suppose that all the pleasures of the world could be brought to these three focal points of life and truth and love, just as the rays of the sun are brought to unity in the sun; and suppose that all the successive pleasures of time could be enjoyed at one and the same now; and suppose that these points of unity on which our hearts and minds and souls would be directed would not merely be three abstractions, but that the focal point in which all the pleasures of life were concentrated would be a life personal enough to be a Father, and that that focal point of truth in which all the pleasures of truth were concentrated, would not merely be an abstract truth, but a truth personal enough to be a Word or a Son, and that that focal point of love in which all the pleasures of love were concentrated would be not merely an abstract love, but a love personal enough to be a Holy Spirit; and suppose that once elevated to that supreme height, happiness would be so freed from limitations that it would include these three as one, not in succession, but with a permanence; not as in time, but as in the timeless—then we would have eternity, then we would have God! The Father, Son, and Holy Ghost: Perfect Life, Perfect Truth, Perfect Love. Then we would have happiness—and that would be heaven.

Will the pleasures of that timelessness with God and that enjoyment of life and truth and love which is the Trinity be in any way comparable to the pleasures of time? Is there anyone on this earth that will tell me about heaven? Certainly there are three faculties to which one might appeal, namely, to what one has seen, to what one has heard, and to what one can imagine. Will heaven surpass all the pleasures of the eye, and the ear, and the imagination? First of all, will it be as beautiful as some of the things that can be seen? I have seen the Villa d'Este of Rome with its long lanes of ilex and laurel, and its great avenues of cypress trees, all full of what might be called the vivacity of quiet and living silence; I have seen a sunset on the Mediterranean when two clouds came down like pillars to form a brilliant red tabernacle for the sun and it glowing like a golden host; I have seen, from the harbor, the towers and the minarets of Constantinople pierce through the

mist which hung over them like a silken veil; I have seen the château country of France and her Gothic cathedrals aspiring heavenward like prayers; I have seen the beauties of the castles of the Rhine, and the combination of all these visions almost makes me think of the doorkeeper of the Temple of Diana who used to cry out to those who entered: "Take heed to your eye," and so I wonder if the things of eternity will be as beautiful as the combined beauty of all the things which I have seen. . . .

I have not seen all the beauties of nature, others I have heard of that I have not seen: I have heard of the beauties of the hanging gardens of Babylon, of the pomp and dignity of the palaces of the doges, of the brilliance and glitter of the Roman forum as its foundations rocked with the tramp of Rome's resistless legions; I have heard of the splendor of the Temple of Jerusalem as it shone like a jewel in the morning sun; I have heard of the beauties of the garden of paradise where fourfold rivers flowed through lands rich with gold and onyx, a garden made beautiful as only God knows how to make a beautiful garden; I have heard of countless other beauties and joys of nature which tongue cannot describe, nor touch of brush convey, and I wonder if all the joys and pleasures of heaven will be as great as the combined beauty of all the things of which I have heard. . . .

Beyond what I have heard and seen, there are things which I can imagine: I can imagine a world in which there never would be pain, nor disease, nor death; I can imagine a world wherein every man would live in a castle, and in that commonwealth of castles there would be a due order of justice without complaint or anxiety; I can imagine a world in which the winter would never come, and in which the flowers would never fade, and the sun would never set; I can imagine a world in which there would always be a peace and a quiet without idleness, a profound knowledge of things without research, a constant enjoyment without satiety; I can imagine a world which would eliminate all the evils and diseases and worries of life, and combine all of its best joys and happiness, and I wonder if all the happiness of heaven would be like the happiness of earth which I can imagine. . . .

Will eternity be anything like what I have seen, or what I have heard or what I can imagine? No, eternity will be nothing like anything I have seen, heard, or imagined. Listen to the voice of God: "Eye hath not seen, nor ear heard, neither hath it entered into the heart of man what things God hath prepared for them that love Him."

# COMMON LIFE IN THE PRESENCE OF GOD

*J. V. Langmead Casserley*

THERE IS a communion, a common life in the presence of God, enjoyed by all those in whose lives the Spirit of God is openly working in the name of Christ. In time things happen one after the other, the generations succeed each other in turn, so that some men are dead before others are born. But we must not suppose that this successiveness, because it is a law of time, is also a universal law which governs the whole realm of being. In a deep sense it is true to say that in the presence of God past, present, and future stand side by side. He is God not of the dead but of the living, for all live unto Him. In the last resort we are all contemporaries. Ancient and modern touch and find fellowship in eternity.

# IX.

# LIVING

# HOPE, HORIZON BEFORE THE SUNRISE

*Pierre Teilhard de Chardin*

WE ARE SOMETIMES inclined to think that the same things are monotonously repeated over and over again in the history of creation. That is because the season is too long by comparison with the brevity of our individual lives, and the transformation too vast and too inward by comparison with our superficial and restricted outlook, for us to see the progress of what is tirelessly taking place in and through all matter and all spirit. Let us believe in Revelation, once again our faithful support in our most human forebodings. Under the commonplace envelope of things and of all our purified and salvaged efforts, a New Earth is being slowly engendered.

One day, the Gospel tells us, the tension gradually accumulating between humanity and God will touch the limits prescribed by the possibilities of the world. And then will come the end. Then the presence of Christ, which has been silently accruing things, will suddenly be revealed—like a flash of light from pole to pole. Breaking through all the barriers within which the veil of matter and the watertightness of souls have seemingly kept it confined, it will invade the face of the earth. And, under the finally liberated action of the true affinities of being, the spiritual atoms of the world will be borne along by a force generated by the powers of cohesion proper to the universe itself and will occupy, whether within Christ or without Christ (but always under the influence of Christ), the place of happiness or pain designated for them by the living structure of the Pleroma. *Sicut fulgur exit ab Oriente et paret usque ad Occidentem . . . Sicut venit diluvium et tulit omnes . . . Ita erit adventus Filii hominis.* Like lightning, like a conflagration, like a flood, the attraction exerted by the Son of Man will lay hold of all the whirling elements in the universe so as to reunite them or subject them to His body. *Ubicumque fuerit corpus congrebuntur et aquilae.*

Such will be the consummation of the divine milieu.

As the Gospel warns us, it would be vain to speculate as to the hour and the modalities of this formidable event. But we have to *expect* it.

Expectation—anxious, collective, and operative expectation of an end of the world, that is to say of an issue for the world—that is perhaps the supreme Christian function and the most distinctive characteristic of our religion.

Historically speaking, that expectation has never ceased to guide the progress of our faith like a torch. The Israelites were constantly expectant, and the first Christians too. Christmas, which might have been thought to turn our gaze toward the past, has only fixed it further in the future. The Messiah who appeared for a moment in our midst only allowed Himself to be seen and touched for a moment before vanishing again, more luminous and ineffable than ever, into the depths of the future. He came. Yet now we must expect Him—no longer a small chosen group among us, but all men—once again and more than ever. The Lord Jesus will only come soon if we ardently expect Him. It is an accumulation of desires that should cause the Pleroma to burst upon us.

Successors to Israel, we Christians have been charged with keeping the flame of desire ever alive in the world. Only twenty centuries have passed since the Ascension. What have we made of our expectancy?

A rather childish haste, combined with the error in perspective which led the first generation of Christians to believe in the immediate return of Christ, has unfortunately left us disillusioned and suspicious. Our faith in the Kingdom of God has been disconcerted by the resistance of the world to good. A certain pessimism, perhaps, encouraged by an exaggerated conception of the original fall, has led us to regard the world as decidedly and incorrigibly wicked. And so we have allowed the flame to die down in our sleeping hearts. No doubt we see with greater or less distress the approach of individual death. No doubt, again, our prayers and actions are conscientiously directed to bringing about "the coming of God's Kingdom." But in fact how many of us are genuinely moved in the depths of their heart by the wild hope that *our* earth will be recast? Who is there who sets a course in the midst of our darkness toward the first glimmer of a *real* dawn? Where is the Christian in whom the impatient longing for Christ succeeds, not in submerging (as it should) the cares of human love and human interests, but even in counterbalancing them? Where is the Catholic as passionately vowed (*by conviction* and not *by convention*) to spreading the hopes of the Incarnation as are many humanitarians to spreading the dream of the new city? We persist in saying that we keep vigil in expectation of the Master. But in reality we should have to admit, if we were sincere, *that we no longer expect anything.*

The flame must be revived at all costs. At all costs we must renew in ourselves the desire and the hope for the great Coming. But where are we to look for the source of this rejuvenation? We shall clearly find it, first and foremost, in an increase of the attraction exercised directly by Christ upon His members. And then *in an increase of the interest,* discovered by our thought, in the preparation and consummation of the *parousia.* And from where is this interest itself to spring? From the perception of *a more intimate connection* between the victory of Christ and the outcome of the work which our human effort here below is seeking to construct.

We are constantly forgetting that the supernatural is a ferment, a soul, and not a complete and finished organism. Its role is to transform "nature"; but it cannot do so apart from the matter which nature provides it with. If the Jewish people have remained turned toward the Messiah for three thousand years, it is because He appeared to them to enshrine the glory of their people. If the disciples of St. Paul lived in perpetual expectation of the great day, that was because it was to the Son of Man that they looked for a personal and tangible solution to the problems and the injustices of life. The expectation of heaven cannot remain alive unless it is incarnate. What body shall we give to our today?

That of a huge and *totally human* hope. Let us look at the earth around us. What is happening under our eyes within the mass of peoples? What is the cause of this disorder in society, this uneasy agitation, these swelling waves, these whirling and mingling currents, and these turbulent and formidable new impulses? Mankind is visibly passing through a crisis of growth. Mankind is becoming dimly aware of its shortcomings and its capacities. . . . It sees the universe growing luminous like the horizon just before sunrise. It has a sense of premonition and of expectation.

# HOPEFUL GROUND

## Sam Keen

SEEMINGLY, the world of the spirit loathes a power vacuum no less than does the political world. When realism prevails and we acknowledge that our infantile strivings to have dominion over all things are doomed to failure, the question of God inevitably arises. If I am not the source of a deathless and victorious power, is there any such power? If I am not God, is there a God? Is there any force, mind, or person working at the heart of things to accomplish what I desire but cannot achieve; to bring order out of chaos, meaning out of contingency, triumph out of tragedy? Or is human history "a tale told by an idiot"?

The question of God is not the question of the existence of some remote infinite being. It is the question of the possibility of hope. The affirmation of faith in God is the acknowledgment that there is a deathless source of power and meaning that can be trusted to nurture and preserve all created good. To deny that there is a God is functionally equivalent to denying that there is any ground for hope. It is therefore wholly consistent for Sartre to say that human beings "must act without hope," or for Camus to warn that hope was the last of the curses which Pandora took from her box. If God is dead, then death is indeed God, and perhaps the best motto for human life is what Dante once wrote over the entrance to hell: "Abandon hope, all ye who enter."

The concept of hope has been so little examined in our time that it is frequently thought to mean the same thing as optimism or illusion or mere agnosticism about the future. There are, however, crucial differences. Optimism is based upon illusion—in the Freudian sense—in that it arises out of a drive for wish fulfillment which ignores contrary evidence. The optimist conspires to ignore the facts because they suggest an interpretation he does not want to make. Contrariwise, the believer's affirmation of a ground for hope is made in the knowledge that by all realistic calculations human history is ultimately tragic. It is in light of this certain knowledge that the believer sets himself to examine his experience to determine whether there is any basis for hoping that what is penultimately the case is not ultimately so.

---

# LOOKING TO THE FUTURE

## Augustine of Hippo

WHAT DISADVANTAGE is it to me not to know when I began to exist, if I know that I exist now and hope to exist in the future? I do not trouble about the past, or think a false opinion about the past a disastrous error. I direct my course to my future, led by the mercy of my Creator. If, therefore, I believe or think falsely about my future state, or about Him with whom I shall be in the future, I must be most careful to guard against this error. The danger is that I may be unable to reach the end I have in view, if I confuse one thing with another.

If I were buying a coat, it would not affect me adversely to have forgotten last winter, but such would be the case, were I not to believe that cold weather will be coming on. So too it will be no hindrance to my soul if it forgets what it may have endured in the past, provided it keeps carefully in mind all for which it is urged to prepare in the future. If, for example, a man was sailing for Rome, it would not matter if he forgot the land from which he set sail, so long as he knew whither to steer from the place at which he was. It would not help him to remember the land from which he set out, if he made a mistake about the port of Rome and was wrecked. In the same way it will do no harm to me to forget the beginning of my life, if I know the end where I can find rest.

Blessed is the man
who trusts in the Lord,
whose hope is in the Lord.
He is like a tree
planted beside the waters
that stretches out its
roots to the stream;
It fears not the heat
when it comes,
its leaves stay green;
In the year of drought
it shows no distress,
but still bears fruit.

JEREMIAH 17: 7-8

# CHARTER OF HOPE

*Hilda Graef*

ALMOST TWO THOUSAND YEARS before our present neopagan fashion of pessimism and despair, St. Paul elaborated a theology of hope: "We are confident even over our afflictions, knowing well that affliction gives rise to endurance, and endurance gives proof of our faith, and a proved faith gives ground for hope. Nor does this hope delude us; the love of God has been poured out in our hearts by the Holy Spirit, whom we have received. Were that hope vain, why did Christ . . . undergo death for us sinners, while we were still powerless to help ourselves? . . . We have died, once for all, to sin; can we breathe its air again? . . . In our baptism, we have been buried with him, died like him, that so, just as Christ was raised up by his Father's power from the dead, we, too, might live and move in a new kind of existence. We have to be closely fitted into the pattern of his Resurrection, as we have been into the pattern of death; we have to be sure of this, that our former nature has been crucified with him, and the living power of our guilt annihilated, so that we are the slaves of guilt no longer. . . . You must not, then, allow sin to tyrannize over your perishable bodies, to make you subject to its appetites. . . . And you, thanks be to God, although you were the slaves of sin once, accepted obedience with all your hearts, true to the pattern of teaching to which you are now engaged. Thus you escaped from the bondage of sin, and became the right-doing instead. . . . At the time when you were the slaves of sin, right-doing had no claim upon you. And what harvest were you then reaping, from acts which now make you blush? Their reward is death. Now that you are free from the claims of sin, and have become God's slaves instead, you have a harvest in your sanctification, and your reward is eternal life. Sin offers death for wages; God offers us eternal life" (Romans 5–6).

We have cited this passage at length, because it may well be called the charter of Christian hope, and it comes like a fresh blast of wind to disperse the fog of despair and *angst* in which so much contemporary literature enshrouds us. St. Paul knew affliction as well as any of us—hunger, shipwreck, persecution had been his experience for years—but far from letting all this produce a state of dread in him, it gives, on the contrary, "rise to endurance." This power of endurance proves the reality of his faith, and this faith gives him grounds for hope, a hope that is not a delusion, but a fact, because Christ has died for us, and in our baptism we have died with Him to sin, we have been raised to a new "kind of existence"—an existence far removed from the existence of the existentialists, for it is an existence in which our human life has found the plenitude of its meaning. It is a supernatural and a moral existence, an existence of "right-doing," the reward of which is eternal life.

Christian hope then, while looking toward eternity, has also its powerful effects on earth, because, hoping in Christ, Christians have died to sin and must not, as St. Paul tells them, allow sin to tyrannize over their perishable bodies, for they are now free from the claims of sin and able to resist it. Authors like Mauriac and Greene take the exact opposite for their subject: the tyranny of sin over the perishable body, man's incapacity of freeing himself from its bondage.

Nietzsche, the German philosopher who proclaimed that "God is dead," taunted Christians for teaching Redemption, but not looking at all as if they were redeemed. He could truthfully have said the same of our contemporary Catholic novelists: their personages profess a religion of Redemption, but their behavior completely contradicts their beliefs; they are as full of crime, gloom, and despair as the characters of their unbelieving fellow writers. But Christianity is not a religion of gloom but of joy, even in this world. The whole New Testament rings with joy: the angel of the Annunciation proclaims tidings of joy; the man who has found the treasure in the field, symbolizing the kingdom of heaven, "for the joy it gives him" sells all his possessions; after the Ascension, the disciples "went back to Jerusalem with great joy"; and St. Paul preaches joy wherever he goes: "May God, the author of our hope, fill you with all joy" (Romans 15:13), "My joy is the joy of you all" (2 Corinthians 2:3), for "the fruit of the spirit is love, joy, peace" (Galatians 5:22). For the life of Christ, which all of us have to reproduce in some way in ourselves, did not end in the Crucifixion, but was consummated in the Resurrection. "We have to be closely fitted into the pattern of his resurrection" says St. Paul; the Christian life is a new life, a kind of "risen life" even in this world. For it simply is not true that such a kind of life cannot be lived here on earth, that here we are only subject to sin, to absurdity, that the death of an innocent child, like that described by Camus in *The Plague*, suffices to destroy anyone's faith. . . .

The hope of union with God in the next world certainly makes the inevitable evils of this world easier to bear, but it is not meant to make men indifferent to the miseries of their neighbor—quite the contrary. If the poor who have patiently borne their misfortunes for the love of God (for this is the condition; poverty in itself is no virtue at all) are promised the reward of heaven, the rich who have been deaf to their needs are threatened with severe punishment. For the Christian hope is the same for the rich and for the poor; and it works in a way that should smooth out the differences: for the rich are taught to share with the poor if they would have eternal life, and the poor are assured of this life if they accept their state with submission to the divine will.

If Christianity does not work out quite like this in practice, this is not the fault of our religion but of human sinfulness, which refuses to obey the commandments of Christ. Nevertheless, our care for the poor, for the sick and the aged, our desires for social justice and the freedom of the individual is a result of the Christian principles still alive in the West; we need only turn our eyes to the East to see what happens if men abandon hope in eternal life in order to establish beatitude on earth.

"Our salvation is founded upon the hope of something. Hope would not be hope at all, if its object were in view; how could a man still hope for something which he sees?" (Romans 8:24). Because the exponents of modern gloom can stare only at visible things, because the invisible is for them unreal, hope is not in them and they can only sink into despair. Even Kierkegaard could only "choose" God in a desperate "leap" into the dark, in fear and anguish, without objective certainty, since, according to him, "truth is subjectivity" and Christianity is the "absolute paradox." But Christian hope does not spring from *angst*, which is quite foreign to it, nor does it require a leap into the dark. For though its object is not "in view," it rests on a sure foundation, for it is "hope in our Lord Jesus Christ" (1 Thessalonians 1:3), who is Himself our hope (1 Timothy 1:1). It is based on the historic fact of our Redemption through Christ, who has given us access to the invisible realities of heaven for which we now hope, but which we shall one day possess.

In the light of this hope all things fall into their place. The sufferings of this world, however severe, will not cause despair, because they must come to an end; our reason, puzzled by so much that seems "absurd," will then be enlightened, our love will be purified and perfected, and this world of ours will be seen not as a transitory stage between nought and nought, but as the way that leads to our true home.

# CREATIVE HOPE: THREE REMARKS

## Johannes B. Metz

(1) Christian hope is not the attempt of reason to pierce through the future and so to rob it of mystery. The man who hopes is not making the irritating claim to know more about the future than others. Christian eschatology therefore is not an ideology of the future. It values precisely the poverty of its knowledge about the future. What distinguishes it from the ideas of the future both in East and West is not that it knows more but rather that it knows less about the hoped-for future of mankind, and that it stands by the poverty of this knowledge. "By faith Abraham obeyed the call to go out to a land destined for himself and his heirs and left home without knowing where he was to go" (Hebrews 11:8).

(2) The creative hope of the Christian does not seek to outbid by its optimism all forms of human alienation or the "pain of finiteness," nor to unmask them as provisional. It concentrates rather on those forms of human alienation which can in no way be removed through any economic and social transformation of situations and destiny, however perfect they may be. For example: the experience of guilt and of evil, or the experience which theology describes with the word "concupiscence."

Here we have an experience of self-alienation which plainly cannot be overcome simply by social and economic means. For man always feels the discrepancy between the level on which he projects to live and that on which he in fact lives, between idea and existence. He constantly falls below the great experiences of his life and does not allow himself to be changed by them, but rather transforms them and levels them down to everyday banalities. As Camus put it: "It seems that great men are less disturbed by pain than by the thought that it does not last." It does not last because we are not equal to its claims and do not remain equal to its claims. In such and similar experiences we become aware of a situation of human self-alienation which cannot be removed or nullified by social, economic, or technical progress. Christian hope strives to remain faithful to such experiences and precisely through them to realize all the painful breadth and depth of its hope against hope.

(3) Finally Christian hope is aware of the greatest risk of all: it is aware of death, before which all glittering promises are threatened and grow dim. Christian hope has been called an anticipated practice for death, practice, that is, in a hope against all hope.

But even this movement of hope should not be narrowed down to an individualistic hope which forgets the world; it has lost its private character or should lose it. This too must take place with a glance on the world, on the world of our brothers, in the self-forgetting oblation of love for others, for the "least of the brethren," in selfless commitment for *their* hope.

For through our love of the community we overcome death in anticipation: "We know that we have passed over from death to life, because we love the brethren" (1 John 3:14). Only one who loses his soul in this way will gain it. Christian hope draws to itself and overcomes the passion of death, which threatens our promises, as it accepts the adventure of brotherly love of the least —in imitation of Christ, whose being is not originally self-perfection, not a *reditio subjecti in se ipsum* but a "being for others" (Bonhoeffer).

Christian hope is creative imitation of this "being for others"; and so it is at the service of creative responsibility for the world.

# HOPE IN AMERICA

## *Jurgen Moltmann*

FOR MANY PEOPLE through the world America represents the *great experiment*. Through their traditions of thousands of years most of the other nations understand themselves as a piece of nature. Culture and nature have become a unity. Every present is burdened with the past. Everywhere one sees the remnants of past times. Next to one of these nations America appears as an artifact. In a very short time after its independence the United States was constructed out of the will and the reason of immigrants. One needs only to compare an American city with a European city in order to observe that "city" is no translation of *polis*, *città*, or *Stadt* but

designates a new phenomenon. One needs only to compare the farmland in the Middle West with Asian farming villages to see that here also a new relationship with nature has emerged. American cultivation and management of land is an experiment with the possibilities of space, of which we spoke at the beginning. The city is an experiment with the possibilities of society.

In the land of unknown possibilities one must experiment in order to probe its latent energies and to discover the best possibilities. The experimental life-style corresponds to the open environment. It is fascinated by the realm of possibility and is itself fascinating. As Boorstin has said, "America lived with the constant belief that something better might turn up. Americans were glad enough to keep things growing and moving. When before had men got so much faith in the unexpected?"

*Life as experiment* means, try it again and again, the future is open for you and the future is gracious to the virtuous. *Life as experiment* means not to accept any piece of reality as final and closed but to go forward in the dynamic of the provisional. *Life*

*as experiment* is the trial-and-error method. History as experiment is the challenge-and-response method. From its very inception America was a great experiment, and up to the present day it understands itself as a great experiment with nature, society, the future, with God. If there is an American life-style which is spread throughout the world today, it is this shape of life which is open to the future, enamored of risk, and experimental.

But one must pay a high price for this *life as experiment*. According to sociological investigations it is the dearest dream of every American to own his own house on his own land, and on the national average every American moves at least every five years. Forty million Americans per year change their address. As John Steinbeck set out on his *Travels with Charlie* he saw in the eyes of his neighbor something he was to discover everywhere in the nation: "A burning desire to go, to move, to get underway, anyplace away from Here. They spoke quietly of how they wanted to go someday, to move about, free and unanchored, not toward something, but away from something" (p. 10). But in order to be a person in movement, one must cut off one's roots and live without relationships. The fascinating mobility of the American legs costs the bitter rootlessness of the American soul. Vance Packard has described this *Nation of Strangers* with an abundance of statistics. He found: "While the footlooseness of Americans as pioneers was a source of vitality and charm, several of the new forms that the accelerating rootlessness of Americans is taking should be the cause for alarm." He has thereby overlooked, I suspect, the fact that modern rootlessness is the consequence of the old footlooseness and the necessary price for an experimental life-style. As the great experiment, America can only be a society of torn roots.

*Life as experiment* costs not only this price of loneliness in one's own life but also the sacrifice of many other lives. An experiment is only an attempt. One must be able to repeat an experiment. One should, therefore, take into account the failures. One can learn from errors in order to try again from scratch. When one transfers this experimental attitude to real life, one can immediately see its limits. *Medical experiments* on the living, which can lead to life or death and which can leave behind irreparable damage, are morally suspect. It would be better for politicians to abstain from *political experiments*. Was Vietnam merely a *military experiment*? What about the dead then? One cannot experiment with catastrophe.

Making an experiment means leaving everything open and in suspension. But when it comes to a matter of life and death, then the point of no return has been reached. Then it is no longer a question of an experiment but an emergency. Death is not an experiment, for one cannot make a new beginning with it. Therefore, life is also not an experiment, for it is once for all.

Not to be able to live, to love, and to die with one's whole heart but to be able only to experiment with life, love, and death is the kind of detached life-style to which one is forced by the messianism with which America has entered the stage of world history. The messianic *dynamic of the provisional* creates the strength of America, but the *provisional life* is also the weakness of America. To live with a dream and a hope in its realization is something great and extraordinary.

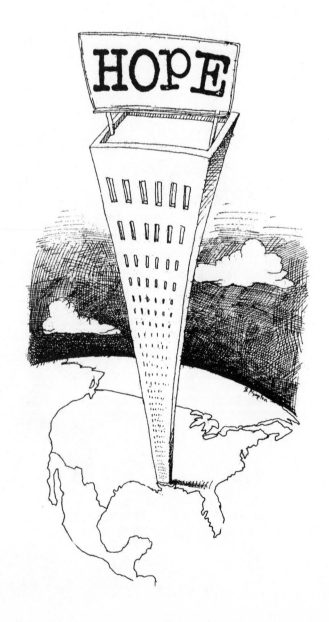

# THE LORD'S PRAYER, PRAYER OF HOPE

## *Augustine of Hippo*

OF ALL THE MATTERS which are to be believed in the true spirit of faith, only those pertain to hope which are contained in the Lord's Prayer. For, "cursed be every one," so the Holy Scriptures testify, "that placeth his hope in man." It follows that one who puts his hope in himself is likewise held by the bond of this curse. We should, therefore, beg of the Lord alone for whatsoever we may hope to accomplish ourselves in the way of good works, or hope to obtain as a reward for good deeds alone.

Wherefore, according to the evangelist Matthew the Lord's Prayer appears to contain seven petitions, three of which request eternal goods, the remaining four, temporal goods necessary for the attainment of the eternal. For, when we say: "Hallowed be Thy name, Thy kingdom come, Thy will be done on earth as it is in heaven" (which latter words some have with good reason interpreted to mean "in body and in spirit"), there are things to be retained forever. They are begun here; they are increased in us as we make progress; and in their perfection, a state to be hoped for in the other life, they will be

an everlasting possession. But when we say: "Give us this day our daily bread, and forgive us our debts, as we also forgive our debtors, and bring us not into temptation, but deliver us from evil," who does not see that these things pertain to the necessaries of this life? In that eternal life, therefore, where we hope to be forever, the hallowing of God's name, His kingdom, and His will will abide in everlasting perfection in our souls and bodies. The bread is called "daily bread" for the reason that here below this is a necessity, and that to the extent required by soul and body, whether the term is understood in a spiritual or a physical sense, or in both senses. Here, too, where there is commission of sins, is the place for the remission which we ask. Here are the temptations which allure or urge us to sin. And, lastly, here is the evil from which we pray to be freed. But in that other world none of these things exist.

Now, with the evangelist Luke the Lord's Prayer embraces not seven but five petitions. But of course this does not mean that he disagreed with the other version; rather, by his very brevity he has shown how the seven petitions should be understood. For God's name is hallowed in the spirit; and God's kingdom will come in the resurrection of the flesh. Luke, therefore, by showing that the third petition is to some extent a repetition of the first two, helps us to a better understanding of it by omitting it. He then goes on to state three further petitions: concerning the daily bread, the remission of sins, and the avoidance of temptation. However, what Matthew put in the last place, "but deliver us from evil," Luke omitted, to make us see that it belongs to what was previously said about temptation. In fact, this is why Matthew said "*but* deliver us," not "*and* deliver us," to make clear that we have here practically only one petition: do not this, but this. Thus everyone would know that he is delivered from evil by the fact that he is not led into temptation.

# THE SPIRITUAL SENSE OF THE LORD'S PRAYER

## Mary Baker Eddy

Here let me give what I understand to be the spiritual sense of the Lord's Prayer:

Our Father which art in heaven,
"Our Father-Mother God, all-harmonious,"

Hallowed be Thy name.
"Adorable One."

Thy kingdom come.
"Thy kingdom is come; Thou art ever-present."

Thy will be done in earth, as it is in heaven.
"Enable us to know,—as in heaven, so on earth,
—God is omnipotent, Supreme."

Give us this day our daily bread;

"Give us grace for today; feed the famished affections";

And forgive us our debts, as we forgive our debtors.
"And love is reflected in love";

And lead us not into temptation, but deliver us from evil;
"And God leadeth us not into temptation, but delivereth us from sin, disease, and death."

For Thine is the kingdom, and the power, and the glory, forever.
"For God is infinite, all-power, all Life, Truth, Love, over all, and All."

---

## PRECURSOR OF THE ACROSTIC

### Bamber Gascoigne

THIS SQUARE of letters has been found in several places, including Pompeii in Italy and even faraway Cirencester in England. It appears to be meaningless, but a little re-arrangement will work wonders. "I am Alpha and Omega, the beginning and the ending, saith the Lord." If we remove A and O, twice over, we are left with a group of letters which can be reorganized to spell "Pater Noster," Our Father, also twice over and in the shape of a cross.

```
R O T A S
O P E R A
T E N E T
A R E P O
S A T O R
```

# THREE WAYS TO PRAY THE LORD'S PRAYER

*George Maloney*

THE PERSON would take the text of Scripture and see that the disciples asked Jesus how to pray and he told them when you pray, say, "Our Father, who art in heaven, hallowed be thy name." So, you place yourself with your memory back to the time of our Lord. You try to imagine that you're sitting there listening as he speaks these words. And as you listen, you ask yourself, "What do these words mean to me? What does 'our' mean?" You discursively think, "Jesus and I and all the human race are all brothers and sisters of this one great Father. And I can call him Father, with all these people."

You move gradually to the presence of the Father through Jesus. In discursive prayer, as you activate your imagination and get into that scene, Jesus becomes more vividly present; the Father becomes more vividly present, because as you see Jesus you see the Father mirror-imaged in Jesus' humanity. The whole point of this prayer is to get a feeling, a love of the Father and a love of Jesus. A lot depends on how you can control your distractions so you can really focus on the presence of God coming through those ideas.

As you stay in that affective state, the love of the Father flows toward you. You let that happen; you express your love for the Father, you pray with Jesus, with the saints and the angels, in an adoration of the Father. You go on to the next phrase, when you've exhausted that, and you say, "Who art in heaven. . . . What does 'heaven' mean?" And "Hallowed be thy name. . . ."

Now on the second level, the affective prayer is the beginning of the simplification, where you begin to let go of your own activism, your own discursive activity. Faith and hope and love are developing now. As soon as you say "Father," something resonates deep within you; it stirs up all sorts of feelings. Before you had to get to those feelings step by step, now you've done that type of logical thinking and you can move right into affection.

At this stage of your prayer life, you are centered in a quick way because we've gone through the words and their connotations, so you can jump through this process and get immediately into the presence of God with great feeling. Now you can spend concentrated prayer time with very strong, multiplied feelings. Now, there might be sorrow for ignoring the Father, not letting him be your Father. Thoughts of the Prodigal Son might come up, so there could be great sorrow. And there might be hope, that Jesus has come to bring us back to the Father.

After some time of such prayer, the feelings kind of merge into one act of great faith, hope, and love. That's when you would be moving from affective prayer to the beginning stages of contemplative prayer that I call the prayer of faith. Here is where you have the anima-type of listening. This admits of a very long process; it can go on for years and years: you are gradually moving away from any images and any of your own controlled activities and you are evolving into a greater surrender and openness to God. His presence comes to you, now, not because you feel through affections or you see through your own discursive powers. Rather, there's a darkening of those powers. The affections dry up. There's aridity usually. There is a darkening of your intellectual powers—not that you couldn't discursively think about God. But psychologically you reach a stage of deepening faith where you don't want to think about God, you just want to be with him because faith tells you he's here. To go back and go through the whole process again would be very painful psychologically for a person who is in the area of deeper faith.

So the person just stays in God's presence, day after day, being centered, and his greatest activity is just to push his consciousness to want to be there, to want to surrender to God without any words, without any feelings even, but just totally at service. If God wants to reveal himself through feelings, okay, but the person is now becoming indifferent to that level. This shows a greater growth in trust, abandoning onself to whatever God wants to do. A person is just totally submissive to God.

That level is the beginning of contemplative prayer. It requires great inner discipline, because it can so easily lend itself to vagueness, instead of true faith. You can wander around and no longer push your consciousness toward God.

# OUR FATHER

## JESUS' FATHER
### Raymond E. Brown

THIS NEW TESTAMENT concept of God's Fatherhood and Christian sonship gives an eschatological tone to the title of the Pater Noster; for if we examine the synoptic gospels carefully, we find that becoming sons of God is something that happens in the last days and in the heavenly kingdom. Luke 20:36 says that there will be no marriage in the next age because those who are worthy to attain that age "cannot die any more, since they are equal to angels and are *sons of God.*" Again, Luke 6:35 promises a heavenly reward to those who love their enemies: "Your reward will be great, and you will be *sons of the Most High.*" The beatitudes promise heavenly rewards to various groups among the followers of Jesus; the peacemakers are blessed, "for they shall be called sons of God" (Matthew 5:9). In the explanation of the parable of the weeds in the field (Matthew 13:37–43), we find that at the close of the age, when the angels are sent forth, there is a separation between the sons who enter the kingdom of their Father (verses 38, 43) and the sons of the Evil One.

Hence, if in the Pater Noster the Christians can address God as "Father," it is because they are anticipating their state of perfection, which will come at the close of this age. They are anticipating the coming of God's eschatological kingdom, which is already incipient in the preaching of Jesus. It is no accident that in the beatitudes . . . the parallel to the promise that the peacemakers shall be called the sons of God is the promise that the poor in spirit shall inherit the kingdom of God. And so, the community that says the Our Father is not the Jewish nation but the poor, the sick, and the needy who accept Jesus' preaching of the kingdom, a kingdom prepared by the Father through Jesus (Luke 22:29–30).

## WHO WILL GIVE ME WINGS LIKE A DOVE?
### Gregory of Nyssa

"WHO WILL give me wings like a dove?" says the great David somewhere in the Psalms. This I, too, would say, boldly using the same words. Who will give me those wings, that my mind may wing its way up to the heights of these noble words? Then I would leave behind the earth altogether and traverse all the middle air; I would reach the beautiful ether, come to the stars, and behold all their orderly array. But not even there would I stop short, but, passing beyond them, would become a stranger to all that moves and changes, and apprehend the stable Nature, the immovable Power which exists in its own right, guiding and keeping in being all things, for all depend on the ineffable will of the Divine Wisdom. So first my mind must become detached from anything subject to flux and change and tranquilly rest in motionless repose, so as to be rendered akin to Him who is perfectly unchangeable; and then it may address Him by this most familiar name and say: Father.

# THIS TIME OF REPENTANCE

*Søren Kierkegaard*

FATHER IN HEAVEN! What is a man without Thee! What is all that he knows, vast accumulation though it be, but a chipped fragment if he does not know Thee! What is all his striving, could it even encompass a world, but a half-finished work if he does not know Thee: Thee the One, who art one thing and who art all! So may Thou give to the intellect, wisdom to comprehend that one thing; to the heart, sincerity to receive this understanding; to the will, purity that wills only one thing. In prosperity may Thou grant perseverance to will one thing; amid distractions, collectedness to will one thing; in suffering, patience to will one thing. Oh, Thou that givest both the beginning and the completion, may Thou early, at the dawn of day, give to the young man the resolution to will one thing. As the day wanes, may Thou give to the old man a renewed remembrance of his first resolution, that the first may be like the last, the last like the first, in possession of a life that has willed only one thing. Alas, but this has indeed not come to pass. Something has come in between. The separation of sin lies in between. Each day, and day after day something is being placed in between: delay, blockage, interruption, delusion, corruption. So in this time of repentance may Thou give the courage once again to will one thing.

## YOUR HEAVENLY FATHER

*Andrew Murray*

*Our Father which art in heaven.*
—Luke 11:2

How SIMPLE, HOW BEAUTIFUL, this invocation which Christ puts upon our lips! And yet how inconceivably rich in its meaning, in the fullness of the love and blessing it contains.

Just think what a book could be written of all the memories there have been on earth of wise and loving fathers. Think of what this world owes to the fathers who have made their children strong and happy in giving their lives to seek the welfare of their fellowmen. And then think how all this is but a shadow—a shadow of exquisite beauty, but still but a shadow of what the Father in heaven is to His children on earth.

What a gift Christ bestowed on us when He gave us the right to say: "Father!" "The Father of Christ," "Our Father," "My Father."

And then, "Our Father in heaven," our Heavenly Father. We count it a great privilege as we bow in worship to know the Father comes near to us where we are upon earth. But we soon begin to feel the need of rising up to enter into His holy presence in heaven, to breathe its atmosphere, to drink in its spirit, and to become truly heavenly minded. As we in the power of thought and imagination leave earth behind, and in the power of the Holy Spirit enter the holiest of all, where the seraphs worship, the word "Heavenly Father" takes on a new meaning, and our hearts come under an eternal influence.

As we then gather up our thoughts of what fatherhood on earth has meant, and hear the voice of Christ saying, "How much more," we feel the distance there is between the earthy picture and the heavenly reality, and can only bow in lowly, loving adoration, "Father, our Father, my Father." And only thus can full joy and power come to us as we rest rejoicingly in the word: "How much more shall your Heavenly Father give the Holy Spirit to them that ask him?"

Oh, for grace to cultivate a heavenly spirit, and daily to prove we are children who have a Father in heaven, and who love day by day to dwell in His holy presence!

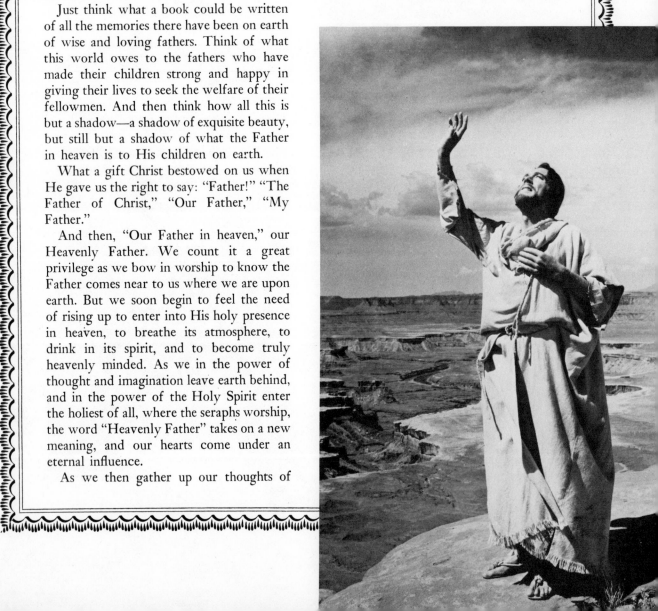

## THE DIVINE ENVIRONMENT

### Carlo Carretto

FROM THE DAWN to the sunset of His earthly life, the presence of the Father was the "divine environment" of Jesus. From His baptism in the Jordan, when, as He came up out of the water, "he saw the sky rent in two and the Spirit descending on him like a dove. Then a voice came from the heavens: 'You are my beloved Son. On you my favor rests'" (Mark 1:10), until His death on Calvary, "Father, into your hands I commit my spirit" (Luke 23:46), the presence of the Father was Jesus' point of reference for His interior life, for His contemplation, for His discourse. How many nights did He go out under the stars just to be alone with the Father; how many times words of union with Him came to His lips: "Father, it is true. You have graciously willed it so" (Matthew 11:26). He exulted in the Father's actions: "Father, Lord of heaven and earth, to you I offer praise; for what you have hidden from the learned and the clever you have revealed to the merest children" (Matthew 11:25); he confirmed his vocation to give revelation and witness for the Father: "Everything has been given over to me by my Father. No one knows the Son but the Father, and no one knows the Father but the Son—and anyone to whom the Son wishes to reveal him" (Matthew 11:27).

So, if we accept Jesus as Son of God, we must also accept the Father as a quite distinct presence. The gospels are quite incomprehensible if we exclude the dialogue, the relationship between Jesus and His Father. It is a symbol, a model of each dialogue and relationship between us and God.

---

## A PHYSICAL PLACE OR A SPIRITUAL CONCEPT?

### Origen

WHEN IT IS SAID that the Father of the saints is in heaven, it must not be understood that He is circumscribed by a bodily form and has a habitation in heaven. For if He were so contained, God would be less the heavens, since the heavens would be enclosing Him. Rather must we believe that by the ineffable power of His divinity all things are contained and maintained by Him. In general, too, the passages which taken literally might be understood by the uninitiated to mean that God is in a place must be taken properly as conveying great spiritual concepts about God. Such passages are the following found in the Gospel according to John: "Before the festival day of the pasch, Jesus knowing that His hour was come, that He should pass out of this world to the Father: having loved His own who were in the world, He loved them unto the end." And a little further on: "Knowing that the Father had given Him all things into His hands and that He came from God and goeth to God." And later on: "You have heard that I said to you: I go away," and "I come unto you. If you loved me, you would indeed be glad because I go to the Father." And again further on: "And now I go to Him that sent me, and none of you asketh me: Whither goest Thou?" If these passages are to be taken in a local sense, it is clear that the following must be taken in the same way: "Jesus answered and said to them: If any man love me, he will keep my word. And my Father will love him, and we will come to him and will make our abode with him."

## THE CELESTIAL EQUATION

*Augustine of Hippo*

LET THE NEW PEOPLE called to an eternal inheritance use the language of the New Testament and say: "Our Father, who art in heaven"—that is, among the saints and the just. God is not tied down to space or place. The heavens, truly enough, are the most excellent physical bodies of the universe; just the same, bodies they are, and bodies can be only in space. But if God's place is believed to be in the heavens as the more elevated parts of the universe, then the birds count more than we, for their life is lived nearer to God. However, it is not written: "God is nigh to men on high" or "to the mountain dwellers"; but it is written, "The Lord is nigh unto them that are of a contrite heart"; and that refers rather to humility. And just as the sinner has been called earth, when to him it was said: "Earth thou art and unto earth thou shalt return"; so, on the other hand, the just can be called heaven, for to the just it is said: "For the temple of God is holy, which you are." Wherefore, if God dwells in His temple and the saints are His temple, the words "who art in heaven" are rightly said to be the equivalent of "who art in the saints." And this equation is a most appropriate one, indicating as it does that there is as much difference spiritually between a sinner and a saint as there is materially between heaven and earth. . . .

---

## THE FATHERLAND FROM WHICH WE HAVE FALLEN

*Gregory of Nyssa*

IN THE STORY of the young man who left his father's home and went away to live after the manner of swine the Word shows the misery of men in the form of a parable which tells of his departure and dissolute life; and He does not bring him back to his former happiness until he has become sensibly aware of his present plight and entered into himself, rehearsing words of repentance. Now these words agree as it were with the words of the prayer, for he said, "Father, I have sinned against heaven and before thee." He would not have added to his confession the sin against heaven, if he had not been convinced that the country he had left when he sinned was heaven. Therefore this confession gave him easy access to the father, who ran toward him and embraced and kissed him. And this signifies the yoke of the Word, which had been placed on man through the mouth, that is to say, through the tradition of the Gospel, after he had thrown off the first yoke of the commandment by shaking himself free of the protecting law. And he put on him the robe, not another one, but the first robe, of which he had been deprived by his disobedience, when he had tasted of the forbidden fruit and seen his own nakedness. The ring on his hand, because of the carved stone, signifies the regaining of the Image. But he also protects his feet with shoes so that if he approaches the head of the serpent, it may not bite into his naked heel. Thus the return of the young man to his Father's home became to him the occasion of experiencing the loving kindness of his Father; for this paternal home is the heaven against which, as he says to his Father, he has sinned. In the same way it seems to me that if the Lord is teaching us to call upon the Father in heaven, He means to remind you of our beautiful fatherland. And by thus putting into your mind a stronger desire for these good things, He sets you on the way that will lead you back to your original country.

## REACHABLE, YET UNREACHABLE

*Simone Weil*

HE IS OUR FATHER. There is nothing real in us which does not come from him. We belong to him. He loves us, since he loves himself and we are his. Nevertheless he is our Father who is in heaven—not elsewhere. If we think to have a Father here below it is not he, it is a false God. We cannot take a single step toward him. We do not walk vertically. We can only turn our eyes toward him. We do not have to search for him, we only have to change the direction in which we are looking. It is for him to search for us. We must be happy in the knowledge that he is infinitely beyond our reach. Thus we can be certain that the evil in us, even if it overwhelms our whole being, in no way sullies the divine purity, bliss, and perfection.

## AN HONORIFIC QUALITATIVE

*Raymond E. Brown*

IN MATTHEW'S TITLE there is a second qualification of "Father," i.e., "who art in heaven." Here again Matthew is close to Jewish prayer formulae which use "heavenly" as an honorific qualitative to give God His proper place and to distinguish Him from "our father Abraham." Lohmeyer, however, suggests that in Matthew this is no mere formalism, but rather a sign of the eschatological times when God's presence is no longer localized in a place like Sinai, Zion, or Gerizim. As Jesus said to the Samaritan woman, "The hour is coming when you will worship the Father neither on this mountain Gerizim nor in Jerusalem" (John 4:21).

# HALLOWED BE THY NAME

## GOOD WORKS GLORIFY

### Gregory of Nyssa

THE PRAYER SAYS, in effect, let the Name of His dominion which I invoke be hallowed in me, "that men may see your good works and glorify your Father who is in Heaven." Who would be so absurdly unreasonable as not to glorify God if he sees in those who believe in Him a pure life firmly established in virtue? I mean a life purged from all stain of sin, above any suspicion of evil and shining with temperance and holy prudence. A man who leads such a life will oppose fortitude to the assaults of the passions; since he partakes of the requirements of life only as far as necessary, he is in no way softened by the luxuries of the body and is an utter stranger to revelry and laziness as well as to boastful conceit. He touches the earth but lightly with the tip of his toes, for he is not engulfed by the pleasurable enjoyments of its life, but is above all deceit that comes by the senses. And so, even though in the flesh, he strives after the immaterial life. He counts the possession of virtues the only riches, familiarity with God the only nobility. His only privilege and power is the mastery of self so as not to be a slave of human passions. He is saddened if his life in this material world be prolonged; like those who are seasick he hastens to reach the port of rest.

How could anyone who sees such a man fail to glorify the Name invoked by such a life? Therefore if I pray "Hallowed be Thy Name," I ask that these words may effect in me things such as these: May I become through Thy help blameless, just and pious, may I abstain from every evil, speak the truth, and do justice. May I walk in the straight path, shining with temperance, adorned with incorruption, beautiful through wisdom and prudence. May I meditate on the things that are above and despise what is earthly, showing forth the angelic way of life. These and similar things are comprised in this brief petition by which we pray to God: "Hallowed be Thy Name." For a man can glorify God in no other way save by his virtue which bears witness that the Divine Power is the cause of his goodness.

---

## DIVINE, NOT HUMAN, ACTION

### Raymond E. Brown

COMING NOW to the first petition, we find that it is not a new concept; for the *Qaddish* resembles it very closely: "May His great name be magnified and sanctified in the world." But when we try to uncover the exact meaning of this petition of the Pater Noster, we are faced with a problem: Is the primary agent in the sanctification man or God? Many writers, including St. Augustine and Luther, have understood it as a prayer that men would come to bless God's name. Yet the fact that this petition is a prayer addressed to God suggests that it concerns divine action, a request for God to make manifest the sanctity of His own name. A study of the Old Testament background and the New Testament parallels makes the latter interpretation, we believe, virtually certain.

# HOLINESS ITSELF

## Simone Weil

GOD ALONE has the power to name himself. His name is unpronounceable for human lips. His name is his word. It is the Word of God. The name of any being is an intermediary between the human spirit and that being; it is the only means by which the human spirit can conceive something about a being that is absent. God is absent. He is in heaven. Man's only possibility of gaining access to him is through his name. It is the Mediator. Man has access to this name, although it also is transcendent. It shines in the beauty and order of the world and shines in the interior light of the human soul. This name is holiness itself; there is no holiness outside it; it does not therefore have to be hallowed. In asking for its hallowing we are asking for something that exists eternally, with full and complete reality, so that we can neither increase nor diminish it, even by an infinitesimal fraction. To ask for that which exists, that which exists really, infallibly, eternally, quite independently of our prayer, that is the perfect petition. We cannot prevent ourselves from desiring; we are made of desire; but the desire that nails us down to what is imaginary, temporal, selfish, can, if we make it pass wholly into this petition, become a lever to tear us from the imaginary into the real and from time into eternity, to lift us right out of the prison of self.

---

# WOVEN INTO THE DIVINE WORLD

## Evelyn Underhill

OUR FATHER which art in heaven, hallowed be Thy Name! That tremendous declaration, with its unlimited confidence and unlimited awe, governs everything else.

What a contrast this almost inarticulate act of measureless adoration is, to what Karl Barth calls the dreadful prattle of theology. Hallowed be Thy Name: not described, or analyzed, be Thy Name. Before that Name, let the most soaring intellects cover their eyes with their wings, and adore. Compared with this, even the coming of the Kingdom and the doing of the Will are side issues; particular demonstrations of the Majesty of the Infinite God, on whom all centers, and for whom all is done. People who are apt to say that adoration is difficult, and it is so much easier to pray for practical things, might remember that in making this great act of adoration they are praying for extremely practical things: among others, that their own characters, homes, social contacts, work, conversation, amusements, and politics may be cleansed from imperfection, sanctified. For all these are part of God's Universe; and His Name must be hallowed in and through them, if they are to be woven into the Divine world, and made what they were meant to be.

## EXPLAINED BY THE SECOND COMMANDMENT

*Martin Luther*

WHAT ... DOES IT MEAN to hallow the name of God? This: when our teaching and life are Christian and godly. The purpose of the second commandment is to cause us not to curse, swear, and lead people astray, as the sectarians do, but rather to praise and call upon this name. Those who misuse the name of God for deceiving and lying profane and desecrate the name of God, just as it used to be said that churches were desecrated when a fight had taken place in them. God's name is hallowed, therefore, when one calls upon him, prays, praises, and magnifies him, preaches about the Lord that is he merciful and helps us in peril and otherwise. Therefore the first petition in the Lord's Prayer is explained by the second commandment. In short, when one teaches and lives Christianly, that is, when one does not curse, swear, and so on.

## NOT YET HALLOWED

*Origen*

WHETHER THIS signifies that what is prayed for has not yet happened, or, if it has happened, implies that it does not persist and asks that it should be preserved, it is clear from the text itself that the name of the Father is not yet hallowed and that we are bidden to say in Matthew and Luke: "Hallowed be Thy Name."

## REGARD AS HALLOWED

*Augustine of Hippo*

THIS PETITION is not so worded as if God's name were not already holy, but that men may regard it as holy, that is, that God may become so familiar to them that they will esteem nothing more holy and dread nothing more than to offend that name. And certainly, because it was said: "In Judea God is known; His name is great in Israel," this is not to be understood as if God were less in one place and more in another; but there His name is great where it is mentioned because of the greatness of His majesty. So, too, there His name is pronounced holy where it is mentioned with reverence and the fear of offending Him. And this is precisely what is now transpiring: the Gospel by being made known among all the different nations even in our own times commends the name of the God through the operation of His Son.

# THY KINGDOM COME

## KING OF RIGHTEOUSNESS

### Martin Luther

JUST AS the name of God is holy in itself and we still must pray that it may be holy among us, so the kingdom of God comes, whether we pray or not. But we should pray, in order that I too may be a part of those in whom the name of God is hallowed, that God's kingdom may come also to me and his will be done in me. Christ is the king of righteousness and life against the devil, sin, death, and all evil conscience. He has given us his holy Word, that it may be preached, in order that we might believe in him and live holy lives. Therefore we must pray that this may become effective and powerful, that the Word may go out into the world with power, that many may come into this kingdom and learn to believe and thus become partakers of redemption from death, sin, and hell. The first petition is that God's name be not blasphemed, but rather [honored]. The second is that this may also bear fruit, that his name be so hallowed that his kingdom will come in us and we become members of his kingdom. But God's kingdom comes to us in two ways: first, here, through the Word, and secondly, in that the future, eternal life is given to us. This is a strong petition when it is expressed in German: Dear Father, grant thy pure Word, that it may be purely preached throughout the world, and then grant grace and power that it may also be accepted and the people believe. The first concerns the Word and the second the fruit of the Word. For, if the Word is preached but not accepted, the kingdom of God does not come. It is an obscure prayer because it is so Hebraically expressed. These are the two greatest needs. Here on [earth] God's kingdom comes through the beginning of faith and there [in eternity] through the revelation of eternal life. These are the two greatest petitions of this prayer, both of which are comprehended [in Christ's saying:] "Seek first his kingdom" [Matthew 6:33]. Here we pray that his name and kingdom may remain with us.

## ENERGY, DRIVE, PURPOSE

### Evelyn Underhill

THY WILL BE *done*—Thy Kingdom *come*! There is energy, drive, purpose in those words; an intensity of desire for the coming of perfection into life. Not the limp resignation that lies devoutly in the road and waits for the steamroller; but a total concentration on the total interests of God, which must be expressed in action. It is useless to utter fervent petitions for that Kingdom to be established and that Will be done, unless we are willing to do something about it ourselves. As we walk through London we know very well that we are not walking through the capital of the Kingdom of Heaven. Yet we might be, if the conviction and action of every Christian in London were set without any conditions or any reluctance toward this end; if there were perfect consistency, whatever it cost—and it is certain that the cost would not be small —between our spiritual ideals and our social and political acts.

# THE HAPPY ENTHRONEMENT OF REASON

## Origen

EVERY SAINT, being ruled by God as his king and obedient to the spiritual laws of God, as it were, dwells within himself as in a well-ordered city. The Father is present to him, and Christ reigns with the Father in the soul that is perfect according to the words mentioned by me a little earlier: "We will come to him and will make our abode with him." And by the kingdom of God, I believe, is meant the happy enthronement of reason and the rule of wise counsels; and by the "kingdom" of Christ, the saving words that reach those who hear, and the accomplished works of justice and the other virtues. For the Son of God is Word and Justice. On the other hand, every sinner is subject to tyranny under "the prince of this world," since every sinner is a slave to "this present wicked world" in not giving himself over to Him "who gave Himself for our sins, that He might deliver us from this present wicked world," and might deliver us "according to the will of God and Our Father"—as is said in the Epistle to the Galatians. He who is subject to the tyranny of "the prince of this world" is also under the reign of sin because he has sinned voluntarily. Hence Paul bids us not to submit to sin that would rule over us; and we are told this as follows: "Let not sin therefore reign in your mortal body, so as to obey the lusts thereof."

# SMOKE AND WAX

## Gregory of Nyssa

IN THE following clause we pray that God's Kingdom should come. Could this really mean that He who *is* King of the Universe should *become* King? He who is always the same and incapable of change, since He could not find anything better into which to change? What, then, does this prayer mean that asks for the Kingdom of God?

If we ask that the Kingdom of God may come to us, the meaning of our request is this: I would be a stranger to corruption and liberated from death; would that I were freed from the shackles of sin and that death no longer lorded it over me. Let us no more be tyrannized by evil so that the adversary may not prevail against me and make me his captive through sin. But may Thy Kingdom come to me, so that the passions which still rule me so mercilessly may depart from me, or rather may be altogether annihilated. For "As smoke vanisheth, so shall they vanish away"; and "as wax melteth . . . so shall they perish." The smoke which dissolves in the air leaves no trace of its existence, nor can wax be found anymore once it has been in the fire. But as the latter, having nourished the flame with its own substance, has evaporated into the air, and as the smoke has disappeared into complete nothingness, so, when the Kingdom of God comes upon us, all the things that now hold sway will cease to exist. Thus darkness vanishes before the presence of light, and illness passes when health has been established. The passions cease to be troublesome when *apatheia* has appeared; death is undone and corruption is no more when life and incorruption reign in us unopposed.

# THE FINAL KINGDOM

*Raymond E. Brown*

THIS PETITION, too, has its echo in the *Qaddish* . . . : "May He establish His kingdom in your days." There is little doubt here that God is the primary agent in causing the kingdom to come. The real problem is whether this petition of the Pater Noster deals primarily with a question of everyday growth of the kingdom or with the definitive reign of God at the end of the world. On a purely grammatical basis, the aorist is more favorable to the latter.

The Old Testament does not precisely speak of the coming of God's kingdom, but it does promise a universal kingship of God (Jeremiah 10:7, 10; Malachi 1:14). Isaiah 24:23 connects the signs of the last times, like the darkening of the sun and moon, with the reign of the Lord of Hosts on Mt. Zion and the manifesting of His glory. Daniel 7:18 has the saints of the Most High receiving the kingdom after all the earthly kingdoms have passed away. Thus, already in the Old Testament, divine kingship has eschatological overtones.

In the New Testament, the establishment of God's kingdom is to a certain extent identical with Jesus' coming, for His ministry opens with the announcement that the kingdom of God is at hand. Yet, if Jesus through His word and work established God's dominion on this earth, the fulness of that kingdom cannot come until Jesus returns again to destroy the prince of this world. As long as Satan has power in this world, God's dominion is not perfected (Luke 4:6; 1 John 5:19).

We believe that the petition "May your kingdom come" concerns this final coming of God's kingdom. Actually, the expression "kingdom come" does not occur frequently in the Gospels; but when it does, it refers primarily to the eschatological coming. We have "coming" and "kingdom" joined in Mark 9:1: "There are some standing here who will not die before they see the kingdom of God come with power" (the parallel in Matthew 16:28 interprets this eschatologically: ". . . before they see the Son of Man coming in His kingdom"). At the Last Supper (Luke 22:18) Jesus says: "I shall not drink of the fruit of the vine until the kingdom of God comes." While not using *erchesthai*, Luke 21:31 is interesting; in speaking of the signs of the last days, it says: "When you see these things take place, you know that the kingdom of God is near."

When the Christian community utters the second petition of the Pater Noster, it is identifying itself with the divine plan. The Christians are not primarily asking that God's dominion come into their own hearts . . . but that God's universal reign be established—that destiny toward which the whole of time is directed.

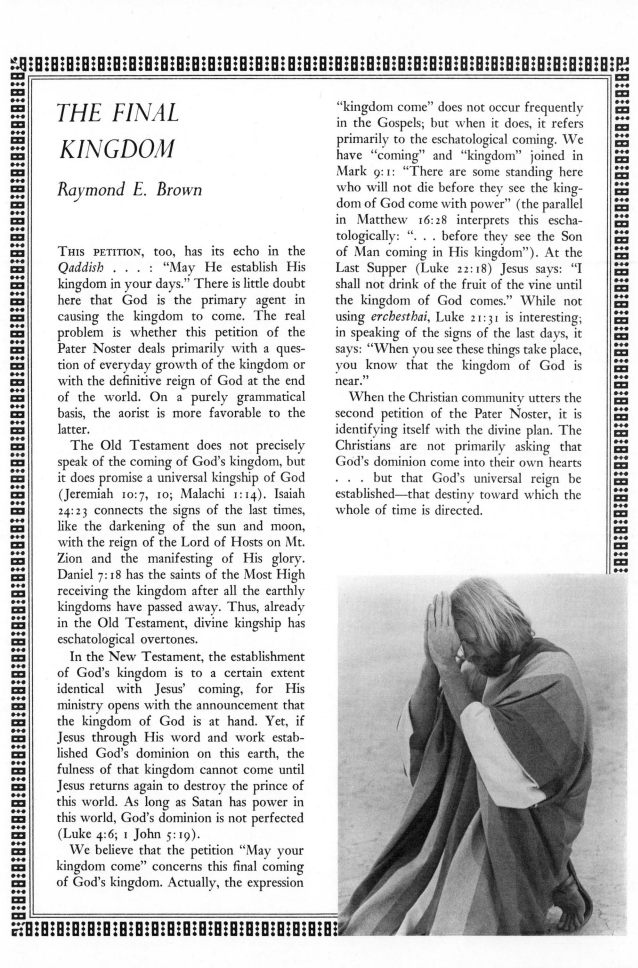

## THE VISIBLE KINGDOM

*Augustine of Hippo*

THE WORDS "Thy kingdom come" do not imply that God is not reigning now. But it might be said that with "come" we should supply "upon the earth." As if God were not even now reigning on earth and has not been doing so ever since the world was created! "Come," then, must be taken to mean "may it be made manifest to men." Just as light that is present is absent to the blind or to those who shut their eyes, so the kingdom of God, though it never departs from the earth, yet is absent to those who know nothing about it. To none, however, will ignorance of God's kingdom be permitted when His only begotten will come from heaven, not merely so that He is recognizable by the intellect, but visibly as the Man of the Lord to judge the living and the dead. After this judgment, that is, when the selection of the just and their separation from the unjust has been made, God will so dwell in the just that there will be no need for anyone to be taught by man but "they shall all," as it is written, "be taught of God." Then will the blessed life be made perfect in all respects in the saints for eternity, even as now the most holy and blessed angels in heaven with God alone to enlighten them are wise and blessed, because the Lord promised this also to His followers: "In the resurrection," He says, "they shall be as the angels in heaven."

## A LONGING CRY

*Simone Weil*

THIS CONCERNS something to be achieved, something not yet here. The Kingdom of God means the complete filling of the entire soul of intelligent creatures with the Holy Spirit. The Spirit bloweth where he listeth? We can only invite him. We must not even try to invite him in a definite and special way to visit us or anyone else in particular, or even everybody in general; we must just invite him purely and simply, so that our thought of him is an invitation, a longing cry. It is as when one is in extreme thirst, ill with thirst; then one no longer thinks of the act of drinking in relation to oneself, or even of the act of drinking in a general way. One merely thinks of water, actual water itself, but the image of water is like a cry from our whole being.

## REVELATION OF GOD'S HEART

*Watchman Nee*

WE ARE to pray this. "Thy kingdom come!" If his kingdom would come of itself, we should not have been given that command. But God's people are to pray, for his work is done in response to their cry. "Thy will be done!" Yes, but where? "On earth," for this is the only place where today God's will is not done. Then how can God's kingdom be brought down here? By the created will, in union with the Uncreated Will, seeking the displacement of the rebellious will of the devil. For prayer is always three-sided. It involves someone prayed to, someone prayed for, and someone prayed against; and on earth there is someone to pray against—a will that is opposed to God's.

# THY WILL BE DONE ON EARTH AS IT IS IN HEAVEN

## THREE MEANINGS

### Augustine of Hippo

THIS MEANS: "As Thy will is in the angels who are in heaven so that in every respect they remain close to Thee and fully enjoy Thee with no error bedimming their wisdom, no misery frustrating their blessedness, so may it be accomplished in Thy saints who are on earth and have been made from the earth as respects their body and, though they are to be taken up to be transformed and to dwell in heaven, are yet on earth."

There is also a reflection of this in the hymn of the angels: "Glory to God in the highest and on earth peace to men of good will." Thus when our good will has gone before by following Him when He calls, the will of God is accomplished in us as it is in the heavenly angels. Thus no adversity stands in the way of our happiness; and this is peace.

Again, "Thy will be done," correctly interpreted, means "let obedience be given to Thy precepts"—"on earth as it is in heaven," that is, "by men as it is by angels." For that the will of God is being done when His precepts are obeyed the Lord Himself affirms when He says: "My meat is to do the will of Him who sent me"; and often: "I have not come to do my own will, but the will of Him that sent me"; and when He said: "Behold my mother and behold my brethren; and whosoever shall do the will of God, he is my brother and mother and sister." And therefore, in those at least who do God's will is the will of God accomplished—not because they make God will but because they do as He wills, that is, they act according to His will.

There is also the other acceptations: "Thy will be done on earth as it is in heaven," that is, as in the holy and just, so also in sinners. This, moreover, can be taken in two ways: either that we also pray for our enemies—for how else are they to be reckoned against whose will it is that the Christian and Catholic name is being spread? —and then to say "Thy will be done on earth as it is in heaven" amounts to saying: "As the just so also may the sinners do Thy will, in order that they may be converted to Thee"; or "Thy will be done on earth as it is in heaven," that is, so that to each may be given his due; and this will take place at the Last Judgment when the sheep will be separated from the goats—the just receiving a due reward, the sinners, the damnation due them.

## OBEDIENCE TO THE COURSE OF EVENTS

*Simone Weil*

WE ARE ONLY absolutely, infallibly certain of the will of God concerning the past. Everything that has happened, whatever it may be, is in accordance with the will of the almighty Father. That is implied by the notion of almighty power. The future also, whatever it may contain, once it has come about, will have come about in conformity with the will of God. We can neither add to nor take from this conformity. In this clause, therefore, after an upsurging of our desire toward the possible, we are once again asking for that which is. Here, however, we are not concerned with an eternal reality such as the holiness of the Word, but with what happens in the time order. Neverthless we are asking for the infallible and eternal conformity of everything in time with the will of God. After having, in our first petition, torn our desire away from time in order to fix it upon eternity, thereby transforming it, we return to this desire which has itself become in some measure eternal, in order to apply it once more to time. Whereupon our desire pierces through time to find eternity behind it. That is what comes about when we know how to make every accomplished fact, whatever it may be, an object of desire. We have here quite a different thing from resignation. Even the word *acceptance* is too weak. We have to desire that everything that has happened should have happened, and nothing else. We have to do so, not because what has happened is good in our eyes, but because God has permitted it, and because the obedience of the course of events to God is in itself an absolute good.

## DEFEND US FROM THE DEVIL

*Martin Luther*

WHEN YOU PRAY this petition you must look askance at a gang, which is called the devil and his mates, who would hinder the kingdom of God. For the father of a household should not only support his own but also defend them. And so it is here; even if we already prayed the first two greatest petitions, the devil nevertheless cannot endure that the Word should be preached and people accept it. Here he has his poisoned arrows: he has the opposing world and our flesh, which is lazy. The will of the pope, the emperor, the princes, the devil, and our flesh prevents the will of God from being done. What we pray is: Dear Father, defend us from the devil and his cohorts and from our lazy flesh which would hinder thy will, and grant grace that thy gospel may go forth unhindered. Thus we are shown in these three petitions our need with regard to God, but in such a way that it redounds to our benefit. God's name is not only hallowed in itself, but in me. Likewise, God's kingdom not only comes of itself and his will is done not only of itself, but rather in order that God's kingdom may come in me, that God's will may be done in me, and his name be hallowed in me.

## PURITY ABOVE, PASSION BELOW

### Gregory of Nyssa

SINCE . . . THE LIFE above is passionless and pure, whereas this wretched life here below is immersed in all manner of passions and miseries, it should be clear that the city above, being pure from all evil, is firmly established in the good Will of God. For where there is no evil there must necessarily be the good. But our life, which has fallen away from sharing the good things, has at the same time fallen away from the Divine Will. Therefore the prayer teaches us thus to purify our life from evil that the will of God may rule in us without hindrance, in the same way as it does in the life of heaven. In other words: As Thy Will is done by the thrones and principalities and powers and dominations and all the supramundane hosts, where no evil hinders the action of the good, so may the good be accomplished also in us. Thus, when all evil has been removed, Thy Will may be accomplished in our souls in all things.

## THE ALLEGORICAL INTERPRETATION

### Origen

IF ONE understands "heaven" allegorically and maintains that it stands for Christ, and "earth" for the church (for who is as worthy to be throne of the Father as Christ? And what can be compared to the church as a footstool for the feet of God?), he will easily solve the difficulties raised. We say that each member of the church must pray that he may accomplish the will of the Father as Christ did, who came to do the will of the Father and accomplished it perfectly. For in being "joined to Him" we can become "one spirit" with Him, and consequently accomplish the will of God so that it will be fulfilled on earth as it is in heaven. "He who is joined to the Lord," according to Paul, "is one spirit." I believe that this interpretation, if considered carefully, is not lightly to be put aside.

## THE ULTIMATE PERFECTION

### Raymond E. Brown

THE ULTIMATE GOAL of this plan is the redemption of the universe, the subjecting of all things to the Father's will in the Person of Jesus Christ (Ephesians 1:20–22), for it is to Jesus that all power in heaven and on earth has been given (Matthew 28:18). We may now see the full impact of the third petition of the Pater Noster: "May your will come about 'on earth as in heaven.'" If God created heaven and earth according to His will (Genesis 1:1; Revelation 4:11), that will concerns the ultimate perfection of heaven and earth. As Colossians 1:20 phrases it, it is God's pleasure to reconcile to Himself all things whether on earth or in heaven, through Jesus Christ. God's will shall have come about when there is a new heaven and a new earth, when the heavenly city comes down and weds itself to the people of God (Revelation 21:1–3).

# GIVE US THIS DAY OUR DAILY BREAD

## SIMPLE FARE

### Gregory of Nyssa

Do YOU REALIZE the whole scope of the Divine teaching? How much doctrine is not compressed into this short sentence! Does He not clearly proclaim in these words something like this to His listeners: Men, let yourselves no longer be distracted by desiring vanities; stop heaping toil upon toil for yourselves. The needs of your nature are but few; you owe food to your flesh—a trivial thing and easily procured, if you content yourselves with what is necessary. Why do you lay yourselves under so much tribute? Why do you submit to the yoke of paying so many fines? Mining silver, digging gold, and searching for transparent stones—for no other purpose save that your stomach, this perpetual tax collector, may live daintily through all this. Yet it needs only bread to supply the needs of the body. But you go on business to the Indies and venture out upon strange seas; you go on a voyage every year only to bring back flavorings for your food, without realizing that the enjoyment of the spices goes no further than the palate. In the same way the loveliness of sight or smell or taste presents the senses with very transitory delight; except for the palate, there is no difference in the foods consumed, for nature changes all things equally into an evil smell. Do you see the end of fine cookery? Do you realize what are the results of wizard flavorings? Ask for bread because life needs it, and you owe it to the body because of your nature. But all those superfluous things that have been invented by men given to luxury are weeds sown in besides. The seed sown by the Master of the house is corn, from which bread is made. Luxuries, however, are the tares sown in by the enemy with the wheat. If men refuse to satisfy their nature by what is necessary they are truly choked, as Scripture says somewhere, by the pursuit of vanities; for if the soul is perpetually occupied with these things it remains atrophied itself.

# BREAD OF THE FUTURE

*Raymond E. Brown*

WE MAY AGREE that the Christian community was marked with poverty; but we believe that in this need the Christians yearned, not for the bread of this world, but for God's final intervention and for that bread which would be given at the heavenly table. In the Gospels, God's supplying men with food is frequently in terms of an eschatological banquet. "Blessed is he who shall eat bread in the kingdom of God" (Luke 14:15). "Blessed are you that hunger now, for you shall be satisfied"; as mentioned, the rewards of the beatitudes are heavenly ones (Luke 6:21). "Many shall come from East and West and sit at the table with Abraham, Isaac, and Jacob in the kingdom of heaven" (Matthew 8:11). "As my Father appointed a kingdom for me, so I appoint for you to eat and drink at my table in the kingdom" (Luke 22:29–30). . . . We notice that the bread of the kingdom is promised to the Christians; therefore they could petition for it as "*our bread.*" The request for it "today" expresses the urgency of the eschatological yearning of the persecuted and impoverished Christians.

# SPIRITUAL FOOD

*Augustine of Hippo*

WE SHOULD INTERPRET "daily bread" as spiritual food, namely, the divine precepts which we are to think over and put into practice each day. It is of this that the Lord says: "Labor for the food which perisheth not." And this food is now called "daily" as long as this temporal life goes on through days succeeding days departing. And verily as long as the disposition of the soul alternates now to the higher now to the lower, that is, now to the spiritual now to the material, much like a person who now has a good meal and again is obliged to go hungry: so long is bread a daily necessity that by it the hungry may be refreshed and the failing quickened. And thus, as our body in this life, namely, before the transformation that is to come, sensing its decline, renews itself by means of food, in like manner also the soul, since by reason of its temporal propensities it suffers wear and tear, so to speak, in its striving after God, is restored by the food of God's precepts. Moreover, "Give us this day" was said to mean "as long as it is called today," that is, in this temporal life. Conversely, after this life we shall be fed on spiritual food forever, so that then there will be no reason to speak of "daily bread," because there the fleeting rotation of time which makes day succeed day—whence the term "today"—will not exist. But as it is said: "Today if you shall hear His voice," which the apostle in his Epistle to the Hebrews interprets "as long as it is called today," so here, too, we should interpret "Give us *this day*." If, however, a person chooses to take this sentence as referring also to food necessary to the body or to the Sacrament of the Lord's Body, all three ought to be taken conjointly, that is to say, in the same breath we are to ask for our daily bread—both that which is necessary for the body and the consecrated visible bread and the invisible bread of the word of God.

## THE TRUE BREAD

### Origen

IN THE GOSPEL according to John He says to those who had come to Capernaum seeking for Him: "Amen, amen, I say to you, you seek [me], not because you have seen miracles, but because you did eat of the loaves and were filled." He who has eaten of the bread blessed by Jesus and is filled with it tries all the more to understand the Son of God more perfectly, and hastens to Him. Hence His admirable command: "Labor not for the meat which perisheth, but for that which endureth unto life everlasting, which the Son of man will give you." And when those who were listening to this asked Him, saying: "What shall we do that we may work the works of God? Jesus answered and said to them: This is the work of God, that you believe in Him whom He hath sent." Now God "hath sent His Word, and healed them"—obviously the sick—as it is written in the Psalms. Those who believe in the Word do the works of God which are "meat that endureth unto life everlasting." And "my Father," He says, "giveth you the true bread from heaven. For the bread of God is that which cometh down from heaven and giveth life to the world." The "true bread" is that which nourishes the true man, the "man created" after "the image of God," and through which he who is nourished by it is made "to the image of Him that created him." What is more nourishing for the soul than the Word? And what is more precious for the mind of him that understands it than the wisdom of God? And what is in better accord with rational nature than truth?

## IN PEACE, BREAD

*Martin Luther*

WHEN YOU PRAY this petition turn your eyes to everything that can prevent our bread from coming and the crops from prospering. Therefore extend your thoughts to all the fields and do not see only the baker's oven. You pray, therefore, against the devil and the world, who can hinder the grain by tempest and war. We pray also for temporal peace against war, because in times of war we cannot have bread. Likewise, you pray for government, for sustenance and peace, without which you cannot eat: Grant, Lord, that the grain may prosper, that the princes may keep the peace, that war may not break out, that we may give thanks to thee in peace. Therefore it would be proper to stamp the emperor's or the princes' coat-of-arms upon bread as well as upon money or coins. Few know that this is included in the Lord's Prayer. Though the Lord gives bread in sufficient abundance even to the wicked and godless, it is nevertheless fitting that we Christians should know and acknowledge that it comes from God, that we realize that bread, hunger, and war are in God's hands. If he opens his hand, we have bread and all things in abundance; if he closes it, then it is the opposite. Therefore, do not think that peace is an accidental thing: it is the gift of God.

## OUR BREAD IS CHRIST

*Simone Weil*

CHRIST IS our bread. We can only ask to have him now. Actually he is always there at the door of our souls, wanting to enter in, though he does not force our consent. If we agree to his entry, he enters; directly we cease to want him, he is gone. We cannot bind our will today for tomorrow; we cannot make a pact with him that tomorrow he will be within us, even in spite of ourselves. Our consent to his presence is the same as his presence. Consent is an act; it can only be actual, that is to say in the present. We have not been given a will that can be applied to the future. Everything not effective in our will is imaginary. The effective part of the will has its effect at once; its effectiveness cannot be separated from itself. The effective part of the will is not effort, which is directed toward the future. It is consent; it is the "yes" of marriage. A "yes" pronounced within the present moment and for the present moment, but spoken as an eternal word, for it is consent to the union of Christ with the eternal part of our soul.

# AND FORGIVE US
# OUR DEBTS, AS WE FORGIVE
# OUR DEBTORS

## DEBITS
## AND CREDITS

### Augustine of Hippo

THAT BY DEBTS sins are meant is evident either from what the Lord Himself says: "Thou shalt not go out thence till thou repay the last farthing"; or from the fact that He calls debtors those who had been reported to Him as having lost their life, some of them in the collapse of the tower and others whose blood Herod had mingled with their sacrifice. For He said that men thought these were debtors beyond measure, that is, were sinners; and He added: "I say to you, unless you do penance you shall all likewise perish." Here, therefore, it is not financial indebtedness that each is urged to remit, but to forgive whatever another has committed against him. As to debts of money, we are told to remit these by that precept rather which has been mentioned above: "If a man will contend with thee in judgment and take away thy coat, let go thy garment also unto him." Nor is it required in that passage to remit the debt to everyone who owes us money, but only to him who is so disinclined to pay it that he would rather go to court. "But the servant of the Lord," as the Apostle says, "must not wrangle." Therefore, when a person is unwilling to pay back a debt of money either of his own accord or when notice to pay is served upon him, his debt is to be canceled. Now, his reluctance to pay will be owing to one of two reasons: either because he does not have it, or because he is miserly and covetous of another's property. In either case poverty is involved: in the former, poverty of means; in the latter, poverty of soul. Whoever, therefore, remits a debt to such a person remits it to one who is poor, and performs a Christian work with due observance of the precept to be prepared in mind to lose what is owed him. For if a person makes every effort, discreetly and calmly, to obtain repayment—bent not so much on benefiting from the money as to effect improvement in a man to whom it is without doubt harmful to have the wherewithal to pay and yet not to do so —not only will he not sin, but will confer a great benefit by his endeavor to prevent the other, who is set upon making another's money his gain, from suffering the loss of his faith. And that is so much more a serious matter that there is no comparison. Hence, too, it is understood that in this fifth petition, "Forgive us our debts as we forgive our debtors," there is no reference to money as such, but to all the things regarding which a person does us wrong; and in this reference money is included. For he sins against you who refuses to pay back money he owes you when he has means to do so. But if you do not forgive this sin, you will not be able to say: "Forgive us as we also forgive"; and if you do forgive, you see that he who is commanded to offer such a prayer is admonished also in regard to forgiving a money debt.

# COMPLETE FORGIVENESS

*Raymond E. Brown*

IT IS INTERESTING to see how often in the Gospels forgiveness of debts or sins is connected with the judgment. In the Sermon on the Mount, which is also Matthew's setting for the Pater Noster, we hear (5:23-25) that the Christian should be reconciled to his brother who has something against him, ". . . lest your accuser hand you over to the judge, and the judge to the guard, and you be put in prison. Truly, I say to you, you will never get out till you have paid the last cent." Again, Luke 6:37 has a parallelism between judgment and forgiveness: "Judge not and you will not be judged . . . forgive, and you will be forgiven." The best illustration of our petition is the parable of the unforgiving servant (Matthew 18:23-35). The king who wishes to settle debts with his servants is obviously God, and the atmosphere is that of judgment. The parable points out that God's forgiveness of the servant has a connection to that servant's forgiveness of his fellow servant. When this brotherly forgiveness fails, he is given to the torturers until he pays his debt.

This leads us to the second clause of our petition: "as we have forgiven our debtors" (or "as we now forgive our debtors"—one action). Once more, the Gospel background of fraternal obligations favors an eschatological interpretation, for the failure to deal properly with one's brother is frequently spoken of in terms of judgment. The description par excellence of the Last Judgment is Matthew 25:31-46, which describes the sentence being passed before the throne of the Son of man. The criterion of judgment is precisely our dealings with one another. In the same mood, Matthew 5:21-22 lists faults against one's brother which make one liable to judgment and hellfire. In the Lazarus story (Luke 16:19-31), the eternal judgment against the rich man is based on his enjoyment of wealth, instead of employing it in what Lucan theology emphasizes is the only proper way: giving it to the poor.

# SINS AND SINNERS

*Martin Luther*

In the fourth petition you pray against that need which the poor body has for bread, which it cannot get along without. It includes every peril which may hinder bread from coming to us. Now comes our life, which we cannot lead without sinning. Here is the greatest need of all, and we pray: "Forgive us our debts." Not that he does not give it without our prayer, for he has given us baptism, and in his kingdom there is nothing but forgiveness of sins. But it is to be done in order that we may acknowledge it. For the flesh is anxious for the belly and has evil lusts and loves, hatred, anger, envy, and wicked whims, so that we sin daily in words, deeds, and thoughts, in what we do and fail to do. No one does what he should do. So we get stuck in the mire of being proud and thinking that we are thoroughly holy people. Therefore he says here: None of you is good. All of you, no matter how holy and great you are, must say: "Forgive us our debts." Therefore one must pray God to give us a conscience unafraid, which is assured that its sins are forgiven. . . .

"As we also have forgiven our debtors." God has promised the forgiveness of sins. Of that you must be certain and sure, insofar as you [also forgive your neighbor]. If you have someone whom you do not forgive, you pray in vain. Therefore let each one look to his neighbor, if he has been offended by him, and forgive him from the heart; then he will be certain that his sin too has been forgiven. Not that you are forgiven on account of your forgiveness, but freely, without your forgiveness, your sins are forgiven. He, however, enjoins it upon you as a sign, that you may be assured that, if you forgive, you too will be forgiven.

# HOLY AUDACITY

*Gregory of Nyssa*

Do you realize to what height the Lord raises His hearers through the words of the prayer, by which he somehow transforms human nature into what is Divine? For he lays down that those who approach God should themselves become gods. Why, He says, do you go to God crouching with fear like a slave because your conscience pricks you? Why do you shut out holy audacity which is inherent in the freedom of the soul because it has been joined to its very essence from the beginning? Why do you seek to flatter with words Him who brooks no flattery? Why do you offer language of abject servility to Him who regards only deeds? Yet you may lawfully say whatever is worthy of God, because your mind is free in its own right. Be yourself your own judge, give yourself the sentence of acquittal. Do you want your debts to be forgiven by God? Forgive them yourself, and God will ratify it. For your judgment of your neighbor, which is in your power, whatever it may be, will call forth the corresponding sentence upon you. What you decide for yourself will be confirmed by the Divine judgment.

# OUR DEBTS, OUR DEBTORS

## Origen

WHEN A MAN owes a debt, he either pays it or defaults. In our life it is the same—we can pay our debts, we can default. There are those who owe nothing to anybody. Some pay most of what they owe and [remain in debt for a little. Others] pay a little and remain in debt for most of what they owe. And some may pay nothing and owe all. He who pays all and owes nothing may discharge his obligation within a certain time and requires a remission of debts incurred before that time. Such a remission can reasonably be obtained by one who does his best by a certain time to discharge all obligations as yet unpaid. . . .

But if we are in debt to so many, it is also true that there are some who are in debt to us. Some have obligations toward us as their fellow men; others as to their fellow citizens; some as to fathers; others as to sons; and in addition, some as wives to their husbands, and as friends to friends. Therefore when some of our many debtors to us may prove rather tardy in the matter of discharging their obligations toward us, we shall act with humanity, not remembering their debts to us, but rather those that we owe ourselves in which we have often failed—not only our debts to men, but those also to God Himself. When we but recall the debts which we have not discharged but have refused to pay: debts incurred when the time went by in which we ought to have done certain things for our neighbor, we shall be more sympathetic to those who are debtors to ourselves and who have not discharged their debt; and especially so if we do not allow ourselves to forget our transgressions of God's law, and our "iniquity spoken on high"—spoken either through ignorance of the truth or because of dissatisfaction with circumstances that overtook us.

# AND LEAD US NOT INTO TEMPTATION

## THE TEMPTER

### Gregory of Nyssa

IT SEEMS TO ME that the Lord calls the evil one by many different names according to the distinctions between the evil actions. He names him variously devil, Beelzebub, Mammon, prince of this world, murderer of man, evil one, father of lies, and other such things. Perhaps, therefore, here again one of the names devised for him is "temptation," and the juxtaposition of clauses confirms this assumption. For after saying, "Lead us not into temptation," He adds that we should be delivered from evil, as if both words meant the same. For if a man who does not enter into temptation is quite removed from evil, and if one who has fallen into temptation is necessarily mixed up with evil, then temptation and the evil one mean one and the same thing. What therefore does the exhortation of the prayer teach us? That we should be separated from the things that belong to this world; as somewhere else He says to the disciples: "The whole world is seated in wickedness." Therefore if a man desires to be free from wickedness, he will necessarily separate himself from the world. For temptation finds no opportunity for touching the soul unless this preoccupation with worldly things be held out to greedy men like a bait on the hook of evil.

## USEFULNESS OF TEMPTATION

### Origen

THE GIFTS which our soul has received are unknown to everyone except God. They are unknown even to ourselves. Through temptations they become known. Thereafter we can no longer be ignorant of what we are: we know ourselves and can be aware, if we but cooperate, of our wrongdoings. We can also give thanks for the benefits conferred upon us and made manifest by temptations. Temptations that come upon us serve the purpose of showing us who we really are and making manifest "the things that are in our heart." This is made clear by what the Lord says in the book of Job and what is written in Deuteronomy, as follows: "Do you think I should have treated you otherwise but to make you appear just?" And in Deuteronomy: "He afflicted thee with want, and gave thee manna for thy food," and "brought thee through the desert wherein there was the serpent that bit, and the scorpion, and thirst, that the things that were in thy heart might be made known."

# TEMPTATION WITH PERMISSION

## Augustine of Hippo

TEMPTATIONS COME through Satan not by his power but with God's permission, either to punish men for their sins or in the plan of the Lord's mercy to put them on probation and trial. Moreover, it makes a very great difference into what sort of temptation the individual falls. For example, Judas, who sold his Master, did not fall into one of the same nature as Peter, who by an obsession of fear denied Him. There are temptations that are but human, I believe, when a person, though meaning well, yet through human frailty fails to live up to some resolve or becomes irritated with a brother in his zeal to correct him, going just a little beyond the limits set him by Christian composure. Concerning such the apostle says; "Let no temptation take hold on you but such as is human"; while he also says: "And God is faithful, who would not let you be tempted above that which you are able, but will also make with temptation issue that you may be able to bear it." By this statement he quite clearly shows that we are not to pray that we may not be tempted, but that we may not be led into temptations. For we are led into them if they are such as we cannot endure. But when dangerous temptations, into which it is our undoing to be brought and led, arise from either temporal fortune or misfortune, no one is broken down by the visitation of adversity who does not succumb to the lure of prosperity.

# FROM CONFIDENCE
# TO FEAR

## Simone Weil

THE ONLY TEMPTATION for man is to be abandoned to his own resources in the presence of evil. His nothingness is then proved experimentally. Although the soul has received supernatural bread at the moment when it asked for it, its joy is mixed with fear because it could only ask for it for the present. The future is still to be feared. The soul has not the right to ask for bread for the morrow, but it expresses its fear in the form of a supplication. It finishes with that. The prayer began with the word "Father," it ends with the word "evil." We must go from confidence to fear. Confidence alone can give us strength enough not to fall as a result of fear. After having contemplated the name, the kingdom, and the will of God, after having received the supernatural bread and having been purified from evil, the soul is ready for that true humility which crowns all virtues. Humility consists of knowing that in this world the whole soul, not only what we term the ego in its totality, but also the supernatural part of the soul, which is God present in it, is subject to time and to the vicissitudes of change. There must be absolute acceptance of the possibility that everything natural in us should be destroyed. But we must simultaneously accept and repudiate the possibility that the supernatural part of the soul should disappear. It must be accepted as an event that would come about only in conformity with the will of God. It must be repudiated as being something utterly horrible. We must be afraid of it, but our fear must be as it were the completion of confidence.

# THE FINAL BATTLE

## Raymond E. Brown

WE ARE NOT dealing with a question of daily temptation (which, after all, is the lot of the Christian and must be endured: James 1:2, 12) but with the final battle between God and Satan. . . .

Are we, then, to think that the Christian community, which suffered so much for Christ, was not willing to face the final battle with Satan? Reflection shows us that there is no question of timidity here, but real insight into the nature of this terrible struggle to come. Paul warned the Ephesians (6:12–13) that they were not fighting against flesh and blood, but against a whole array of superhuman powers, and that it would take the whole armor of God to withstand them. True, Christ defeated Satan in principle on the cross; but before Satan would release his hold on this earth, there would come such tribulation as has not been seen since the world's creation. As Christ Himself admitted, if the Lord had not shortened the days of this tribulation, no human being would be saved. But He added by way of encouragement that the days have been shortened for the sake of the elect (Mark 13:19–20). And the text of Revelation 3:10 . . . shows Christ promising to keep His faithful Christians from the trial. Therefore, asking for preservation from the final diabolic onslaught is simply following Christ's directions.

# BUT DELIVER US
# FROM EVIL

## WHEN DEATH SLIP-SLIDES

*Augustine of Hippo*

WE MUST PRAY not only that we may not be led into the evil from which we are free —which is asked for in the sixth place—but that we may also be delivered from the evil into which we have already been led. And when this has been accomplished, nothing will remain to inspire dread nor will any temptation at all have to be dreaded. And yet in this life, as long as we are bearers of this mortality into which we were led by the inducement of the serpent, there is no hope of accomplishing this. But that it will be accomplished someday is a hope that should be entertained; and this is the hope which is not seen, whereof when the apostle discussed it he said: "But hope that is seen is not hope." Yet the wisdom which is granted in this life also is not to be despaired of by the faithful servants of God. And it is this—that with the utmost care we shun what from the Lord's revelation we know we must avoid and that with a most intense devotion we strive after what from God's revelation we know we should strive after. For thus when death itself slips from us the last burden of our mortality in our appointed time, the blessedness of the whole man will be brought to pass, a blessedness that was begun in this life and which to grasp and attain someday we now expend every effort.

## DELIVER US FROM WAR

*John Paul II*

"DELIVER US from evil"! Reciting these words of Christ's prayer, it is very difficult to give them a different content from the one that opposes peace, that destroys it, that threatens it. Let us pray therefore: Deliver us from war, from hatred, from the destruction of human lives! Do not allow us to kill! Do not allow use of those means which are in the service of death and destruction and whose power, range of action, and precision go beyond the limits known hitherto. Do not allow them to be used ever! "Deliver us from evil!" Defend us from war! From any war. Father, who are in Heaven, Father of life and Giver of peace, the Pope, the son of nation which, during history, and particularly in our century, has been among those more sorely tried in the horror, the cruelty, and the cataclysm of war, supplicates you. He supplicates you for all peoples in the world, for all countries and for all continents. He supplicates you in the name of Christ, the Prince of Peace.

# ENLARGEMENT

## Origen

IN THE WORDS, "Lead us not into temptation," Luke seems to me to have implied also the idea, "Deliver us from evil." And surely it is likely that the Lord spoke pithily to the disciple, who was already rather advanced in knowledge, but more explicitly to the multitude, who had need of more detailed instruction. Now, God "delivers us from evil," not when the Adversary does not attack us at all with his own devices, whatever they may be, and the ministers of his will, but rather when we overcome him through taking a courageous stand in face of whatever befalls us. This is also our interpretation of the words: "Many are the afflictions of the just; but out of them all doth He deliver them." God delivers us from afflictions, not when afflictions no longer beset us—as Paul says, "In all things we are afflicted," as much as to say that at no time are we without affliction—but rather, when "we are afflicted, we are" through God's help "not distressed." To be "afflicted" indicates, according to a certain Hebraic idiom, a critical situation that arises against one's will. To be "distressed," however, indicates a state arising from one's will, inasmuch as one is overcome by, and yields to, affliction. And so Paul quite rightly says: "In all things we are afflicted, but are not distressed." We have the same idea, I think, in the Psalms: "When I was in affliction, Thou hast enlarged me." For through the cooperation and presence of the Word of God encouraging and saving us, our mind through God's help is made joyful and courageous in the time of trial; and this experience is called "enlargement."

## SICKNESS, POVERTY, DEATH

### Martin Luther

WE RECEIVE EVIL from everything which hurts us. Its whole meaning points to the devil. We can sum it up this way: Deliver us from the wicked devil, who hinders everything we have previously been talking about; from that wicked one, evil one, deliver us! Nevertheless, you must include in this "evil" everything on earth which is evil, such as sickness, poverty, death, whatever evil there is in the dominion of Satan, of which there is very much on earth. For who can count all the evils? A child becomes sick, and so forth. In short: Deliver us from the devil! Then the name of God will be hallowed, his kingdom come, and his will be done, and we shall be delivered from all things.

## BAIT NOT, HOOK NOT

### Gregory of Nyssa

THE SEA is often dangerous on account of its mighty waves, but not to those who are far removed from it. Fire destroys, but only if inflammable matter is near it. War is full of danger, but only to those who take part in the battle. As, therefore, a man who wants to escape the terrible calamities of war prays not to become involved in it, and another one who fears fire asks not to find himself in such; as a third one who abhors the sea prays that he may not be obliged to go on a voyage; so also he who fears the assault of the evil one should pray that he may not fall into it. But since, as we have said before, Scripture says that the world is seated in wickedness, and as the occasions for temptation arise from worldly preoccupations, therefore if a man prays truly to be delivered from evil, he asks that he may be far from temptation. For no one would swallow the hook unless he had first gulped down the bait in his greed. But let us rise and say to God, "Lead us not into temptation"—that is to say, into the evils of the world—"but deliver us from evil" which holds sway in this world; from which may we be delivered by the grace of Christ, for His is the power and glory with the Father and the Holy Spirit, now and always, and for ever and ever. Amen.

## SONS VERSUS SONS

### Raymond E. Brown

THE WHOLE WORLD is in the power of Satan (1 John 5:19); but the Christian has the promise that through God's begetting he will be protected from the Evil One (5:18), and this is what prompts him to utter the petition of the Pater Noster. Faced with the awesome power of the strong one, the Christian begs for help of a stronger (Matthew 12:28–29). He has asked for the coming of his Father's kingdom, but he knows that in that decisive moment the sons of the Evil One will be drawn up against the sons of the kingdom (Matthew 13:38). And so he begs his Father, not only to spare him the trial of that terrible struggle, but also to wrench him free from the power of Satan.

# FOR THINE IS THE KINGDOM, AND THE POWER, AND THE GLORY, FOREVER

# THE BLESSED COMMUNITY

## Thomas R. Kelly

"SEE HOW THESE CHRISTIANS love one another" might well have been a spontaneous exclamation in the days of the apostles. The Holy Fellowship, the Blessed Community, has always astonished those who stood without it. The sharing of physical goods in the primitive church is only an outcropping of a profoundly deeper sharing of a Life, the base and center of which is obscured to those who are still oriented about self rather than about God. To others, tragic to say, the very existence of such a Fellowship within a common Life and Love is unknown and unguessed. In its place, psychological and humanistic views of the essential sociality and gregariousness of man seek to provide a social theory of church membership. From these views spring church programs of mere sociability and social contacts. The precious word *Fellowship* becomes identified with a purely horizontal relation of man to man, not with that horizontal-vertical relationship of man to man *in God*.

But every period of profound rediscovery of God's joyous immediacy is a period of emergence of this amazing group interknittedness of God-enthralled men and women who know one another *in Him*. It appeared in vivid form among the early Friends. The early days of the evangelical movement showed the same bondedness in love. The disclosure of God normally brings the disclosure of the Fellowship. We don't create it deliberately; we find it and we find ourselves increasingly within it as we find ourselves increasingly within Him. It is the holy matrix of "the communion of the saints," the body of Christ which is His church. William C. Braithwaite says, in the Rowntree Series, that it was a tragic day when the Quakers ceased to be a Fellowship and became a Society of Friends. Yet ever within that society, and ever within the Christian church, has existed the Holy Fellowship, the Blessed Community, an *ekklesiola in ekklesia*, a little church within the church.

Yet still more astonishing is the Holy Fellowship, the Blessed Community, to those who are within it. Yet can one be surprised at being *at home*? In wonder and awe we find ourselves already interknit within unofficial groups of kindred souls. A "chance" conversation comes, and in a few moments we know that we have found and have been found by another member of the Blessed Community. Sometimes we are thus suddenly knit together in the bonds of a love far faster than those of many years' acquaintance. In unbounded eagerness we seek for more such fellowship, and wonder at the apparent lethargy of mere "members."

In the Fellowship cultural and educational and national and racial differences are leveled. Unlettered men are at ease with the truly humble scholar who lives in the Life, and the scholar listens with joy and openness to the precious experiences of God's dealing with the workingman. We find men with chilly theologies but with glowing hearts. We overleap the boundaries of church membership and find Lutherans and Roman Catholics, Jews and Christians, within the Fellowship. We reread the poets and the saints, and the Fellowship is enlarged. With urgent hunger we read the Scriptures, with no thought of pious exercise, but in order to find more friends for the soul. We brush past our historical learning in the Scriptures, to seize upon those writers who lived in the Center, in the Life and in the Power. Particularly does devotional literature become illuminated, for the *Imitation of Christ*, and Augustine's *Confessions*, and Brother Lawrence's *Practice of the Presence of God* speak the language of the souls who live at the Center. Time telescopes and vanishes, centuries and creeds are overleaped. The incident of death puts no boundaries to the Blessed Community, wherein men live and love and work and pray in that Life and Power which gave forth the Scriptures. And we wonder and grieve at the overwhelmingly heady preoccupation of religious people with problems, problems, unless they have first come into the Fellowship of the Light.

The final grounds of holy Fellowship are in God. Lives immersed and drowned in God are drowned in love, and know one another in Him, and know one another in love. God is the medium, the matrix, the focus, the solvent. As Meister Eckhart suggests, he who is wholly surrounded by God, enveloped by God, clothed with God, glowing in selfless love toward Him—such a man no one can touch except he touch God also. Such lives have a common meeting point; they live in a common joyous enslavement. They go back into a single Center where they are at home with Him and with one another. It is as if every soul had a final base, and that final base of every soul is one single Holy Ground, shared in by all. Persons in the Fellowship are related to one another through Him, as all mountains go down into the same earth.

# HOPEFULLY

## *William Griffin*

"HOPEFULLY" IS A WEED, an *herba inutilis*, a *flora non grata*, in the linguistic landscape. It is gagroot, skunk cabbage, broadleaved goldenrod. It makes Charles Kuralt's ears tingle; it makes Harold Taylor physically ill; it makes A. B. Guthrie, Jr., homicidal; it makes Richard Edes Harrison suicidal; it makes Stanley Kunitz adverbicidal. It is the most horrible usage of our time, and hence should be banned forever from standard English and American gardens.

Parenthetically, for some of the opinions on this most controversial word I am indebted to the *Harper Dictionary of Contemporary Usage* (1975), the editors of which polled 136 prominent English and American authors.

Presumably, what agitates these otherwise sensible people is that the usage of the word often exceeds its definition. Traditionally, an adverb has been a word that modifies a verb, an adjective, or another adverb. When it does so, it is welcome in the formalest gardens, the tiniest terrariums. When it doesn't, it is sprayed trammeled, uprooted.

Syntactically, and it doesn't take a foundation grant for a comprehensive study of ten thousand English and American adverbs to establish this, most adverbs do not modify other elements in a sentence; they simply grow by themselves. Like Queen Anne's lace and hairy Solomon's seal, they flourish in the woodlands and wetlands of contemporary speech and prose.

Intuitively, and it doesn't take a Wordsworthian or Thoreauvian ramble across the English or American countryside to perceive this; "hopefully" is not a weed, not an unuseful plant, not an unwelcome flower. Like forget-me-nots or touch-me-nots, it is a wildflower with a taxonomy and a syntax all its own.

Patronizingly, Orville Prescott finds the word illiterate; filially, Peter Prescott finds it ungrammatical; hopelessly, Edwin Newman perspires to prove the nonexistence of the word by positing the nonusage of its contrary. Astonishingly, these gentlemen seem in their pursuit of the trivium and quadrivium never to have come into smart contact with an absolute: that is to say, a clause, phrase, or word upon which the design if not the logic of a sentence depends.

Preteritionally, absolutes are as old as literature, grammar, and logic. Genitive absolutes abound in Xenophon's histories, and ablative absolutes adorn Cicero's orations: constructions that are both adverbial in nature and expressive of time, condition, cause, concession, and probably half a dozen other modes of thought.

Compositionally, the adverbial absolute has often been confused with clauses like "it is to be hoped" and phrases like "in a hopeful manner." Purely and simply, however, it is but a single word. Placed first in a sentence and followed always by a comma, it indicates the timber or tone of the voice or pen of the speaker or writer. "Hopefully, my novel will sell well" is a usage John L'Heureux is unable to resist.

Speracidally, Phyllis McGinley, Leo Rosten, Hal Borland, T. Harry Williams, and the other death-of-hope grammarians are gathering to ignite the woodlands and drain the wetlands, to level the hills and even the valleys. When they finish their work, there will be nothing left on the literary plain, except perhaps the sort of stubbly prose found in Edwin Newman's *Strictly Speaking* (a garden variety of adverbial absolute if there ever was one)—a fate worse than sign language in a leper colony.

Speradically, even if they were to be successful with their bulldozers and cropdusters, even if they were to eradicate adverbial absolutes from the world beyond the privet hedge and terrarial bowl, they would appear again in a few months' time; not only "hopefully" but also "wistfully" and "endearingly," "whimsically" and "capriciously," "metaphorically" and "hyperbolically," "fascistically" and "anarchistically," "subliminally" and "subconsciously," "pussyfootingly" and "caterwaulingly," "bicentenially" and "tricentenially," "firstly" and "lastly."

Eschatologically, the perfect endtime adverb is "hopefully."

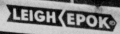

# BIOGRAPHIES

ADAMNAN OF IONA (627–704), born in Ireland, entered the famous monastery on Iona, an island off the coast of Scotland. A contemporary described him as "a man of tears and penitence, devoted in prayer, diligent, watchful, and learned in God's holy Scriptures."

AELRED OF RIEVAULX (1110–1167) decided at the age of twenty-four to leave the service of King David of Scotland and join the Cistercian monks in England. His two important works are *The Mirror of Charity* and *Spiritual Friendship*.

CLEVELAND AMORY is not only a successful columnist and nonfiction writer but also the founder and president of the Fund for Animals.

ARNOBIUS OF SICCA, in the diocese of Africa, underwent a conversion to Christianity sometime at the end of the third or beginning of the fourth century. He stated his *Case Against the Pagans* in seven books.

W. H. AUDEN (1907–1973), an Anglo-American author, wrote plays, essays, and even an opera libretto, but he is best known as a poet and an anthologist of poetry.

AUGUSTINE OF HIPPO (354–430), fathered a child with his mistress and sired a host of bad habits before his dramatic conversion in 387; he was baptized by Ambrose, bishop of Milan; in 391 he was ordained to the priesthood; in 395 he was consecrated to the episcopate of Hippo, diocese of Africa. Among his voluminous and stylish writings are a spiritual biography entitled *Confessions*, treatises against a variety of heresies, and a theologically utopian work entitled *City of God*.

WILLIAM BARCLAY (1907–1978) was for many years minister of Trinity Church, Renfrew, Scotland, and dean of the faculty of divinity, University of Glasgow. Among his voluminous and insightful writings are the *Daily Study Bible* series, *The King and the Kingdom*, and *Jesus of Nazareth*.

BASIL OF CAESAREA (c. 330–379) was, according to *The Oxford Dictionary of Saints*, "a theologian of distinction, a monastic founder, and diocesan bishop of extraordinary ability." All this in Caesarea, Cappadocia, Asia Minor.

RICHARD BAXTER (1615–1691), an English Nonconformist divine, penned many works of evangelical piety, the most popular among the Puritans being *The Saints' Everlasting Rest* (1650).

AMBROSE BIERCE (1842–1914?) was an American satirist, journalist, and short-story writer. *The Devil's Dictionary* (1911), published in 1906 under the title *The Cynic's Word Book*, is a collection of sardonic definitions.

LORAINE BOETTNER, a graduate of Princeton Theological Seminary, has a number of books to his credit. Among them are *The Reformed Doctrine of Predestination* (1932), *Studies in Theology* (1947), *Immortality* (1956), and *Roman Catholicism* (1962).

JAMES MONTGOMERY BOICE has degrees from Harvard, Princeton Theological Seminary, and the University of Basel. He is an author, a religious broadcaster, and pastor of Tenth Presbyterian Church in Philadelphia.

BONAVENTURE (1221–1274) was a Franciscan friar, bishop, and cardinal. According to *The Oxford Dictionary of Saints*, "he stressed the importance of an affective rather than a purely rational approach to the divine mysteries." Among his writings are essays on mysticism as well as treatises on dogma.

P. J. BOUDREAUX (dates unknown) was a French Jesuit preacher and pastor in nineteenth-century France.

PAUL BRAND is, according to *Christianity Today*, "a skilled and inventive hand surgeon, and most major textbooks on hand surgery contain chapters by him." He began his career as a missionary surgeon in India, specializing in the treatment of leprosy. The last ten years he has spent at a leprosarium in the United States at the Public Health Service Hospital in Carville, Louisiana.

JAMES BREIG is a freelance writer who contributes frequently to *US Catholic*.

ARLINE BRECHER is a freelance writer who contributes regularly to *The National Enquirer*.

RAYMOND E. BROWN, a Catholic priest, is Auburn Professor of Biblical Studies at Union Theological Seminary. Among his many books are the Anchor Bible volume on the Gospel of John and *The Birth of the Messiah*.

MALCOLM W. BROWNE writes on science and scientific developments for *The New York Times*.

JOHN BUNYAN (1628–1688), while in prison for dissenting from the Church of England, wrote, among other things, *Pilgrim's Progress*, an allegorical tale of a Christian's pilgrimage through this world to the next. A compendium of evangelical theology, it has been read by more Christians than any other book (only the Bible excluded).

THOMAS CAMPION (1567–1620), an Englishman, was a physician by vocation but by avocation he was a poet, composer, and lutenist.

CARLO CARRETTO renounced security and civilization at the age of forty-four to search for his own soul in the Sahara. There he joined the Little Brothers of Jesus, a monastic group founded by Charles de Foucauld. Among his writings are *Letters from the Desert*, *Love Is for Living*, and *The God Who Comes*.

J. V. LANGMEAD CASSERLEY (1909–1978), a Church of England cleric, taught dogmatic theology for many years at General Theological Seminary in New York City. He is perhaps best remembered for his spiritual autobiography entitled *No Faith of My Own*.

ARTHUR C. CLARKE, an Englishman who now calls Sri Lanka his home, has written both fiction and nonfiction on space and the modern age. He is perhaps best known for coauthoring the screenplay of *2001: A Space Odyssey*.

COLUMBA OF IONA (521–597), an Irish monk who was forced to leave home only to found a monastery on Iona, a small island off the coast of Scotland. Iona soon became the hub of missionary activity and cultural accomplishment in the area.

W. A. CRISWELL, a graduate of Southern Baptist Theological Seminary, served various pastorates in Oklahoma and Texas before becoming pastor of the First Baptist Church of Dallas in 1944. Among his many books are *Expository Sermons on Revelation* in five volumes.

CYPRIAN OF CARTHAGE (c. 200–258), in the last thirteen years of his life, was ordained a priest, proclaimed a bishop, and rendered a martyr. According to *The*

*Oxford Dictionary of Saints*, he "insisted on discreet compassion, on the unity of the Church, and the need for obedience and loyalty."

JEAN DANIÈLOU (1905–1974) was a French Jesuit priest, theologian, and in the last years of his life a cardinal. Among his many works are *Holy Pagans of the Old Testament* and *The Lord of History*.

DANIEL DEFOE (1660?–1731), associated at one time or another during his life with twenty-six periodicals, has been called the father of modern journalism. He also wrote novels (*Robinson Crusoe*) and poetry ("The True-born Englishman").

JAMES DICKEY has achieved measures of success as an advertising executive, novelist, and poet.

EMILY DICKINSON (1830–1886), unpublished in her lifetime and unknown at her death, stands today in the front rank of American poets.

*Didache*, title of the Greek work also called *The Teaching of the Twelve Apostles*. Written sometime between A.D. 50 and 150, it is a catechism of instruction for those wishing to become Christians.

*Documents of Vatican II* contains all sixteen official texts promulgated by the Ecumenical Council, 1963–1965.

JOHN DONNE (1572–1631), English poet and Anglican divine, mixed metaphysics and ministry in his poems (*Holy Sonnets*) and sermons (*Devotions*).

JOANNES ECKHART (c. 1260–c. 1328), also known as Meister Eckhart, was a German Dominican theologian whose mysticism tended to harmonize holiness and learning.

MARY BAKER EDDY (1821–1910) was founder of the Christian Science movement. *Science and Health* (later entitled *Science and Health with a Key to the Scriptures*), the textbook of Christian Science, was published in 1875.

JACQUES ELLUL, noted theologian and lay member of the Reformed Church of France, is professor of law and history at the University of Bordeaux. Among his score of books are *Hope in Time of Abandonment* and *Apocalypse: The Book of Revelation*.

*Everyman* is the title of a fifteenth-century English morality play. Its author is unknown; its plot may have been filched from a Dutch play of the same title; and its moral is that good deeds are the only friends a man can count on to accompany him beyond the grave.

FREDERICK WILLIAM FABER (1814–1863), a convert from Canterbury to Rome, became a priest of the Oratory, a religious congregation with houses in London and Birmingham. *The Creator and the Creature*, perhaps his spiritual classic, is representative of nineteenth-century piety.

MARK FACKLER, a graduate of Westmont College and the University of Minnesota, is a writer-editor working in Wheaton, Illinois.

MINUCIUS FELIX (second and third centuries) was a lawyer from Christian Africa who went to Rome to earn his fortune. Sometime toward the beginning of the third century he composed *The Octavius*, a prose dialog which had under its sophisticated philosophical veneer a solid apology for Christianity.

J. MASSYNGBERDE FORD is professor of New Testament studies at the University of Notre Dame. *Revelation* is her contribution to the Anchor Bible series.

W. HERSCHEL FORD, a leader in the Southern Baptist Convention, pastor of churches in El Paso and Dallas, has written more than forty volumes of "simple sermons."

ARNOLD GARSON is a staff writer on the *Des Moines Sunday Register*.

BAMBER GASCOIGNE, a British television executive, has authored several books, among them *The Christians*.

ROBERT W. GLEASON, a Jesuit priest, teaches dogmatic theology at Fordham University. Among his books are *The World to Come*, *Yahweh*, and *The God of the Old Testament*.

YVONNE GOULET is a freelance writer who contributes frequently to magazines like *Sign* and *US Catholic*.

HILDA GRAEF (dates unknown) translated from Greek into English *The Lord's Prayer • The Beatitudes by St. Gregory of Nyssa*, one of the volumes in the Paulist Press Ancient Christian Writers series.

BILLY GRAHAM is the American evangelist whose messages on radio and television, whose books and crusades have reached people all around the world for decades.

FREDERICK C. GRANT (1891–1974) taught at Union Theological Seminary, edited the *Anglican Theological Review*, served as rector of Trinity Church in Chicago, and officiated as dean of Seabury-Western Theological Seminary. He wrote more than twenty books, among them *Basic Christian Beliefs*.

GREGORY OF NAZIANZUS (329–389) was monk, priest, and eventually bishop of Constantinople. He endorsed the orthodoxy propounded by the Council of Nicea. Having resigned the bishopric, a hotbed of heresy, he spent his declining years gardening and writing; he died in bed.

GREGORY OF NYSSA (c. 330–c. 395) went to school in Athens, hub of the intellectual universe, but spent the last twenty-five years of his life at the edge of the Christian world, in Nyssa near Armenia. He defended the Council of Nicea against the Arians and wrote ascetical works of great spiritual depth.

WILLIAM GRIFFIN, a senior editor at Macmillan Publishing Co., Inc., has originated and edited the following anthologies: *The Joyful Christian: 127 Readings* by C. S. Lewis; *The Whimsical Christian: 114 Readings* by Dorothy L. Sayers; *The Newborn Christian* by J. B. Phillips; and *The Electronic Christian: 105 Readings* by Fulton J. Sheen.

ROMANO GUARDINI (1885–1968), a Catholic priest, taught philosophy at the University of Munich. Among his many books are *The Lord*, *The Last Things*, and *The Faith and Modern Man*.

BARBARA GRIZZUTI HARRISON is author of *Visions of Glory: A History and a Memory of Jehovah's Witnesses*.

VAN A. HARVEY, formerly chairman of the graduate program in religion at Southern Methodist University, is now a professor of religious studies at Stanford University.

WALTER HILTON (died 1396), was an English Augustinian monk whose *Scale of Perfection* ranks among the most important mystical compositions of the medieval era.

ANTHONY A. HOEKEMA, a graduate of Calvin Theological Seminary and Princetown Theological Seminary, has been professor of systematic theology at Calvin Theological Seminary, Grand Rapids, Michigan, since 1958. He is author of a number of books, among which are *The Four Major Cults* and *Holy Spirit Baptism.*

GERARD MANLEY HOPKINS (1844–1898) was a Jesuit priest who taught literature in British and Irish schools. His poetry, privately circulated during his lifetime, has won for him a reputation of excellence and influence since its publication in 1918.

HERMAN A. HOYT is chancellor and professor of Christian theology at Grace Theological Seminary and Grace College, Winona Lake, Indiana. Among his books is *The End Times.*

JACOPONE DA TODI (1230?–1306), Italian religious poet, who began his adult life as a lawyer representing indigent clients and ended it as a hermit writing mystical poems.

ROBERT JASTROW, director of NASA's Goddard Institute for Space Studies, is the author of *Until the Sun Dies* and *God and the Astronomers.*

JEROME (c. 341–420) was educated in the best Roman tradition, decided to become a monk, and rendered into intelligible Latin the Hebrew and Greek texts of the Old and New Testaments. Among his other writings are scriptural commentaries, biographies of celebrated monks, and a considerable correspondence.

ARTHUR D. KATTERJOHN is an associate professor at Wheaton College where he is chairman of the orchestral instruments department of the conservatory of music.

SAM KEEN wrote "Hope in a Posthuman Era" for *Christian Century* in 1967, while associate professor of philosophy and Christian faith at Louisville Presbyterian Seminary.

THOMAS R. KELLY (1893–1941), a Quaker, countered a great personal failure with increased ascetical observance. The result was the sort of abandonment generally found among mystics. *A Testament to Devotion,* his spiritual classic, was assembled after his death by Douglas Steere.

THOMAS À KEMPIS (c. 1379–1471) was a German monk who spent most of his days in the library of a Dutch monastery, copying the works of others and composing works of his own. Among the latter has traditionally been included *The Imitation of Christ.*

SØREN KIERKEGAARD (1813–1855), a Danish philosopher and theologian, lived an outwardly uneventful but inwardly intense life. His works fall into two categories, esthetic and religious, his journals containing his deepest insights.

RONALD A. KNOX (1888–1957), Catholic chaplain at Oxford University from 1926 to 1939, is perhaps best remembered for his translation of the Bible and for *Enthusiasm: A Chapter in the History of Religion with Special Reference to the Seventeenth and Eighteenth Centuries.*

JACQUES LACARRIÈRE, author of a number of books on historical and philosophical subjects, has translated modern and classical Greek literature into contemporary French.

GEORGE ELDON LADD is professor of New Testament exegesis and theology at Fuller Seminary in Pasadena. Among his publications are *The Presence of the Future* and *The Blessed Hope.*

TIM LAHAYE is pastor of Scott Memorial Baptist Church and president of Christian Heritage College, both in San Diego.

WILLIAM LAW (1686–1761) was an Anglican divine who devoted himself to the practice of pious exercises and gave spiritual direction to aged ladies. His spiritual classic is entitled *A Serious Call to a Devout and Holy Life.*

IGNACE LEPP (1909–1966) told of his dramatic conversion in *From Karl Marx to Jesus Christ.* By profession he was a psychoanalyst, and after his ordination to the priesthood, he attempted to show the compatibility of accepted concepts of psychoanalysis and Christian teachings.

ZOLA LEVITT, a Hebrew Christian, is a speaker and evangelist for the American Board of Missions to the Jews. He has collaborated with Thomas S. McCall on *The Coming Russian Invasion of Israel* and *Raptured.*

C. S. LEWIS (1898–1963) was professor of medieval and renaissance literature at both Oxford and Cambridge universities. In addition to *The Space Trilogy* and *The Chronicles of Narnia,* he has written scholarly works like *English Literature in the Sixteenth Century* and apologetical works like *Mere Christianity* and *The Problem of Pain.*

H. P. LIDDON, author of *Advent in St. Paul's,* was rector of St. Paul's, London, at the turn of the twentieth century.

HAL LINDSEY was educated at the University of Houston and the Dallas Theological Graduate School. His books, all of which have been best sellers, have dealt in one way or another with rapture, tribulation, and the millennium.

DAVID W. LOTZ is Washburn Professor of Church History at Union Theological Seminary in New York City.

JOHN LOVELL, JR., was professor of English at Howard University where he was associate dean of the College of Liberal Arts through 1969. Among his publications is *Black Song: The Story of How the Afro-American Spiritual Was Hammered Out.*

IGNATIUS LOYOLA (1491–1556), a Spanish soldier who underwent a dramatic conversion while recovering from a leg wound, went on to live a life of severe personal austerity and to found the Society of Jesus, popularly known as the Jesuits.

SISTER LUCIA is a nun who, as one of three children, was reported in 1917 to have seen a vision of Mary the mother of Jesus at Fatima, Portugal. Among the things Mary is reported to have shown the children was a vision of hell.

MARTIN LUTHER (1483–1546) was a German monk who took exception to, among other things, the marketing of indulgences and the nature of the papacy. At Wittenberg and later at Worms he made his protestations public. Those who agreed with him in principle and went their own ways were the first Protestants. As an author, he was prolific.

GEORGE MACDONALD (1824–1905), was a Scottish novelist, poet, and Christian writer, whose more than fifty published volumes exercised tremendous influence on C. S. Lewis.

MARGARET MACDONALD (?1815–1937?) was a member of the Scottish Church in 1830 when she was reported to have had a revelation of rapture and tribulation. Her own account of the vision first appeared in print in 1840.

GEORGE MALONEY is an American Jesuit priest who was ordained in the Russian rite. Unable to enter the Soviet Union for many years, he taught Eastern Christian spirituality at Fordham University. He now devotes his time to lecturing and spiritual counseling.

*Martyrdom of St. Polycarp* is the story, in letter form, of the death which the bishop of Smyrna suffered in A.D. 155 at the hands of the Roman authorities in Asia.

THOMAS S. McCALL, a graduate of Dallas Theological Seminary, is head of the southwestern branch of the American Board of Missions to the Jews and is minister at the Beth Sar Shalom in Dallas.

ABIGAIL McCARTHY is a writer, lecturer, and columnist for *Commonweal*.

JOHN L. McKENZIE, a Catholic priest and scholar, is author of *Dictionary of the Bible* and of half a dozen other books dealing with the Scriptures.

ARTHUR McNALLY, a Passionist priest, was editor of *Sign* magazine for many years.

METHODIUS was a Christian teacher, perhaps a bishop and martyr, who flourished in the latter half of the third century. "Thecla's Hymn," an epithalamium on the wedding of Christ and his Church, is part of *Symposium*, a sophisticated allegorical work with Platonic sprinkles.

JOANNES B. METZ, a priest and professor of fundamental theology at the University of Münster, is a highly original thinker and one of the exponents of the theology of hope.

WILLIAM MILLER (1782–1849) was an American sectarian leader who, when the day of judgment did not come in 1843 or 1844 as he had prophesied, founded the Second Adventist Church in 1845.

JOHN MILTON (1608–1674) would have become a minister if the ritualism of the Church of England had been more to his taste. Instead, he maintained his interest in religious affairs, accepted a post in Cromwell's government, and later, when his eyesight failed, concentrated on writing the epic poems *Paradise Lost* and *Paradise Regained*.

JURGEN MOLTMANN has been professor of systematic theology at the University of Tübingen, Germany, since 1967. Among his books are *The Theology of Hope* and *The Church in the Power of the Spirit*.

L. L. MORRIS, principal of Ridley College, Melbourne, Australia, is one of the contributors to *The New Bible Dictionary*.

ANDREW MURRAY (1828–1906) pastored Dutch Reformed churches throughout South Africa from 1850 to 1906. His preaching ability was legendary; his skill as a devotional writer was extraordinary.

WATCHMAN NEE (1903–1972) and his wife Charity Chang were edifying and apostolic Christians through a fifty-year period of Chinese history most inhospitable to Christians. He is known in the West chiefly for volumes of devotional writings that have found their way into English.

JOHN HENRY NEWMAN (1801–1890) was an Anglican divine who made the pilgrimage to Rome, eventually being appointed cardinal. He was a theologian who stressed the certainty and development of doctrine. He was a pastor whose sermons were mainly simple treatments of gospel themes.

NICHOLAS OF CUSA (1401–1464), a priest, bishop, and cardinal, was a humanist, philosopher, and theologian.

ORIGEN (c. 185–253) was an educator and priest in both Alexandria and Caesarea. Among his writings are scriptural exegesis and ascetical works. His father was martyred for the faith; he exhorted others to prepare

for martyrdom; he may have been martyred himself.

GEORGE OTIS was a senior executive in the electronic and aerospace industries before becoming a lay teacher, writing four books, and traveling half a million miles for the Lord.

PAULINE OF NOLA (c. 355–431) spent the last thirty-six years of his life in a monastery near Naples where he led an austere life and wrote hortatory letters and didactic poems.

J. BARTON PAYNE (1922–1979) was a professor in graduate studies at Wheaton College in Wheaton, Illinois, where he taught Old Testament subjects and the Hebrew language.

J. B. PHILLIPS is translator of *The New Testament in Modern English* and author of a host of other books. A priest in the Episcopal Church since 1931, he now resides in retirement in Swanage, Dorset, England.

KARL RAHNER is a German Jesuit priest and theologian. The author of many books, his complete list of publications is in excess of 3,000 items.

MARJORIE REEVES, author of *The Influence of Prophecy in the Later Middle Ages: A Study in Joachinism*, teaches at Oxford University.

JOHN A. T. ROBINSON is a New Testament scholar and bishop of the Church of England. The book of his that attracted most attention was *Honest to God* (1963) in which he expressed controversial, even revolutionary, interpretations of some articles of orthodox faith.

*Roman Ritual* is the priest's handbook for administration of the sacraments and for other liturgical functions.

ELISABETH KUBLER ROSS is a psychiatrist who took the pennies off the eyes of the living so that they might look at death and dying with some intelligence and not a little compassion. *Death and Dying* is the title of her best-selling book.

RUFINUS (345–410), who numbered among his friends Jerome and Augustine of Hippo, was a learned man who spent much of his time translating Greek theological writings into Latin. Perhaps his best-known work is *Commentary on the Apostles' Creed*.

FRANZ SEIBEL, author of numerous articles on dogmatic and pastoral theology, is prior of a Carmelite monastery in Germany.

GEORGE BERNARD SHAW (1856–1950), British playwright born in Ireland, is considered by some to be the best dramatist since Shakespeare. Of greatest interest to eschatologists is *Don Juan in Hell*, the interlude in *Man and Superman* (1905) in which the Devil expresses a number of extraordinary opinions.

F. J. SHEED began his preaching career more than fifty years ago on a soapbox in London. Theology with sanity is the hallmark of his style, which is shown to best effect in his most recent book *Christ in Eclipse: A Clinical Study of the Good Christian*.

FULTON J. SHEEN is the Roman Catholic bishop who in the 1950s got better television ratings than Milton Berle. He is also the author of more than sixty books covering all phases of Christian doctrine and practice.

GERTRUDE GRACE SILL has lectured at the Metropolitan Museum of Art and at the Frick Museum in New York City; she teaches at Fairfield University in Connecticut and is the author of *A Handbook of Symbols in Christianity*.

JUNE SINGER is a psychoanalyst practicing in Chicago. Her *Boundaries of the Soul* explains how C. G. Jung's psychology works in practice.

DAVID STEINDL-RAST is a Benedictine monk who writes and lectures frequently on prayer.

PIERRE TEILHARD DE CHARDIN (1881–1955) was a French Jesuit priest who, through a much-traveled, much-travailed life, managed to keep his sanity and probably achieved a measure of sanctity. *The Phenomenon of Man* and *The Divine Milieu*, which were published after his death, contain a unique blend of archaeology, cosmology, theology, and mysticism.

TERESA OF ÁVILA (1512–1582) was a Spanish Carmelite nun whose mystical relationship with the heavenly bridegroom is described in the greatest detail in *The Way of Perfection* and *The Castle of the Soul*.

TERTULLIAN (c. 160–c. 230) was a Roman theologian and Christian apologist whose view of sin and forgiveness was more rigorous than the Church's. His pithiest sentence "the blood of martyrs is the seed of the Church" is also his most widely known.

HELMUT THIELICKE, professor of theology at the University of Hamburg, Germany, lectures frequently in the United States. He is presently at work on the third and final volume of his masterpiece entitled *Theological Ethics*.

THEOPHILUS OF ANTIOCH (died 180s) was the author of several apologetical works, only one of which is extant. In *Letter to Autolycus* he contrasts the best in Christianity with the worst of pagan culture in the hope that the facts will speak for themselves.

LEWIS THOMAS, president of the Memorial Sloan-Kettering Cancer Center in New York, is author of the best-selling book *The Lives of a Cell*.

THOMAS OF CELANO (1200–1253) was a Franciscan, a poet, and the first biographer of Francis of Assisi. When authorship of the "Dies Irae" is debated, his is the name most often mentioned. Algernon Charles Swinburne translated the poem into English.

EVELYN UNDERHILL (1875–1941), a convert to the Anglican communion, spent much of her life devoted to religious work, visiting the poor, and directing souls. Her several books on mysticism have become classics.

SIMONE WEIL (1909–1943), French by birth, Jewish by heritage, Roman Catholic by conviction if not in practice, died believing that Christ on the cross was the bridge between God and man.

THOMAS WELCH was, at the time of the accident described in *Oregon's Amazing Miracle* (1976), an engineer's helper for a lumber company near Portland, Oregon.

JOHN WESLEY (1703–1791), declaring that the world was his parish, traveled a quarter of a million miles during the last fifty years of his life, preaching the gospel to whoever would listen. He is the chief founder of Methodism.

JOHN WESLEY WHITE is a Canadian evangelist, sometime associate of Billy Graham, and a student of end-time prophecy.

ROBERT K. WILCOX, former religion editor of *The Miami News*, won the Supple Memorial Award for religion newswriting in 1970. He is the author of *Shroud* and *The Mysterious Deaths at Ann Arbor*.

DAVID WILKERSON, whose experiences with rebellious and drug-oriented youth in New York resulted in the best-selling *The Cross and the Switchblade*, has founded Teen Challenge centers all across the United States. World Evangelistic Crusades is also his foundation, with headquarters at Lindale, Texas.

LEON J. WOOD, professor of Old Testament studies and dean of the Grand Rapids Baptist Bible Seminary, is author of *Is the Rapture Next?* and *The Bible & Future Events*.

# SOURCES AND PERMISSIONS

## TEXT

*Sources and permissions are expressed in their entirety only the first time they appear.*

**ADORATION OF THE LAMB AND HYMN OF THE CHOSEN**
The Revelation of St. John the Divine 14:1-3; 19:1, 3-4. Scripture quotations with headings have been taken from the Authorized King James version.

**ALLEGORICAL INTERPRETATION, THE**
From *Prayer* as it appears in *Prayer · Exhortation to Martyrdom* by Origen. Translated and annotated by John J. O'Meara. New York: Newman Press, 1954. Reprinted with permission of Paulist Press.

**ALPHA AND THE OMEGA, THE**
From "Christ, the Alpha and Omega" as it appears in *The Documents of Vatican II*. Edited by Walter M. Abbott. Reprinted with permission of America Press, Inc., 106 West 56th Street, New York, New York, 10019. Copyright © 1966. All rights reserved.

**AMILLENNIALISM**
Taken from Anthony A. Hockema's contribution to *The Meaning of the Millennium: Four Views*. Edited by Robert G. Clouse. Copyright © 1977 by InterVarsity Christian Fellowship and used with permission of InterVarsity Press.

**ANIMALS HAVE SOULS JUST LIKE OTHER PEOPLE**
From *The Case Against the Pagans*, volume 1, by Arnobius of Sicca. Translated and annotated by George E. McCracken. New York: Newman Press, 1949. Reprinted with permission of Paulist Press.

**ANTICIPATING THE END**
From *The Beginning of the End* by Tim LaHaye. Wheaton, Illinois: Tyndale House Publishers, 1977. Reprinted with permission.

**ANTICHRIST IN THE NEW TESTAMENT**
It appears as "Antichrist" by L. L. Morris in *The New Bible Dictionary*. Edited by J. D. Douglas. Grand Rapids, Michigan: Wm. B. Eerdmans Publishing Co., 1962. Reprinted with permission.

**ANTISEPTIC FIRE**
From *Letters to Malcolm: Chiefly on Prayer*. Copyright © 1963, 1964 by the estate of C. S. Lewis and/or C. S. Lewis. Reprinted with per-

mission of Harcourt Brace Jovanovich, Inc.

**APOCALYPTICAL SIGNS**
From *WW III: Signs of the Impending Battle of Armageddon* by John Wesley White. Copyright © 1977 by the Zondervan Publishing House. Used with permission.

**APOCATASTASIS**
From *A Handbook of Theological Terms* by Van A. Harvey. Reprinted with permission of Macmillan Publishing Co., Inc. Copyright © 1964 by Van A. Harvey.

**APPREHENSIVE DEFENDANT, THE**
From *A Commentary on the Apostles' Creed* by Rufinus. Translated and annotated by J. N. D. Kelly. New York: Newman Press, 1954. Reprinted with permission of Paulist Press.

**ARKANSAS, 1976**
From the Associated Press as quoted in *Human Scandals* by Brad Holland. New York: Thomas Y. Crowell Co., 1977. Reprinted with permission.

**ARMAGEDDON I IS WORLD WAR III**
From *WW III*.

**AS MANY GO TO HELL AS HEAVEN**
Article by Arline Brecher, as it appears in the *National Enquirer* (August 15, 1978). Reprinted with permission.

**AS THE WIND WHIRLS**
From *The Poems of St. Paulinus of Nola*. Translated by P. G. Walsh. New York: Newman Press, 1975. Reprinted with permission of Paulist Press.

**AT EVENING WE SHALL BE JUDGED BY LOVE**
From *The World to Come* by Robert W. Gleason. New York: Sheed & Ward, Inc., 1958. Reprinted with permission.

**AWE AND EXPECTANCY**
From *Expository Sermons on Revelation* by W. A. Criswell. Copyright © 1962, 1963, 1964, 1965, 1966 by Zondervan Publishing House. Used with permission.

**BAIT NOT, HOOK NOT**
From *The Lord's Prayer*, as it appears in *The Lord's Prayer · The Beatitudes* by St. Gregory of Nyssa. Translated and annotated by Hilda C. Graef. New York: Newman Press, 1954. Reprinted with permission of Paulist Press.

**BEATIFIC VISION, THE**
From *The Happiness of Heaven* by

P. J. Boudreaux, Chicago: Loyola University Press, 1962. Baltimore: John Murphy & Co., 1872.

**BIBLICAL CLIMAX**
From *My Answer* by Billy Graham. Garden City, N.Y.: Doubleday & Co., Inc., 1960. Reprinted with permission.

**BLESSED COMMUNITY, THE**
From *A Testament of Devotion* by Thomas R. Kelley, as it appears in *The Doubleday Devotional Classics*, volume 3. Edited by E. Glenn Hinson. Garden City, N.Y.: Doubleday & Co., Inc., 1978.

**BLOODBATH AT ARMAGEDDON**
From *The Vision* by David Wilkerson. Copyright © 1974 by David Wilkerson Youth Crusades. Published by Pyramid Publications for Fleming H. Revell Company.

**BOOK OF ACTIONS, BOOK OF LIFE**
From *Apocalypse: The Book of Revelation* by Jacques Ellul. Translated by George W. Schreiner. New York: Seabury Press, 1977. English translation copyright © 1977 by Seabury Press, Inc. Used with permission of the publisher.

**BREAD OF THE FUTURE**
From *New Testament Essays* by Raymond E. Brown. Reprinted with permission of Macmillan Publishing Co., Inc. Copyright © 1965 by Macmillan Publishing Co., Inc.

**BUT A SONIC BOOM**
From *WW III*.

**BY GOD'S FINGER**
From *Orations* by Gregory of Nazianzus, as it appears in *The Later Christian Fathers*. Edited and translated by Henry Bettenson. London: Oxford University Press, 1970. Reprinted with permission.

**CARTHAGE, A.D. 200 and CARTHAGE, A.D. 250**
As quoted in *Men Possessed by God: The Story of the Desert Monks of Ancient Christendom* by Jacques Lacarrière. Translated by Roy Monkcom. Garden City, N.Y.: Doubleday & Co., Inc., 1964.

**CAUGHT UP TOGETHER**
The First Epistle of Paul the Apostle to the Thessalonians 4:16-18.

**CELESTIAL CITY, THE**
From *Pilgrim's Progress and Christiana's Progress for Devotional Reading* by John Bunyan. Edited by Clara E. Murray. Grand Rapids, Mich.: Baker Book House, 1976. Reprinted with permission.

CELESTIAL EQUATION, THE
From *The Lord's Sermon on the Mount* by St. Augustine. Translated by John J. Jepson. New York: Newman Press, 1948. Reprinted with permission of Paulist Press.

CHARTER OF HOPE
From *Modern Gloom and Christian Hope* by Hilda Graef. Chicago: Henry Regnery Co., 1959. Copyright © 1959 by Hilda Graef. Reprinted with permission of Curtis Brown Ltd.

CITY OF GOD, THE
From *The City of God* by St. Augustine, as it appears in *The Soul Afire: Revelations of the Mystics*. Edited by H. A. Reinhold. New York: Pantheon Books, 1973. Reprinted with permission.

COME ALIVE WITH PEPSI
Reprinted with permission from *Campus Life*, magazine. Copyright © 1978 by Youth for Christ International, Wheaton, Illinois.

COMFORTABLE DOCTRINE, A
From *The Creator and the Creature: or, The Wonders of Divine Love* by Frederick William Faber. Westminster, Md.: Newman Press, 1961. First published in 1858.

COMMON LIFE IN THE PRESENCE OF GOD
From *No Faith of My Own* by J. V. Langmead Casserley. London: Longmans, Green and Co., 1950. Reprinted with permission.

COMPLETE FORGIVENESS
From *New Testament Essays*

CONTINUING JUDGMENT, THE
From *The City of God* by St. Augustine, as it is quoted in *The Later Christian Fathers*. Edited and translated by Henry Bettenson. London: Oxford University Press, 1970. Reprinted with permission.

CREATIVE HOPE
From "Creative Hope" by Johannes B. Metz, as it appears in *Cross Currents* (Spring, 1967). Reprinted with permission.

DAY IN COURT
From "Judgement in the Psalms" in *Reflections on the Psalms*. Copyright © 1958 by C. S. Lewis. Reprinted with permission of Harcourt Brace Jovanovich, Inc.

DAY OF THE LORD, DAY OF CHRIST
From *The Last and Future World* by James Montgomery Boice. Copyright © 1974 by Zondervan Publishing House. Used with permission.

DAY OF WRATH, THE
A poem by Columbia of Iona, as it appears in *The Soul of Fire: Revelations of the Mystics*.

DEATH AS FULFILLMENT
From *Death and Its Mysteries* by Ignace Lepp. Translated and with an introduction by Bernard Murchland. New York: Macmillan Publishing Co., Inc., 1968. Reprinted

with permission of the publisher. Translation copyright © 1968 by Macmillan Publishing Co., Inc.

DEATH OF A FRIEND
From Book IV of *The Confessions of Saint Augustine*. Translated by Edward B. Pusey. New York: Collier Books, 1961.

DEATH, THE RESULT OF LIFE
From "God's Astounding Laws of Nature: An Interview with Paul Brand" by Philip Yancey, *Christianity Today* (December 1, 1978). Copyright © 1978 by *Christianity Today*. Reprinted with permission.

DEATH, THE RESULT OF SIN
Reprinted with permission of Macmillan Publishing Co., Inc., from *Miracles: A Preliminary Study* by C. S. Lewis. Copyright © 1947 by Macmillan Publishing Co., Inc.; renewed 1975 by Arthur Owen Barfield and Alfred Cecil Harwood.

DEATHDAY AS BIRTHDAY
From "The Martyrdom of Saint Polycarp," as it appears in: *The Didache; The Epistle of Barnabas; The Epistles and The Martyrdom of St. Polycarp; The Fragments of Papias; The Epistle to Diognetus*. Translated and annotated by James A. Kleist. New York: Newman Press, 1948. Reprinted with permission of Paulist Press.

DEBITS AND CREDITS
From *The Lord's Sermon on the Mount*.

DEFEND US FROM THE DEVIL
From *Martin Luther: Selections from His Writings*. Edited and with an introduction by John Dillenberger. New York: Quadrangle Books, Inc., 1961. Reprinted with permission.

DELIVER US FROM WAR
From homily delivered by Pope Paul II on January 1, 1979, as it appeared in *Osservatore Romano*, (English edition, January 8, 1979), p. 1.

DEPARTURE OR ARRIVAL
From *For This Day: 365 Meditations* by J. B. Phillips. Waco, Tex.: Word Books, 1975. Reprinted with permission.

DEVIL ON DANTE AND MILTON, THE
From "Don Juan in Hell" in *Man and Superman* by Bernard Shaw as it appears in *Complete Plays and Prefaces*, volume 1. New York: Dodd, Mead & Company, 1963. Reprinted with the permission of the Society of Authors on behalf of the Bernard Shaw estate.

DEVIL'S ENVY, THE
From *Table Talk* by Martin Luther, as it appears in *Luther's Works*. Edited and translated by Theodore G. Tappert. Philadelphia: Fortress Press, 1967. Reprinted with permission.

DIABOLICAL DEFINITION, A

From *The Devil's Dictionary* by Ambrose Bierce. New York: Albert & Charles Boni, Inc., 1911.

DIALOGUE OF THE BODY WITH THE SOUL, WHICH IS LEADING IT TO JUDGMENT
A poem by Jacopone da Todi; it appears in *Lyrics of the Middle Ages*. Edited by Hubert Creekmore. New York: Grove Press, Inc., 1959. Reprinted with permission.

DIES IRAE
A poem by Thomas of Celano, translated by Algernon Charles Swinburne; it appears in *Lyrics of the Middle Ages*.

DIE WHEN YOU ARE ALIVE
Excerpt from "Learning To Die" by Brother David Steindl-Rast, *Parabola: Myth and the Quest for Meaning*, volume 2, number 1. Copyright © 1977. Reprinted with permission of the author.

DISMAL SITUATION, THE
From *Paradise Lost*, as it appears in *The Complete Poetical Works of John Milton*. Edited with introduction and notes by Harris Francis Fletcher. Boston: Houghton Mifflin Co., 1941.

DIVINE ENVIRONMENT, THE
From *The God Who Comes* by Carlo Carretto. Translated by Rose Mary Hancock. Maryknoll, N.Y.: Orbis Books, 1974. Reprinted with permission.

DIVINE, NOT HUMAN, ACTION
From *New Testament Essays* by Raymond E. Brown.

DON JUAN IN HELL
From "Don Juan in Hell" in *Man and Superman*.

DRESSING FOR THE PARTY
From *The Waiting Father: The Parables of Jesus* by Helmut Thielicke. Translated, with an introduction, by John W. Doberstein. New York: Harper & Row, 1975. Copyright © 1959 by John W. Doberstein. Reprinted with permission of the publisher.

EASY AT THE HOUR OF DEATH
From *A Serious Call to a Devout Life* by William Law. Introduction by G. W. Bromiley. William B. Eerdmans Publishing Co., 1966. Reprinted with permission.

ENDTIME MUSICAL, AN
It appeared as "A Chorus Line," a review by William Griffin, *Sign* (March 1976). Copyright © 1976 by *Sign*, Union City, N.J. All reproduction rights reserved.

ENERGY, DRIVE, PURPOSE
From *The Spiritual Life* by Evelyn Underhill. New York: Harper & Row.

ENIGMAS OR SYMBOLS
From *Apocalypse*.

ENLARGEMENT
From *Prayer · Exhortation to Martyrdom*.

ESCHATOLOGICAL RESSURECTION, THE

From *The Last Things: An Escha-tology for Laymen* by George El-don Ladd. Grand Rapids, Mich.: Wm. B. Eerdmans Publishing Co., 1978. Reprinted with permission.

ESCHATOLOGY AND HISTORY
From *The Power and the Wisdom.*

ESCHATOLOGY, APOCALYPTIC AND PRO-PHETIC
Reprinted with permission of Mac-millan Publishing Co., Inc., from *Basic Christian Beliefs* by Frederick C. Grant. Copyright © 1960 by Frederick C. Grant.

ESCHATOLOGY IN A NUTSHELL
From *Foundations of Christian Faith: An Introduction to the Idea of Christianity* by Karl Rahner. Translated by William V. Dych. New York: Seabury Press, 1978. English translation copyright © 1978 by Seabury Press, Inc. Used with permission of the publisher.

ESCHATOLOGY REALIZED AND UNREAL-IZED
From *Ring of Truth* by J. B. Phillips. Acknowledgment is made to Harold Shaw Publishers for per-mission to reprint material from the 1977 North American edition of *Ring of Truth* by J. B. Phillips. Copyright © 1967 by J. B. Phillips, Hodder & Stoughton, Ltd., Lon-don.

EXCELLENCIES OF THE SAINTS' REST
From *The Saints' Everlasting Rest* by Richard Baxter as it appears in Volume I of *The Doubleday De-votional Classics.* Edited by E. Glenn Hinson. Garden City, N.Y.: Doubleday & Co., Inc., 1978.

EXPECTATION IN A NUTSHELL
From *The Divine Milieu: An Essay on the Interior Life* by Pierre Teil-hard de Chardin. Copyright © 1960 by Wm. Collins Sons & Co., Lon-don, and by Harper & Row, New York. Reprinted by permission of Harper & Row.

EXPLAINED BY THE SECOND COMMAND-MENT
From *Martin Luther: Selections from His Writings.*

EVERYMAN'S PRAYER
From *Everyman*, as it appears in *Medieval and Tudor Drama.* Edited, with introductions and moderniza-tions, by John Gassner. Copyright © 1963 by Bantam Books, Inc. Re-printed with permission of the pub-lisher. All rights reserved.

FACE OF GOD, THE
From *The Vision of God* by Nich-olas of Cusa, as it appears in *The Soul Afire.*

FALSE PROPHET
Revelation 13:11–18.

FATHERLAND FROM WHICH WE HAVE FALLEN, THE
From *The Lord's Prayer.*

FEAR OF COLLECTIVE DEATH

From *Death and Its Mysteries* by Ignace Lepp.

FIFTH SEAL, THE
Revelation 6:9–11.

FIFTH TRUMPET, THE
Revelation 9:1–10.

FIFTH VIAL, THE
Revelation 16:10–11.

FINAL BATTLE, THE
From *New Testament Essays.*

FINAL KINGDOM, THE
From *New Testament Essays.*

FIRE AND ICE
From *The Poetry of Robert Frost* edited by Edward Connery Lathem. Copyright © 1923, 1969 by Holt, Rinehart and Winston. Copyright © 1951 by Robert Frost. Reprinted with permission of Holt, Rinehart and Winston.

FIRE OF PURGATORY, THE
From *Love Is for Living* by Carlo Carretto. Translated by Jeremy Moiser. Maryknoll, N.Y.: Orbis Books, 1977. Reprinted with per-mission.

FIRST FIVE MINUTES AFTER DEATH, THE
From *Advent in St. Paul's* by H. P. Liddon. London: Longmans, 1899.

FIRST MAN'S DISOBEDIENCE, THE
From "To Autolycus" by The-ophilus of Antioch, as it appears in *The Teachings of the Church Fathers.* Edited by John R. Willis. New York: Herder and Herder, 1966. Reprinted with permission.

FIRST RAPTURE, THEN WRATH
From *The Tribulation People* by Arthur D. Katterjohn with Mark Fackler. Copyright © 1974 by Crea-tion House, Carol Stream, Illinois, 60187. Used with permission.

FIRST SEAL, THE
Revelation 6:1–2.

FIRST TRUMPET, THE
Revelation 8:7.

FIRST VIAL, THE
Revelation 16:2.

FIVE STAGES OF DYING, THE
Reprinted with permission of Mac-millan Publishing Co., Inc., from *On Death and Dying* by Elisabeth Kubler Ross. Copyright © 1969 by Elisabeth Kubler Ross.

FOURTH SEAL, THE
Revelation 6:7–8.

FOURTH TRUMPET, THE
Revelation 8:12.

FOURTH VIAL, THE
Revelation 16:8–9.

FROM CONFIDENCE TO FEAR
From *The Simone Weil Reader.* Edited by George A. Panichas. Copyright © 1977. Reprinted with permission of David McKay Co., Inc.

FUNERAL SERVICE
From the *Roman Ritual*, as it ap-pears in *The Soul Afire: Revela-tions of the Mystics.* Edited by

H. A. Reinhold. New York: Pan-theon Books, 1973. Reprinted with permission.

GATE OF HELL, THE
From Dante's *The Inferno*, trans-lated by John Ciardi. Copyright © 1954 by John Ciardi. Reprinted by arrangement with New American Library, Inc., New York.

GEHENNA
Reprinted with permission of Mac-millan Publishing Co., Inc., from *Dictionary of the Bible* by John L. McKenzie. Copyright © 1965 by Macmillan Publishing Co., Inc.

GENERAL RECKONING, THE
From *Everyman.*

GLORIFIED BODIES
From *The Bible & Future Events: An Introductory Survey of Last-Day Events* by Leon J. Word. Copyright © 1973 by Zondervan Publishing House. Used with per-mission.

GLORIOUS INBREAKING OF GOD, THE
From *The Incredible Cover-Up: The True Story on the Pre-Trib Rapture* by Dave MacPherson. Copyright © 1975 by Logos Inter-national. All rights reserved. Used with permission.

GOD OF THE SPARROW
From *Life Essential: The Hope of the Gospel* by George MacDonald. New York: E. Appleton & Co., 1892.

GOD'S APPRAISAL
From *Everyman.*

GOOD WORKS GLORIFY
From *The Lord's Prayer.*

GRACIOUS JUDGE, THE
From *Waiting on God: Daily Mes-sages for a Month* by Andrew Mur-ray. Chicago: Moody Press, no date available.

GREAT WHITE THRONE, THE
Revelation 20:11–15.

GREATEST PHANTASMAGORIA, THE
From *But That I Can't Believe!* by John A. T. Robinson. London: Collins Fontana Books, 1967. Re-printed with permission.

HALF AN HOUR'S SILENCE IN HEAVEN
Reprinted by permission from *Daily Secrets of Christian Living* by Andrew Murray, compiled by Al Bryant, published and copyright © 1978 by Bethany Fellowship, Inc., Minneapolis, Minnesota, 55438.

HALO, NIMBUS, AUREOLE
Reprinted with permission of Mac-millan Publishing Co., Inc., from *A Handbook of Symbols in Chris-tian Art* by Gertrude Grace Sill. Copyright © 1975 by Gertrude Grace Sill.

HAPPY DEATH, A
"Hers" by Abigail McCarthy, the *New York Times* (November 23, 1978). Copyright © 1978 by The

New York Times Company. Reprinted with permission.

HAPPY ENTHRONEMENT OF REASON, THE
From *Prayer* as it appears in *Prayer: Exhortation to Martyrdom*.

HARROWING OF HELL, THE
From *Medieval anl Tudor Drama*. Edited, with introductions and modernizations, by John Gassner. Copyright © 1963 by Bantam Books, Inc. Reprinted with permission of Bantam Books, Inc. All rights reserved.

HEAVEN IN SCRIPTURE
From "Heaven" by L. L. Morris in *The New Bible Dictionary*.

HEAVEN OF ANIMALS, THE
Copyright © 1961 by James Dickey. Reprinted from *Poems: 1957–1967* by permission of Wesleyan University Press. "The Heaven of Animals" first appeared in the *New Yorker*.

HEAV'M IN GOSPEL SONG
Reprinted with permission of Macmillan Publishing Co., Inc., from *Black Song: The Forge and the Flame* by John Lovell, Jr. Copyright © 1972 by John Lovell, Jr.

HELL
From *Selected Poetry of W. H. Auden*. New York: Random House /Vintage Books, 1971.

HOLINESS ITSELF
From *The Simone Weil Reader*.

HOLLAND, 1533
From *Enthusiasm: A Chapter in the History of Religion* by Ronald A. Knox. New York: Oxford University Press, 1950. Reprinted with permission.

HOLY AUDACITY
From *The Lord's Prayer*.

HONORIFIC QUALITATIVE, AN
From *New Testament Essays* by Raymond E. Brown.

HOPE, HORIZON BEFORE THE SUNRISE
From *The Divine Milieu*.

HOPE IN AMERICA
From "Hope in America" by Jurgen Moltmann, as it appears in *Commonweal* (August 5, 1977). Reprinted with permission.

HOPEFUL GROUND
From "Hope in a Posthuman Era" by Sam Keen. Copyright © 1967 by the Christian Century Foundation. Reprinted with permission from *The Christian Century* (January 25, 1967).

HOW GOD IS HEAVEN
From *The City of God* by Augustine of Hippo as it is quoted in *The Later Christian Fathers*.

HOW JESUS IS HEAVEN
From *The Scale of Perfection* by Walter Hilton, abridged and presented by Illtyd Trethowan. Copyright © by Walter Hilton. Reprinted with permission of Geoffrey Chapman, a division of Cassell Ltd.

IF ANIMALS HAVE NO SOULS
From *Animail* by Cleveland Amory. Introduction by Mary Tyler Moore. Copyright © 1976 by Cleveland Amory. Reprinted with permission of the publisher, E. P. Dutton.

IN A TWINKLING
The First Epistle of Paul the Apostle to the Corinthians 15:51–53.

IN PEACE, BREAD
From *Martin Luther: Selection from His Writings*.

IN THE STOREHOUSE OF YOUR MEMORY
From *Go to Heaven* by Fulton J. Sheen. New York: McGraw-Hill Book Co., Inc., 1960. Reprinted with permission.

INTERMEDIATE STATE, THE
From *Parochial and Plain Sermons*, volume 3, by John Henry Newman. London: Longmans, Green, and Co., 1899.

INTERPRETATIONS OF THE KINGDOM
From *The Meaning of the Millennium: Four Views*.

INTOLERABLE DOCTRINE, THE
From *The Problem of Pain* by C. S. Lewis. New York: Macmillan Publishing Co., Inc., 1943. Reprinted with permission of the publisher.

IOWA POLL: HEAVEN OR HELL, THE
From the article of the same title by Arnold Garson, as it appeared in the *Des Moines Sunday Register* (December 25, 1977). Copyright © 1977 by the Des Moines Register and Tribune Company. Reprinted with permission.

IS HELL STILL A BURNING ISSUE?"
From "Hell: Still a Burning Question?" by James Breig, *U.S. Catholic* (November 1977). Reprinted with permission of Claretian Publications, 221 West Madison Street, Chicago, Illinois, 60606.

ITALY, 1260
From *The Influence of Prophecy in the Later Midlle Ages: A Study in Joachimism* by Marjorie Reeves. Oxford: Clarendon Press, 1969. Reprinted with permission.

JESUS' FATHER
From *New Testament Essays*.

JOYFUL FIRE, A
A quotation from Catherine of Genoa, as it appears in *The Soul Afire*.

JUDGMENT OF THE GREAT WHITE THRONE
From *Simple Sermons on Heaven, Hell, and Judgment* by W. Herschel Ford. Copyright © 1969 by Zondervan Publishing House. Used with permission.

JUMBLING SEEDS AND SOWING THEM
From *A Commentary on the Apostles' Creed*.

KINDLY FIRE, A
From *Orations*.

KING OF RIGHTEOUSNESS
From *Martin Luther: Selections from His Writings*.

KINGDOM SOCIETY, THE
From *Decision*. Copyright © 1965 by the Billy Graham Evangelistic Association. Reprinted with permission.

LAST THINGS HAVE ALREADY BEGUN, THE
From *The Lord of History: Reflections on the Inner Meaning of History* by Jean Danielou. Translated by Nigel Abercrombie. Chicago: Henry Regnevy Co., 1958. Reprinted with permission.

LAZARUS SYNDROME, THE
The Gospel According to St. John, 12:39–44.

LIKE THE COMING OF SUMMER
From Loraine Boettner's contribution to *The Meaning of the Millennium*.

LONDON, 1934
From *New Testament Christianity* by J. B. Phillips. Copyright © 1969 by J. B. Phillips. Reprinted with permission of Macmillan Publishing Co., Inc.

LONG-AWAITED BRIGHTNESS, THE
From *The Tree of Life*, as it appears in *The Soul's Journey into God · The Tree of Life · The Life of St. Francis* by Bonaventure. Translation and introduction by Ewert Cousins. Preface by Ignatius Brady. New York: Paulist Press, 1978. Reprinted with permission.

LONG HABIT OF LIVING, THE
From *The Lives of a Cell* by Lewis Thomas. Copyright © 1973 by the Massachusetts Medical Society. Originally appeared in the *New England Journal of Medicine*. All rights reserved. Reprinted with permission of Viking/Penguin, Inc.

LONGING CRY, A
From *The Simone Weil Reader*.

LOOKING TO THE FUTURE
From *The Problem of Free Choice* by St. Augustine. Translated and annotated by Mark Pontifex. New York: Newman Press, 1955. Reprinted with permission of Paulist Press.

LORD'S PRAYER, PRAYER OF HOPE, THE
From *Faith, Hope, and Charity* by St. Augustine. Translated and annotated by Louis Arand. New York: Newman Press, 1947.

LUMBERMAN'S EXPERIENCE, A
From *Oregon's Amazing Miracle* by Thomas Welch. Dallas: Christ for the Nations, Inc., 1976.

MARRIAGE OF THE KING'S SON—A PARABLE
Matthew 22:2–14.

MARRIAGE SUPPER
Revelation 19:6–9.

MEANING OF THE MEDITATION ON HELL
From *Spiritual Exercises* by Karl Rahner. Translated by Kenneth Baker. New York: Herder and Herder, 1965. Reprinted with permission.

MEDITATION ON HELL, A
From *The Spiritual Exercises of Saint Ignatius*. Translated by Thomas Corbishley. New York: P. J. Kennedy & Sons, 1963. Reprinted with permission of Anthony Clarke Books, Wheathampstead, Hertfordshire, England.

MILLENNIAL MADNESS
From *Freedom's Ferment: Phases of American Social History from the Colonial Period to the Outbreak of the Civil War* by Alice Felt Tyler. New York: Harper & Row, 1944.

MILLENNIAL MANAGEMENT POSITIONS AVAILABLE
From *Millennium Man* by George Otis. Copyright © 1974 Bible Voice, Inc. Used with permission.

MILLENNIALISM
From George Eldon Ladd's contribution to *The Meaning of the Millennium*.

MISSING LIMBS
From *The Terminal Generation* by Hal Lindsey with C. C. Carlson. Copyright © 1976 by Fleming H. Revell Company.

MOSES AND LUTHER AT THE LAST JUDGMENT
From *Table Talk*.

NEW ENGLAND, 1843
From *Freedom's Ferment*.

NEW YORK, 1914
From *Visions of Glory: A History and a Memory of Jehovah's Witnesses* by Barbara Grizzuti Harrison. Copyright © 1978 by Barbara Grizzuti Harrison. Reprinted with permission of Simon & Schuster, a division of Gulf & Western Corporation.

NIGHT I DREAMED OF JUDGMENT, THE
From *The Letters of St. Jerome*. Translated by Charles Christopher Mierow. Introduction and notes by Thomas Comerford Lawler. New York: Newman Press, 1963. Reprinted with permission of Paulist Press.

NINE BILLION NAMES OF GOD, THE
From *The Nine Billion Names of God* by Arthur C. Clarke. Copyright © 1953 by Ballantine Books, Inc. Reprinted with permission of Harcourt Brace Jovanovich, Inc.

NINE LAST THINGS, THE
From "Heaven and Hell in the Christian Tradition" by David W. Lotz, as it appears in *Religion in Life* (Spring 1979). Reprinted with permission.

NO MORE TEARS FOREVER
From *The Joyful Heart: Daily Meditations* by Watchman Nee. Wheaton, Ill.: Tyndale House Publishers, Inc., 1977. Reprinted with permission.

NOT A FICKLE KAZOO
From *The Tribulation People*.

NOT YET HALLOWED
From *Prayer*.

NOW IS THE TIME TO WORK
From *The Imitation of Christ* by Thomas à Kempis. Translated by Ronald Knox and Michael Oakley. New York: Sheed & Ward, Inc., 1959. Reprinted with permission.

NUNS'S GLIMPSE, A
From *Fatima in Lucia's Own Words: Sister Lucia's Memoirs*. Edited by Louis Kondor, with an introduction by Joaquin M. Alonso. Translated by the Dominican Nuns of Perpetual Rosary. Cambridge, Mass.: The Ravensgate Press, 1976.

OBEDIENCE TO THE COURSE OF EVENTS
From *The Simone Weil Reader*.

OLIVET DISCOURSE, THE
Matthew 24:1-14.

ONE TWINKLING BUT SEVEN MOMENTS
From *The Beginning of the End*.

OPEN 24 HOURS
From "Hell: Open 24 Hours" by Arthur McNally, *Sign*. (March 1978). Copyright © 1978 by *Sign*, Union City, New Jersey. All reproduction rights reserved.

OPENING THE GATES OF DEATH
From *A Commentary on the Apostles' Creed*.

OUR BREAD IS CHRIST
From *The Simone Weil Reader*.

OUR DEBTS, OUR DEBTORS
From *Prayer*.

OUR SECOND BODY
From *No Faith of My Own*.

OUT OF MY SOUL'S DEPTH
A poem by Thomas Campion, as it appears in *A Book of Religious Verse*. Edited by Helen Gardner. New York: Oxford University Press, 1972.

PAROUSIA, EPIPHANY, APOCALYPSE
From *The Imminent Appearing of Christ* by J. Barton Payne. Grand Rapids, Mich.: Wm. B. Eerdmans Publishing Co., 1962. Reprinted with permission.

PARTICULAR JUDGMENT
From *The Moral Universe* by Fulton J. Sheen. Milwaukee: Bruce Publishing Co., 1936. Reprinted with permission.

PHRYGIA, A.D. 150
From *Men Possessed by God*.

PHYSICAL PLACE OR SPIRITUAL CONCEPT?
From *Prayer*.

PITFUL OF FIRE FOREVER, A
The Gospel According to St. Mark 9:43-48.

POOR SOULS
From *The Last Things concerning Death, Purification after Death, Resurrection, Judgment, and Eternity*. Translated by Charlotte E. Forsyth and Grace B. Branham, New York: Pantheon Books, 1954. Reprinted with permission.

POSTMILLENNIALISM
From Loraine Boettner's contribu-tion to *The Meaning of the Millennium*.

PRECURSOR OF THE ACROSTIC
From *The Christians* by Bamber Gascoigne. Copyright © 1977 by Bamber Gascoigne. Reprinted with the permission of William Morrow & Company.

PREMILLENNIALISM
Taken from Herman A. Hoyt's contribution to *The Meaning of the Millennium*.

PURGATORY IN SCRIPTURE
*From* "Purgatory: An Interpretation" by Franz Seibel, *Theology Digest*, volume 26 (Spring 1978). Reprinted with permission.

PURITY ABOVE, PASSION BELOW
From *The Lord's Prayer*.

PUTTING THE BODY BACK TOGETHER
From *Faith, Hope, and Charity*.

RAPTURE IN SCRIPTURE
From *The Bible & Future Events*.

REACHABLE, YET UNREACHABLE
From *The Simone Weil Reader*.

REGARD AS HALLOWED
From *The Lord's Sermon on the Mount*.

RESURRECTED BODY, THE
From *The Last Things*.

RESURRECTION OF CHURCH SAINTS
From *The Bible & Future Events*.

RESURRECTION OF THE BODY, NOT THE FLESH
From *Basic Christian Beliefs*.

RESURRECTION OF THE SENSES
From *The Weight of Glory and Other Addresses* by C. S. Lewis. Copyright © 1949 by Macmillan Publishing Co., Inc.; renewed 1977 by Arthur Owen Barfield. Reprinted with permission of Macmillan Publishing Co., Inc.

REVELATION OF GOD'S HEART
From *A Table in the Wilderness: Daily Meditations* by Watchman Nee. Wheaton, Ill.: Tyndale House Publishers, 1978. Reprinted with permission.

RIGHT HAND AND THE LEFT, THE
From *Letters of St. Paulinus of Nola*, volume 2. Translated and annotated by P. G. Walsh. New York: Newman Press, 1967. Reprinted with permission of Paulist Press.

SAINT'S VISION, A
From *The Autobiography of St. Teresa of Avila*. Translated and edited by E. Allison Peers. Copyright © 1946, Sheed and Ward, Inc., New York. Reprinted with permission.

SATAN IN THE NEW TESTAMENT
From *Dictionary of the Bible*.

SCOTLAND, A.D. 700
From *An Irish Precursor to Dante* by C. S. Boswell (London, 1908), as it is quoted in *Saint Francis: Nature Mystic* by Edward A. Armstrong. Copyright © 1973 by the Regents

of the University of California. Reprinted with permission of the University of California Press.

SCROLL, THE BOOK, WHAT IS IT? THE
From *Apocalypse*.

SEALS, TRUMPETS, BOWLS
From *Expository Sermons on Revelation*.

SECOND SEAL, THE
Revelation 6:3–4.

SECOND TRUMPET, THE
Revelation 8:8–9.

SECOND VIAL, THE
Revelation 16:3.

SERIOUS BUSINESS OF HEAVEN, THE
From *The Problem of Pain*.

SEVEN SEALS, THE
Revelation 5:1.

SEVEN TRUMPETS, THE
Revelation 8:2–6.

SEVEN VIALS OF WRATH, THE
Revelation 16:1.

SEVENTH SEAL, THE
Revelation 8:1.

SEVENTH TRUMPET, THE
Revelation 9:1.

SEVENTH VIAL, THE
Revelation 16:17–21.

SHEEP AND THE GOATS, THE
The Gospel According to St. Matthew 25:31–46.

SHEOL AND HADES
From *Dictionary of the Bible*.

SICKNESS, POVERTY, DEATH
From *Martin Luther: Selection from His Writings*.

SIGNS OF THE KINGDOM
From *The King and the Kingdom* by William Barclay. Published in the United States by the Westminster Press, 1969. Copyright © 1969 by William Barclay. Used with permission.

SIMPLE FARE
From *The Lord's Prayer*.

SIN INHERITED
The Epistle of Paul the Apostle to the Romans, 5:12.

SINS AND SINNERS
From *Martin Luther: Selections from His Writings*.

SIXTH SEAL, THE
Revelation 6:12–17.

SIXTH TRUMPET, THE
Revelation 9:13.

SIXTH VIAL, THE
Revelation 16:12–16.

SLEEPERS, AWAKE!"
From *The Waiting Father*.

SMOKE AND WAX
From *The Lord's Prayer*.

SOCIAL JOYS OF HEAVEN, THE
From *The Happiness of Heaven*.

SONS VERSUS SONS
From *New Testament Essays*.

SOULS OF DEPARTED SAINTS
From *The City of God* by Augustine of Hippo, as it appears in *The Later Christian Fathers*.

SOULS UNDER THE ALTAR
From *The Anchor Bible: Revelation*. Introduction, translation, and commentary by J. Massyngberde Ford. Garden City, N.Y.: Doubleday & Co., Inc., 1975. Reprinted with permission.

SPIRITUAL FOOD
From *The Lord's Sermon on the Mount*.

SPIRITUAL FRIENDSHIP
From *Spiritual Friendship* by Aelred of Rievaulx. Kalamazoo, Mich.: Cistercian Publications, Inc., 1977. Reprinted with permission.

SPIRITUAL SENSE OF THE LORD'S PRAYER, THE
From *Science and Health with Key to the Scriptures* by Mary Baker Eddy. Copyright © 1906, 1971, renewed 1934, by the Christian Science Board of Directors. Used with permission.

STING OF DEATH, THE
Corinthians, 15:54–57.

SWARMS, WOLVES, AND HATE
From *The Didache*.

SWEET FOREVER, THE
From *The Last Things: An Eschatology for Laymen*.

TEMPTATION WITH PERMISSION
From *The Lord's Sermon on the Mount*.

TEMPTER, THE
From *The Lord's Prayer*.

TEN VIRGINS —A PARABLE, THE
Matthew 25:1–13.

TERMINAL GENERATION, THE
From *The Terminal Generation*.

THAT NATURE IS A HERICLITEAN FIRE AND OF THE COMFORT OF THE RESURRECTION
From *Poems and Prose of Gerald Manley Hopkins*. Selected with an introduction and notes by W. H. Gardner. Baltimore: Penguin Books, 1953.

THECLA'S HYMN
From *The Symposium* by St. Methodius, as it appears in *The Symposium: A Treatise on Chastity* by St. Methodius. Translated and annotated by Herbert Musurillo. New York: Newman Press, 1958. Reprinted with permission of Paulist Press.

THEIR MURDERERS STILL LIVE
From *Expository Sermons on Revelation*.

THIEF IN THE NIGHT
The Second Epistle of Peter the Apostle 3:10–13.

THINKING ABOUT DEATH
From *The Imitation of Christ*.

THIRD SEAL, THE
Revelation 6:5–6.

THIRD TRUMPET, THE
Revelation 8:10–11.

THIRD VIAL, THE
Revelation 16:4–7.

THIS TIME OF REPENTANCE
From *Purity of Heart* by Søren Kierkegaard, as it appears in *The Doubleday Devotional Classics*, volume 3. Edited by E. Glenn Hinson.

Garden City, N.Y.: Doubleday & Co., Inc., 1978.

THREE MEANINGS
From *The Lord's Sermon on the Mount*.

THREE WAYS TO PRAY THE LORD'S PRAYER
From "Exploring Prayer with Father George Maloney" by Arthur N. Winter, *National Catholic Reporter* (November 3, 1978). Reprinted with permission.

TRUE BREAD, THE
From *Prayer*.

TWILIGHT OF THE DAY, THE LIFE, THE WORLD
From *How Modern Should Theology Be?* by Helmut Thielicke. Translated by H. George Anderson, Philadelphia: Fortress Press, 1969. Reprinted with permission.

ULTIMATE EARTH, THE
From *The Phenomenon of Man* by Pierre Teilhard de Chardin. Copyright © 1959 by Wm. Collins Sons & Co. Ltd., London, and by Harper & Row, Publishers, Inc., New York. Reprinted with permission of Harper & Row.

ULTIMATE PERFECTION, THE
From *New Testament Essays*.

UNBRIDLED INEBRIATION
From *The World's Last Night and Other Essays* by C. S. Lewis. New York: Harcourt Brace Jovanovich, Inc., 1952.

UNDYING AND UNQUENCHABLE
From *The Rules Treated Briefly* by Basil of Caesarea, as it appears in *The Later Christian Fathers*.

USEFULNESS OF TEMPTATION
From *Prayer*.

VERITABLE VESUVIUS, A
From *The Octavius of Marcus Minucius Felix*. Translated and annotated by G. W. Clarke. New York: Newman Press, 1974. Reprinted with permission of Paulist Press.

VISIBLE KINGDOM, THE
From *The Lord's Sermon on the Mount*.

WARS AND RUMORS OF WARS
Mark 13:1–8.

WE ARE BORN DYING
From *Boundaries of the Soul: The Practices of Jung's Psychology* by June Singer. Garden City, N.Y.: Anchor Books, 1973. Reprinted with permission.

WEDDING OR RECEPTION
From *The Bible & Future Events*.

WELL IS THE HOUR OF DEATH
From *Faith and Prejudice and Other Unpublished Sermons* by John Henry Newman. Edited by the Birmingham Oratory. New York: Sheed & Ward, 1956. Reprinted with permission of the Oratory.

WHAT IS GOD DOING IN HEAVEN?

From Meister Eckhart, as quoted in *The Soul Afire.*

WHEN AND HOW WILL THE END COME?
It appeared under the title "Doomsday Debate: How Near is the End?" by Malcolm W. Browne in the *New York Times* (November 14, 1978). Copyright © 1978 by The New York Times Company. Reprinted with permission.

WHEN DEATH SLIP-SLIDES
From *The Lord's Sermon on the Mount.*

WHEN JESUS ROSE
From *Shroud* by Robert K. Wilcox. Copyright © 1977 by Robert K. Wilcox. Reprinted with permission of Macmillan Publishing Co., Inc.

WHERE WILL YOU PUT ALL THE MOSQUITOES?
From *The Problem of Pain* by C. S. Lewis.

WHO IS THE ANTICHRIST?
From *The Last and Future World.*

WHO IS THE FALSE PROPHET?
From *The Tribulation People.*

WHO WILL GIVE ME WINGS LIKE A DOVE?
From *The Lord's Prayer.*

WHORE OF BABYLON, THE
Revelation 17:1–18.

WHY FEAR OF HELL IS HEALTHY
From *The Creator and the Creature.*

WHY FEAR OF HELL IS NEUROTIC
From *Death and Its Mysteries.*

WILL I HAVE MY CAT IN HEAVEN?
From *Christ in Eclipse: A Clinical Study of the Good Christian* by F. J. Sheed. Kansas City, Kan.: Sheed Andrews and McMeel, Inc., 1978. Reprinted with permission.

WILL PEOPLE THROW PARTIES IN HEAVEN?
Yvonne Goulet, *U.S. Catholic* (April 1979). Reprinted with permission of Claretion Publications, 221 West Madison Street, Chicago, Illinois, 60606.

WILL THE TALL BE SHORT AND THE THIN BE FAT?
From *Faith, Hope, and Charity.*

WITH A BANG
From "Have Astronomers Found God?" by Robert Jastrow, as it appeared in the *New York Times Magazine* (June 25, 1978). Copyright © 1978 by The New York Times Company. Reprinted with permission.

WITHOUT WARNING
Copyright © 1952 by C. S. Lewis. From *The World's Last Night and Other Essays.*

WORLD IS NOT CONCLUSION, THE
From *Selected Poems and Letters of Emily Dickinson.* Edited by Robert N. Linscott. Garden City, N.Y.: Doubleday & Co., Inc., 1959. Reprinted with permission.

WORLD'S LAST NIGHT, THE
From *The Poems of John Donne.* Edited by Sir Herbert Grierson. London: Oxford University Press, 1933.

WORM AND THE FIRE, THE
From St. Augustine, *City of God* (Book 21, Chapter 9). Translated by G. G. Walsh and D. J. Honan. *Fathers of the Church* series, volume 24. Washington, D.C.: Catholic University of America Press, 1954.

WOVEN INTO THE DIVINE WORLD
From *The Spiritual Life.*

WRATHFUL JUDGE, THE
From *The Tree of Life.*

YOUR HEAVENLY FATHER
From *Daily Secrets of Christian Living* by Andrew Murray. Reprinted with permission.

# SOURCES AND PERMISSIONS*

# ILLUSTRATIONS

i–ii. Used with permission of Macmillan Publishing Co., Inc., from *En Masse* by Hans-Georg Rauch. Copyright © Rowahlt Verlag Gmbh, Reinbeck bei Hamburg, 1974.

v. From poster of W.P.A.'s production of Christopher Marlowe's *Faustus*; as it appears in *Free, Adult, Uncensored: The Living History of the Federal Theatre Project*. Foreword by John Houseman; edited by John O'Connor and Lorraine Brown. Washington, D.C.: New Republic Books, 1978. Reprinted with permission of the Research Center for the Federal Theatre Project, George Mason University, Fairfax, Virginia.

vi. From *The Rime of the Ancient Mariner* by Samuel Taylor Coleridge. Illustrations by Gustave Doré. With a new introduction by Millicent Rose. New York: Dover Publications, Inc., 1970.

vii. From *The Angel Book*. Huntington, Indiana: Our Sunday Visitor Press, 1978.

viii. From *Think Good Thoughts about a Pussycat* by George Booth. New York: Dodd, Mead & Co., 1975.

ix. From *Dante's Inferno Illustrated by Gustave Doré*. With a new introduction by Michael Marsquee. New York: Paddington Press, Ltd., and Two Continents Publishing Group, Ltd., 1976.

x. From *God's Man: A Novel in Woodcuts* by Lynd Ward. New York: St. Martin's Press, 1978. Reprinted with permission.

xi. From *The Rime of the Ancient Mariner*.

xiii. From *Early New England Gravestone Rubbings* by Edmund Vincent Gillon, Jr. New York: Dover Publications, 1960. Reprinted with permission.

xiv. From *I Paint What I See* by Gahan Wilson. Copyright © 1971 by Gahan Wilson. Reprinted with permission of Simon & Schuster, a division of Gulf & Western Corporation.

xvi. From *Sojourners*, August 1979, page 5.

xvii. From Stanley Kubrick's *Dr. Strangelove, Or: How I Learned to Stop Worrying and Love the Bomb* (1964). Courtesy of *Movie Star News*.

xviii. Used with permission of Macmillan Publishing Co., Inc., from *Against the Grain: The Woodcuts of Antonio Frasconi*. Copyright © 1974 by Antonio Frasconi.

2–3. Reprinted with permission of Charles Scribner's Sons from *Battle Lines* by Hans-Georg Rauch. Copyright © 1977 Rowahlt Verlag Gimbh.

4. From *Early New England Gravestone Rubbings*.

7. From Pier-Paolo Pasolini's *The Gospel According to St. Matthew* (1964). Courtesy of *Movie Star News*.

9. From *En Masse*.

10. From *Early New England Gravestone Rubbings*.

11. Drawing by Joan Hall accompanying "Hers" by Abigail McCarthy, the *New York Times* (November 23, 1978), page C2. Copyright © 1978 by The New York Times Company. Reprinted with permission.

13. From *En Masse*.

14. Drawing by Koren; © 1975 The New Yorker Magazine, Inc.

16. From *Early New England Gravestone Rubbings*.

17. "The Joys of the World and the Warning of Death" from *The Complete Woodcuts of Albrecht Dürer*. Edited by Willi Kurth with an introduction by Campbell Dodgson. New York: Dover Publications, Inc., 1963. Reprinted with permission.

18. From *Early New England Gravestone Rubbings*.

19. "Prayer for the Dead" from *A Book of Christian Prayers*, printed by Richard Yardley and Peter Short for Richard Day, London, 1590. As it appears in *Picture Book of Devils, Demons, and Witchcraft* by Ernst and Johanna Lehner. New York: Dover Publications, Inc., 1971. Reprinted with permission.

20. From *Early New England Gravestone Rubbings*.

21. From *Picture Book of Devils, Demons, and Witchcraft*.

22. "The Soul Hovering over the the Body Reluctantly Parting with Life": from *The Grave, A Poem* by Robert Blair. Illustrated by twelve etchings executed by Louis Schiavonetti, from the original inventions of William Blake, 1808.

23 (*top*). From *Amphigorey Too* by Edward Gorey. Copyright © 1975 by Edward Gorey. Reprinted with permission of Condida Donadio & Aside, Inc.

23 (*bottom*), 25. From *Early New England Gravestone Rubbings*.

27. From Jacob Cats' autobiographical poem *An Eighty-Two-Year-Long Life*, published by Jan van der Deyster, Leydin, 1732. It appears in Ernst and Johanna Lehner's *Picture Book of Devils, Demons, and Witchcraft*.

28. From *Early New England Gravestone Rubbings*.

30. "The Descent of Christ into the Grave," from *The Grave, A Poem*.

31 (*top*). "Harrowing of Hell" from *The Complete Engravings, Etchings and Drypoints of Albrecht Dürer*. Edited by Walter L. Strauss. New York: Dover Publications, Inc. Copyright © 1972, 1973. Reprinted with permission.

31 (*bottom*)–33. From *Early New England Gravestone Rubbings*.

36. From *Human Scandals* by Brad Holland (Thomas Y. Crowell). Copyright © 1977 by Brad Holland. Reprinted with permission of Harper & Row Publishers, Inc.

38. From *Early New England Gravestone Rubbings*.

39. Harry Belafonte as Ralph in *The World, the Flesh, and the Devil* (1959). Courtesy of *Movie Star News*.

40–41. Spectators awaiting twilight concert in Central Park, New York City (August 1, 1979). Photograph by Barton Silverman. Reprinted with permission of the *New York Times*.

45. From *I Paint What I See*.

46. From *Great Moments in Architecture* by David Macaulay. Copyright © 1978 by David Macaulay. Reprinted with permission of Houghton Mifflin Company.

47. From *The Anglican Digest*, II Quarter A.D. 1978, page 18. Reprinted with permission.

50 (*left*). From *Early New England Gravestone Rubbings*.

50 (*right*). Illustration by Rockwell Kent. Used through courtesy of

---

* Please note that the sources and/or permissions are given in their entirety only the first time they occur.

the Rockwell Kent Legacies, John F. H. Gorton, director.

52. Cartoon by John Lawing as it appeared in *Christianity Today*. Copyright © 1978 by John V. Lawing, Jr. Used with permission.

53. From *Early New England Gravestone Rubbings*.

55. From *Against the Grain*.

56 (top). Drawing by Gahan Wilson that appeared in an ad for the movie *The End*, starring Burt Reynolds; United Artists, A Transamerica Company; as it appeared on page 49 of the *New York Times* (May 9, 1978).

56 (bottom). From *Phobias & Therapies* by Joseph Farris. Copyright © 1977 by Joseph Farris. Used with permission of Grosset & Dunlap, Inc.

57 (top). Cartoon by Joe Mirachi as it appeared in the *Wall Street Journal*. Reprinted with permission of Cartoon Features Syndicate.

57 (bottom), 59. From *Early New England Gravestone Rubbings*.

60. Culver Pictures, Inc. Used with permission.

62. Copyright © 1978 David Burnett. Reprinted with permission of Contact Press Images, Inc.

63–64. From Frank Capra's *Lost Horizon* (1937). Courtesy of *Movie Star News*.

65. From Charles Jarrot's *Lost Horizon* (1973). Courtesy of *Movie Star News*.

66. From advertisement of the film *The Late Great Planet Earth*, a Pacific International Enterprises release.

69. From *Early New England Gravestone Rubbings*.

70. From Peter Brook's *King Lear* (1970). Courtesy of *Movie Star News*.

71. Drawing by Andrzei Dudzinski as it appeared in the *New York Times Book Review* (November 26, 1978), page 15. Copyright © 1978 by the New York Times Company. Reprinted with permission.

73. From *En Masse*.

75. "The Skeleton Reanimated," from *Night Thoughts or The Complaint and the Consolation*. Illustrated by William Blake; text by Edward Young. Edited, with introduction and commentary, by Robert Essick and Jenijoy La Belle. New York: Dover Publications, Inc., 1975.

77. Bumper Sticker. Emblems, Inc. Copyright © Garland, Texas. Reprinted with permission.

78. From *The Rime of the Ancient Mariner*.

81. Photograph by Gary Settle of band at Rockefeller Center, New York City, printed in the *New York Times* (December 18, 1978). Reprinted with permission.

83. "Resurrection" from *The Complete Engravings, Etchings, and Drypoints of Albrecht Dürer*.

84–85. Imprint of Jesus's body on the linen shroud he was buried in: as it appears to the naked eye (top) and as it appears on a film negative (bottom). Holy Shroud Guild, Esopus, New York. Copyright © Holy Shroud Guild, Bronx, New York. Reprinted with permission.

87. "The Reunion of the Soul & The Body" from *The Grave, A Poem*.

88. Details of Tympanun, left portal, north transept, cathedral of Reims, A.D. 1200. New York Public Library Picture Collection.

89. Reproduced from the collection of the Library of Congress.

90 (left). From Victor Fleming's *The Wizard of Oz (1939)*. Courtesy of *Movie Star News*.

90 (right). From *Sojourners* (February 1979). Used with permission.

91. Photograph by W. Eugene Smith of a cathedral turned into a hospital, Philippine Islands, 1944. *Life* magazine © 1944 Time, Inc. Reprinted with permission.

92. From *Sojourners* (November 1978). Used with permission.

93. Illustration by Peter Lui as it appeared in the May/June 1979 issue of *Faith at Work*. Reprinted with permission.

94. Rockwell Kent.

95. Culver Pictures, Inc. Used with permission.

99. From Federico Fellini's *La Dolce Vita* (1966). Courtesy of *Movie Star News*.

100–101. From *Human Scandals*.

105. From Dante's *Inferno*, illustrated by Gustave Doré. With a new introduction by Michael Marqusée. New York: Paddington Press Ltd. & Two Continents Publishing Group Ltd., 1976.

106. From *The Complete Woodcuts of Albrecht Dürer*.

107. Paul Henried as the Czech underground leader Victor Lazlo in Michael Curtiz's *Casablanca* (1942). The Museum of Modern Art/Film Stills Library. Used with permission.

108. From *En Masse*.

111. From *Human Scandals*.

112. From *Against the Grain: The Woodcuts of Antonio Frasconi*.

114. Allegoric representation of the Four Horsemen of the Apocalypse: War, Hunger, Plague, and Death. From Albrecht Dürer's *Apocalypse*, Nuremberg, 1498. As it appears in *Picture Book of Devils, Demons, and Witchcraft*.

115. Japanese soldier's skull propped up on burned-out Japanese tank destroyed by U.S. marines on Guadalcanal, Solomon Islands, 1942. Photograph by Ralph Morse. *Life*

magazine © 1942 Time, Inc. Reprinted with permission.

116. From *Against the Grain: The Woodcuts of Antonio Frasconi*.

117. Two parishoners are comforted after viewing the bodies of seven missionaries slain at Musami, Rhodesia, in 1977. Religious News Service photo. Used with permission.

118. "The opening of the fifth and sixth seals, the distribution of white garments among the martyrs, and the fall of stars," from *The Complete Woodcuts of Albrecht Dürer*.

120–21. Earthquake in Anchorage, Alaska. Copyright © Bruce Roberts. Rapho/Photo Researchers, Inc. Used with permission.

122. Drawing by Eugene Mihaesco as it appeared in section 4, page 1 of the June 17, 1979, issue of the *New York Times*. Copyright © 1979 by The New York Times Company. Reprinted with permission.

124. "The seven trumpets are given to the angels, and the results of the first four trumpet calls" as it appears in *The Complete Woodcuts of Albrecht Dürer*.

125. From *Battle Lines*.

126–27. From *Great Moments in Architecture*.

128. Drawing by Leon Kortenkamp as it appears in *The Anchor Bible: Revelation*. Introduction, translation, and commentary by J. Massyngberde Ford. Garden City, N.Y.: Doubleday & Co., Inc., 1975. Used with permission.

129. Faith Domergue as Ruth Adams in the clutches of the mutant in Joseph Newman's *This Island Earth*, (1954). Courtesy of *Movie Star News*.

130–31. From *Battle Lines*.

132. "The Battle of the Angels" as it appears in *The Complete Woodcuts of Albrecht Dürer*.

134–35. Oil spill on Normandy beach, France. Rapho/Photo Researchers, Inc. Used with permission.

136. Keenan Wynn in Stanley Kubrick's *Dr. Strangelove, Or: How I Learned to Stop Worrying and Love the Bomb* (1964). Courtesy of *Movie Star News*.

137. From *Against the Grain: The Woodcuts of Antonio Frasconi*.

138. From *Human Scandals*.

140–41. Photograph by Jacques Duquesnay, Sygma. Reprinted with permission.

142–43. "The Harmony of Christian Love: Representing the Dawn of the Millennium." Reproduced from the collection of the Library of Congress.

144, 146, 148. From David Greene's *Godspell* (1973). Courtesy of *Movie Star News*.

152. Photograph of Jeff Fenholt as Jesus in the New York stage pro-

duction of *Jesus Christ Superstar* (1971). Photograph by Eric Meola of *Time* magazine.

154. Photograph by Jeanne Heiberg. Used with permission.

155. Jesus rally held on a farm in Pennsylvania. Religious News Service photo. Used with permission.

157. Photograph by Jeanne Heiberg. Used with permission.

158. Jesus '79 rally held at Shea Stadium, New York. Religious News Service photo. Used with permission.

159 (*top*). Dallas Expo '72, the International Student Congress on Evangelism. Religious News Service photo. Used with permission.

159 (*bottom*), 160. Jesus '79 rally.

161. Jesus rally held on a farm in Pennsylvania.

162. Jesus '79 rally.

163. Dallas, Expo '72.

164. Jesus '79 rally.

167. Tract Evangelistic Crusade, Box 999, Apache Junction, Arizona, 85220.

169. Rockwell Kent.

170 (*left*). Ukrainian wedding procession in New York. Copyright © 1975 Katrina Thomas. Photo Researchers, Inc.

170 (*right*). Copyright © 1978 Suzanne Szasz. Photo Researchers, Inc.

171. Copyright © 1976 by Sam C. Pierson, Jr. Photo Researchers, Inc.

173. "The Adoration of the Lamb and the Hymn of the Chosen" as it appears in *The Complete Woodcuts of Albrecht Dürer*.

175. Armillary Sphere, as it appears in *The Complete Woodcuts of Albrecht Dürer*.

177. "The Day of Judgment" as it appears in *The Grave, A Poem*.

181. Detail from "The Last Judgment," sculpture/relief on the tympanum of the central door of the cathedral of Bourges. Courtesy of New York Public Library picture collection.

183. "The Last Judgment," woodcut by Michael Wolgemut, as it appears in Hartman Schedel's *Liber Cronicarum*, printed by Anton Koberger, Nuremberg, 1493. From *Picture Book of Devils, Demons, and Witchcraft*.

185. London, 1723. Courtesy of New York Public Library picture collection.

186. "Separation of the sheep from the goats." Marble relief from Rome, 4th century. The Metropolitan Museum of Art. Rogers Fund, 1924. Used with permission.

187. From *Early New England Gravestone Rubbings*.

188. Reprinted with permission of Richard Marek Publishers, Inc., from "*. . . and then we'll get him!*"

by Gahan Wilson. Copyright © 1978 by Gahan Wilson.

190. From *Early New England Gravestone Rubbings*.

191. "The Last Judgment" from *The Doré Bible Illustrations: 241 Illustrations* by Gustave Doré. New York: Dover Pubications, Inc., 1974. With a new introduction by Millicent Rose. Reprinted with permission.

193. From "*. . . and then we'll get him!*"

195. Printed and for sale by G. S. Peters, Harrisburg, Pennsylvania (no date). Reproduced from the collection of the Library of Congress.

196-97. Drawing by Seymour Chwast as it appears on page A31 of the April 27, 1979, issue of the *New York Times*. Copyright © 1979 by The New York Times Company. Reprinted with permission.

199. "Sol Justitiae, or the Judge" from *The Complete Engravings, Etchings, and Drypoints of Albrecht Dürer*.

200-201. Drawing in an ad for the Garrett newspaper chain, the *Wall Street Journal* (July 17, 1979).

202-203. Photograph of the original Broadway cast of Michael Bennett's *A Chorus Line* (1976) by Martha Swope. Used with permission.

205. Drawing by Eugene Mihaesco as it appeared on page 7 of the July 8, 1979, issue of the *New York Times Book Review*. Copyright © 1979 by the New York Times Company. Reprinted with permission.

207. From *Early New England Gravestone Rubbings*.

209. From Dante's *Inferno*.

210. Reprinted from the collection of the Library of Congress.

212. Drawing by Richter. Copyright © 1978 by The New Yorker Magazine, Inc.

215. Reproduced from the collection of the Library of Congress.

214. Drawing by Dedini. Copyright © 1970 The New Yorker Magazine, Inc.

216. Copyright © 1974 by Dedini. *The American Cartoon Album*, Dodd, Mead & Co.

217. Reproduced from the collection of the Library of Congress.

218. "The Eternal Lamentation of the Damned" from *The Complete Woodcuts of Albrecht Dürer*.

219 (*left*). From Dante's *Inferno*.

219 (*right*). From *1800 Woodcuts by Thomas Bewick and His School*. Edited by Blanche Cirkev and the editorial staff of Dover Publications. With an introduction by Robert Hutchinson. New York: Dover Publications, Inc., 1962. Used with permission.

220. Drawing by Garrett Price. Copyright © 1945, 1973, by The New Yorker Magazine, Inc.

223-24. From *The Parables of Our Lord and Saviour Jesus Christ*. With pictures by John Everett Millais; engraved by the brothers Dalziel. With a new introduction by Mary Lutyens. New York: Dover Publications, Inc., 1975. Reprinted with permission.

226. "Hell" by Pieter Brueghel (1557). New York Public Library picture collection. Used with permission.

227. Reprinted with the permission of the American Nuclear Energy Council.

228-29. From *Le grant kalendrier et compost des Bergiers*, printed by Nicolas Le Rouge, Troyes, 1496; as it appears in *Picture Book of Devils, Demons, and Witchcraft*.

232-34. From *Dante's Inferno Illustrated by Gustave Doré*.

235. Drawing by Elliott Banfield as it appeared on page 9 of the June 24, 1979, issue of the *New York Times Book Review*. Copyright © 1979 by The New York Times Company. Reproduced with permission.

236, 238. From *Phobias & Therapies*.

241. Illustration from Doré's *Divine Comedy*.

243. "Dante and Beatrice with the Blessed Souls," illustration from *Comedia dell' Inferno, del Purgatorio, & del Paradiso* by Alighieri Dante, published by Giovanni Maria Sessa e Fratelli, Venice, 1578. Reprinted with permission the Metropolitan Museum of Art; gift of Francis L. Cater, 1958.

245. From *God's Man: A Novel in Woodcuts* by Lynd Ward. New York: St. Martin's Press, Inc., 1978. Reprinted with permission.

246. Drawing by Ed Fisher. Copyright © 1979 The New Yorker Magazine, Inc.

249. Reproduced from the collection of the Library of Congress.

250-51. Drawing by Susannah Kelly from the *New York Times International Economic Survey* (February 4, 1979), page 9. Copyright © 1979 by The New York Times Company. Reprinted with permission.

252. "The Fight of the City of Satan (Babylon) against the City of God (Sion)," from Aurelius Augustinus' *De Trinitate. De Civitate Die*, printed by Johann Amerbach, Basle, 1489. As it appears in *Picture Book of Devils, Demons, and Witchcraft*.

253 (*left*). From the *Des Moines Sunday Register* (December 25, 1977). Used with permission.

253 (*right*). From *Early New England Gravestone Rubbings*.

255. From *The Complete Woodcuts of Albrecht Dürer*.

256. From *Early New England Gravestone Rubbings*.

257. "The seven angels with a cross

and the six keys, with which they have opened heaven to the six works of mercy, receive a soul into heaven." From *Bruder Claus* by Nikolaus von der Fluhe, Max Ayrer, Nuremberg, 1488. As it appears in *The Complete Woodcuts of Albrecht Dürer*.

258. From *I Paint What I See*.

260. Woodcut from Hartmann Schedel's *Liber Chronicarum*, published in Nuremberg, Germany, 1493. Illustrated by Michael Wolgemut and Wilhelm Pleydenwurff. Rare Book and Special Collections Division, Library of Congress.

263. Drawing by Koren. Copyright © 1970 The New Yorker Magazine, Inc.

264–65. Drawing by Rea Irvin. Copyright © 1931, 1959, The New Yorker Magazine, Inc.

268. Drawing by Koren. Copyright © 1970 by The New Yorker Magazine, Inc.

271. "The Meeting of a Family in Heaven" from *The Grave, A Poem*.

272. "The Austrian Saints" as it appears in *The Complete Woodcuts of Albrecht Dürer*.

274. From *En Masse*.

275. Cartoon by Brenda Burbank as it appeared in *"Can You Type?"* A *Cartoon Portfolio from the Wall Street Journal*. Edited by Charles Preston; introduction by Robert L. Bartley. Princeton, N.J.: Dow Jones Books, 1977. Reprinted with permission of Cartoon Features Syndicate.

276. Sketch of scene from Marc Connelly's *The Green Pastures* (1936).

281. Drawing by Philippe Wiesbrecker as it appeared in the *New York Times Book Review* (May 6, 1979), page 9. Copyright © 1979 by the New York Times Company. Reprinted with permission.

283. Rockwell Kent.

287. Reproduced from the collection of the Library of Congress.

289. Drawing by Bob Cole, *the New York Times* (February 11, 1979). Copyright © 1979 by the New York Times Company. Reprinted with permission.

290. Drawing in *Commonweal* (August 5, 1977), page 481. Reprinted with permission.

291. Reproduced from the collection of the Library of Congress.

295. From Pasolini's *Gospel According to St. Matthew*.

296. From George Stevens' *The Greatest Story Ever Told* (1965). Courtesy of *Movie Star News*.

299. From Nicholas Ray's *King of Kings* (1962). Courtesy of *Movie Star News*.

301–302. From Stevens' *The Greatest Story Ever Told*.

305. From Johnny Cash's *The Gospel Road* (1973). Courtesy of *Movie Star News*.

307–308. From Stevens' *The Greatest Story Ever Told*.

311. From Cash's *The Gospel Road*.

313. From Pasolini's *The Gospel According to St. Matthew*.

314. Used with permission of Sturbridge Village.

316. From Cecil B. De Mille's *The King of Kings* (1927). Courtesy of *Movie Star News*.

318, 320. From Norman Jewison's *Jesus Christ Superstar* (1973). Courtesy of *Movie Star News*.

323, 325. From Pasolini's *Gospel According to St. Matthew*.

328. From Greene's *Godspell*.

334. Reprinted with permission of Joseph G. Farris.

342. From *God's Man*.

347–348. From *The Rime of the Ancient Mariner*.